A PEANUTS CHRISTMAS

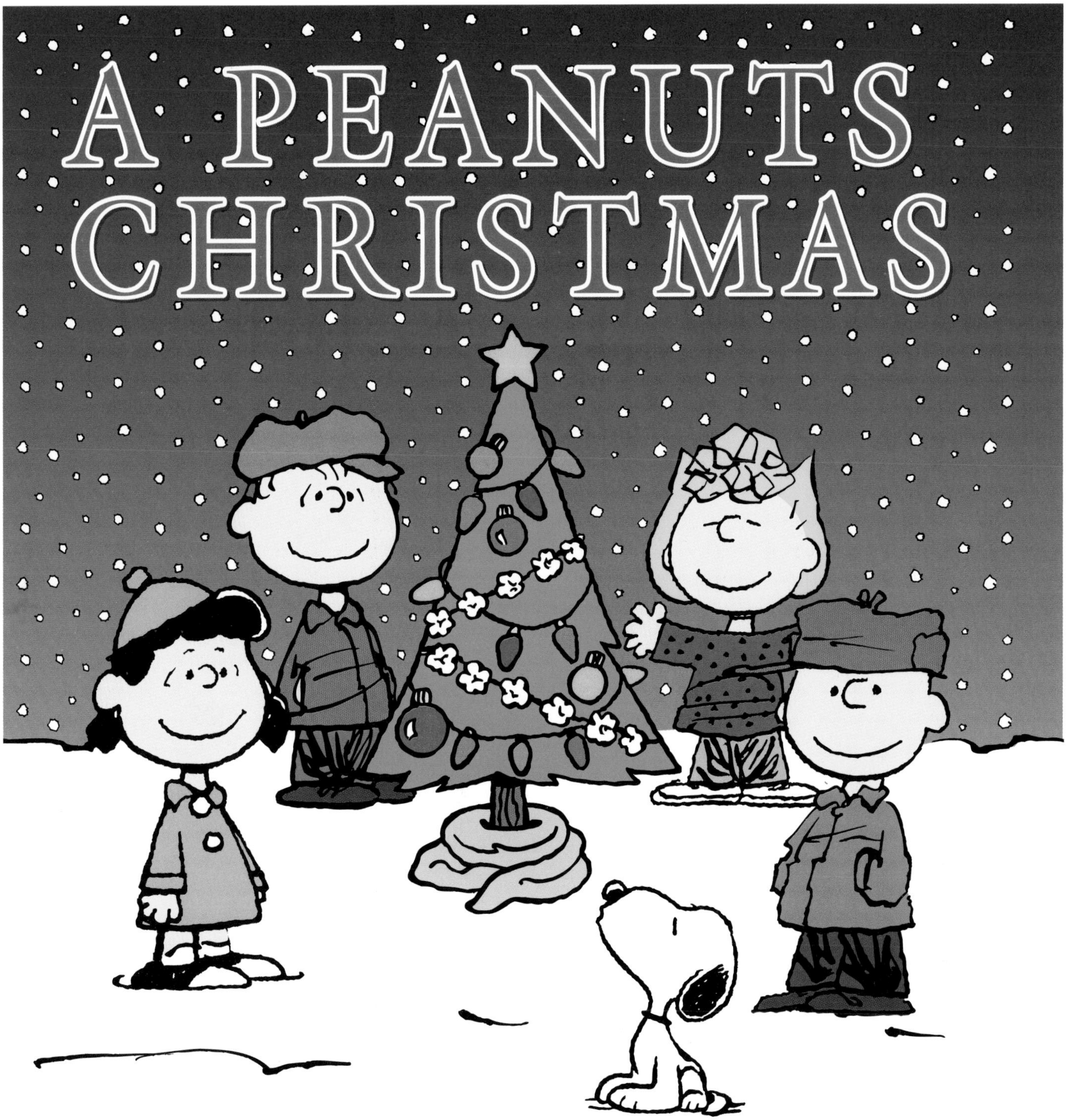

BY CHARLES M. SCHULZ

BALLANTINE BOOKS • NEW YORK

A Ballantine Book
Published by The Ballantine Publishing Group
Copyright © 2002 by United Feature Syndicate, Inc.

All rights reserved under International and Pan-American Copyright Conventions. Published in the United States by The Ballantine
Publishing Group, a division of Random House, Inc., New York, and simultaneously in Canada by Random House of Canada Limited, Toronto.
The comic strips in this book were originally published in newspapers worldwide.

Ballantine and colophon are registered trademarks of Random House, Inc.

www.ballantinebooks.com
www.snoopy.com

Library of Congress Control Number: 2002094135

ISBN 0-345-45351-4

Book Design by HRoberts Design
Jacket Design by United Media

Manufactured in the United States of America

First Edition: November 2002

10 9 8 7 6 5 4 3 2 1

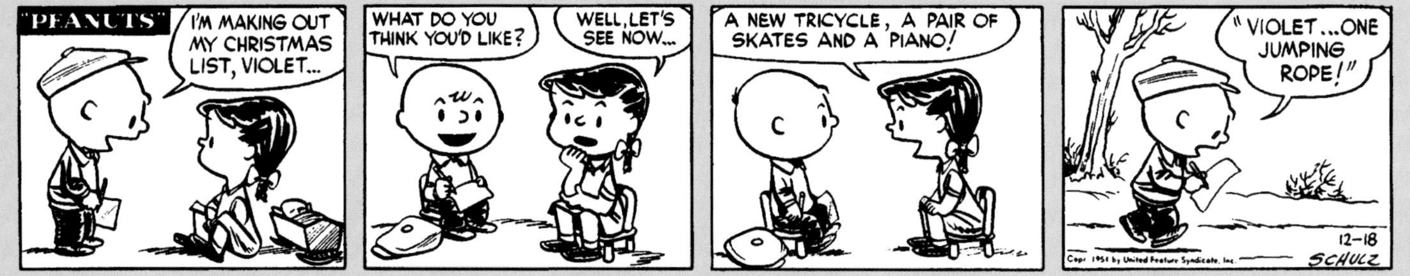
"PEANUTS"
I'M MAKING OUT MY CHRISTMAS LIST, VIOLET...
WHAT DO YOU THINK YOU'D LIKE?
WELL, LET'S SEE NOW...
A NEW TRICYCLE, A PAIR OF SKATES AND A PIANO!
"VIOLET...ONE JUMPING ROPE!"
12-18
Copr 1951 by United Feature Syndicate, Inc.
SCHULZ

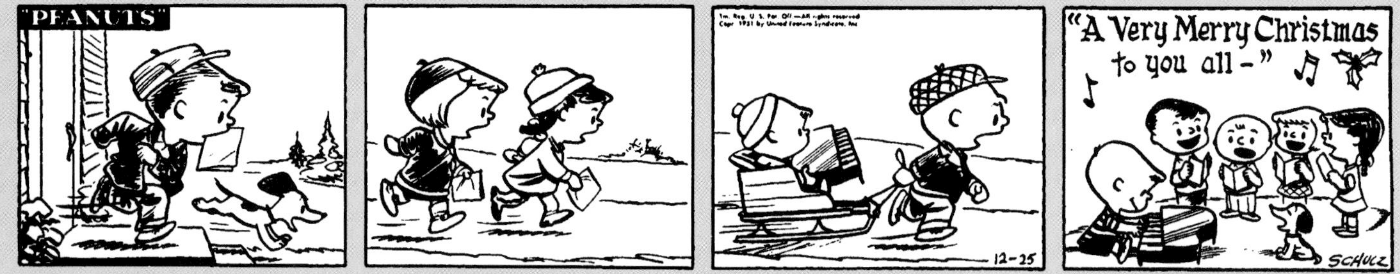
"PEANUTS"
Tm. Reg. U. S. Pat. Off.—All rights reserved
Copr 1951 by United Feature Syndicate, Inc
12-25
"A Very Merry Christmas to you all–"
SCHULZ

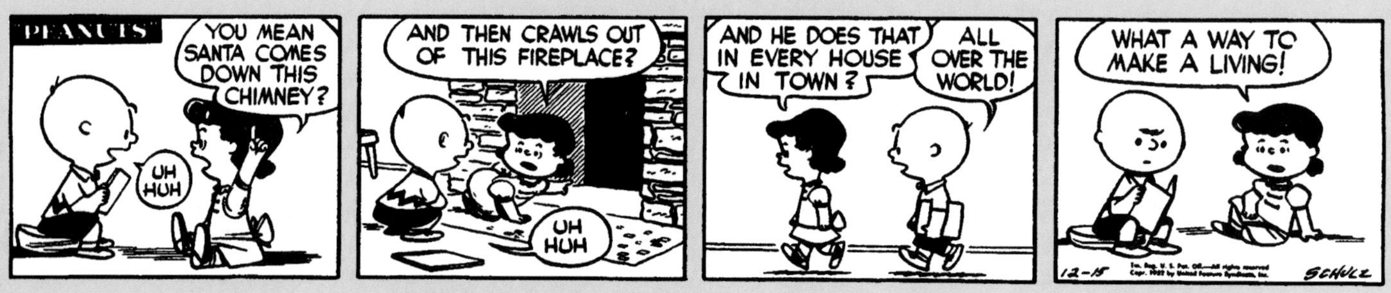
"PEANUTS"
YOU MEAN SANTA COMES DOWN THIS CHIMNEY?
UH HUH
AND THEN CRAWLS OUT OF THIS FIREPLACE?
UH HUH
AND HE DOES THAT IN EVERY HOUSE IN TOWN?
ALL OVER THE WORLD!
WHAT A WAY TO MAKE A LIVING!
12-15
Tm. Reg. U. S. Pat. Off.—All rights reserved
Copr. 1952 by United Feature Syndicate, Inc.
SCHULZ

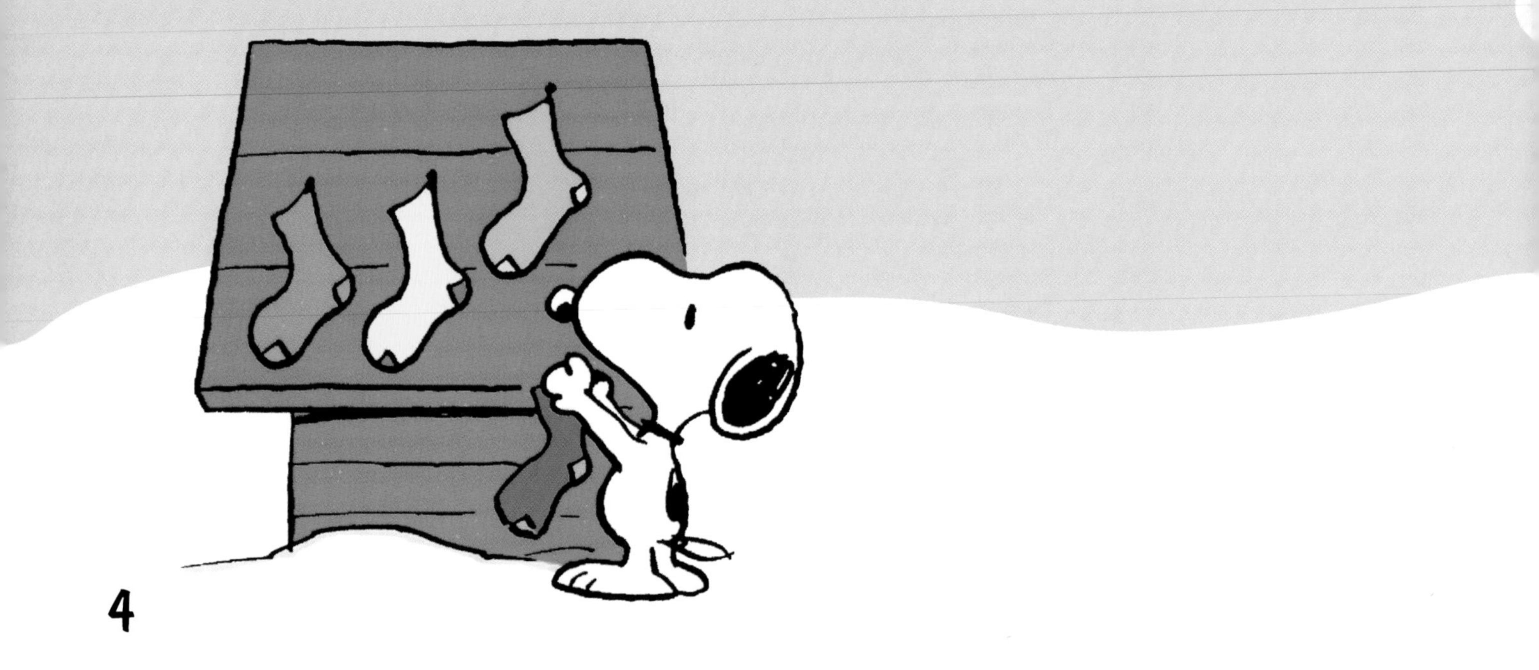

PEANUTS
IS THIS YOUR LETTER TO SANTA CLAUS?
UH HUH..
IT SOUNDS A LOT LIKE THE ONE YOU WROTE LAST CHRISTMAS
IT IS...
I HAVE A FORM LETTER THAT GOES OUT EVERY YEAR!
12-16
SCHULZ

PEANUTS
I DECIDED TO WRITE A NEW LETTER TO SANTA CLAUS
SNIF-SNIF-*SOB*
OH, BOO-HOO-HOO-HOO!
WAAH!
PRETTY HEART-RENDING, ISN'T IT?
12-17
SCHULZ

PEANUTS
"'TWAS THE NIGHT BEFORE CHRISTMAS...
AND ALL THROUGH THE HOUSE NOT A CREATURE WAS STIRRING, NOT EVEN A MOUSE..."
BEFORE I CONTINUE, HERE IS A BRIEF WORD FROM THE SPONSOR...
WOULD YOU LIKE TO BUY A MAGAZINE?
10¢
12 24
SCHULZ

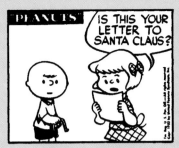

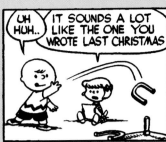

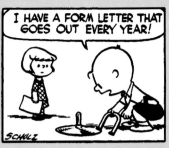

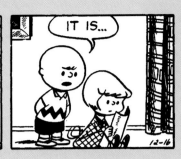

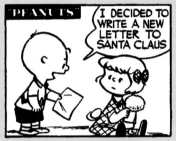

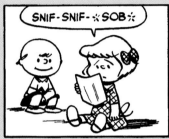

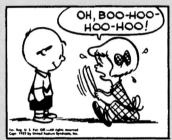

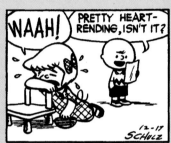

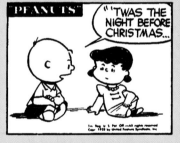

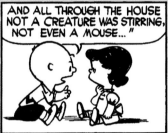

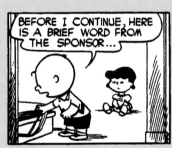

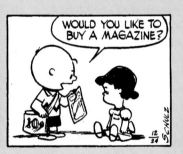

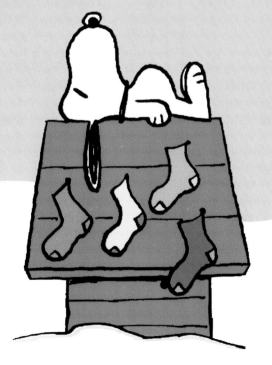

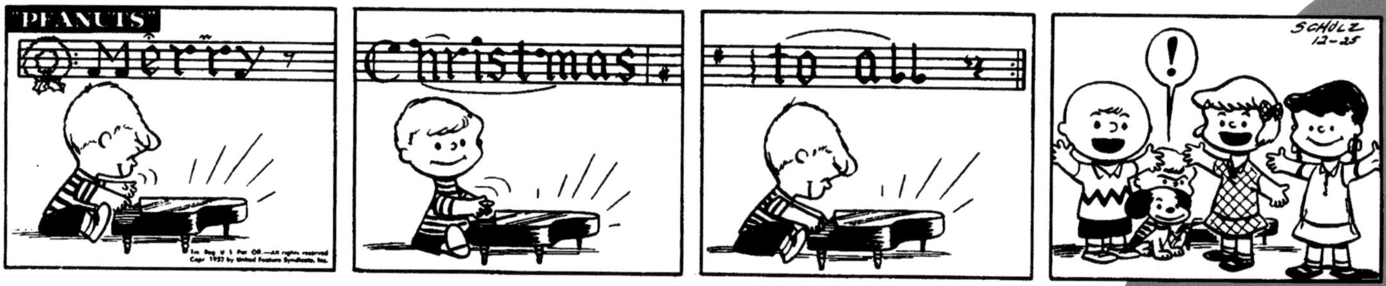
"PEANUTS"
Merry
Christmas
to all
!
SCHULZ 12-25

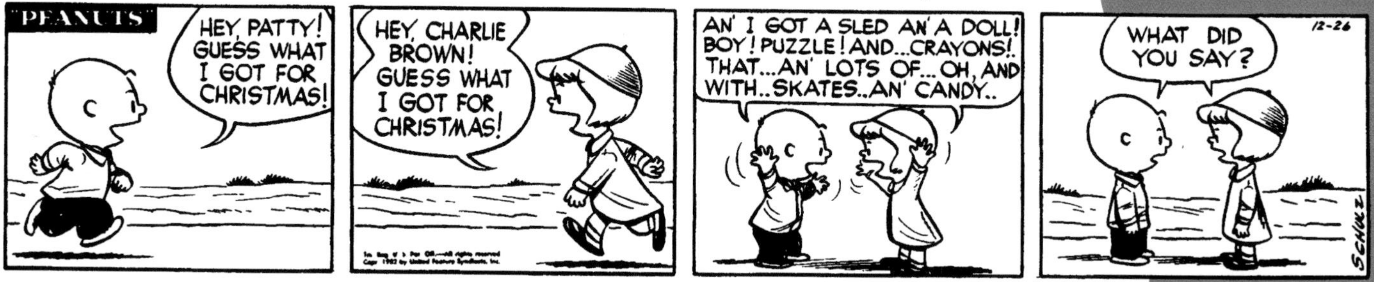
"PEANUTS"
HEY, PATTY! GUESS WHAT I GOT FOR CHRISTMAS!
HEY, CHARLIE BROWN! GUESS WHAT I GOT FOR CHRISTMAS!
AN' I GOT A SLED AN' A DOLL! BOY! PUZZLE! AND...CRAYONS!. THAT...AN' LOTS OF...OH, AND WITH..SKATES..AN' CANDY..
12-26
WHAT DID YOU SAY?
SCHULZ

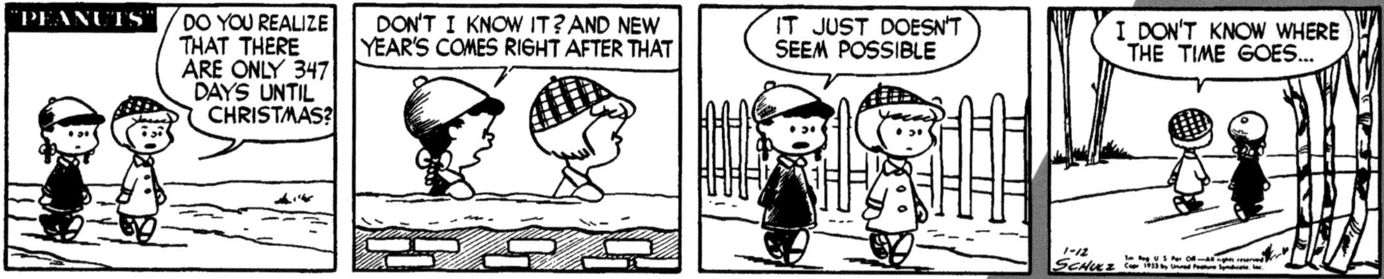
"PEANUTS"
DO YOU REALIZE THAT THERE ARE ONLY 347 DAYS UNTIL CHRISTMAS?
DON'T I KNOW IT? AND NEW YEAR'S COMES RIGHT AFTER THAT
IT JUST DOESN'T SEEM POSSIBLE
I DON'T KNOW WHERE THE TIME GOES...
1-12 SCHULZ

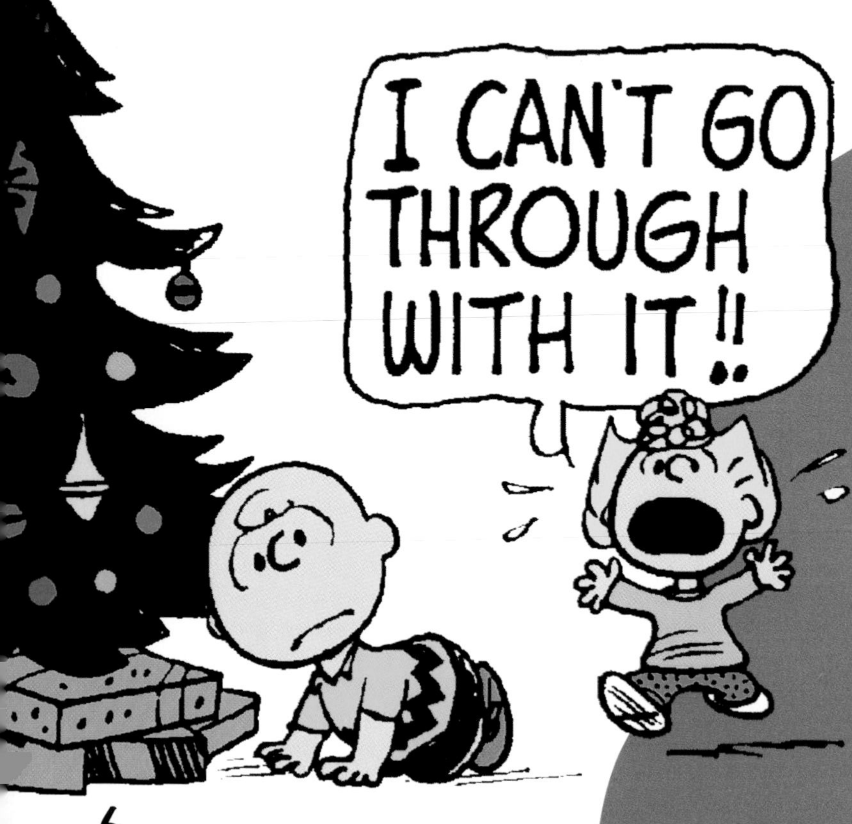
I CAN'T GO THROUGH WITH IT!!

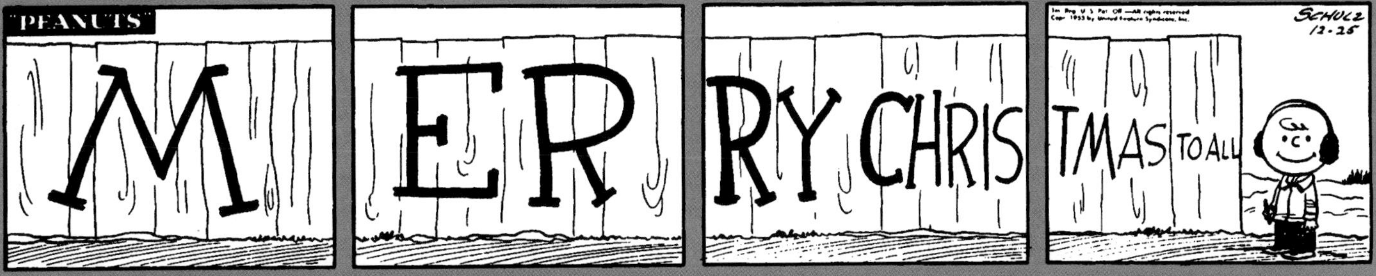
"PEANUTS"
MERRY CHRISTMAS TO ALL
SCHULZ 12-25

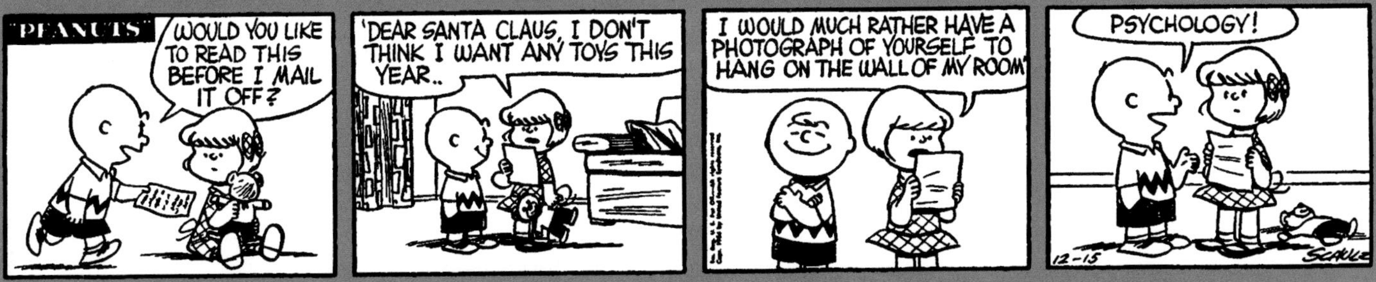
"PEANUTS"
WOULD YOU LIKE TO READ THIS BEFORE I MAIL IT OFF?
'DEAR SANTA CLAUS, I DON'T THINK I WANT ANY TOYS THIS YEAR..
I WOULD MUCH RATHER HAVE A PHOTOGRAPH OF YOURSELF TO HANG ON THE WALL OF MY ROOM'
PSYCHOLOGY!
12-15
SCHULZ

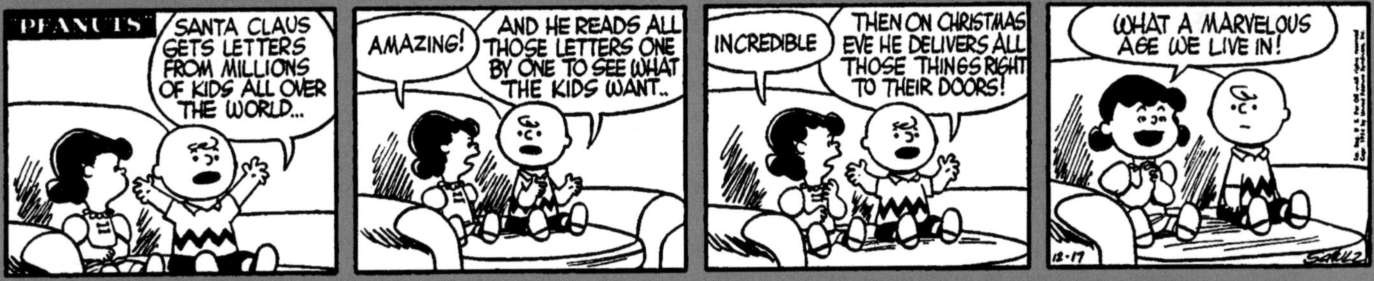
"PEANUTS"
SANTA CLAUS GETS LETTERS FROM MILLIONS OF KIDS ALL OVER THE WORLD...
AMAZING!
AND HE READS ALL THOSE LETTERS ONE BY ONE TO SEE WHAT THE KIDS WANT..
INCREDIBLE
THEN ON CHRISTMAS EVE HE DELIVERS ALL THOSE THINGS RIGHT TO THEIR DOORS!
WHAT A MARVELOUS AGE WE LIVE IN!
12-17
SCHULZ

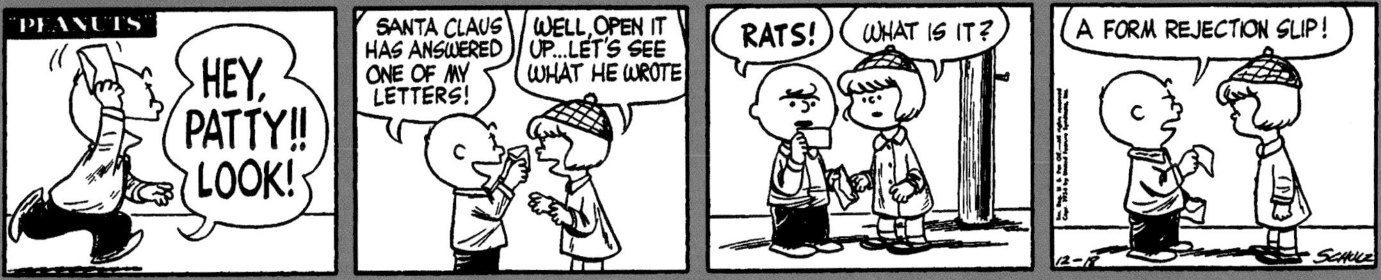
"PEANUTS"
HEY, PATTY!! LOOK!
SANTA CLAUS HAS ANSWERED ONE OF MY LETTERS!
WELL, OPEN IT UP...LET'S SEE WHAT HE WROTE
RATS!
WHAT IS IT?
A FORM REJECTION SLIP!
12-18
SCHULZ

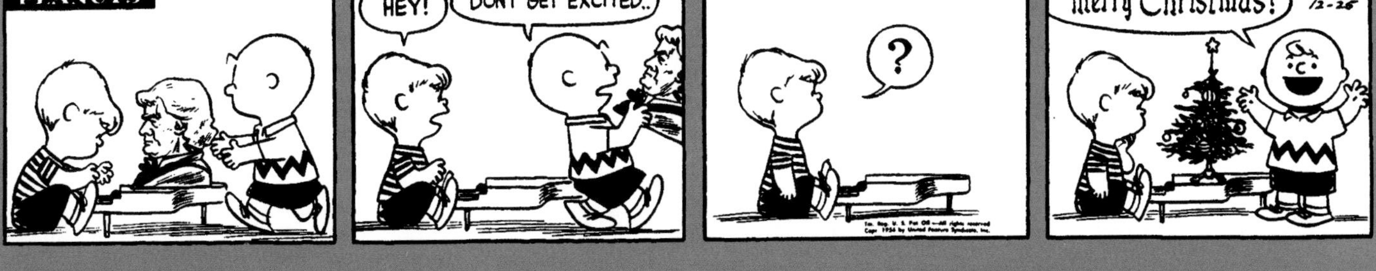
"PEANUTS"
HEY!
DON'T GET EXCITED..
?
'Merry Christmas!'
SCHULZ 12-25

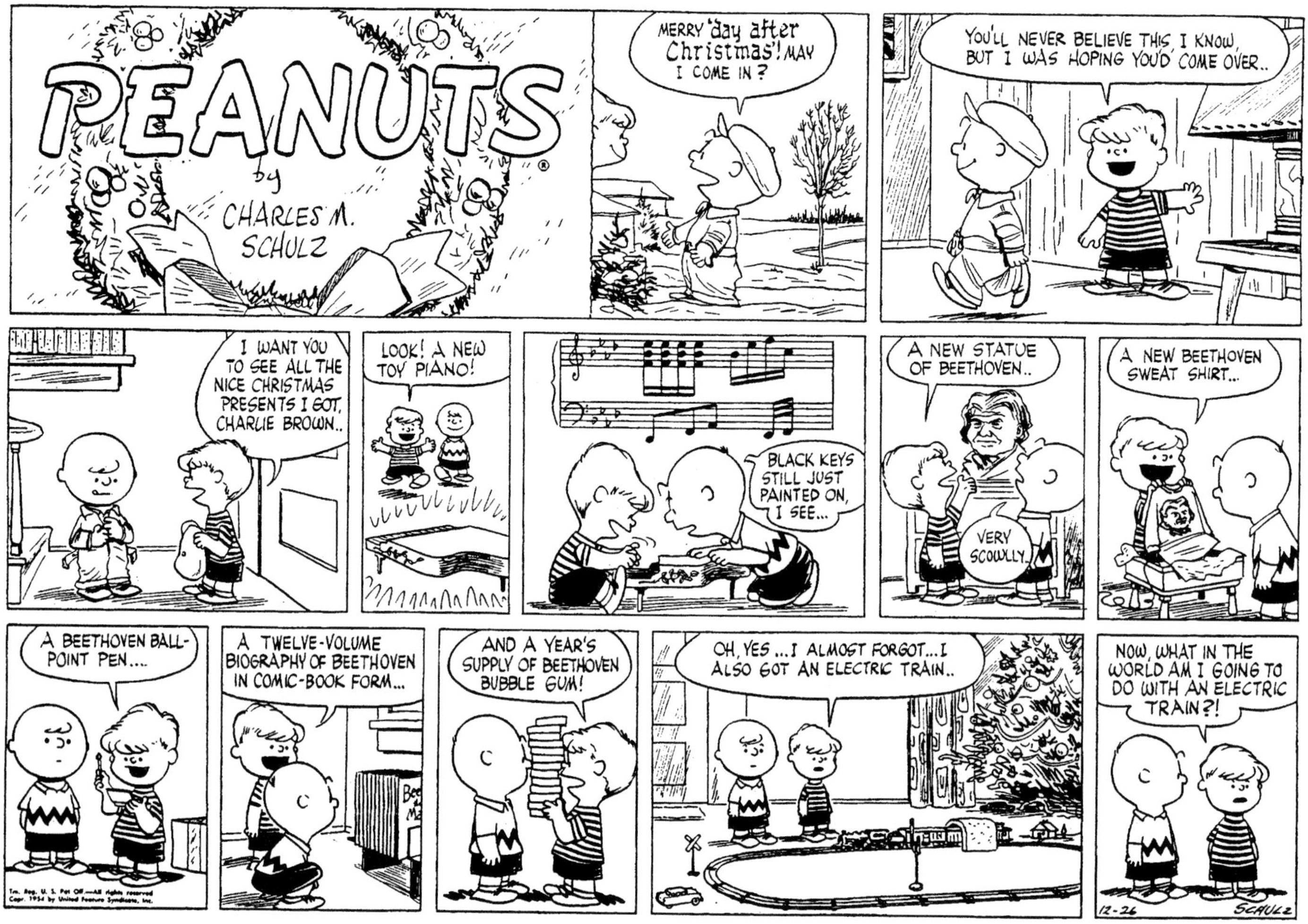
PEANUTS
by CHARLES M. SCHULZ
MERRY 'day after Christmas'! MAY I COME IN?
YOU'LL NEVER BELIEVE THIS, I KNOW, BUT I WAS HOPING YOU'D COME OVER..
I WANT YOU TO SEE ALL THE NICE CHRISTMAS PRESENTS I GOT, CHARLIE BROWN..
LOOK! A NEW TOY PIANO!
BLACK KEYS STILL JUST PAINTED ON, I SEE...
A NEW STATUE OF BEETHOVEN..
VERY SCOWLLY..
A NEW BEETHOVEN SWEAT SHIRT...
A BEETHOVEN BALL-POINT PEN....
A TWELVE-VOLUME BIOGRAPHY OF BEETHOVEN IN COMIC-BOOK FORM...
AND A YEAR'S SUPPLY OF BEETHOVEN BUBBLE GUM!
OH, YES ...I ALMOST FORGOT...I ALSO GOT AN ELECTRIC TRAIN..
NOW, WHAT IN THE WORLD AM I GOING TO DO WITH AN ELECTRIC TRAIN?!
Tm. Reg. U. S. Pat. Off.—All rights reserved
Copr. 1954 by United Feature Syndicate, Inc.
12-26
SCHULZ

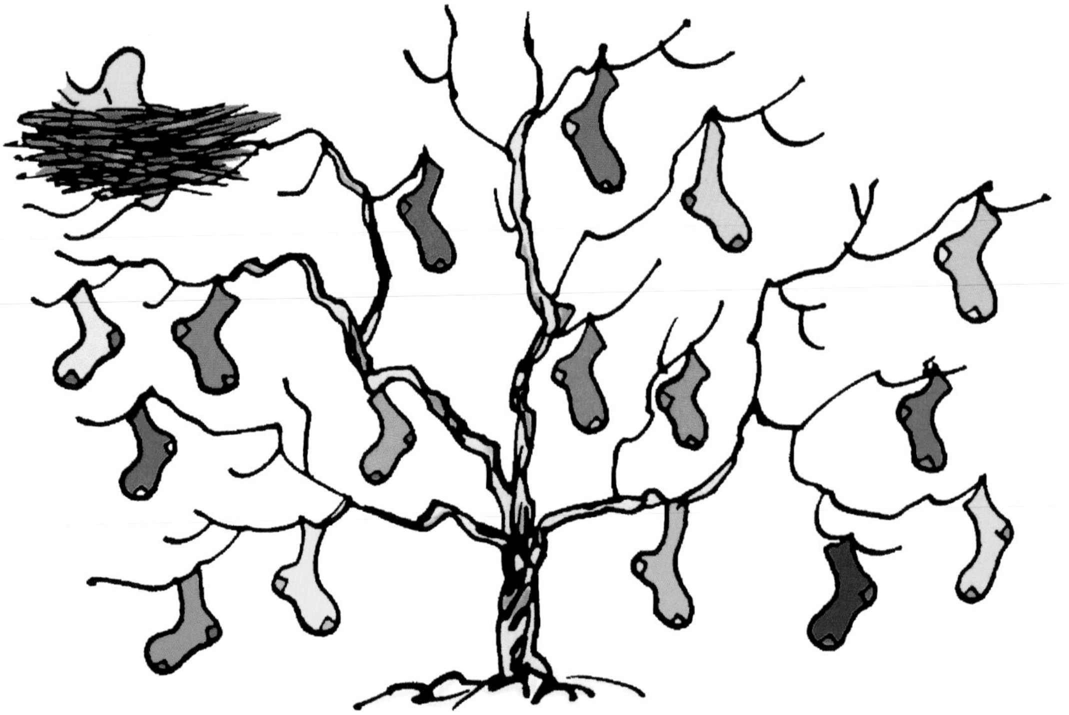

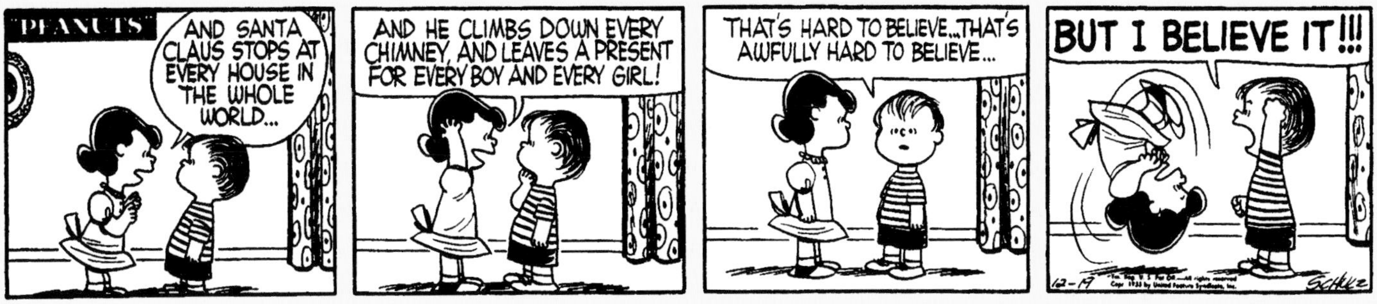
"PEANUTS"
AND SANTA CLAUS STOPS AT EVERY HOUSE IN THE WHOLE WORLD...
AND HE CLIMBS DOWN EVERY CHIMNEY, AND LEAVES A PRESENT FOR EVERY BOY AND EVERY GIRL!
THAT'S HARD TO BELIEVE...THAT'S AWFULLY HARD TO BELIEVE...
BUT I BELIEVE IT!!!
12-17
SCHULZ

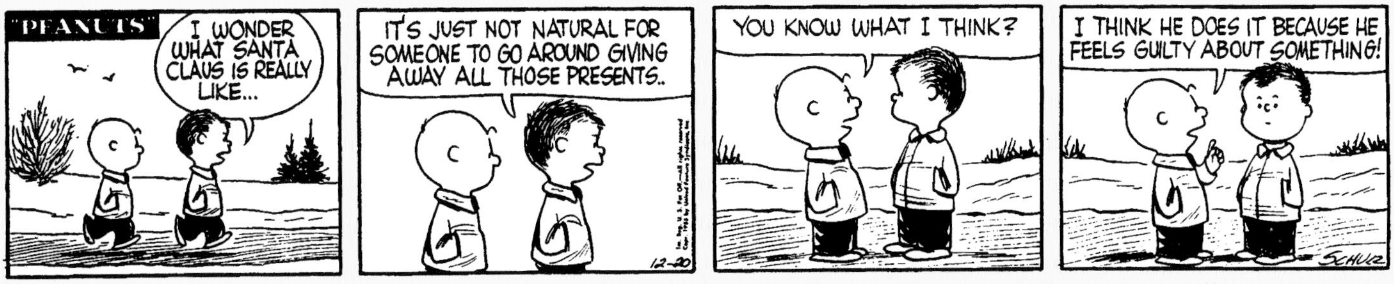
"PEANUTS"
I WONDER WHAT SANTA CLAUS IS REALLY LIKE...
IT'S JUST NOT NATURAL FOR SOMEONE TO GO AROUND GIVING AWAY ALL THOSE PRESENTS..
12-20
YOU KNOW WHAT I THINK?
I THINK HE DOES IT BECAUSE HE FEELS GUILTY ABOUT SOMETHING!
SCHULZ

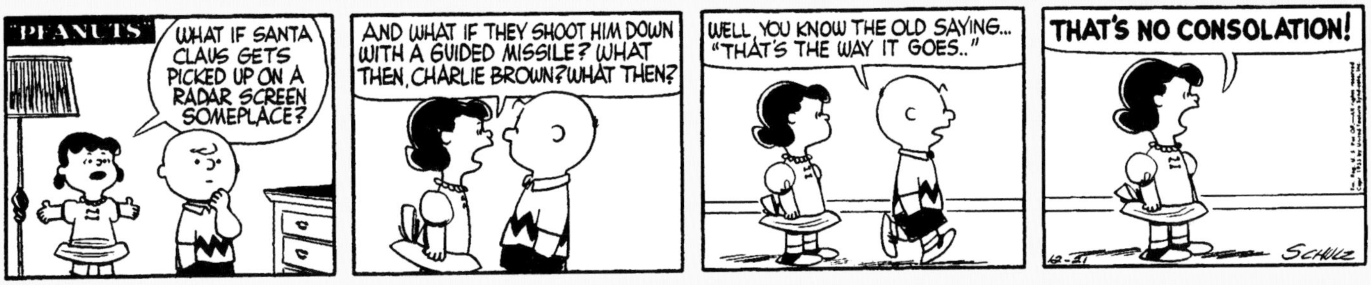
"PEANUTS"
WHAT IF SANTA CLAUS GETS PICKED UP ON A RADAR SCREEN SOMEPLACE?
AND WHAT IF THEY SHOOT HIM DOWN WITH A GUIDED MISSILE? WHAT THEN, CHARLIE BROWN? WHAT THEN?
WELL, YOU KNOW THE OLD SAYING... "THAT'S THE WAY IT GOES.."
THAT'S NO CONSOLATION!
12-21
SCHULZ

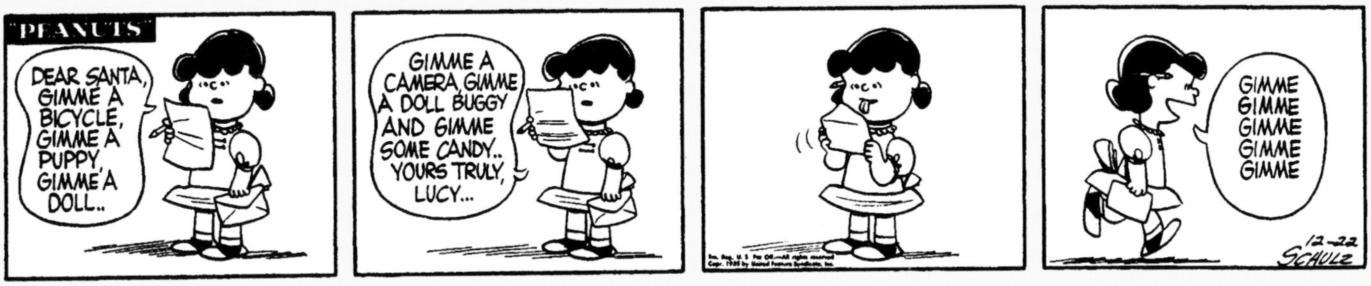
"PEANUTS"
DEAR SANTA, GIMME A BICYCLE, GIMME A PUPPY, GIMME A DOLL..
GIMME A CAMERA, GIMME A DOLL BUGGY AND GIMME SOME CANDY.. YOURS TRULY, LUCY...
GIMME GIMME GIMME GIMME GIMME
12-22
SCHULZ

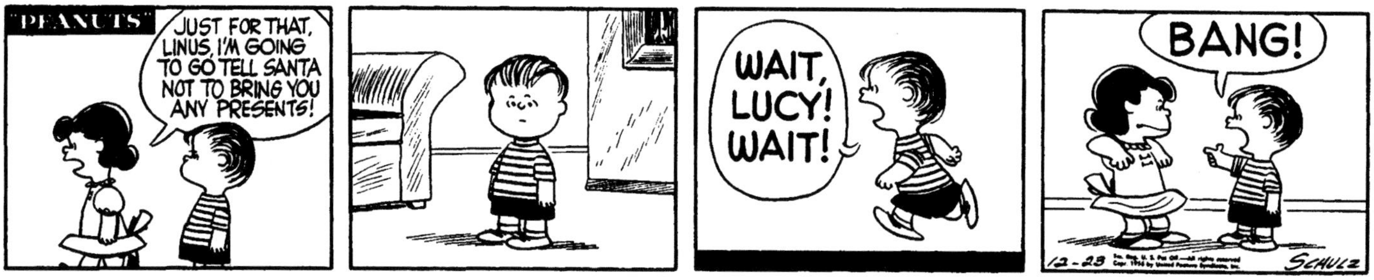
PEANUTS
JUST FOR THAT, LINUS, I'M GOING TO GO TELL SANTA NOT TO BRING YOU ANY PRESENTS!
WAIT, LUCY! WAIT!
BANG!
12-23
SCHULZ

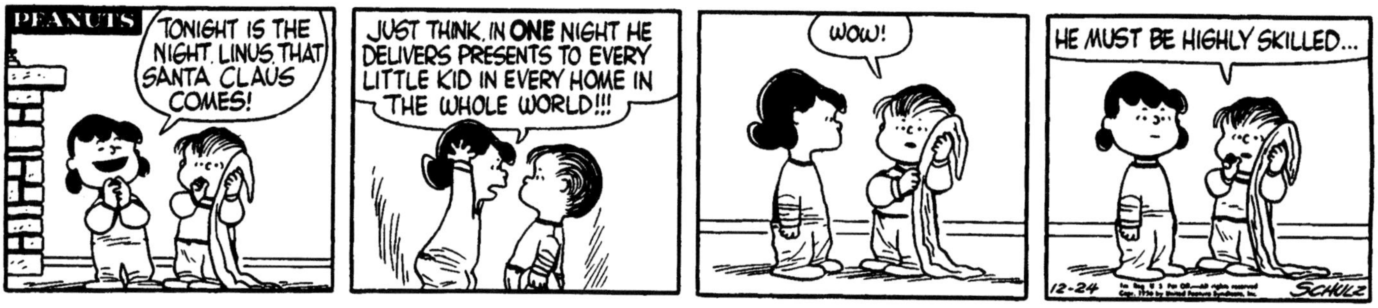
PEANUTS
TONIGHT IS THE NIGHT, LINUS, THAT SANTA CLAUS COMES!
JUST THINK, IN ONE NIGHT HE DELIVERS PRESENTS TO EVERY LITTLE KID IN EVERY HOME IN THE WHOLE WORLD!!!
WOW!
HE MUST BE HIGHLY SKILLED...
12-24
SCHULZ

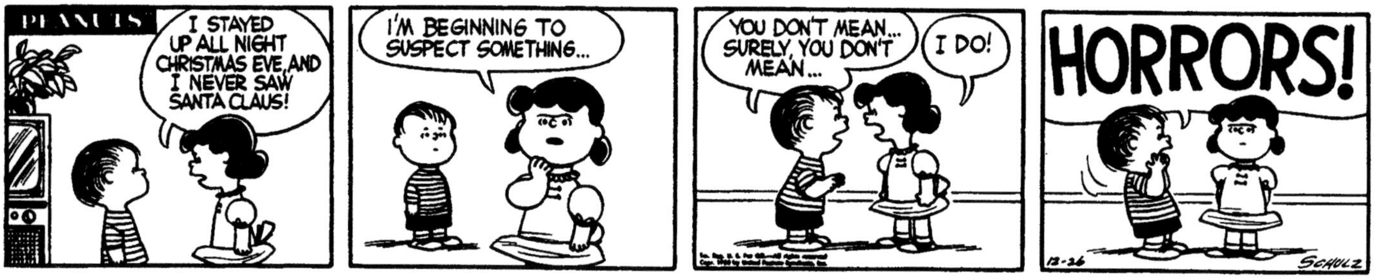
PEANUTS
I STAYED UP ALL NIGHT CHRISTMAS EVE, AND I NEVER SAW SANTA CLAUS!
I'M BEGINNING TO SUSPECT SOMETHING...
YOU DON'T MEAN... SURELY, YOU DON'T MEAN...
I DO!
HORRORS!
12-26
SCHULZ

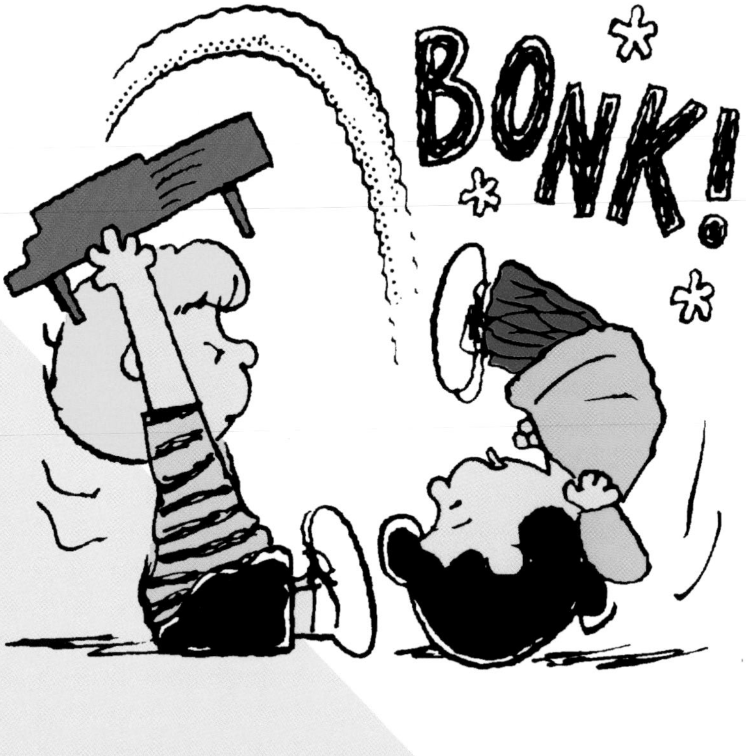
BONK!

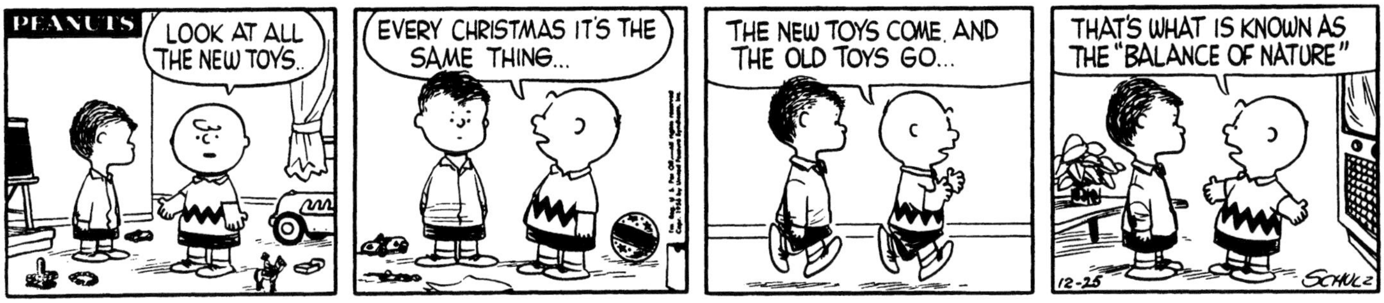
PEANUTS
LOOK AT ALL THE NEW TOYS..
EVERY CHRISTMAS IT'S THE SAME THING...
THE NEW TOYS COME, AND THE OLD TOYS GO...
THAT'S WHAT IS KNOWN AS THE "BALANCE OF NATURE"
12-25
SCHULZ

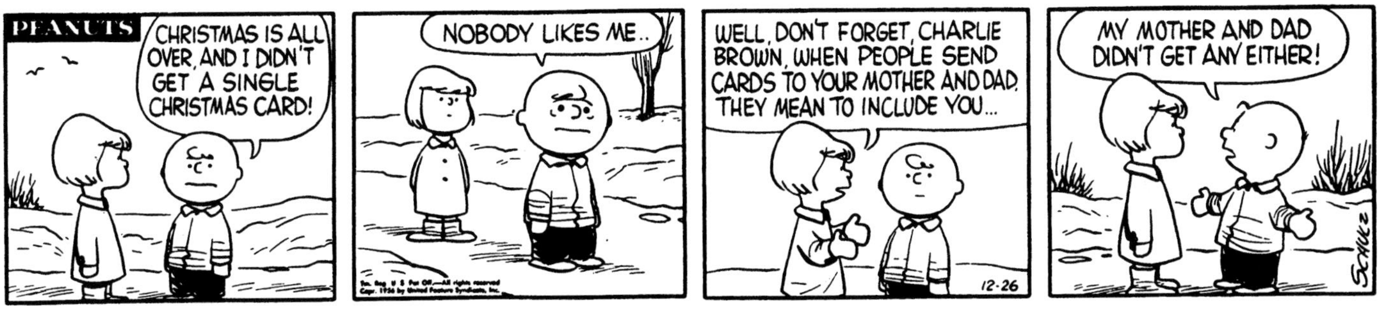
PEANUTS
CHRISTMAS IS ALL OVER, AND I DIDN'T GET A SINGLE CHRISTMAS CARD!
NOBODY LIKES ME..
WELL, DON'T FORGET, CHARLIE BROWN, WHEN PEOPLE SEND CARDS TO YOUR MOTHER AND DAD, THEY MEAN TO INCLUDE YOU...
12-26
MY MOTHER AND DAD DIDN'T GET ANY EITHER!
SCHULZ

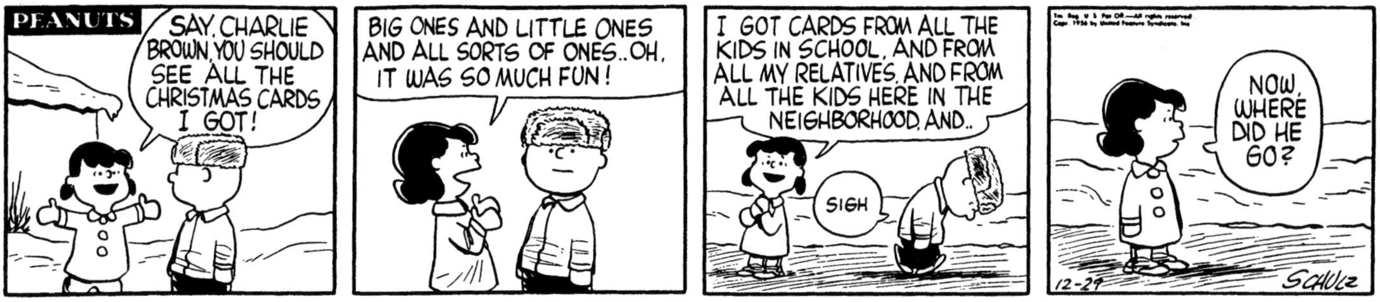
PEANUTS
SAY, CHARLIE BROWN, YOU SHOULD SEE ALL THE CHRISTMAS CARDS I GOT!
BIG ONES AND LITTLE ONES AND ALL SORTS OF ONES..OH, IT WAS SO MUCH FUN!
I GOT CARDS FROM ALL THE KIDS IN SCHOOL, AND FROM ALL MY RELATIVES, AND FROM ALL THE KIDS HERE IN THE NEIGHBORHOOD, AND..
SIGH
NOW, WHERE DID HE GO?
12-29
SCHULZ

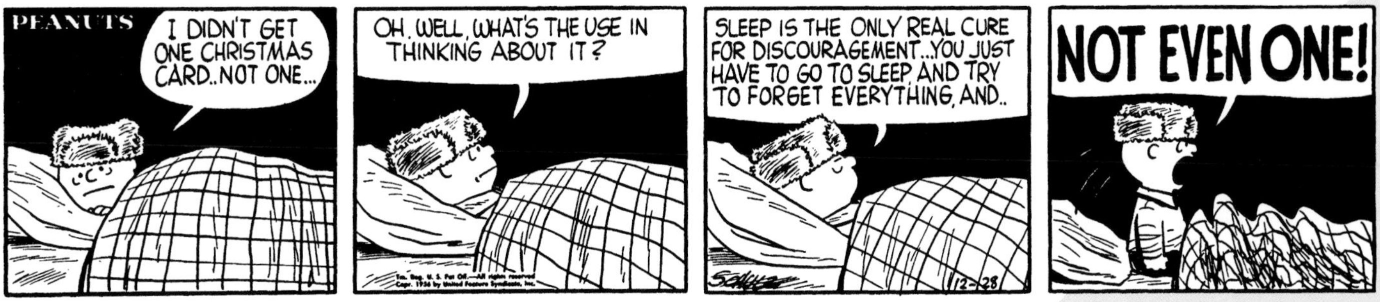
PEANUTS
I DIDN'T GET ONE CHRISTMAS CARD..NOT ONE...
OH, WELL, WHAT'S THE USE IN THINKING ABOUT IT?
SLEEP IS THE ONLY REAL CURE FOR DISCOURAGEMENT...YOU JUST HAVE TO GO TO SLEEP, AND TRY TO FORGET EVERYTHING, AND..
12-28
NOT EVEN ONE!

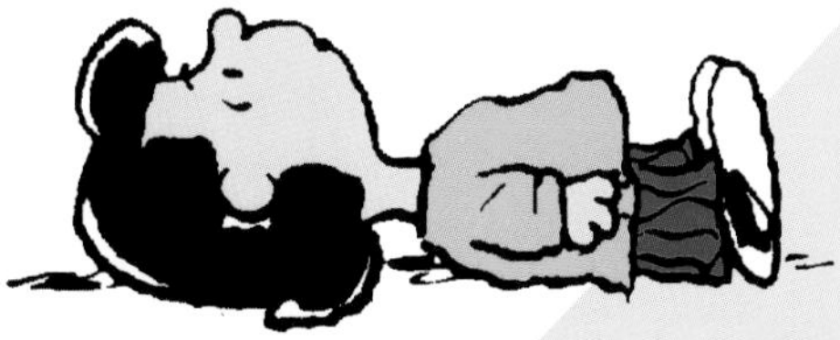

PEANUTS
I'M SO SORRY, CHARLIE BROWN..
ABOUT WHAT?
I HEARD YOU DIDN'T GET A SINGLE CHRISTMAS CARD...
OH I FINALLY GOT ONE ALL RIGHT...
UH, HUH...
I'M THE ONLY PERSON I KNOW WHO HAD TO GO OUT AND BUY HIMSELF A CHRISTMAS CARD!
12-29
SCHULZ

PEANUTS
WELL, LINUS.. HAVE YOU DONE ALL YOUR CHRISTMAS SHOPPING?
WHY SHOULD I DO ANY CHRISTMAS SHOPPING?
I'M NOT INTERESTED IN GIVING... I'M ONLY INTERESTED IN 'GITTING'
GIT GIT GIT GIT!
12-23
SCHULZ

PEANUTS
Christmas Greetings FROM SHERMY...
LUCY
PIG-PEN
VIOLET
PATTY
Tm. Reg. U. S. Pat Off.—All rights reserved Copr. 1957 by United Feature Syndicate, Inc
SNOOPY
SCHROEDER
12-25
LINUS
AND GOOD OL' CHARLIE BROWN
SCHULZ

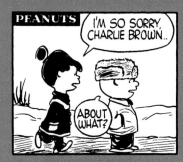

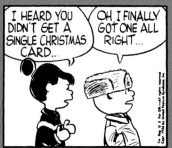

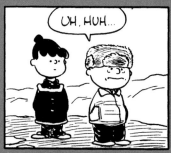

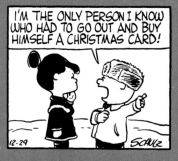

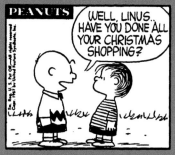

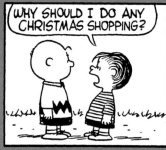

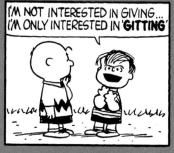

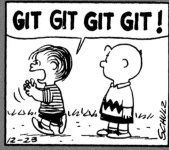

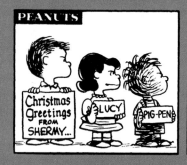

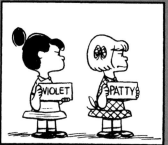

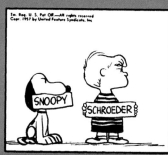

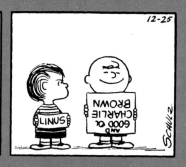

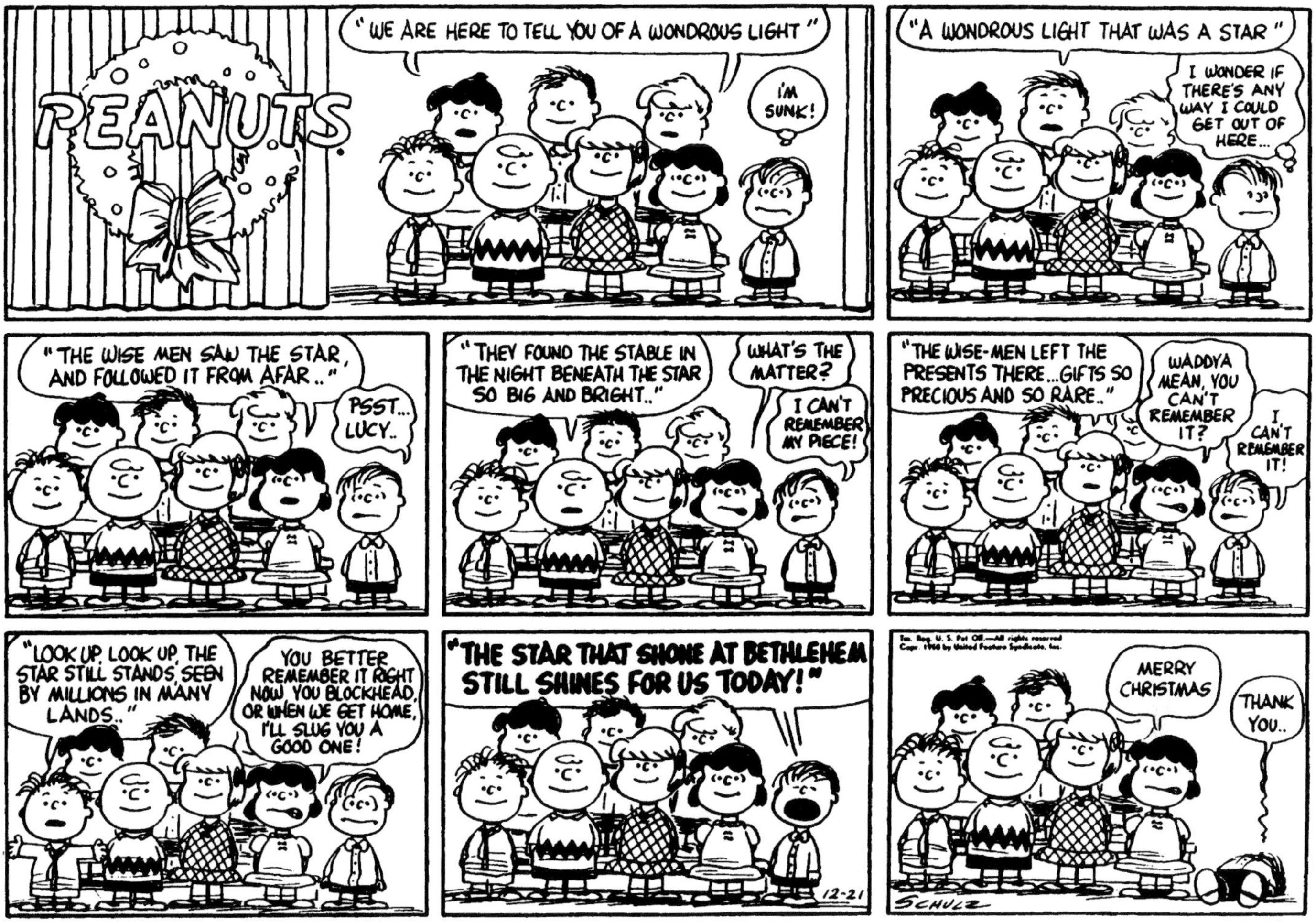
PEANUTS
" WE ARE HERE TO TELL YOU OF A WONDROUS LIGHT "
I'M SUNK!
" A WONDROUS LIGHT THAT WAS A STAR "
I WONDER IF THERE'S ANY WAY I COULD GET OUT OF HERE...
" THE WISE MEN SAW THE STAR, AND FOLLOWED IT FROM AFAR .. "
PSST... LUCY..
" THEY FOUND THE STABLE IN THE NIGHT BENEATH THE STAR SO BIG AND BRIGHT.. "
WHAT'S THE MATTER?
I CAN'T REMEMBER MY PIECE!
" THE WISE-MEN LEFT THE PRESENTS THERE...GIFTS SO PRECIOUS AND SO RARE.. "
WADDYA MEAN, YOU CAN'T REMEMBER IT?
I CAN'T REMEMBER IT!
" LOOK UP, LOOK UP, THE STAR STILL STANDS, SEEN BY MILLIONS IN MANY LANDS.. "
YOU BETTER REMEMBER IT RIGHT NOW YOU BLOCKHEAD, OR WHEN WE GET HOME, I'LL SLUG YOU A GOOD ONE!
" THE STAR THAT SHONE AT BETHLEHEM STILL SHINES FOR US TODAY! "
12-21
MERRY CHRISTMAS
THANK YOU..
SCHULZ

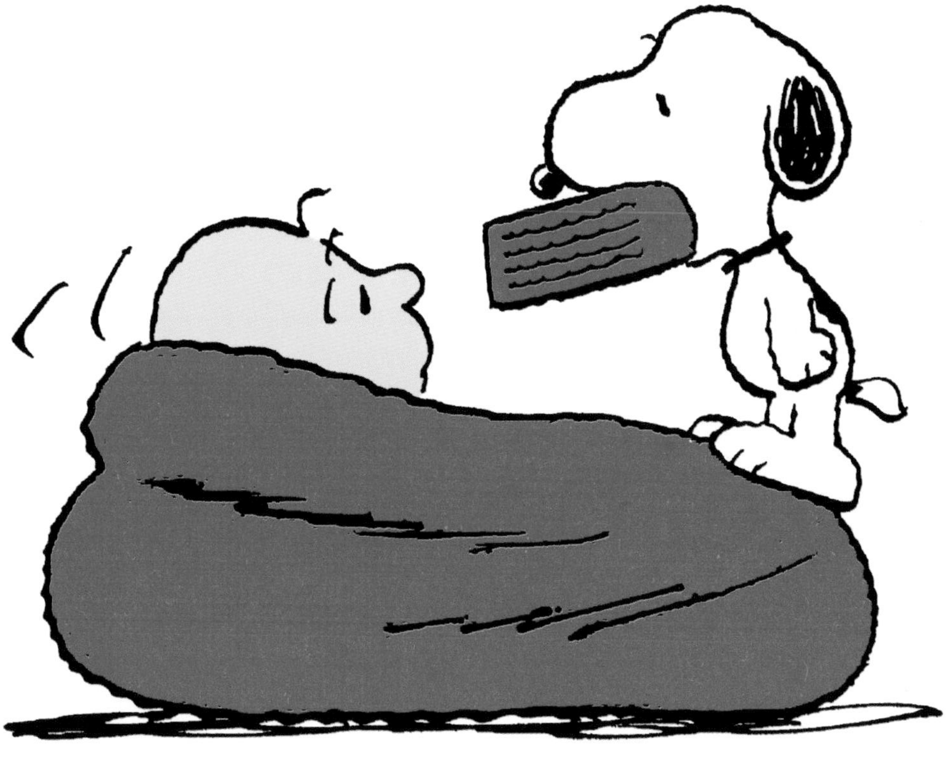

PEANUTS
by SCHULZ
YES, SIR... LONG PANTS SURE DO MAKE THE MAN!
WELL, HOW DO I LOOK?
FINE...IT'S THE FIRST TIME I'VE SEEN YOU IN A WHITE SHIRT IN SIX MONTHS!
NOW ARE YOU SURE YOU KNOW YOUR PIECE FOR THE CHRISTMAS PROGRAM?
I KNOW IT BACKWARDS AND FORWARDS AND SIDEWAYS AND UPSIDE DOWN! I COULD SAY IT IN MY SLEEP!
YEAH, WELL, I REMEMBER LAST YEAR..YOU ALMOST GOOFED THE WHOLE PROGRAM!
WELL, THIS IS THIS YEAR, AND THIS YEAR I WON'T FORGET!
"AND THE ANGEL SAID UNTO THEM, FEAR NOT: FOR, BEHOLD, I BRING YOU GOOD TIDINGS OF GREAT JOY WHICH SHALL BE TO ALL PEOPLE."
SAY, THAT'S PRETTY GOOD..
I TOLD YOU I KNEW IT.. I HAVE A MEMORY LIKE THE PROVERBIAL ELEPHANT!
WELL, I'M GOING ON AHEAD TO THE CHURCH...I'LL SEE YOU THERE...
12-20
"...FOR, BEHOLD, I BRING YOU GOOD TIDINGS OF GREAT JOY WHICH SHALL BE TO ALL PEOPLE." WHAT A MEMORY!!!
WHAT IN THE WORLD? I THOUGHT YOU JUST LEFT?
I DID, BUT I CAME BACK..
I FORGOT WHERE THE CHURCH IS!
SCHULZ

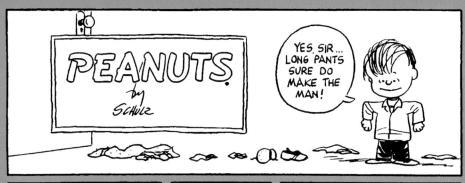

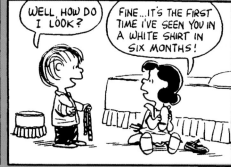

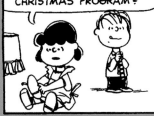

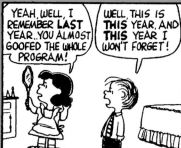

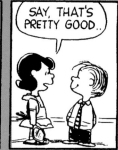

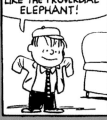

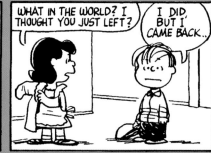

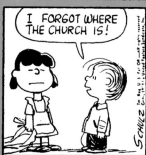

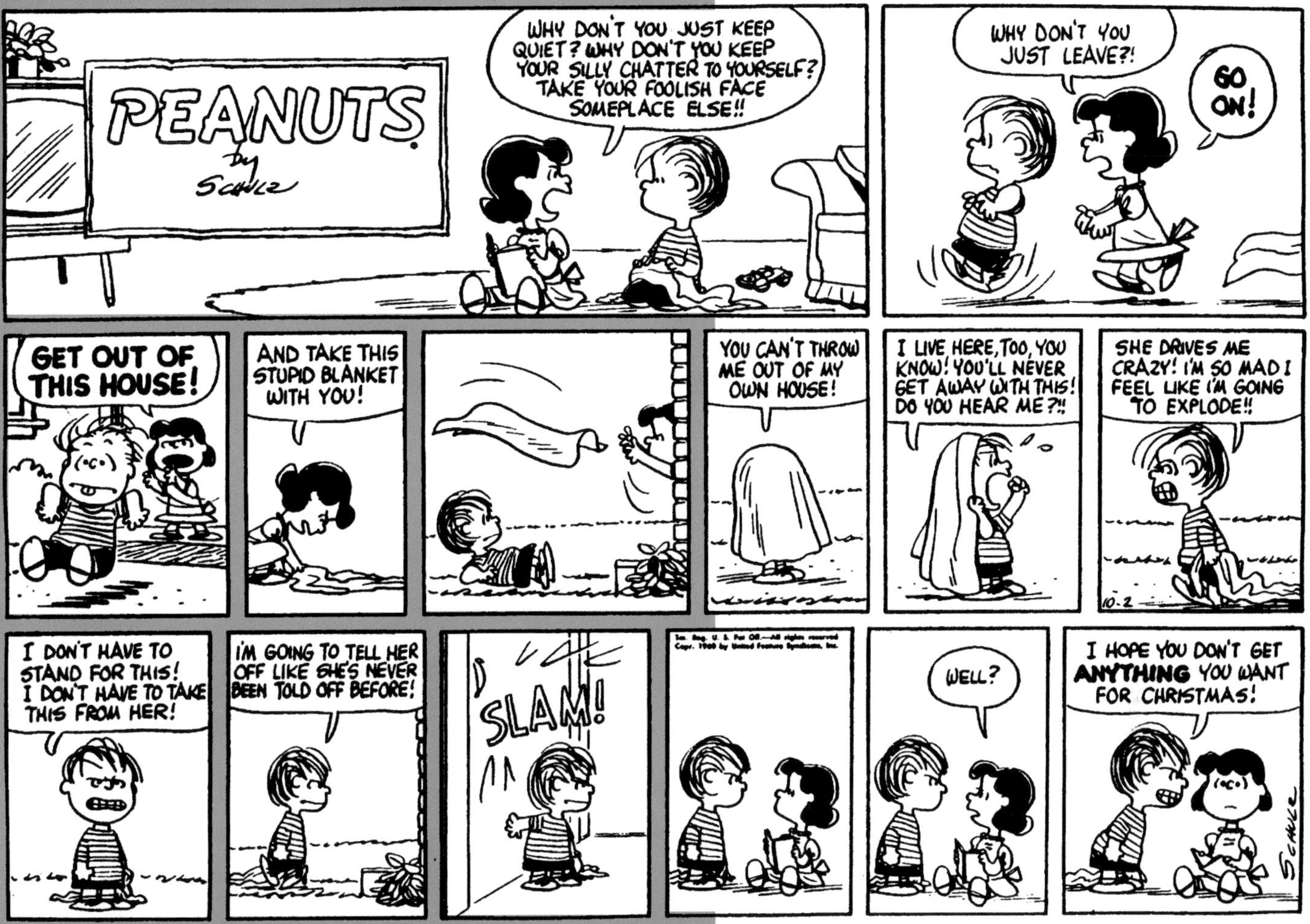
PEANUTS
by Schulz
WHY DON'T YOU JUST KEEP QUIET? WHY DON'T YOU KEEP YOUR SILLY CHATTER TO YOURSELF? TAKE YOUR FOOLISH FACE SOMEPLACE ELSE!!
WHY DON'T YOU JUST LEAVE?!
GO ON!
GET OUT OF THIS HOUSE!
AND TAKE THIS STUPID BLANKET WITH YOU!
YOU CAN'T THROW ME OUT OF MY OWN HOUSE!
I LIVE HERE, TOO, YOU KNOW! YOU'LL NEVER GET AWAY WITH THIS! DO YOU HEAR ME?!!
SHE DRIVES ME CRAZY! I'M SO MAD I FEEL LIKE I'M GOING TO EXPLODE!!
10-2
I DON'T HAVE TO STAND FOR THIS! I DON'T HAVE TO TAKE THIS FROM HER!
I'M GOING TO TELL HER OFF LIKE SHE'S NEVER BEEN TOLD OFF BEFORE!
SLAM!
WELL?
I HOPE YOU DON'T GET **ANYTHING** YOU WANT FOR CHRISTMAS!
SCHULZ

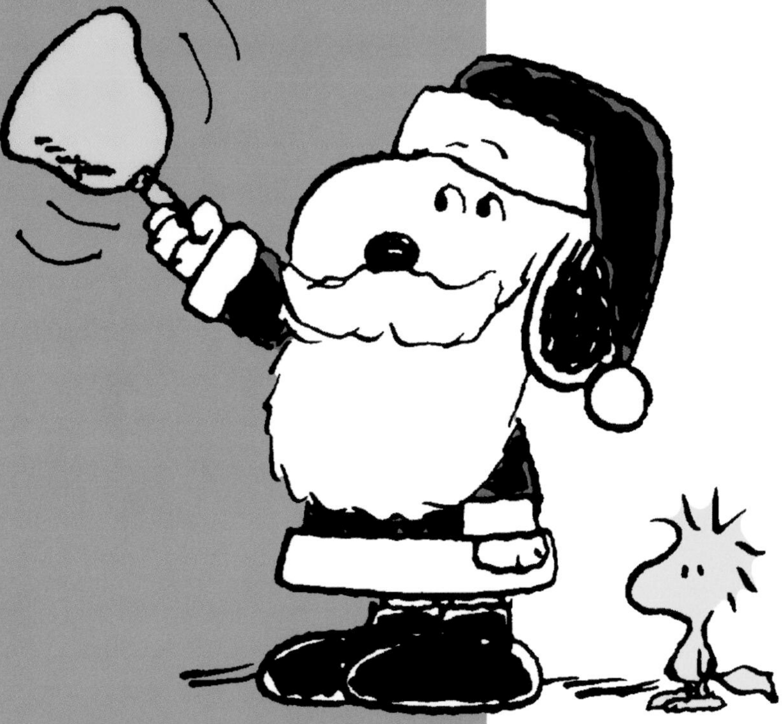

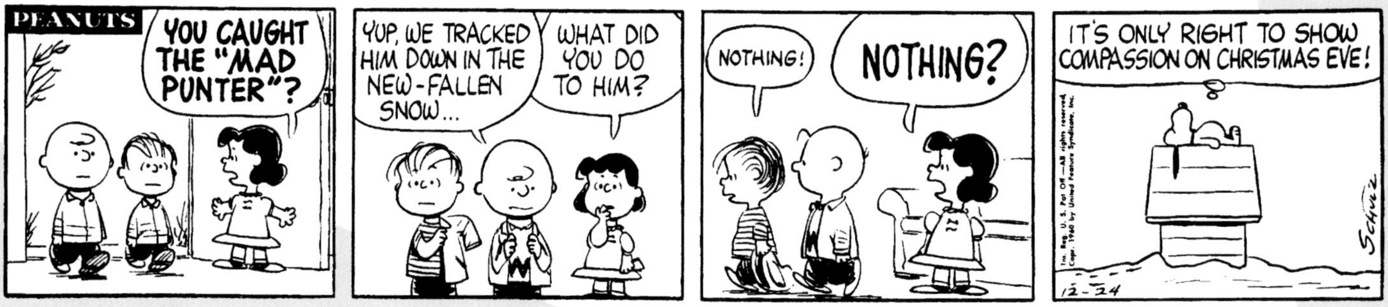
PEANUTS
YOU CAUGHT THE "MAD PUNTER"?
YUP, WE TRACKED HIM DOWN IN THE NEW-FALLEN SNOW...
WHAT DID YOU DO TO HIM?
NOTHING!
NOTHING?
IT'S ONLY RIGHT TO SHOW COMPASSION ON CHRISTMAS EVE!
SCHULZ
12-24

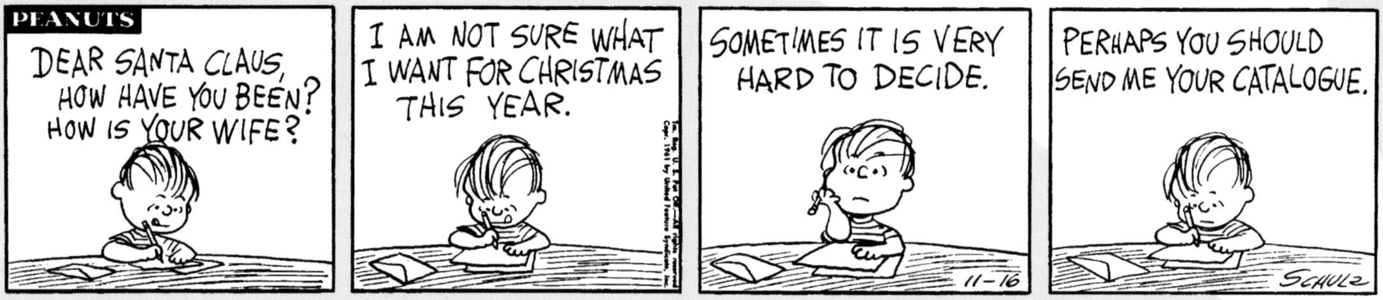
PEANUTS
DEAR SANTA CLAUS, HOW HAVE YOU BEEN? HOW IS YOUR WIFE?
I AM NOT SURE WHAT I WANT FOR CHRISTMAS THIS YEAR.
SOMETIMES IT IS VERY HARD TO DECIDE.
11-16
PERHAPS YOU SHOULD SEND ME YOUR CATALOGUE.
SCHULZ

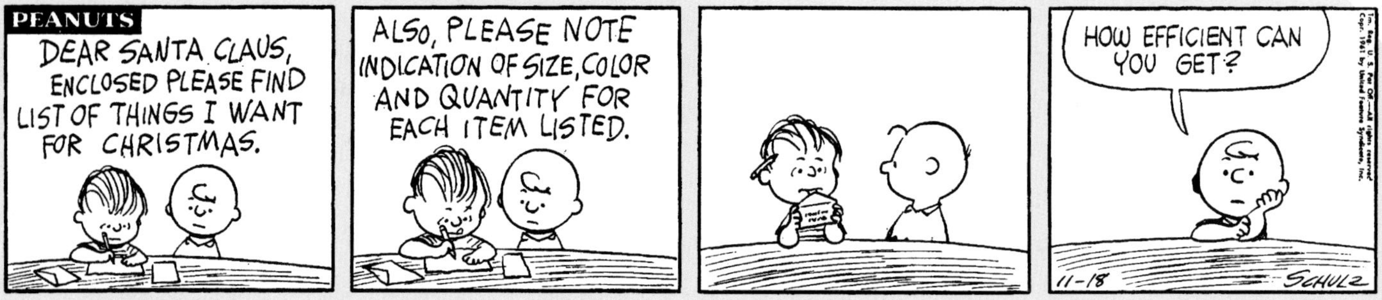
PEANUTS
DEAR SANTA CLAUS, ENCLOSED PLEASE FIND LIST OF THINGS I WANT FOR CHRISTMAS.
ALSO, PLEASE NOTE INDICATION OF SIZE, COLOR AND QUANTITY FOR EACH ITEM LISTED.
HOW EFFICIENT CAN YOU GET?
11-18
SCHULZ

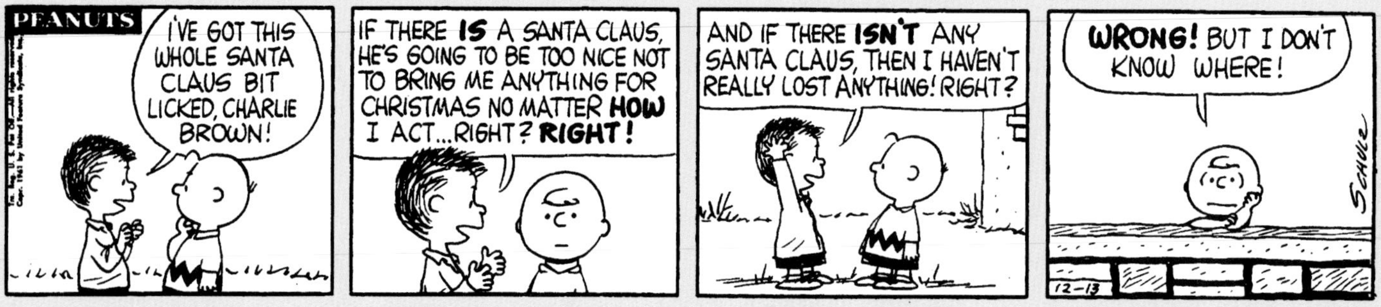
PEANUTS
I'VE GOT THIS WHOLE SANTA CLAUS BIT LICKED, CHARLIE BROWN!
IF THERE IS A SANTA CLAUS, HE'S GOING TO BE TOO NICE NOT TO BRING ME ANYTHING FOR CHRISTMAS NO MATTER HOW I ACT...RIGHT? RIGHT!
AND IF THERE ISN'T ANY SANTA CLAUS, THEN I HAVEN'T REALLY LOST ANYTHING! RIGHT?
WRONG! BUT I DON'T KNOW WHERE!
SCHULZ
12-13

PEANUTS
THIS IS MY "GIT" LIST, CHARLIE BROWN..
THESE ARE ALL THE THINGS I FIGURE I'M GONNA "GIT" FOR CHRISTMAS FROM MY TWO GRAMPAS AND TWO GRAMMAS AND EIGHT UNCLES AND AUNTS!
12-14
WHERE'S YOUR "GIVE" LIST?
MY WHAT?
I KNEW IT!
SCHULZ

PEANUTS
AND THEN, ON CHRISTMAS EVE, SANTA CLAUS COMES DOWN THE CHIMNEY..
HE LEAVES THE TOYS ON THE HEARTH, GOES BACK UP THE CHIMNEY AND FLIES OFF THROUGH THE AIR IN HIS SLED!
Tm. Reg. U. S. Pat. Off.—All rights reserved
Copr. 1961 by United Feature Syndicate, Inc.
12-22
SOMEHOW, I SENSE AN ELEMENT OF DOUBT..
SCHULZ

HELP
HELP
HELP

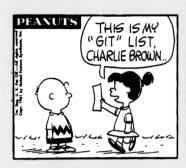

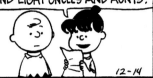

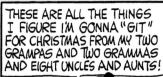

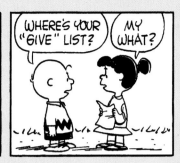

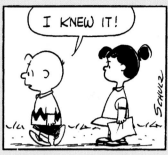

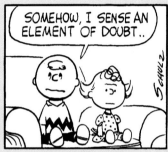

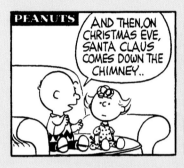

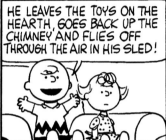

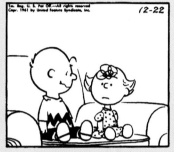

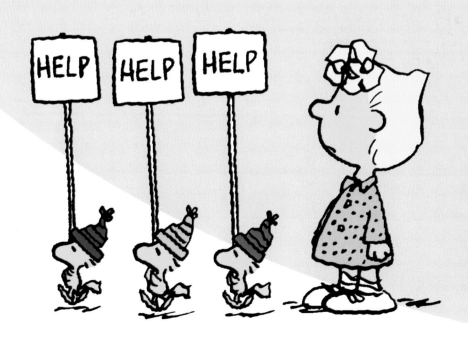

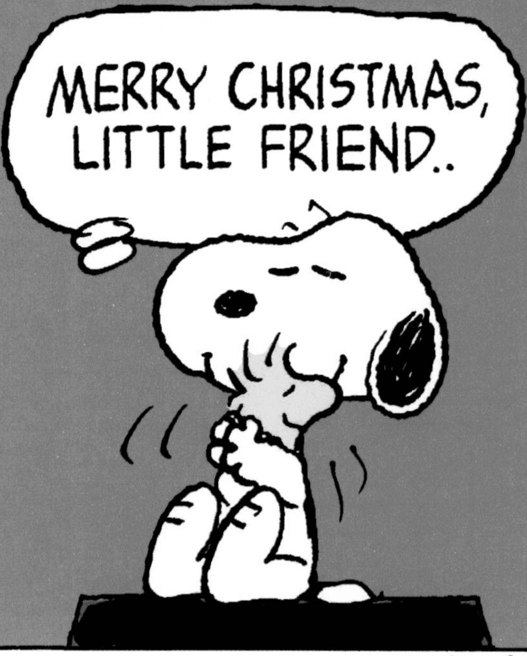
MERRY CHRISTMAS, LITTLE FRIEND..

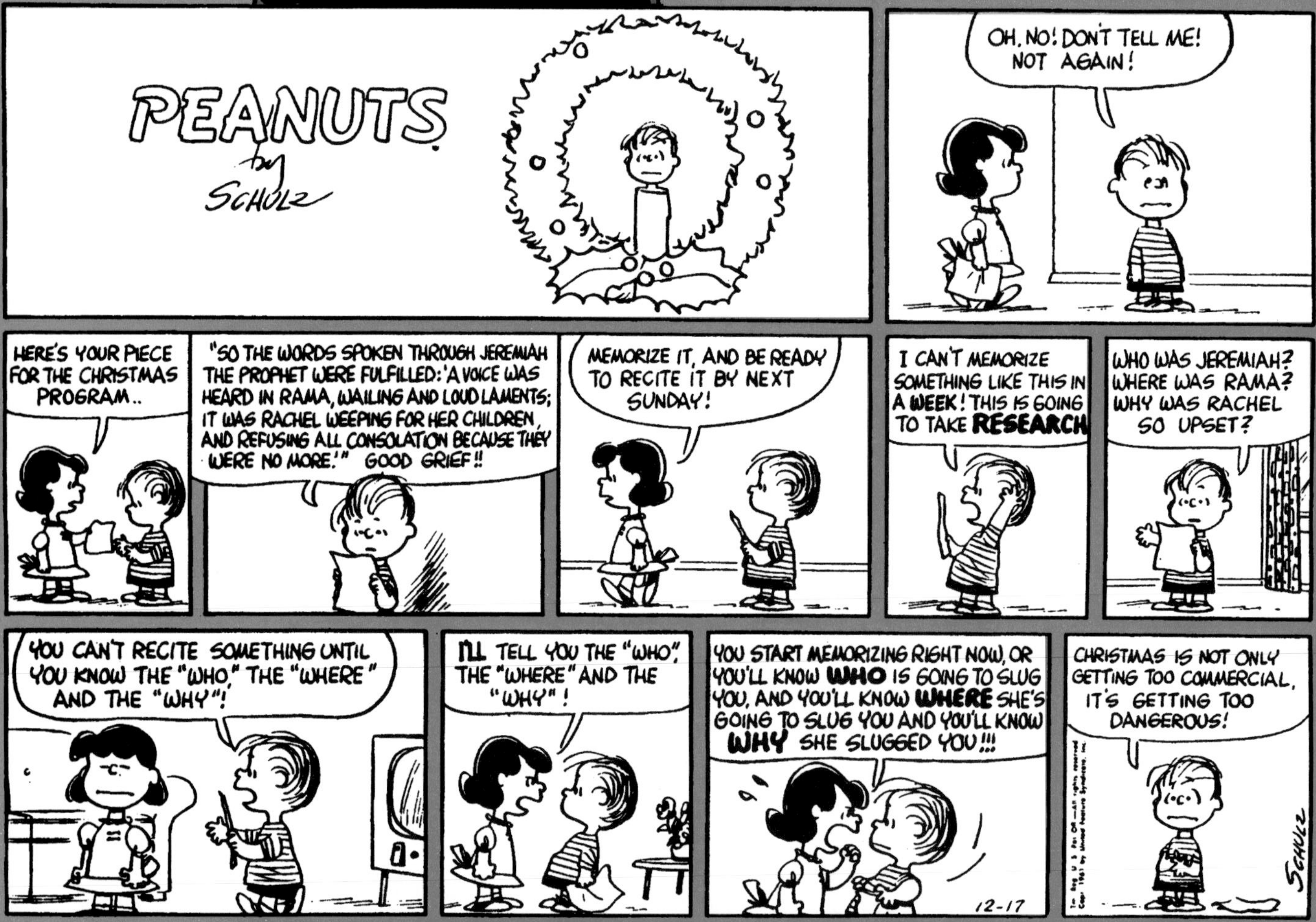
PEANUTS
by SCHULZ
OH, NO! DON'T TELL ME! NOT AGAIN!
HERE'S YOUR PIECE FOR THE CHRISTMAS PROGRAM..
"SO THE WORDS SPOKEN THROUGH JEREMIAH THE PROPHET WERE FULFILLED: 'A VOICE WAS HEARD IN RAMA, WAILING AND LOUD LAMENTS; IT WAS RACHEL WEEPING FOR HER CHILDREN, AND REFUSING ALL CONSOLATION BECAUSE THEY WERE NO MORE.'" GOOD GRIEF!!
MEMORIZE IT, AND BE READY TO RECITE IT BY NEXT SUNDAY!
I CAN'T MEMORIZE SOMETHING LIKE THIS IN A WEEK! THIS IS GOING TO TAKE RESEARCH
WHO WAS JEREMIAH? WHERE WAS RAMA? WHY WAS RACHEL SO UPSET?
YOU CAN'T RECITE SOMETHING UNTIL YOU KNOW THE "WHO," THE "WHERE" AND THE "WHY"!
I'LL TELL YOU THE "WHO", THE "WHERE" AND THE "WHY"!
YOU START MEMORIZING RIGHT NOW, OR YOU'LL KNOW WHO IS GOING TO SLUG YOU, AND YOU'LL KNOW WHERE SHE'S GOING TO SLUG YOU AND YOU'LL KNOW WHY SHE SLUGGED YOU!!!
12-17
CHRISTMAS IS NOT ONLY GETTING TOO COMMERCIAL, IT'S GETTING TOO DANGEROUS!
SCHULZ

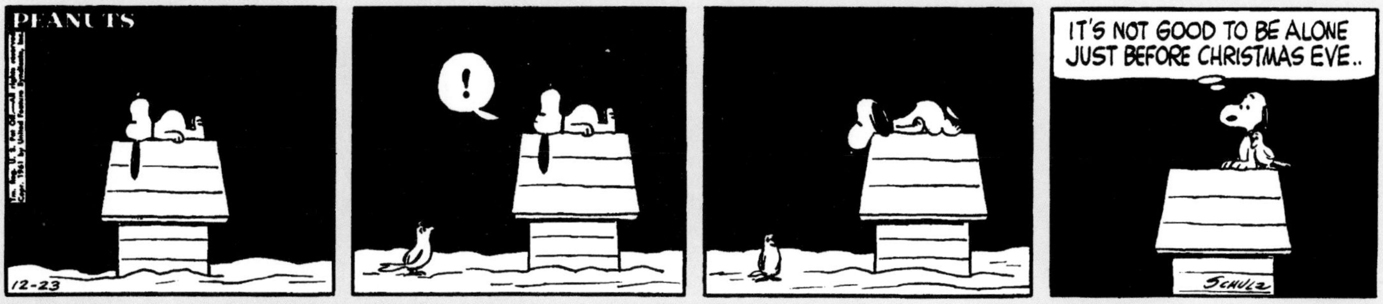
PEANUTS
12-23
!
IT'S NOT GOOD TO BE ALONE JUST BEFORE CHRISTMAS EVE..
SCHULZ

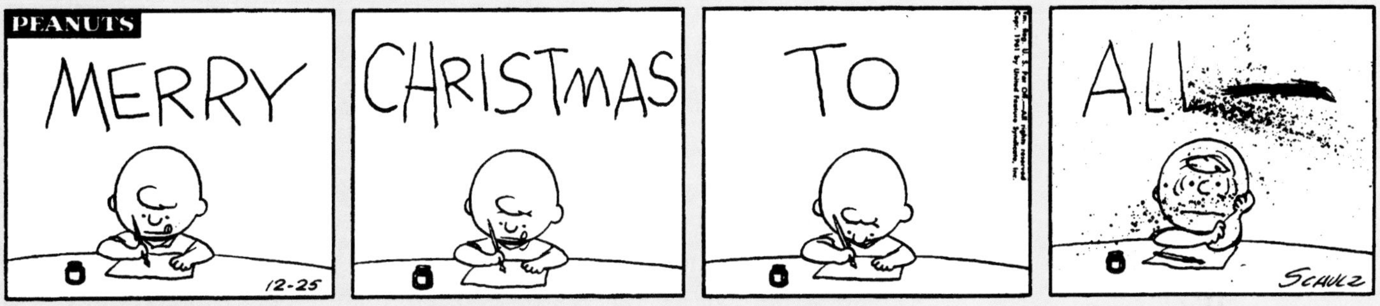
PEANUTS
MERRY
CHRISTMAS
TO
ALL
12-25
SCHULZ

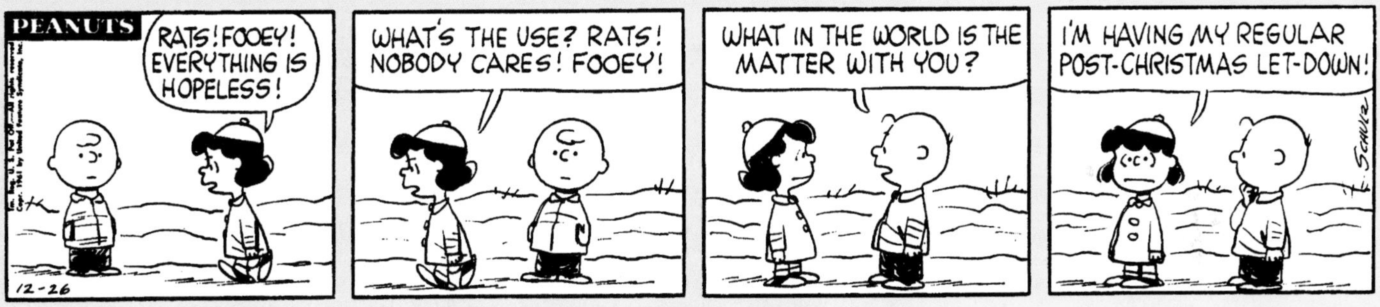
PEANUTS
RATS! FOOEY! EVERYTHING IS HOPELESS!
12-26
WHAT'S THE USE? RATS! NOBODY CARES! FOOEY!
WHAT IN THE WORLD IS THE MATTER WITH YOU?
I'M HAVING MY REGULAR POST-CHRISTMAS LET-DOWN!
SCHULZ

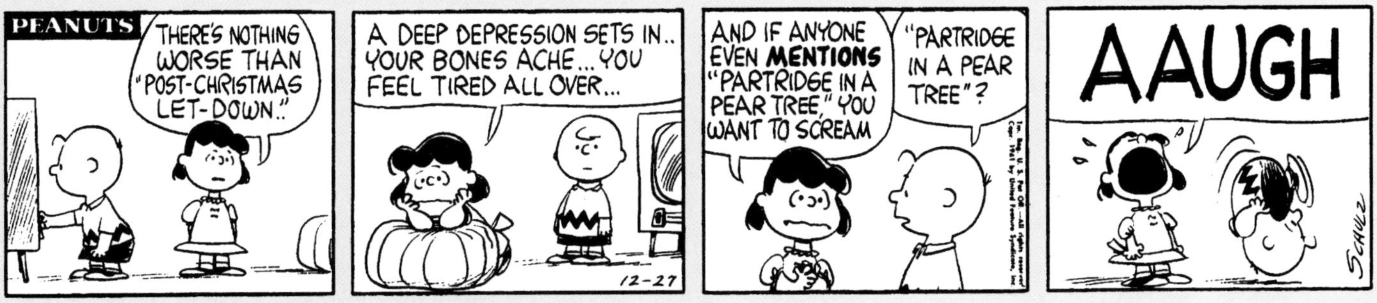
PEANUTS
THERE'S NOTHING WORSE THAN "POST-CHRISTMAS LET-DOWN."
A DEEP DEPRESSION SETS IN.. YOUR BONES ACHE... YOU FEEL TIRED ALL OVER...
12-27
AND IF ANYONE EVEN **MENTIONS** "PARTRIDGE IN A PEAR TREE," YOU WANT TO SCREAM
"PARTRIDGE IN A PEAR TREE"?
AAUGH
SCHULZ

PEANUTS
by SCHULZ
WHAT ARE YOU JUST STANDING AROUND FOR?
AREN'T YOU GOING TO GET READY?
I DON'T KNOW...
WHAT DO YOU MEAN, YOU DON'T KNOW?
I DON'T KNOW IF I'LL BE IN THE CHRISTMAS PROGRAM OR NOT..
ALL RIGHT, THEN, DON'T!
IF HE CAN'T MEMORIZE A SIMPLE LITTLE PIECE, WHY SHOULD I CARE? WHY SHOULD I ALWAYS HAVE TO WORRY ABOUT HIM?!
HE'LL BE THE ONE WHO GETS IN TROUBLE, NOT ME! WHAT DO I CARE?
I'LL LEAVE WITHOUT HIM, THAT'S WHAT I'LL DO!
BOY, THE SIDEWALKS SURE ARE ICY TONIGHT...
BROTHERS ARE A REAL NUISANCE! HE COULD HAVE MEMORIZED THAT PIECE IF HE HAD WANTED TO!
12-24
I DON'T CARE IF HE STAYS HOME! I DON'T CARE IF...
"SO THE WORDS SPOKEN THROUGH JEREMIAH THE PROPHET WERE FULFILLED: 'A VOICE WAS HEARD IN RAMA, WAILING AND LOUD LAMENTS; IT WAS RACHEL WEEPING FOR HER CHILDREN, AND REFUSING ALL CONSOLATION, BECAUSE THEY WERE NO MORE.' MATTHEW 2:17!!
MERRY CHRISTMAS, YOU BLOCKHEAD!
SCHULZ

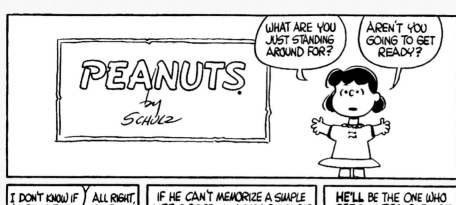

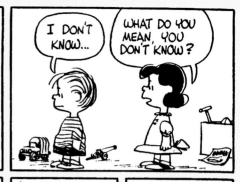

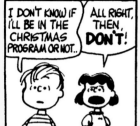

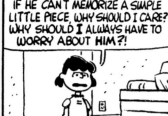

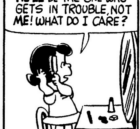

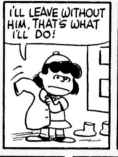

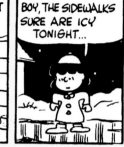

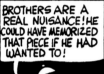

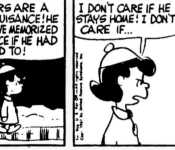

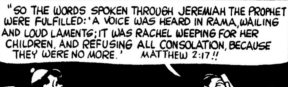

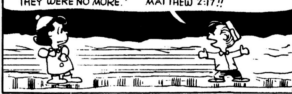

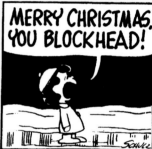

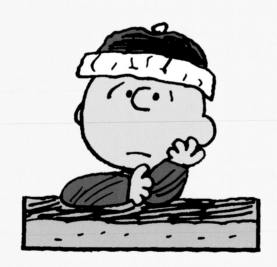

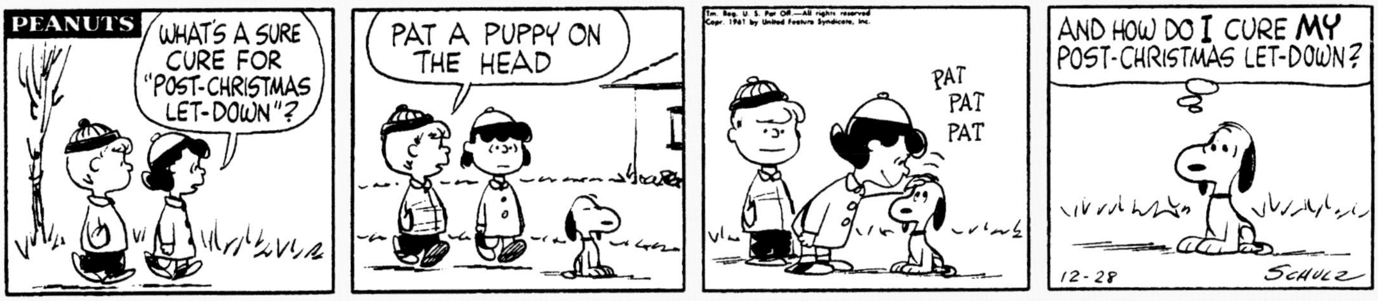
PEANUTS
WHAT'S A SURE CURE FOR "POST-CHRISTMAS LET-DOWN"?
PAT A PUPPY ON THE HEAD
PAT PAT PAT
AND HOW DO I CURE MY POST-CHRISTMAS LET-DOWN?
12-28
SCHULZ

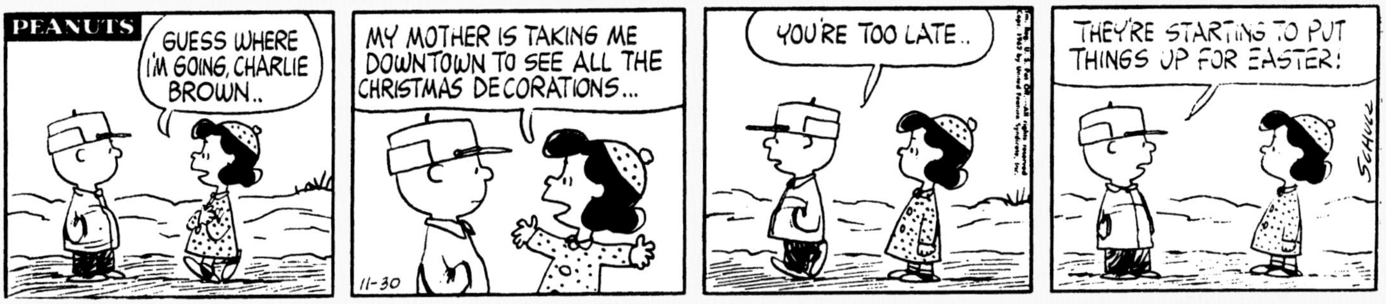
PEANUTS
GUESS WHERE I'M GOING, CHARLIE BROWN..
MY MOTHER IS TAKING ME DOWNTOWN TO SEE ALL THE CHRISTMAS DECORATIONS...
11-30
YOU'RE TOO LATE..
THEY'RE STARTING TO PUT THINGS UP FOR EASTER!
SCHULZ

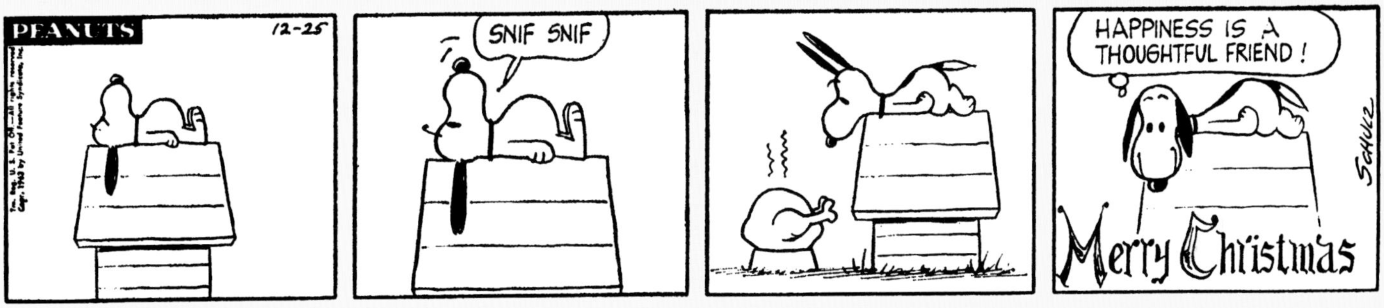
PEANUTS
12-25
SNIF SNIF
HAPPINESS IS A THOUGHTFUL FRIEND!
SCHULZ
Merry Christmas

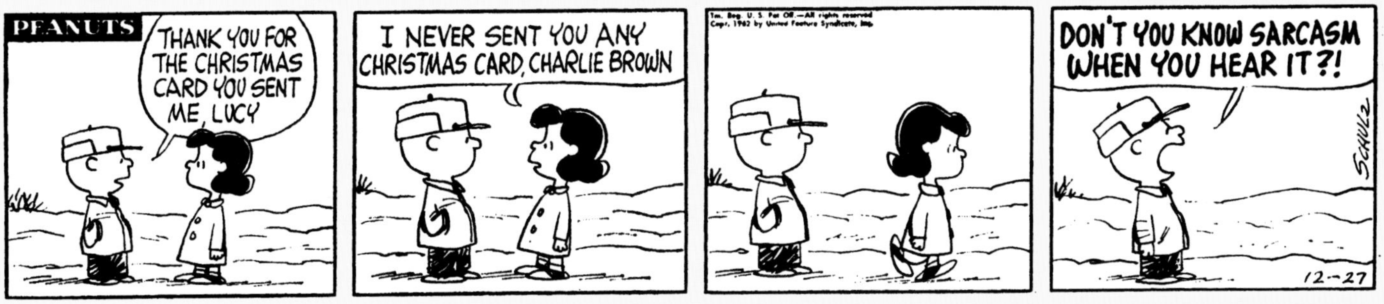
PEANUTS
THANK YOU FOR THE CHRISTMAS CARD YOU SENT ME, LUCY
I NEVER SENT YOU ANY CHRISTMAS CARD, CHARLIE BROWN
DON'T YOU KNOW SARCASM WHEN YOU HEAR IT?!
SCHULZ
12-27

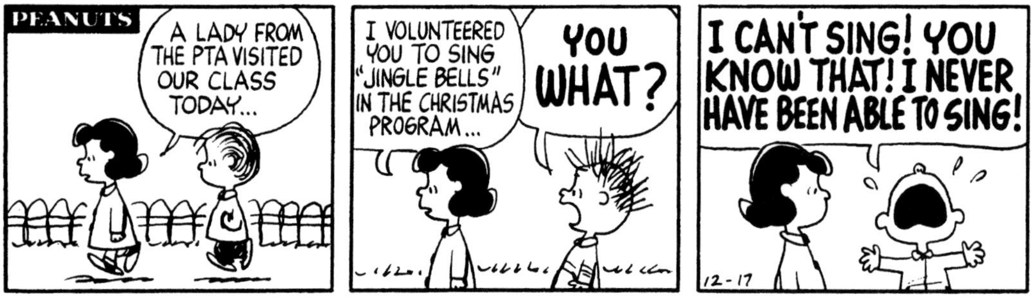
PEANUTS
A LADY FROM THE PTA VISITED OUR CLASS TODAY...
I VOLUNTEERED YOU TO SING "JINGLE BELLS" IN THE CHRISTMAS PROGRAM...
YOU WHAT?
I CAN'T SING! YOU KNOW THAT! I NEVER HAVE BEEN ABLE TO SING!
12-17
LEARN!
SCHULZ

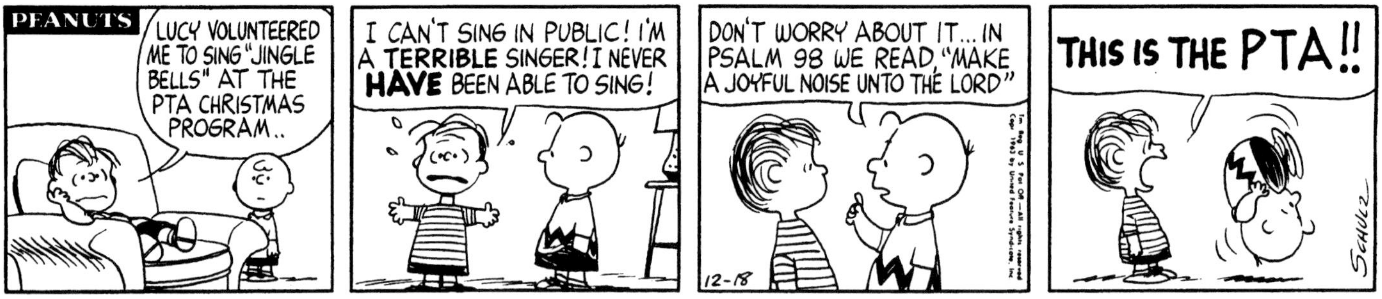
PEANUTS
LUCY VOLUNTEERED ME TO SING "JINGLE BELLS" AT THE PTA CHRISTMAS PROGRAM..
I CAN'T SING IN PUBLIC! I'M A **TERRIBLE** SINGER! I NEVER **HAVE** BEEN ABLE TO SING!
DON'T WORRY ABOUT IT... IN PSALM 98 WE READ, "MAKE A JOYFUL NOISE UNTO THE LORD"
12-18
THIS IS THE PTA!!
SCHULZ

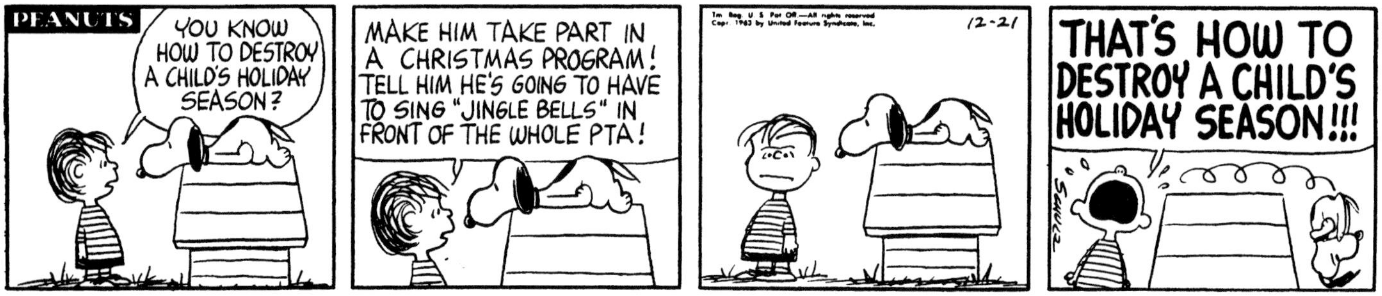
PEANUTS
YOU KNOW HOW TO DESTROY A CHILD'S HOLIDAY SEASON?
MAKE HIM TAKE PART IN A CHRISTMAS PROGRAM! TELL HIM HE'S GOING TO HAVE TO SING "JINGLE BELLS" IN FRONT OF THE WHOLE PTA!
Tm Reg. U. S. Pat. Off.—All rights reserved Copr. 1963 by United Feature Syndicate, Inc.
12-21
THAT'S HOW TO DESTROY A CHILD'S HOLIDAY SEASON!!!
SCHULZ

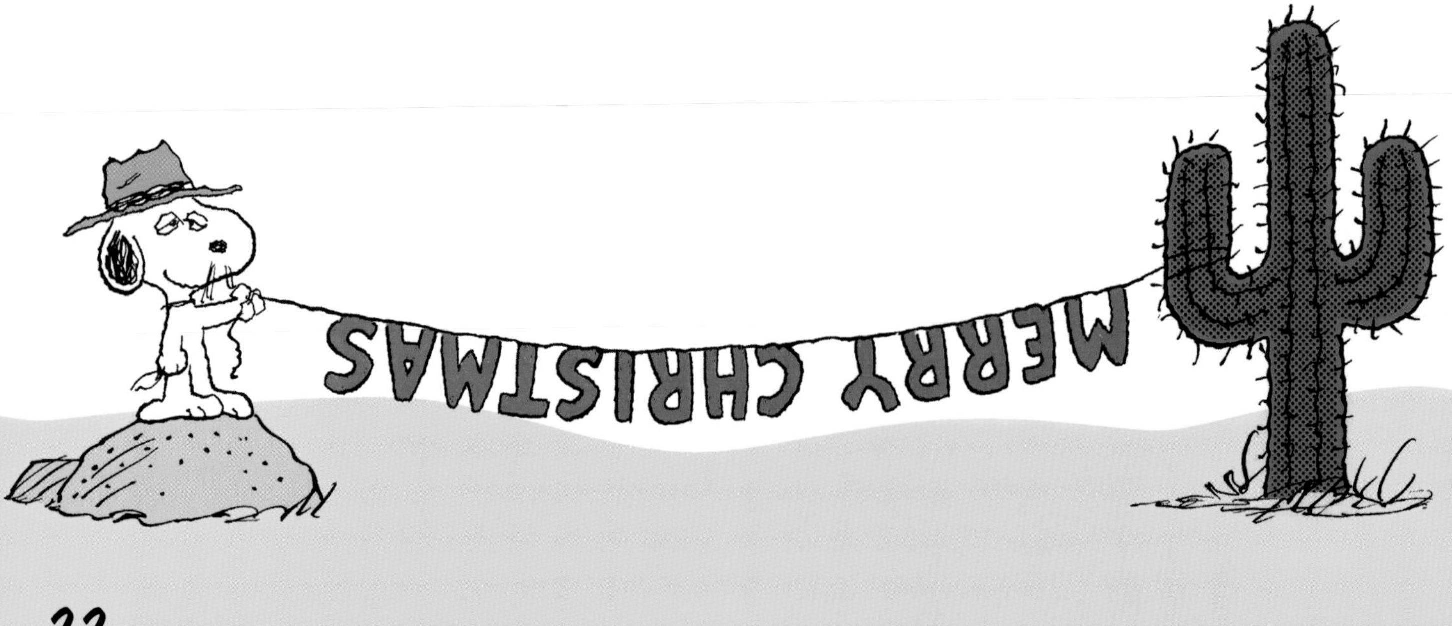
MERRY CHRISTMAS

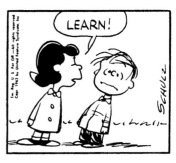

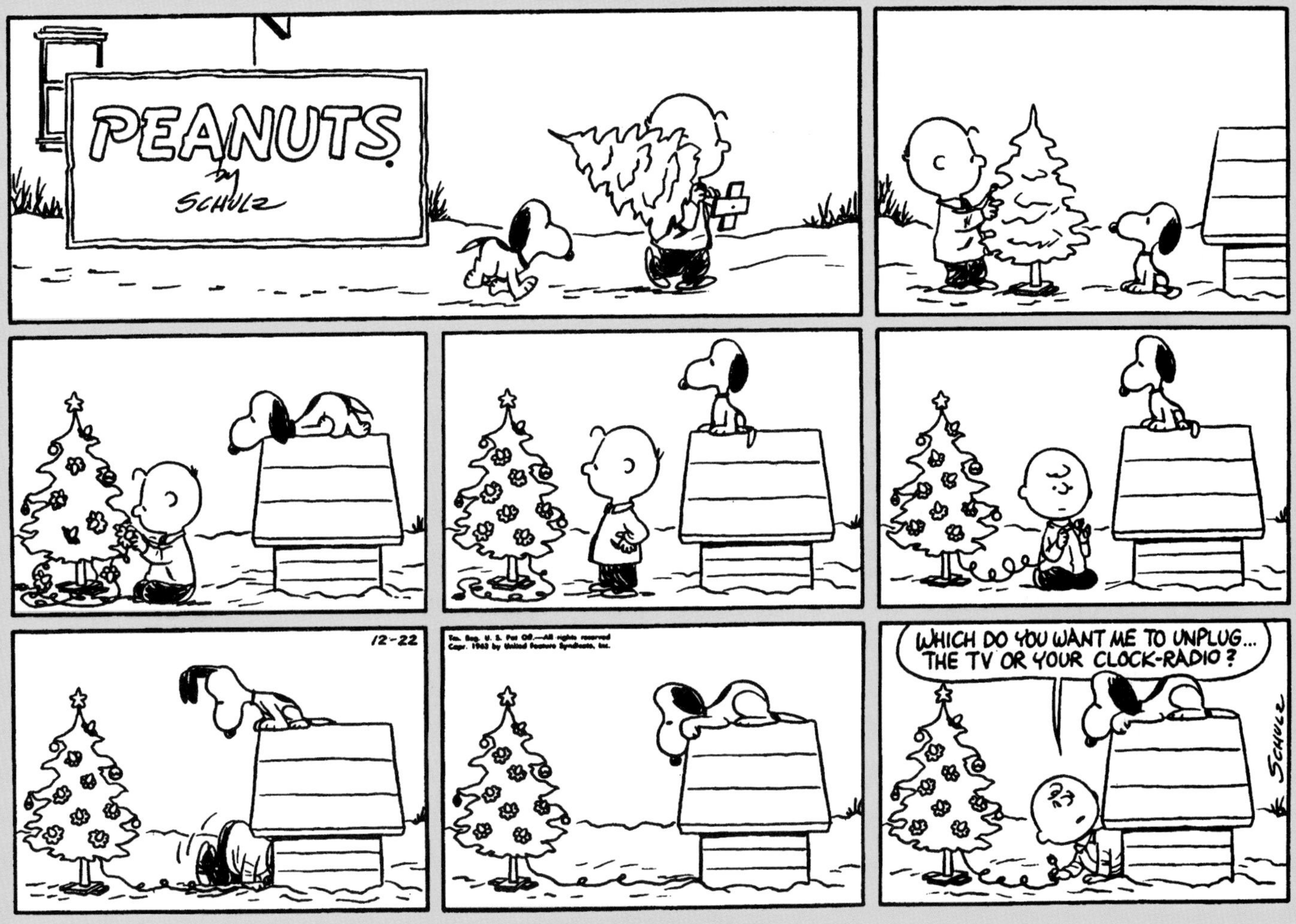
PEANUTS
by
SCHULZ
12-22
WHICH DO YOU WANT ME TO UNPLUG... THE TV OR YOUR CLOCK-RADIO?
SCHULZ

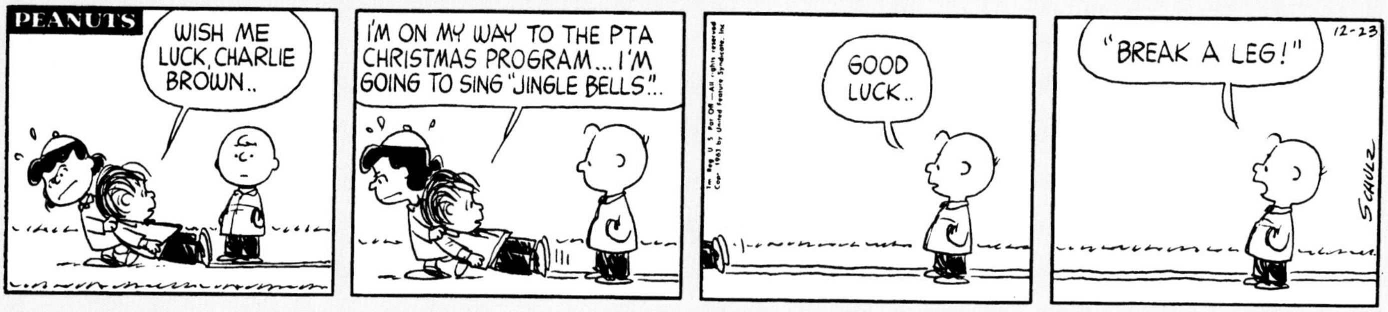
PEANUTS
WISH ME LUCK, CHARLIE BROWN..
I'M ON MY WAY TO THE PTA CHRISTMAS PROGRAM... I'M GOING TO SING "JINGLE BELLS"..
GOOD LUCK..
"BREAK A LEG!"
12-23
SCHULZ

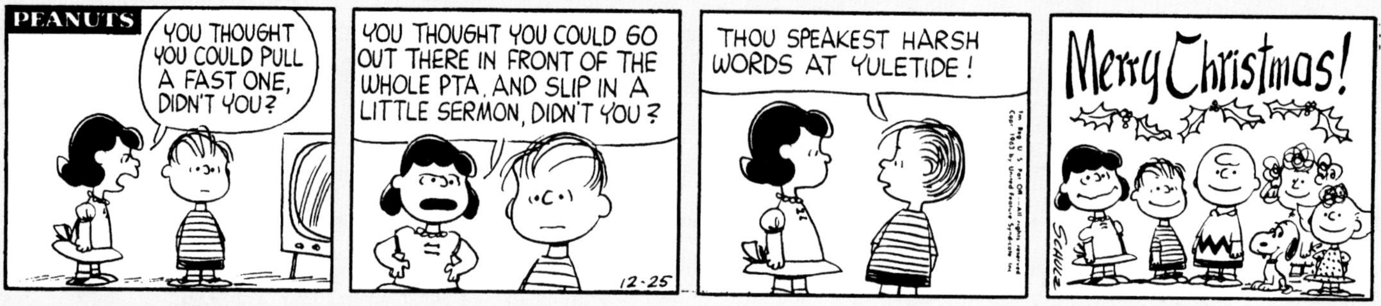
PEANUTS
YOU THOUGHT YOU COULD PULL A FAST ONE, DIDN'T YOU?
YOU THOUGHT YOU COULD GO OUT THERE IN FRONT OF THE WHOLE PTA, AND SLIP IN A LITTLE SERMON, DIDN'T YOU?
12-25
THOU SPEAKEST HARSH WORDS AT YULETIDE!
Merry Christmas!
SCHULZ

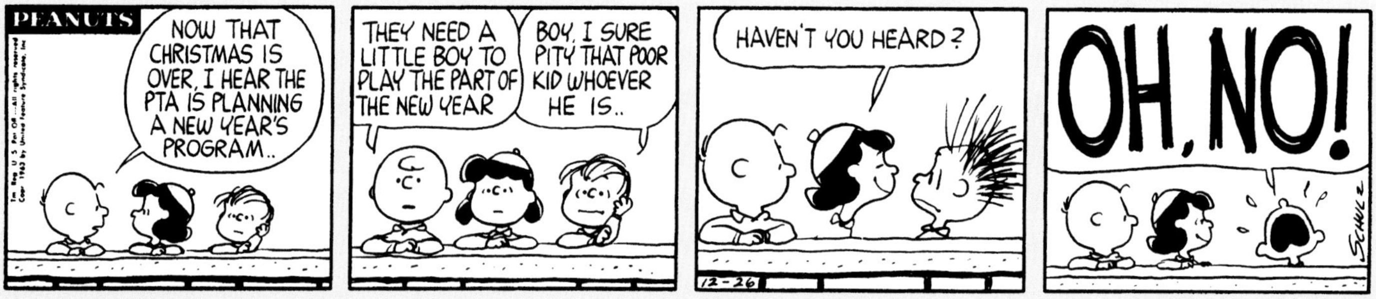
PEANUTS
NOW THAT CHRISTMAS IS OVER, I HEAR THE PTA IS PLANNING A NEW YEAR'S PROGRAM..
THEY NEED A LITTLE BOY TO PLAY THE PART OF THE NEW YEAR
BOY, I SURE PITY THAT POOR KID WHOEVER HE IS..
HAVEN'T YOU HEARD?
12-26
OH, NO!
SCHULZ

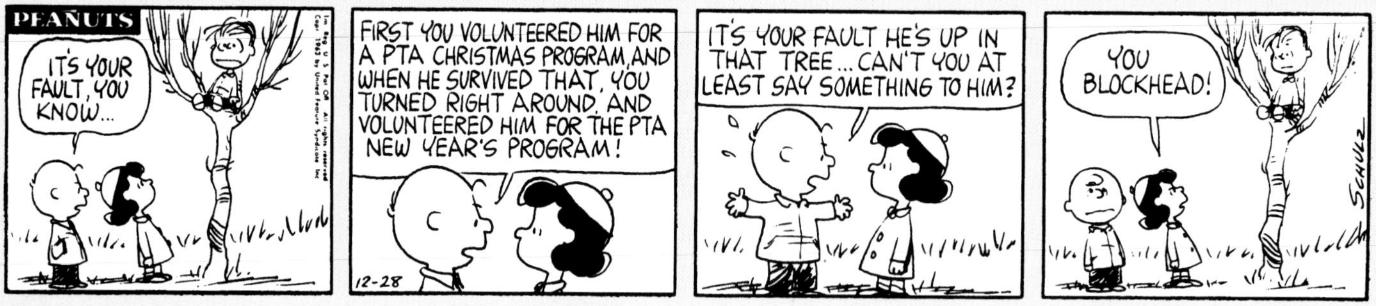
PEANUTS
IT'S YOUR FAULT, YOU KNOW...
FIRST YOU VOLUNTEERED HIM FOR A PTA CHRISTMAS PROGRAM, AND WHEN HE SURVIVED THAT, YOU TURNED RIGHT AROUND, AND VOLUNTEERED HIM FOR THE PTA NEW YEAR'S PROGRAM!
12-28
IT'S YOUR FAULT HE'S UP IN THAT TREE... CAN'T YOU AT LEAST SAY SOMETHING TO HIM?
YOU BLOCKHEAD!
SCHULZ

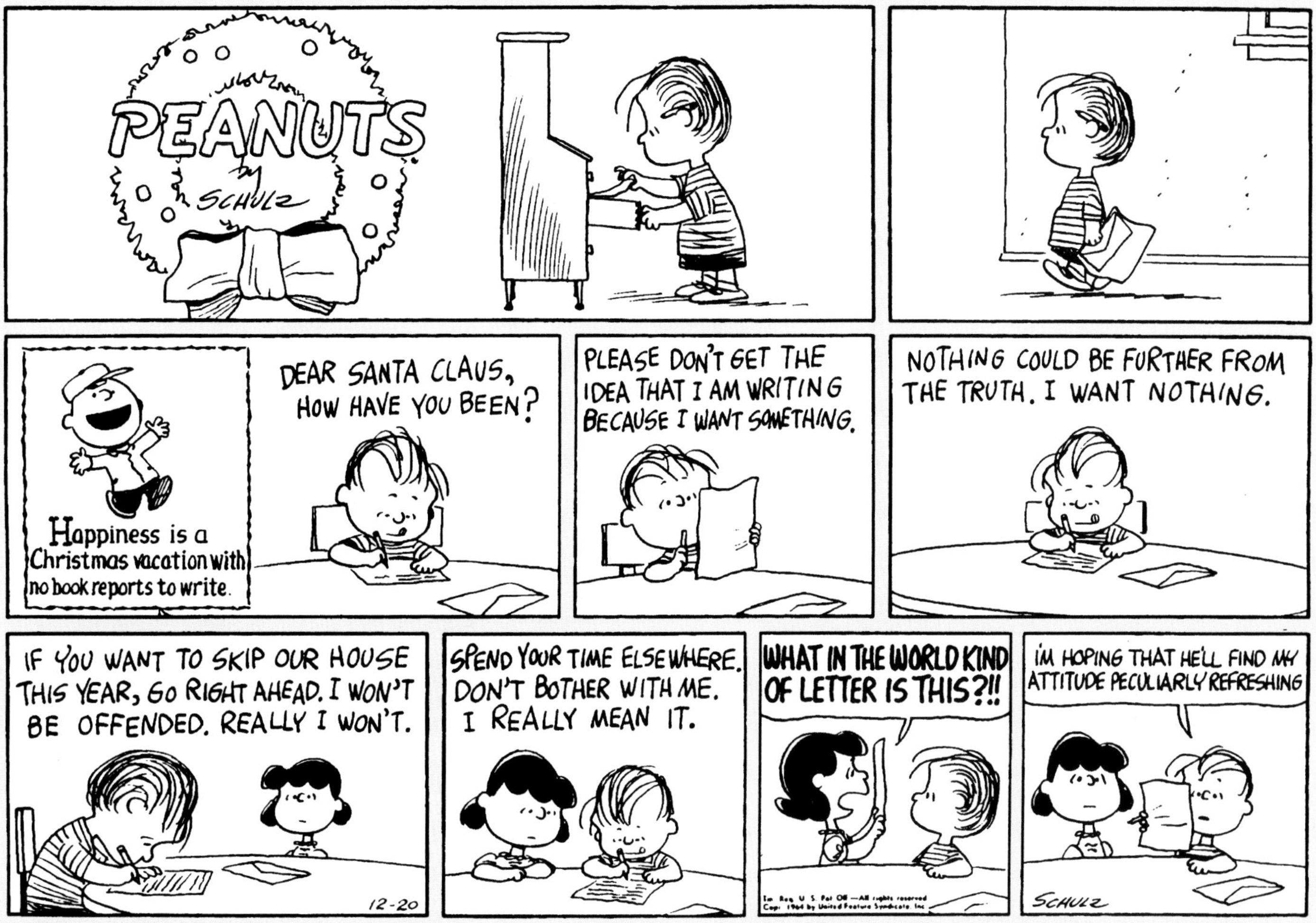
PEANUTS
by SCHULZ
Happiness is a Christmas vacation with no book reports to write.
DEAR SANTA CLAUS, HOW HAVE YOU BEEN?
PLEASE DON'T GET THE IDEA THAT I AM WRITING BECAUSE I WANT SOMETHING.
NOTHING COULD BE FURTHER FROM THE TRUTH. I WANT NOTHING.
IF YOU WANT TO SKIP OUR HOUSE THIS YEAR, GO RIGHT AHEAD. I WON'T BE OFFENDED. REALLY I WON'T.
12-20
SPEND YOUR TIME ELSEWHERE. DON'T BOTHER WITH ME. I REALLY MEAN IT.
WHAT IN THE WORLD KIND OF LETTER IS THIS?!!
I'M HOPING THAT HE'LL FIND MY ATTITUDE PECULIARLY REFRESHING
SCHULZ

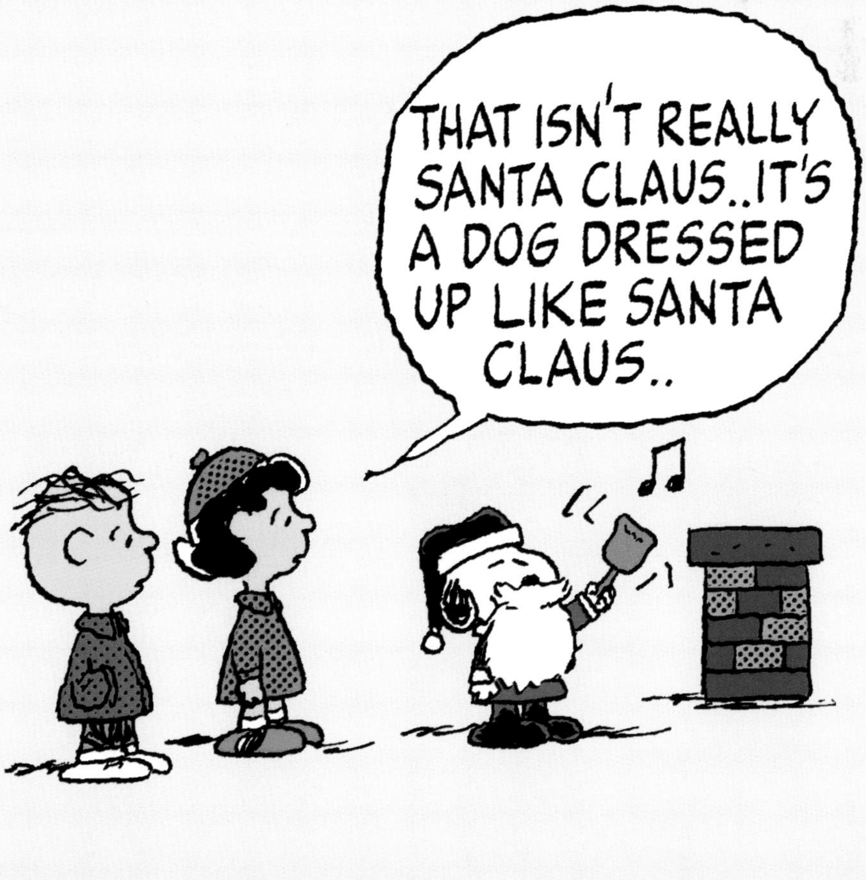
THAT ISN'T REALLY SANTA CLAUS..IT'S A DOG DRESSED UP LIKE SANTA CLAUS..

PEANUTS
by SCHULZ
I CAN'T STAND IT!
Happiness is getting all your Christmas "thank-you" letters written.
HI, CHARLIE BROWN.. COME ON IN...
SEE? JUST LIKE I TOLD YOU....
LOOK AT ALL THIS STUFF...A BICYCLE, GAMES, CLOTHES, BASEBALL EQUIPMENT..
MORE CLOTHES, MORE TOYS, CANDY, BOOKS, A TRANSISTOR RADIO...
THIS IS TERRIBLE! THIS IS MY WORST CHRISTMAS YET!
HOW WILL I EVER DEVELOP ANY CHARACTER?
I ALWAYS GET EVERYTHING I WANT
SCHULZ
12-27

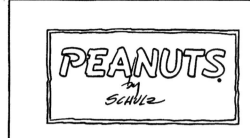

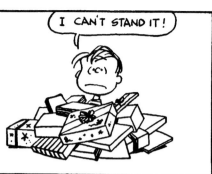

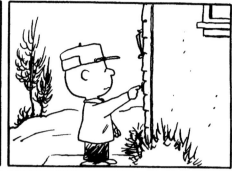

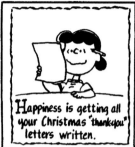

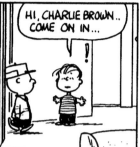

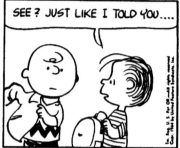

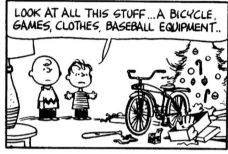

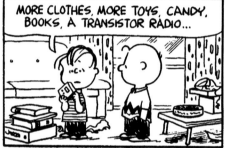

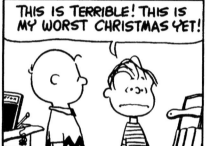

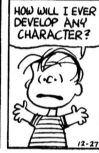

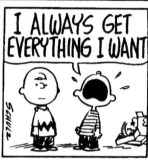

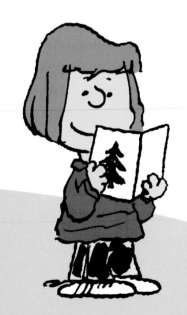

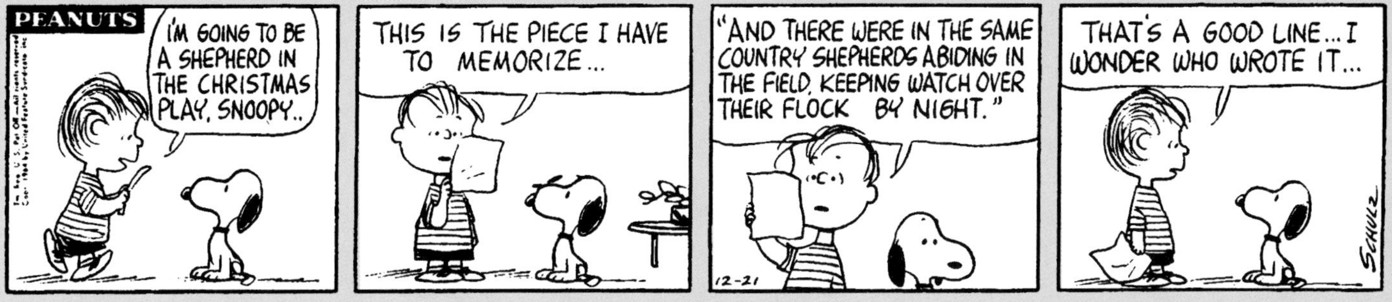
PEANUTS
I'M GOING TO BE A SHEPHERD IN THE CHRISTMAS PLAY, SNOOPY..
THIS IS THE PIECE I HAVE TO MEMORIZE...
"AND THERE WERE IN THE SAME COUNTRY SHEPHERDS ABIDING IN THE FIELD, KEEPING WATCH OVER THEIR FLOCK BY NIGHT."
12-21
THAT'S A GOOD LINE... I WONDER WHO WROTE IT...
SCHULZ

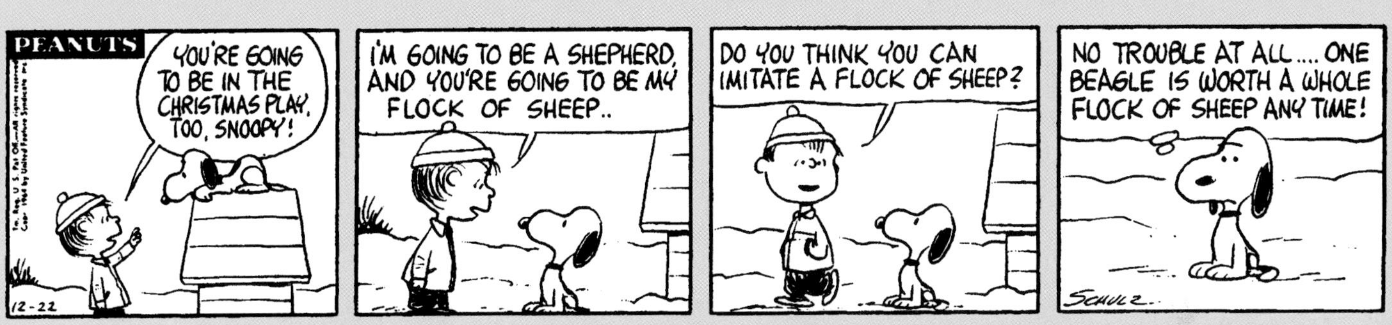
PEANUTS
YOU'RE GOING TO BE IN THE CHRISTMAS PLAY, TOO, SNOOPY!
12-22
I'M GOING TO BE A SHEPHERD, AND YOU'RE GOING TO BE MY FLOCK OF SHEEP..
DO YOU THINK YOU CAN IMITATE A FLOCK OF SHEEP?
NO TROUBLE AT ALL.... ONE BEAGLE IS WORTH A WHOLE FLOCK OF SHEEP ANY TIME!
SCHULZ

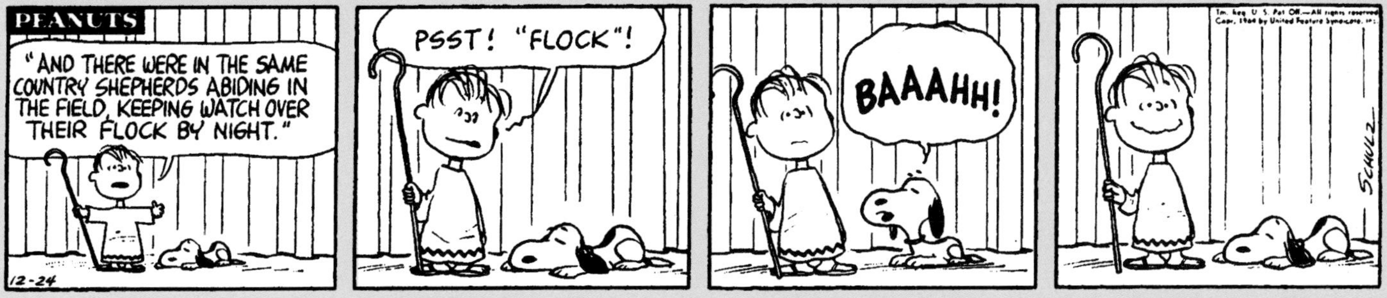
PEANUTS
"AND THERE WERE IN THE SAME COUNTRY SHEPHERDS ABIDING IN THE FIELD, KEEPING WATCH OVER THEIR FLOCK BY NIGHT."
12-24
PSST! "FLOCK"!
BAAAHH!
SCHULZ

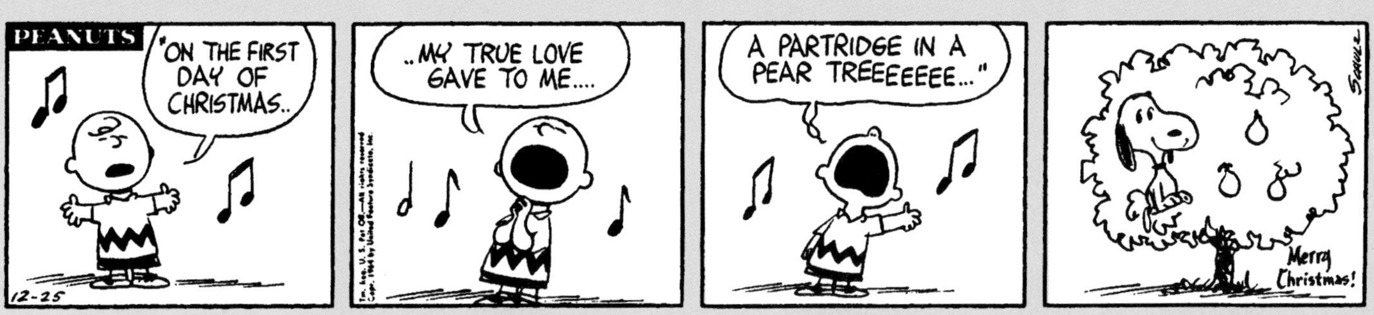
PEANUTS
"ON THE FIRST DAY OF CHRISTMAS..
12-25
..MY TRUE LOVE GAVE TO ME....
A PARTRIDGE IN A PEAR TREEEEEEE..."
SCHULZ
Merry Christmas!

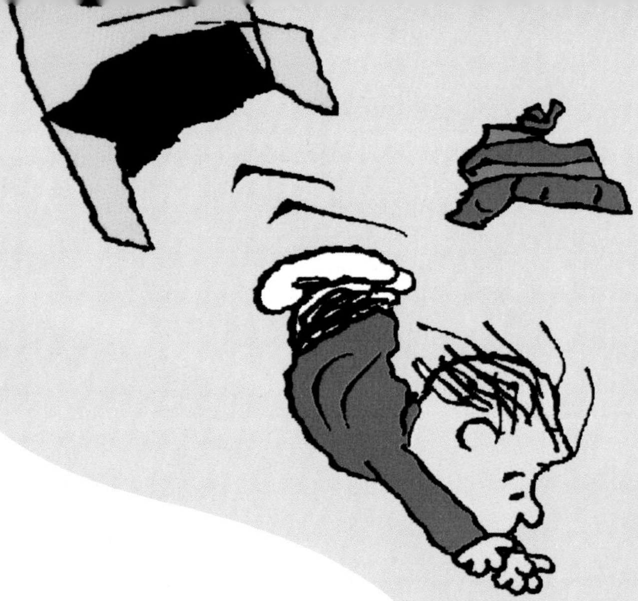

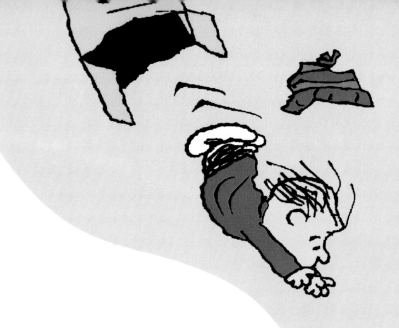

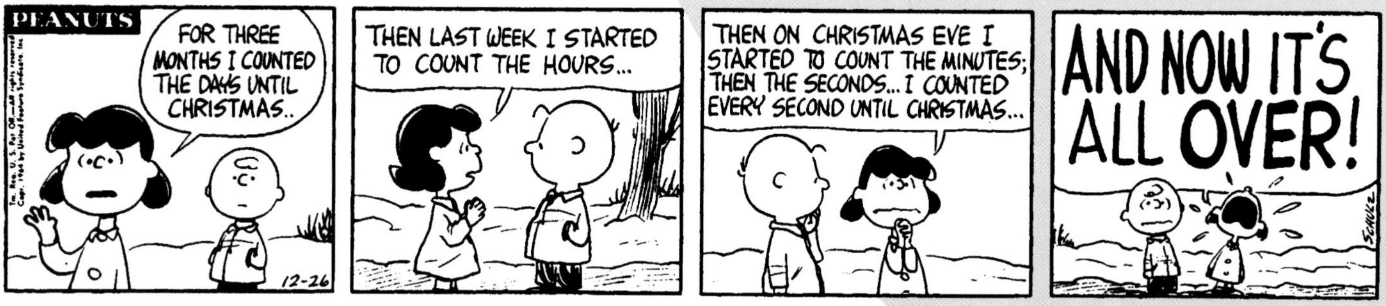
PEANUTS
FOR THREE MONTHS I COUNTED THE DAYS UNTIL CHRISTMAS..
THEN LAST WEEK I STARTED TO COUNT THE HOURS...
THEN ON CHRISTMAS EVE I STARTED TO COUNT THE MINUTES; THEN THE SECONDS... I COUNTED EVERY SECOND UNTIL CHRISTMAS...
AND NOW IT'S ALL OVER!
12-26

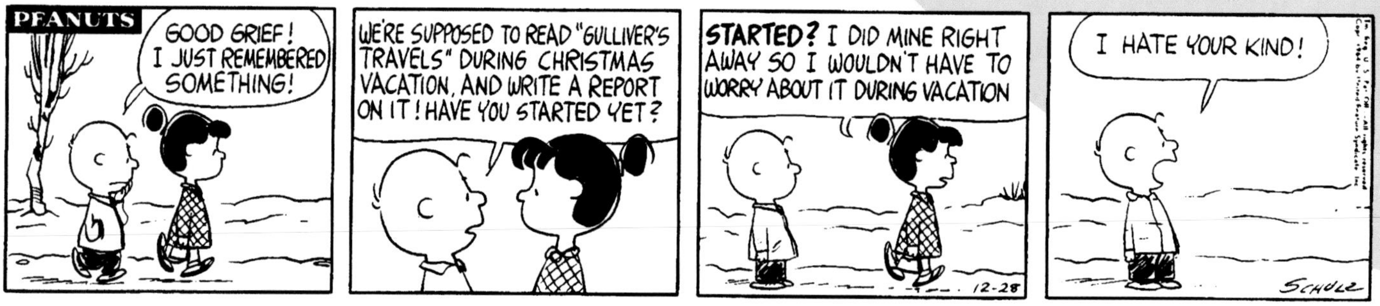
PEANUTS
GOOD GRIEF! I JUST REMEMBERED SOMETHING!
WE'RE SUPPOSED TO READ "GULLIVER'S TRAVELS" DURING CHRISTMAS VACATION, AND WRITE A REPORT ON IT! HAVE YOU STARTED YET?
STARTED? I DID MINE RIGHT AWAY SO I WOULDN'T HAVE TO WORRY ABOUT IT DURING VACATION
I HATE YOUR KIND!
12-28

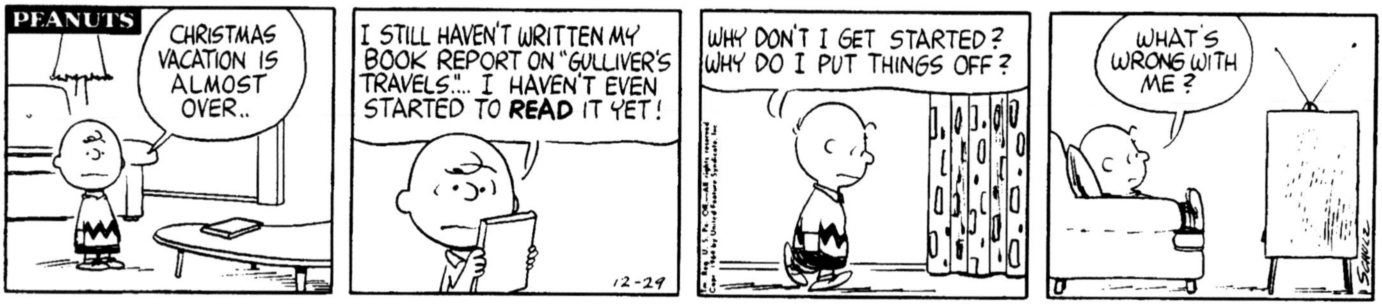
PEANUTS
CHRISTMAS VACATION IS ALMOST OVER..
I STILL HAVEN'T WRITTEN MY BOOK REPORT ON "GULLIVER'S TRAVELS"... I HAVEN'T EVEN STARTED TO **READ** IT YET!
WHY DON'T I GET STARTED? WHY DO I PUT THINGS OFF?
WHAT'S WRONG WITH ME?
12-29

PEANUTS WHAT GRADE DID YOU GET ON YOUR BOOK REPORT, CHARLIE BROWN?

"D MINUS"! THAT'S AS LOW AS YOU CAN GET WITHOUT FAILING!

THE TEACHER SAID IT LOOKED LIKE THE SORT OF REPORT THAT WAS WRITTEN AFTER MIDNIGHT ON THE LAST DAY OF CHRISTMAS VACATION

WHAT COULD I SAY? I CONGRATULATED HER ON HER REMARKABLE PERCEPTIVITY!

PEANUTS

ONLY 6 DAYS UNTIL BEETHOVEN'S BIRTHDAY

ELEVEN DAYS TO THE FIRST DAY OF WINTER

ONLY 12 SHOPPING DAYS UNTIL CHRISTMAS

IT'S UNUSUAL FOR ONE AGENCY TO HAVE ALL THREE ACCOUNTS!

PEANUTS DEAR SANTA CLAUS, HOW ARE ALL YOUR REINDEER? ARE THEY WELL FED?

IS YOUR SLEIGH IN GOOD SHAPE? ARE THE RUNNERS OILED?

THEN GO, MAN... GO!!!

I DON'T THINK I'D BETTER SEND THAT...

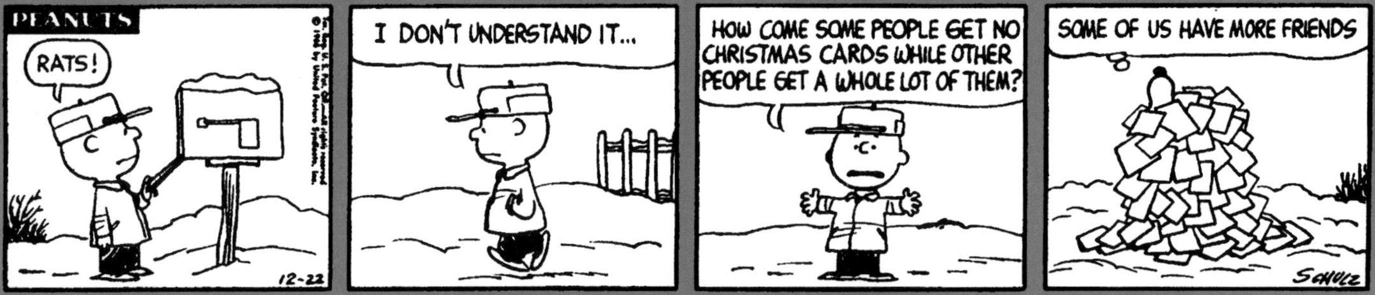
PEANUTS
RATS!
12-22
I DON'T UNDERSTAND IT...
HOW COME SOME PEOPLE GET NO CHRISTMAS CARDS WHILE OTHER PEOPLE GET A WHOLE LOT OF THEM?
SOME OF US HAVE MORE FRIENDS
SCHULZ

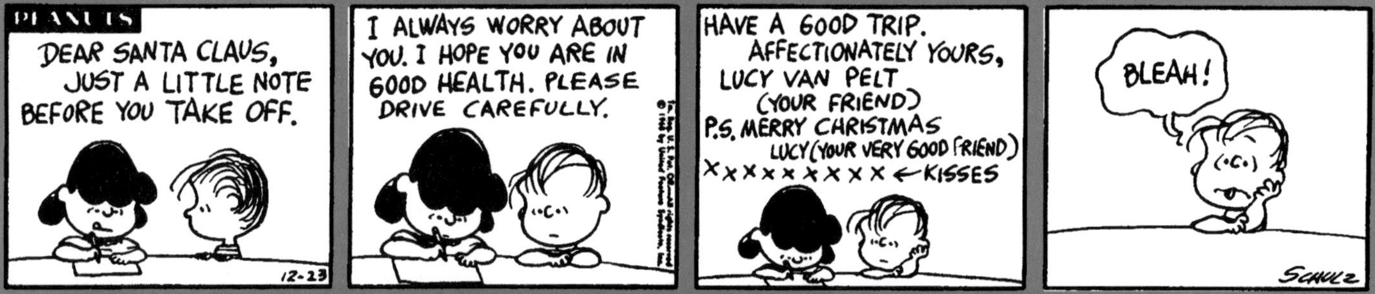
PEANUTS
DEAR SANTA CLAUS,
JUST A LITTLE NOTE BEFORE YOU TAKE OFF.
12-23
I ALWAYS WORRY ABOUT YOU. I HOPE YOU ARE IN GOOD HEALTH. PLEASE DRIVE CAREFULLY.
HAVE A GOOD TRIP.
AFFECTIONATELY YOURS,
LUCY VAN PELT
(YOUR FRIEND)
P.S. MERRY CHRISTMAS
LUCY (YOUR VERY GOOD FRIEND)
XXXXXXXXX ← KISSES
BLEAH!
SCHULZ

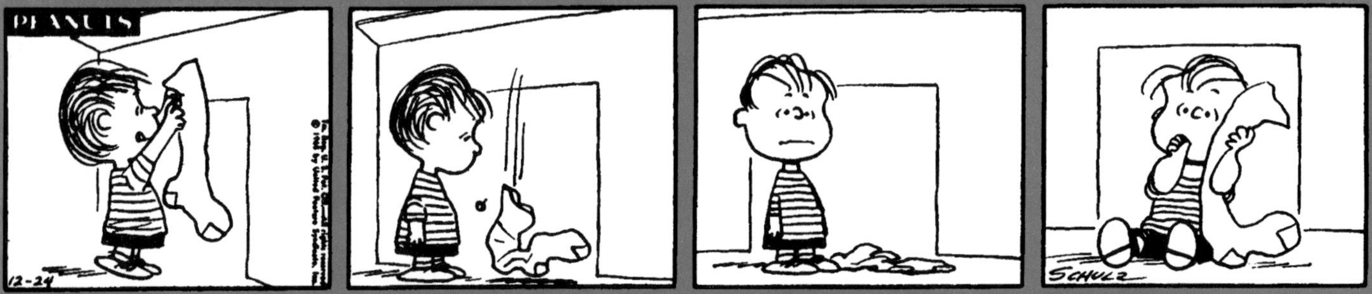
PEANUTS
12-24
SCHULZ

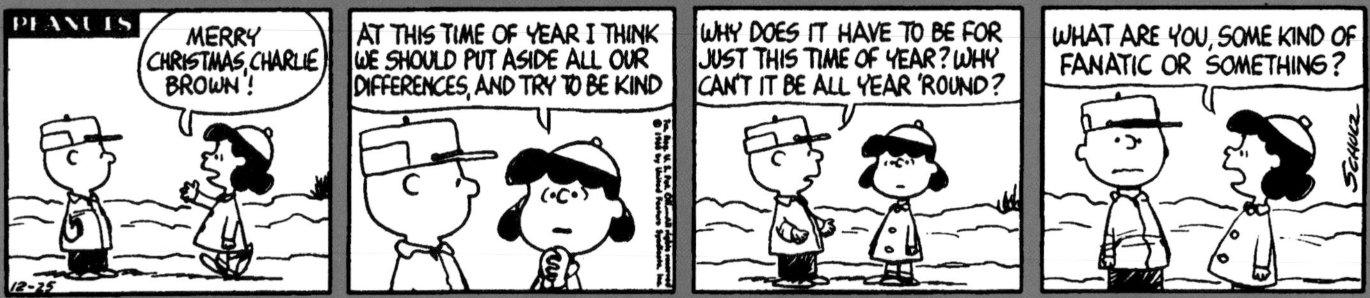
PEANUTS
MERRY CHRISTMAS, CHARLIE BROWN!
12-25
AT THIS TIME OF YEAR I THINK WE SHOULD PUT ASIDE ALL OUR DIFFERENCES, AND TRY TO BE KIND
WHY DOES IT HAVE TO BE FOR JUST THIS TIME OF YEAR? WHY CAN'T IT BE ALL YEAR 'ROUND?
WHAT ARE YOU, SOME KIND OF FANATIC OR SOMETHING?
SCHULZ

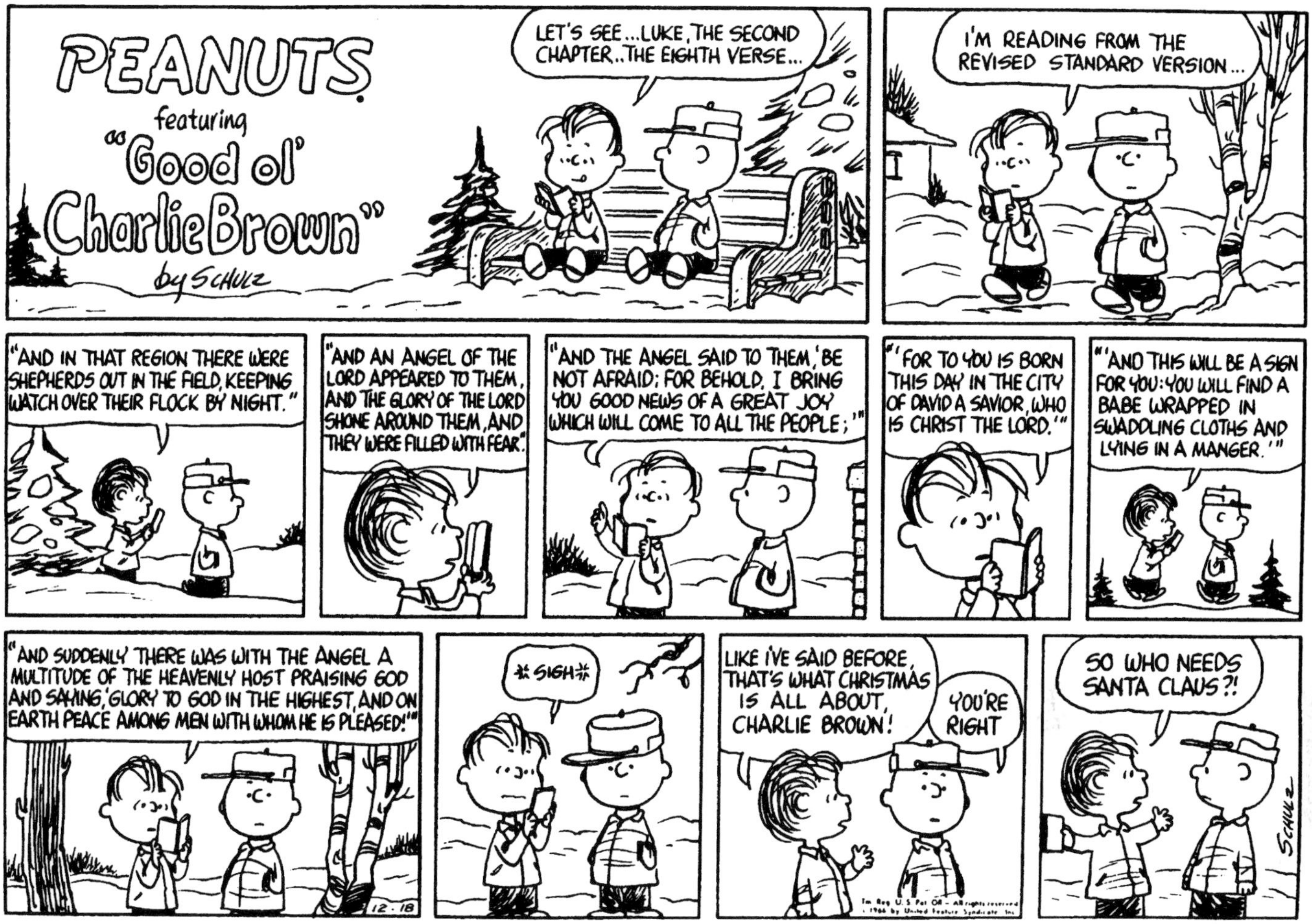
PEANUTS
featuring "Good ol' Charlie Brown"
by SCHULZ
LET'S SEE...LUKE, THE SECOND CHAPTER..THE EIGHTH VERSE...
I'M READING FROM THE REVISED STANDARD VERSION...
"AND IN THAT REGION THERE WERE SHEPHERDS OUT IN THE FIELD, KEEPING WATCH OVER THEIR FLOCK BY NIGHT."
"AND AN ANGEL OF THE LORD APPEARED TO THEM, AND THE GLORY OF THE LORD SHONE AROUND THEM, AND THEY WERE FILLED WITH FEAR."
"AND THE ANGEL SAID TO THEM, 'BE NOT AFRAID; FOR BEHOLD, I BRING YOU GOOD NEWS OF A GREAT JOY WHICH WILL COME TO ALL THE PEOPLE;'"
"'FOR TO YOU IS BORN THIS DAY IN THE CITY OF DAVID A SAVIOR, WHO IS CHRIST THE LORD.'"
"'AND THIS WILL BE A SIGN FOR YOU: YOU WILL FIND A BABE WRAPPED IN SWADDLING CLOTHS AND LYING IN A MANGER.'"
"AND SUDDENLY THERE WAS WITH THE ANGEL A MULTITUDE OF THE HEAVENLY HOST PRAISING GOD AND SAYING, 'GLORY TO GOD IN THE HIGHEST, AND ON EARTH PEACE AMONG MEN WITH WHOM HE IS PLEASED!'"
12·18
SIGH
LIKE I'VE SAID BEFORE, THAT'S WHAT CHRISTMAS IS ALL ABOUT, CHARLIE BROWN!
YOU'RE RIGHT
SO WHO NEEDS SANTA CLAUS?!
SCHULZ

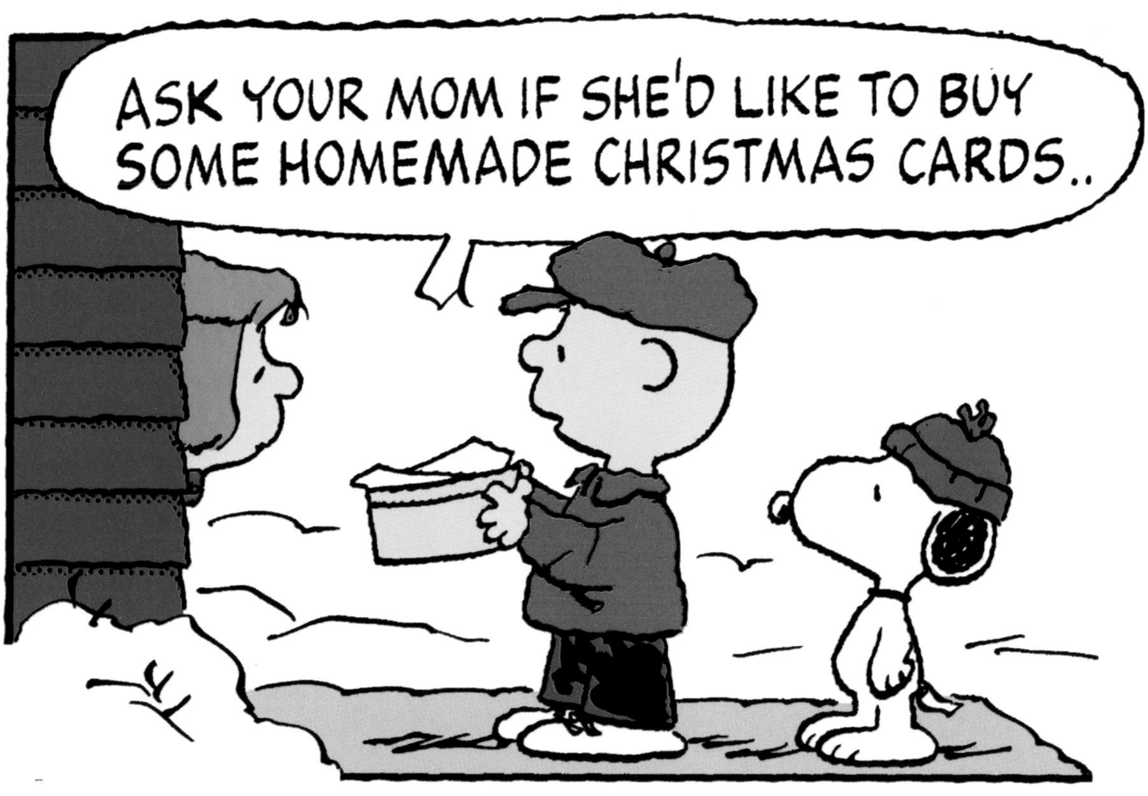
ASK YOUR MOM IF SHE'D LIKE TO BUY SOME HOMEMADE CHRISTMAS CARDS..

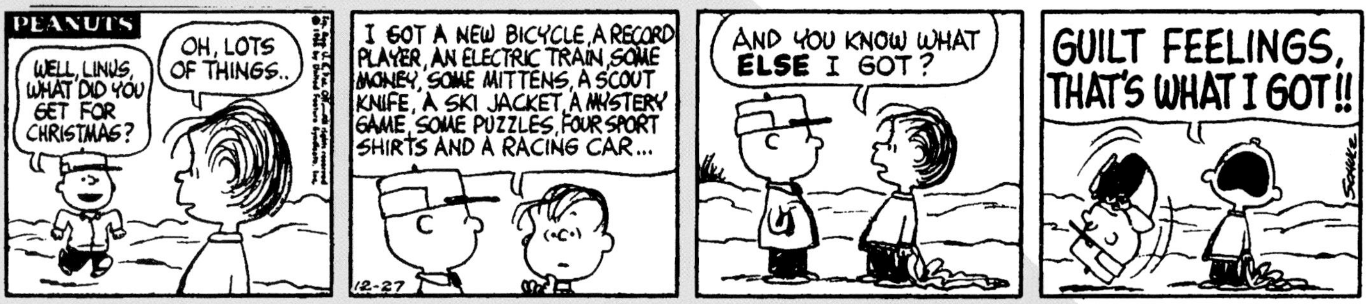
PEANUTS
WELL, LINUS, WHAT DID YOU GET FOR CHRISTMAS?
OH, LOTS OF THINGS..
I GOT A NEW BICYCLE, A RECORD PLAYER, AN ELECTRIC TRAIN, SOME MONEY, SOME MITTENS, A SCOUT KNIFE, A SKI JACKET, A MYSTERY GAME, SOME PUZZLES, FOUR SPORT SHIRTS AND A RACING CAR...
12-27
AND YOU KNOW WHAT ELSE I GOT?
GUILT FEELINGS, THAT'S WHAT I GOT!!
SCHULZ

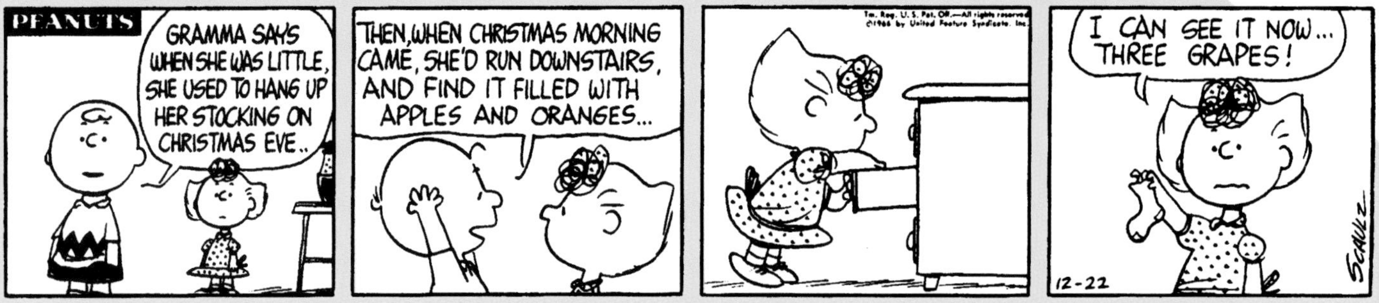
PEANUTS
GRAMMA SAYS WHEN SHE WAS LITTLE, SHE USED TO HANG UP HER STOCKING ON CHRISTMAS EVE..
THEN, WHEN CHRISTMAS MORNING CAME, SHE'D RUN DOWNSTAIRS, AND FIND IT FILLED WITH APPLES AND ORANGES...
I CAN SEE IT NOW... THREE GRAPES!
12-22
SCHULZ

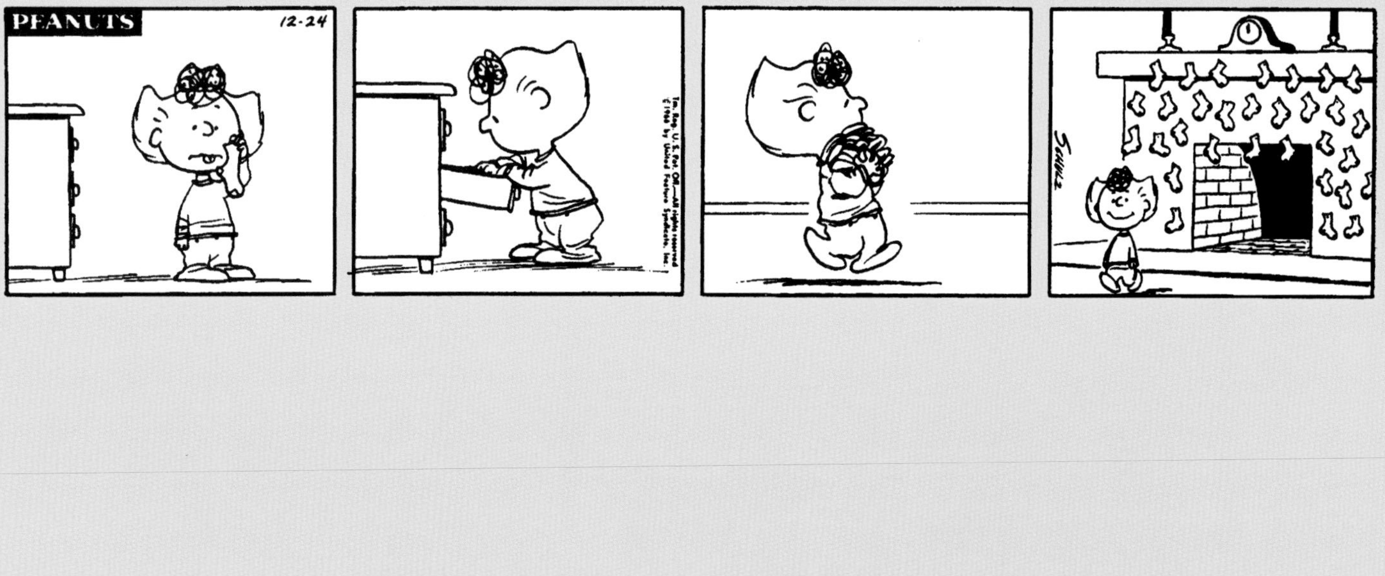
PEANUTS
12-24
SCHULZ

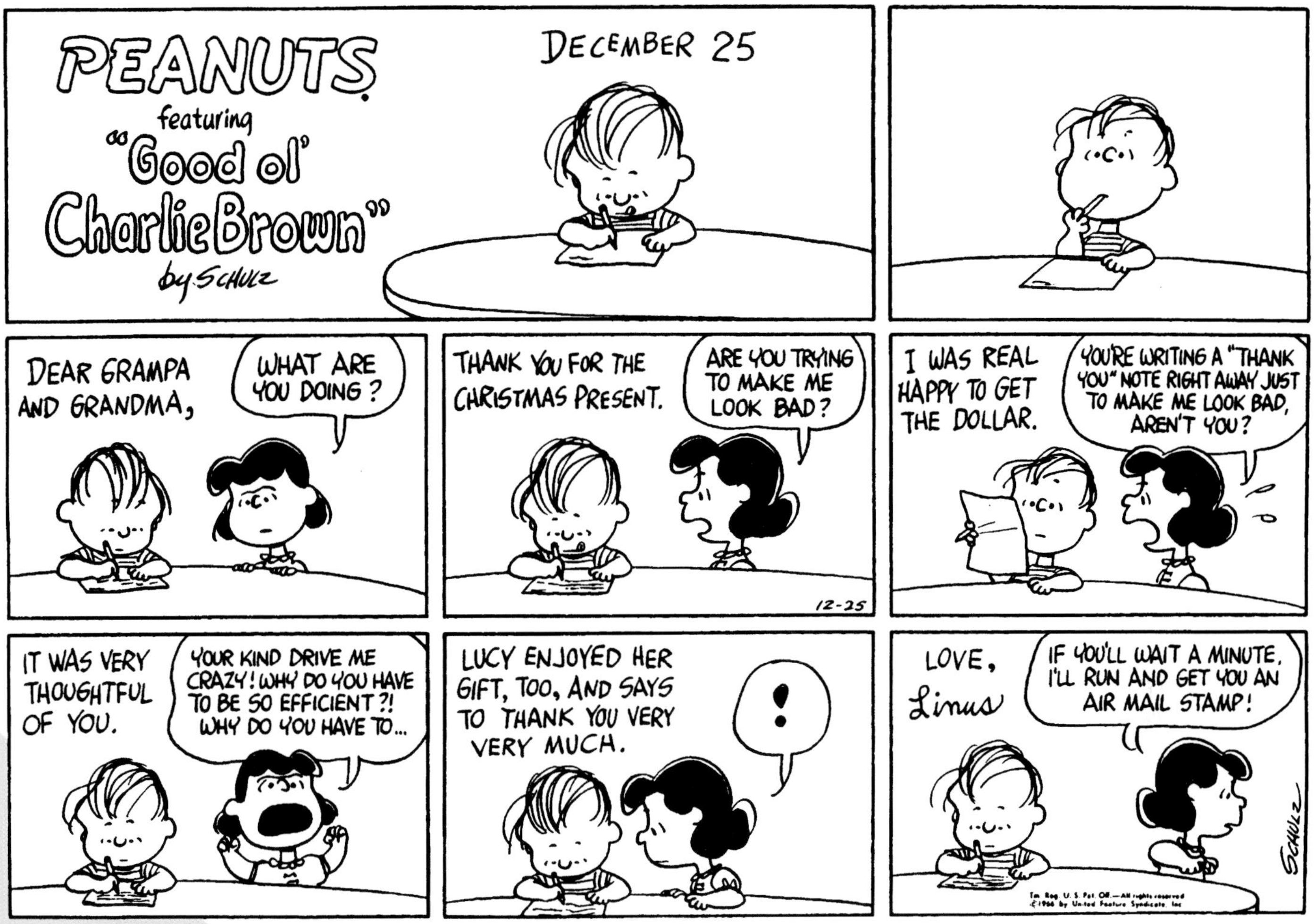
PEANUTS
featuring
"Good ol' Charlie Brown"
by SCHULZ
DECEMBER 25
DEAR GRAMPA AND GRANDMA,
WHAT ARE YOU DOING?
THANK YOU FOR THE CHRISTMAS PRESENT.
ARE YOU TRYING TO MAKE ME LOOK BAD?
12-25
I WAS REAL HAPPY TO GET THE DOLLAR.
YOU'RE WRITING A "THANK YOU" NOTE RIGHT AWAY JUST TO MAKE ME LOOK BAD, AREN'T YOU?
IT WAS VERY THOUGHTFUL OF YOU.
YOUR KIND DRIVE ME CRAZY! WHY DO YOU HAVE TO BE SO EFFICIENT?! WHY DO YOU HAVE TO...
LUCY ENJOYED HER GIFT, TOO, AND SAYS TO THANK YOU VERY VERY MUCH.
!
LOVE, Linus
IF YOU'LL WAIT A MINUTE, I'LL RUN AND GET YOU AN AIR MAIL STAMP!
SCHULZ
Tm. Reg. U.S. Pat. Off.—All rights reserved
©1966 by United Feature Syndicate, Inc.

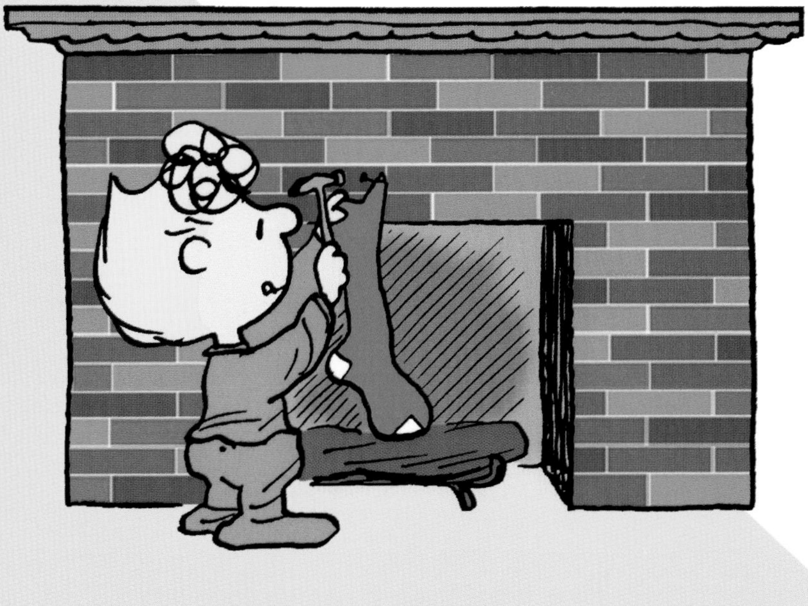

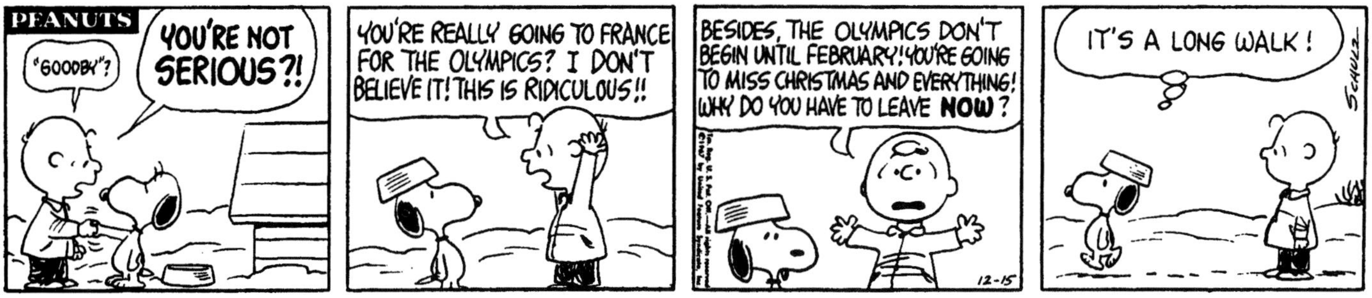
PEANUTS
"GOODBY"?
YOU'RE NOT SERIOUS?!
YOU'RE REALLY GOING TO FRANCE FOR THE OLYMPICS? I DON'T BELIEVE IT! THIS IS RIDICULOUS!!
BESIDES, THE OLYMPICS DON'T BEGIN UNTIL FEBRUARY! YOU'RE GOING TO MISS CHRISTMAS AND EVERYTHING! WHY DO YOU HAVE TO LEAVE NOW?
12-15
IT'S A LONG WALK!
SCHULZ

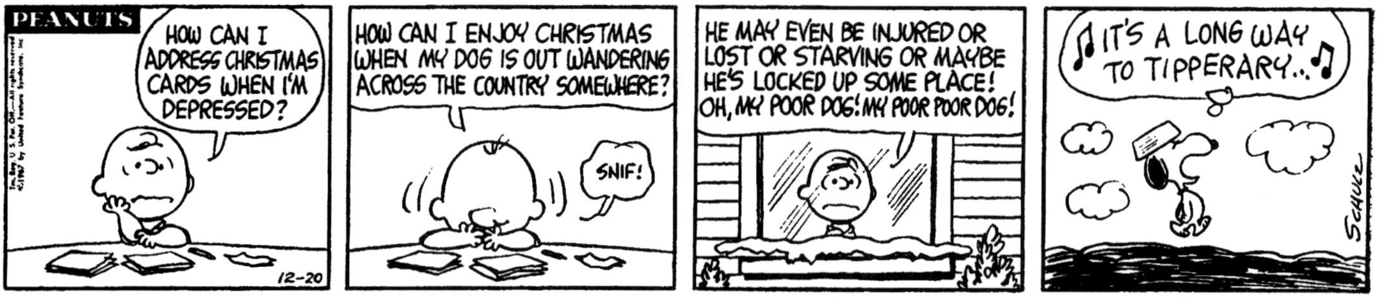
PEANUTS
HOW CAN I ADDRESS CHRISTMAS CARDS WHEN I'M DEPRESSED?
12-20
HOW CAN I ENJOY CHRISTMAS WHEN MY DOG IS OUT WANDERING ACROSS THE COUNTRY SOMEWHERE?
SNIF!
HE MAY EVEN BE INJURED OR LOST OR STARVING OR MAYBE HE'S LOCKED UP SOME PLACE! OH, MY POOR DOG! MY POOR POOR DOG!
♪ IT'S A LONG WAY TO TIPPERARY... ♪
SCHULZ

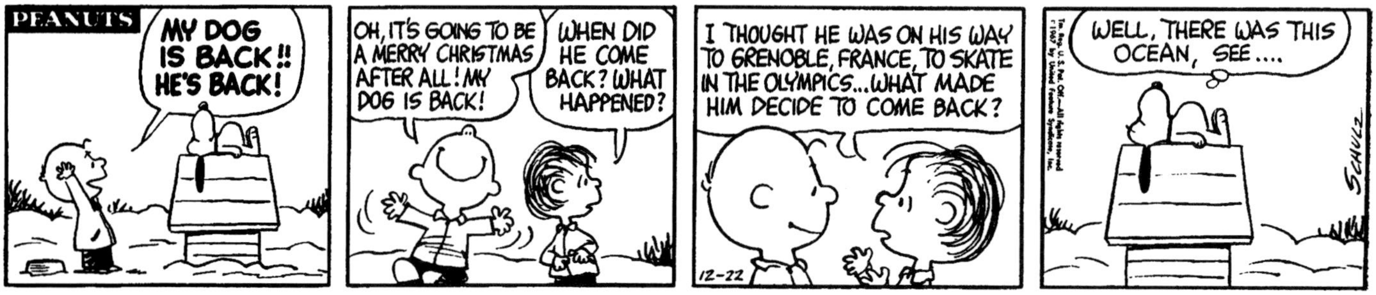
PEANUTS
MY DOG IS BACK!! HE'S BACK!
OH, IT'S GOING TO BE A MERRY CHRISTMAS AFTER ALL! MY DOG IS BACK!
WHEN DID HE COME BACK? WHAT HAPPENED?
I THOUGHT HE WAS ON HIS WAY TO GRENOBLE, FRANCE, TO SKATE IN THE OLYMPICS... WHAT MADE HIM DECIDE TO COME BACK?
12-22
WELL, THERE WAS THIS OCEAN, SEE....
SCHULZ

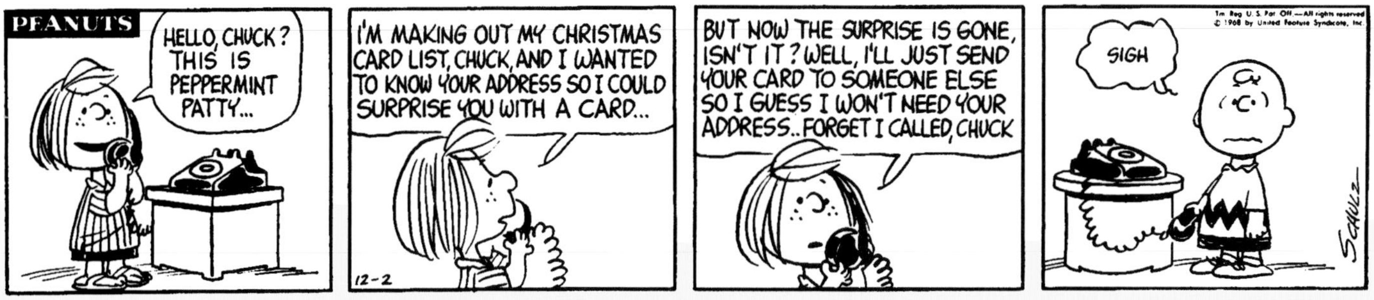
PEANUTS
HELLO, CHUCK? THIS IS PEPPERMINT PATTY...
I'M MAKING OUT MY CHRISTMAS CARD LIST, CHUCK, AND I WANTED TO KNOW YOUR ADDRESS SO I COULD SURPRISE YOU WITH A CARD...
12-2
BUT NOW THE SURPRISE IS GONE, ISN'T IT? WELL, I'LL JUST SEND YOUR CARD TO SOMEONE ELSE SO I GUESS I WON'T NEED YOUR ADDRESS.. FORGET I CALLED, CHUCK
SIGH
SCHULZ

PEANUTS
featuring
"Good ol' Charlie Brown"
by SCHULZ

HERE'S THE WORLD WAR I FLYING ACE IN HIS SOPWITH CAMEL ZOOMING OVER ENEMY LINES..

PRESIDENT WILSON SAID WE'D BE HOME BY CHRISTMAS... HA!

HERE'S THE WORLD WAR I FLYING ACE SITTING IN A LITTLE FRENCH CAFE DRINKING ROOT BEER..HE IS DISGUSTED..

ACTUALLY, WORLD WAR I FLYING ACES VERY SELDOM DRANK ROOT BEER..

WE'LL NEVER GET HOME BY CHRISTMAS! THIS STUPID WAR WILL GO ON FOREVER!

I THINK I'LL TAKE A BOTTLE OF ROOT BEER OVER TO THE ENLISTED MEN... POOR CHAPS, THEY PROBABLY NEED A LITTLE CHEERING UP...

HMM...IT'S BEGINNING TO SNOW...

WHAT'S THAT? THE ENLISTED MEN ARE SINGING CHRISTMAS CAROLS!

THOSE POOR BLIGHTERS ARE CHEERING THEMSELVES UP! THEY DON'T NEED ME!

SUDDENLY THE LONELINESS OF HIS DAYS BECOMES TOO MUCH FOR THE FLYING ACE TO BEAR..HE CRIES OUT IN TERRIBLE ANGUISH...

AAUGH!!

WHAT IN THE WORLD WAS THAT?

LET'S NOT SING ANY MORE CHRISTMAS CAROLS..

IF YOU'RE A LONG WAY FROM HOME, THEY CAN BE VERY DEPRESSING..

SOMETIMES I HAVE NO IDEA WHAT HE'S TALKING ABOUT ???

12-24

PEANUTS
IF YOU'RE GOOD, SANTA CLAUS BRINGS YOU PRESENTS, RIGHT ?
RIGHT
IF YOU'RE NOT GOOD, HE DOESN'T BRING YOU PRESENTS, RIGHT ?
12-21
RIGHT
WRONG! HAVE YOU EVER HEARD OF ONE CASE WHERE THAT ACTUALLY HAPPENED? NEVER!
THAT OLD RASCAL IS BLUFFING!

PEANUTS
Dear Santa Claus,
You can't bluff me.
I know that you are wishy washy. I know that you will bring me presents whether I'm good or whether I am bad.
US MAIL
12-22
INTO THE TEETH OF THE STORM!
US MAIL

PEANUTS
WELL, DID YOU TELL SANTA CLAUS WHAT YOU WANT FOR CHRISTMAS?
Santa HERE TODAY
SURE.. I ALSO WISHED HIM A VERY HAPPY HANUKKAH...
12-23
WE DIDN'T HAVE MUCH TIME, BUT WE DISCUSSED JUDAS MACCABAEUS AND THE CLEANSING OF THE TEMPLE
IT'S NOT OFTEN THAT YOU FIND A SANTA CLAUS WHO'S INTERESTED IN RELIGION ...

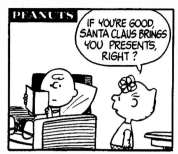

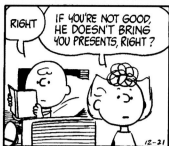

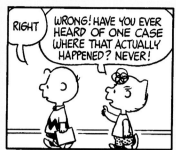

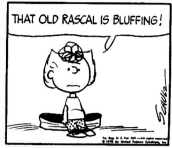

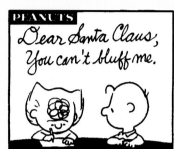

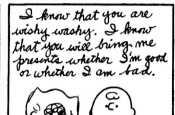

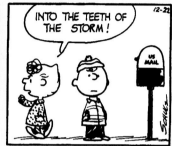

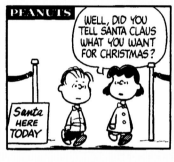

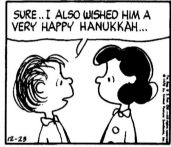

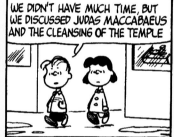

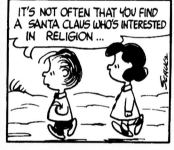

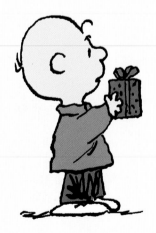

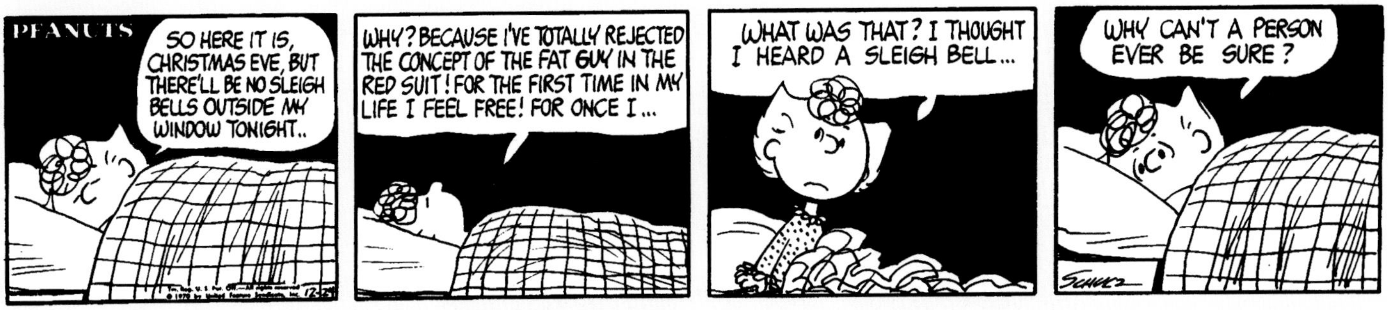
PEANUTS
SO HERE IT IS, CHRISTMAS EVE, BUT THERE'LL BE NO SLEIGH BELLS OUTSIDE MY WINDOW TONIGHT..
WHY? BECAUSE I'VE TOTALLY REJECTED THE CONCEPT OF THE FAT GUY IN THE RED SUIT! FOR THE FIRST TIME IN MY LIFE I FEEL FREE! FOR ONCE I...
WHAT WAS THAT? I THOUGHT I HEARD A SLEIGH BELL...
WHY CAN'T A PERSON EVER BE SURE?
SCHULZ

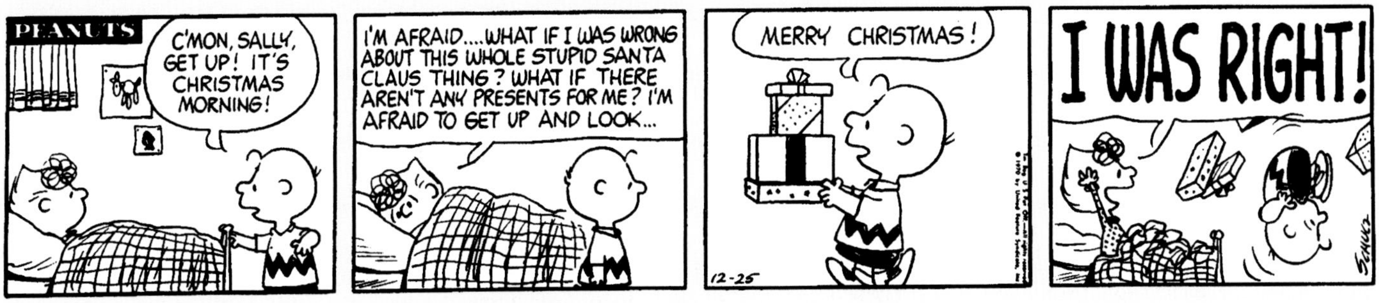
PEANUTS
C'MON, SALLY, GET UP! IT'S CHRISTMAS MORNING!
I'M AFRAID....WHAT IF I WAS WRONG ABOUT THIS WHOLE STUPID SANTA CLAUS THING? WHAT IF THERE AREN'T ANY PRESENTS FOR ME? I'M AFRAID TO GET UP AND LOOK...
MERRY CHRISTMAS!
12-25
I WAS RIGHT!
SCHULZ

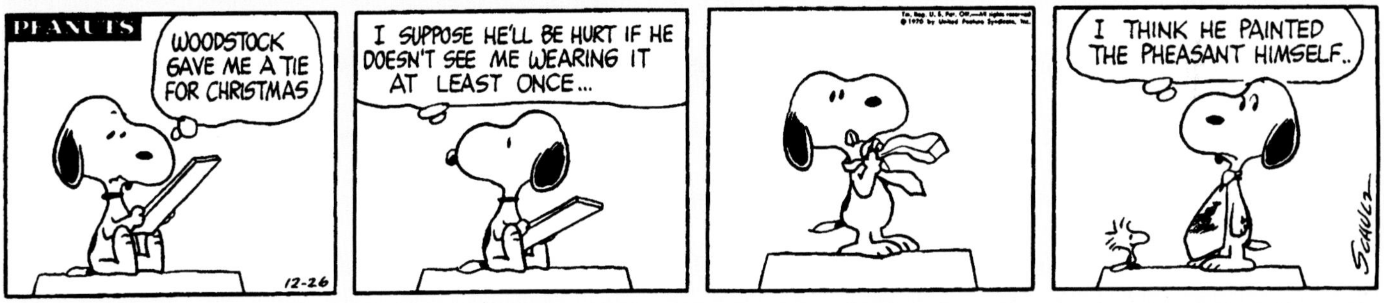
PEANUTS
WOODSTOCK GAVE ME A TIE FOR CHRISTMAS
12-26
I SUPPOSE HE'LL BE HURT IF HE DOESN'T SEE ME WEARING IT AT LEAST ONCE...
I THINK HE PAINTED THE PHEASANT HIMSELF..
SCHULZ

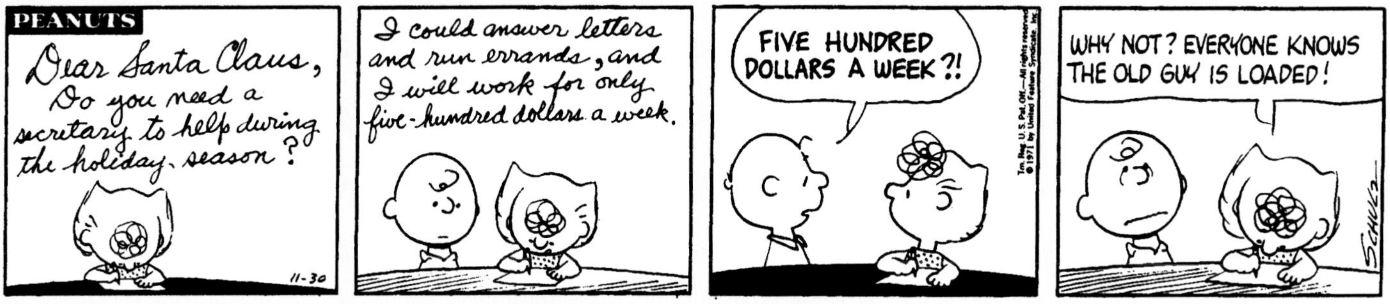
PEANUTS
Dear Santa Claus,
Do you need a secretary to help during the holiday season?
11-30
I could answer letters and run errands, and I will work for only five-hundred dollars a week.
FIVE HUNDRED DOLLARS A WEEK?!
WHY NOT? EVERYONE KNOWS THE OLD GUY IS LOADED!
SCHULZ

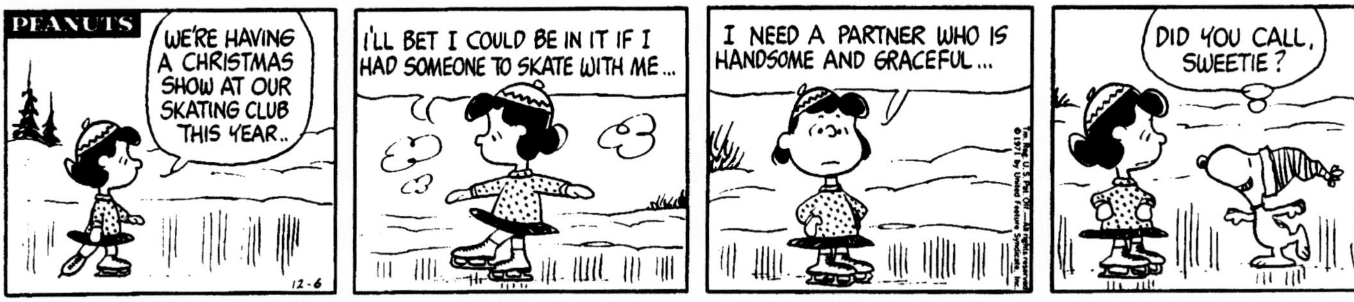
PEANUTS
WE'RE HAVING A CHRISTMAS SHOW AT OUR SKATING CLUB THIS YEAR..
12-6
I'LL BET I COULD BE IN IT IF I HAD SOMEONE TO SKATE WITH ME...
I NEED A PARTNER WHO IS HANDSOME AND GRACEFUL...
DID YOU CALL, SWEETIE?
SCHULZ

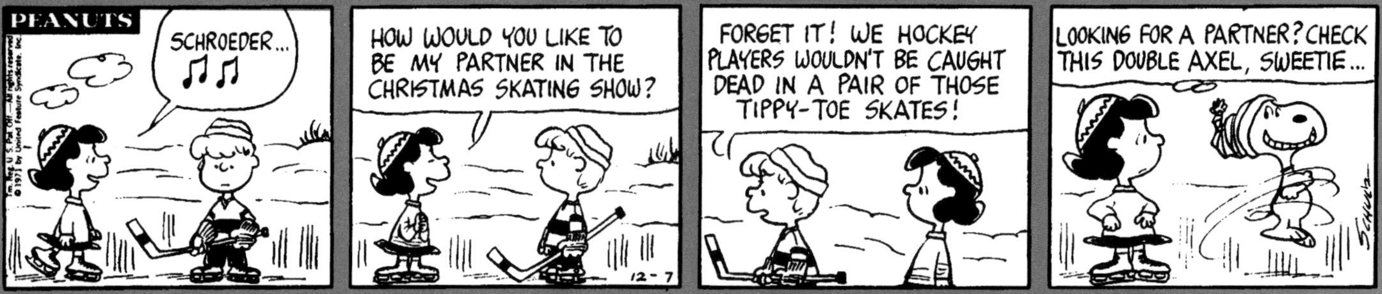
PEANUTS
SCHROEDER... ♫ ♫
HOW WOULD YOU LIKE TO BE MY PARTNER IN THE CHRISTMAS SKATING SHOW?
FORGET IT! WE HOCKEY PLAYERS WOULDN'T BE CAUGHT DEAD IN A PAIR OF THOSE TIPPY-TOE SKATES!
LOOKING FOR A PARTNER? CHECK THIS DOUBLE AXEL, SWEETIE...

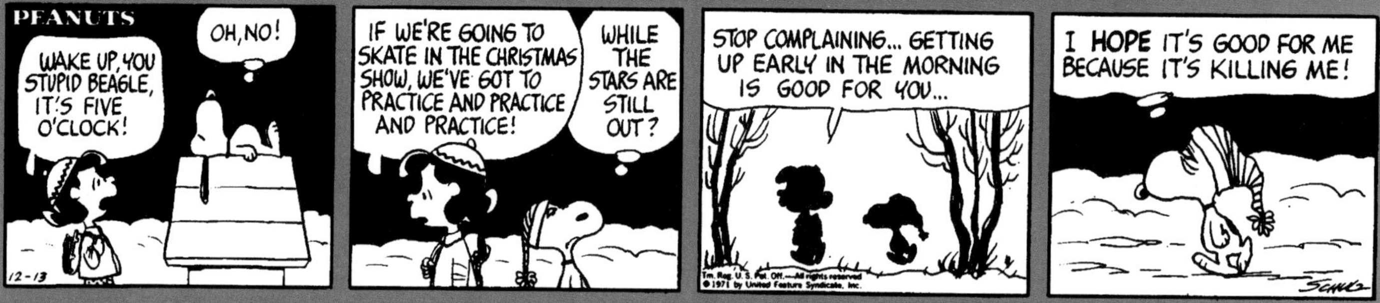
PEANUTS
WAKE UP, YOU STUPID BEAGLE, IT'S FIVE O'CLOCK!
OH, NO!
IF WE'RE GOING TO SKATE IN THE CHRISTMAS SHOW, WE'VE GOT TO PRACTICE AND PRACTICE AND PRACTICE!
WHILE THE STARS ARE STILL OUT?
STOP COMPLAINING... GETTING UP EARLY IN THE MORNING IS GOOD FOR YOU...
I **HOPE** IT'S GOOD FOR ME BECAUSE IT'S KILLING ME!

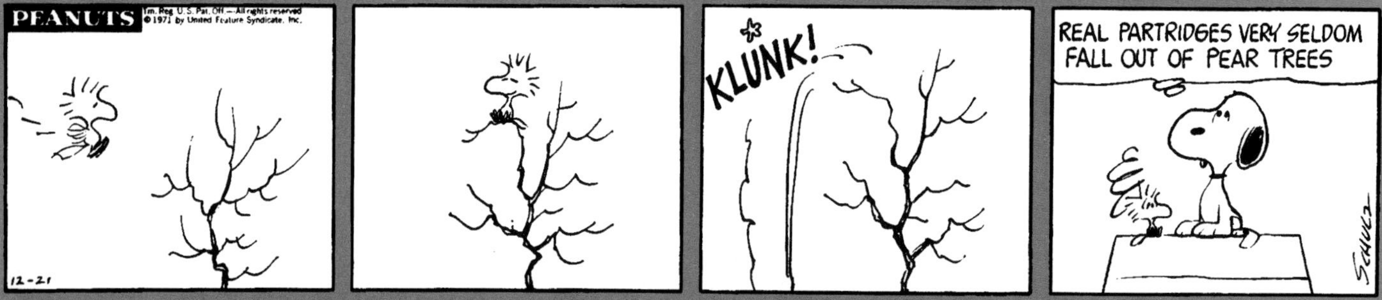
PEANUTS
KLUNK!
REAL PARTRIDGES VERY SELDOM FALL OUT OF PEAR TREES

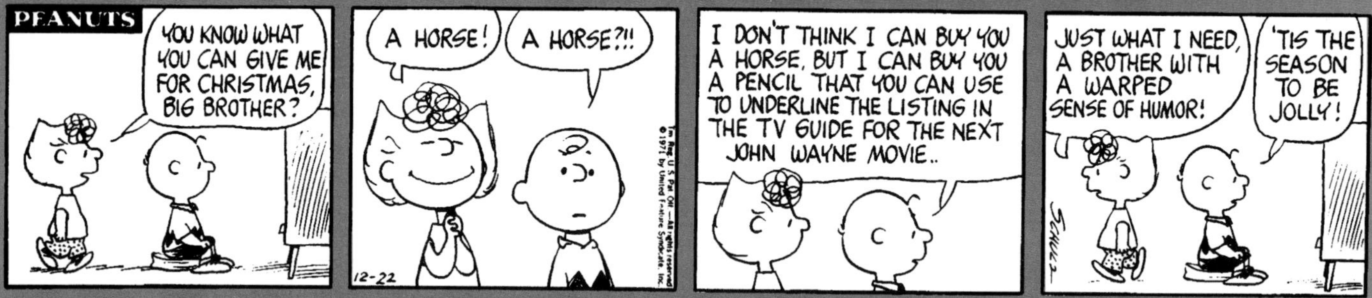
PEANUTS
YOU KNOW WHAT YOU CAN GIVE ME FOR CHRISTMAS, BIG BROTHER?
A HORSE!
A HORSE?!!
I DON'T THINK I CAN BUY YOU A HORSE, BUT I CAN BUY YOU A PENCIL THAT YOU CAN USE TO UNDERLINE THE LISTING IN THE TV GUIDE FOR THE NEXT JOHN WAYNE MOVIE..
JUST WHAT I NEED, A BROTHER WITH A WARPED SENSE OF HUMOR!
'TIS THE SEASON TO BE JOLLY!

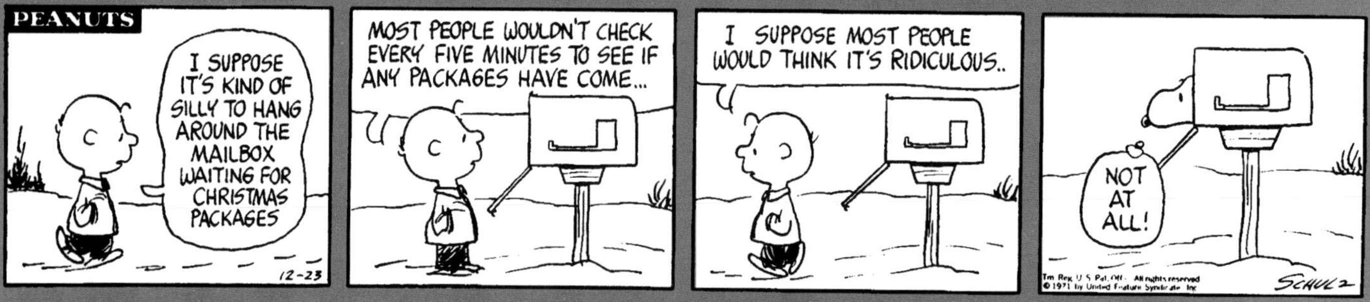
PEANUTS
I SUPPOSE IT'S KIND OF SILLY TO HANG AROUND THE MAILBOX WAITING FOR CHRISTMAS PACKAGES
MOST PEOPLE WOULDN'T CHECK EVERY FIVE MINUTES TO SEE IF ANY PACKAGES HAVE COME...
I SUPPOSE MOST PEOPLE WOULD THINK IT'S RIDICULOUS..
NOT AT ALL!

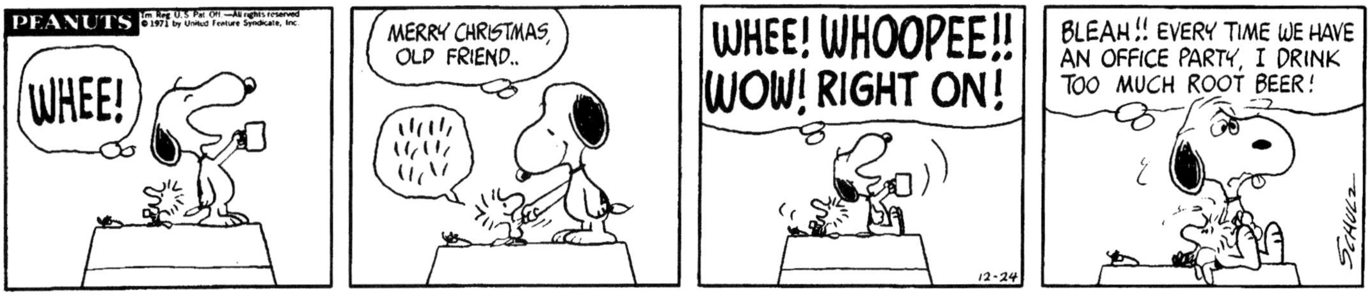
PEANUTS
Tm Reg U.S. Pat Off —All rights reserved © 1971 by United Feature Syndicate, Inc.
WHEE!
MERRY CHRISTMAS, OLD FRIEND..
WHEE! WHOOPEE!! WOW! RIGHT ON!
BLEAH!! EVERY TIME WE HAVE AN OFFICE PARTY, I DRINK TOO MUCH ROOT BEER!
SCHULZ
12-24

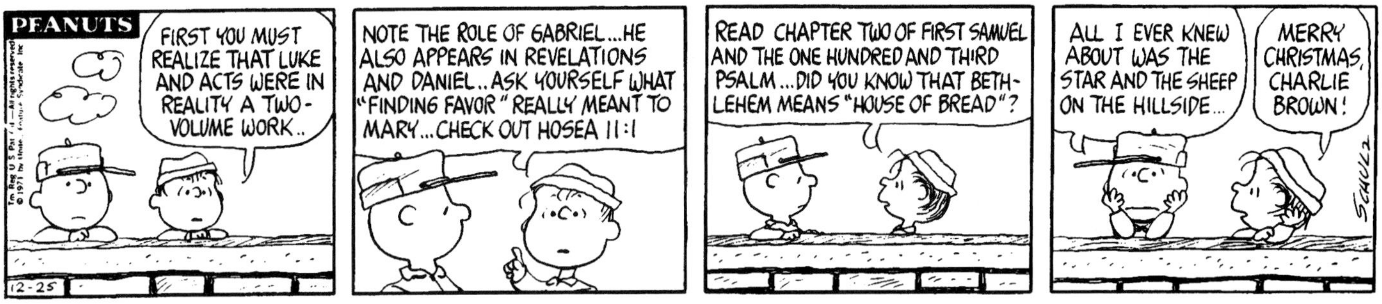
PEANUTS
FIRST YOU MUST REALIZE THAT LUKE AND ACTS WERE IN REALITY A TWO-VOLUME WORK..
NOTE THE ROLE OF GABRIEL...HE ALSO APPEARS IN REVELATIONS AND DANIEL..ASK YOURSELF WHAT "FINDING FAVOR" REALLY MEANT TO MARY...CHECK OUT HOSEA 11:1
READ CHAPTER TWO OF FIRST SAMUEL AND THE ONE HUNDRED AND THIRD PSALM...DID YOU KNOW THAT BETH-LEHEM MEANS "HOUSE OF BREAD"?
ALL I EVER KNEW ABOUT WAS THE STAR AND THE SHEEP ON THE HILLSIDE...
MERRY CHRISTMAS, CHARLIE BROWN!
SCHULZ
12-25

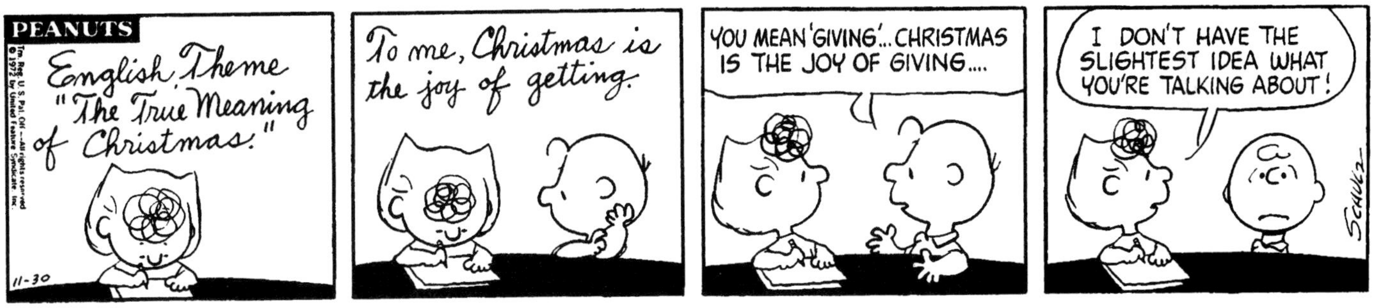
PEANUTS
English Theme "The True Meaning of Christmas."
To me, Christmas is the joy of getting.
YOU MEAN 'GIVING'...CHRISTMAS IS THE JOY OF GIVING....
I DON'T HAVE THE SLIGHTEST IDEA WHAT YOU'RE TALKING ABOUT!
SCHULZ
11-30

"Twas the month before Christmas"

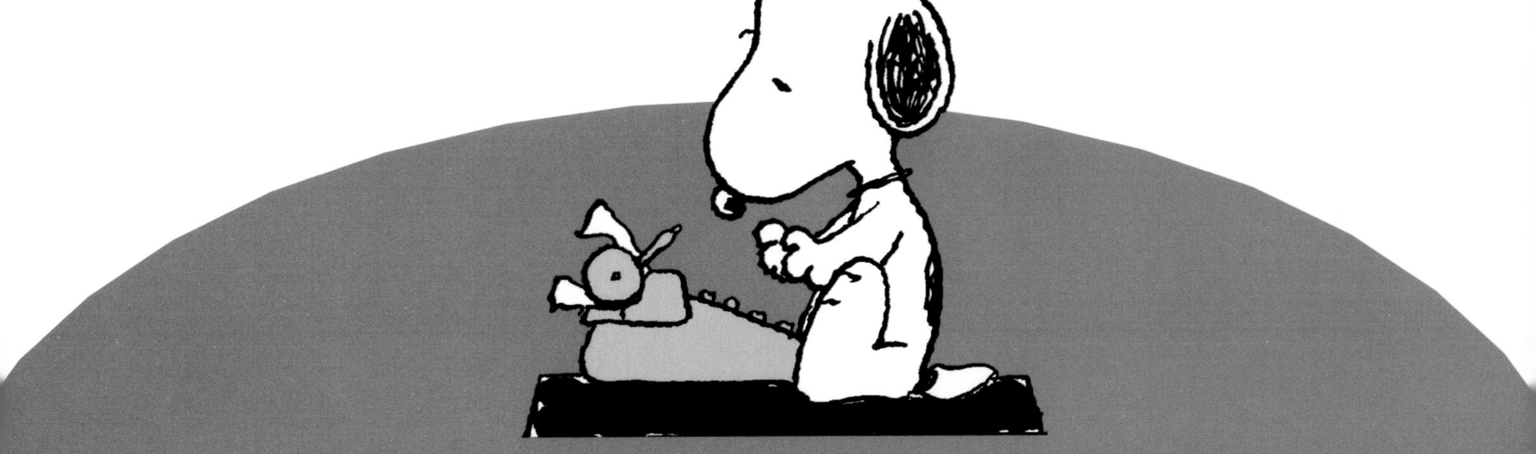

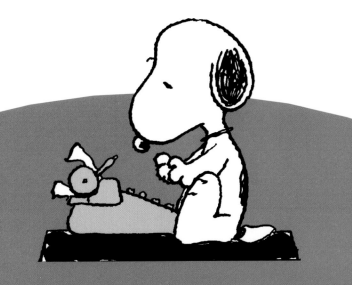

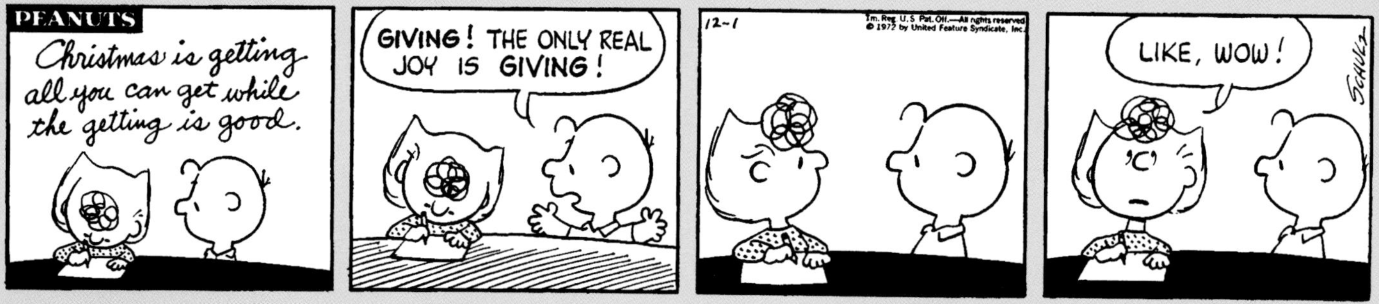
PEANUTS
Christmas is getting all you can get while the getting is good.
GIVING! THE ONLY REAL JOY IS GIVING!
12-1
Tm. Reg. U.S. Pat. Off.—All rights reserved © 1972 by United Feature Syndicate, Inc.
LIKE, WOW!
SCHULZ

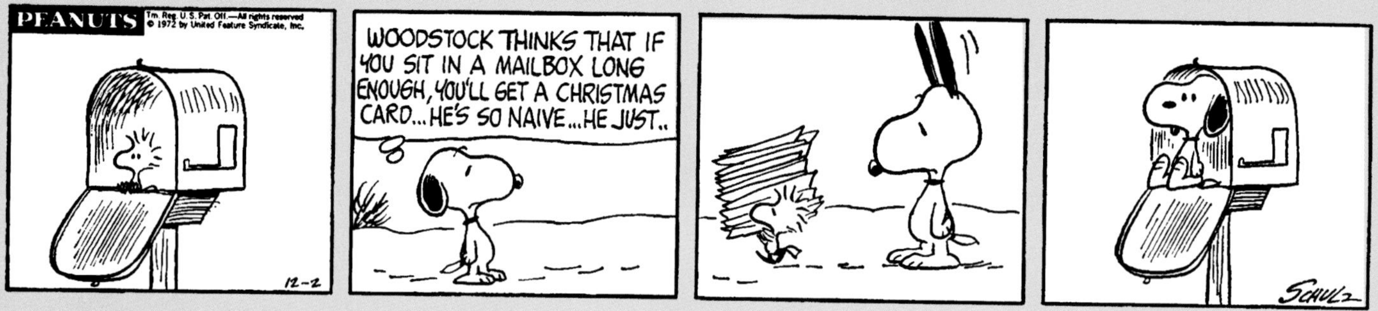
PEANUTS
Tm. Reg. U.S. Pat. Off.—All rights reserved © 1972 by United Feature Syndicate, Inc.
12-2
WOODSTOCK THINKS THAT IF YOU SIT IN A MAILBOX LONG ENOUGH, YOU'LL GET A CHRISTMAS CARD... HE'S SO NAIVE... HE JUST..
SCHULZ

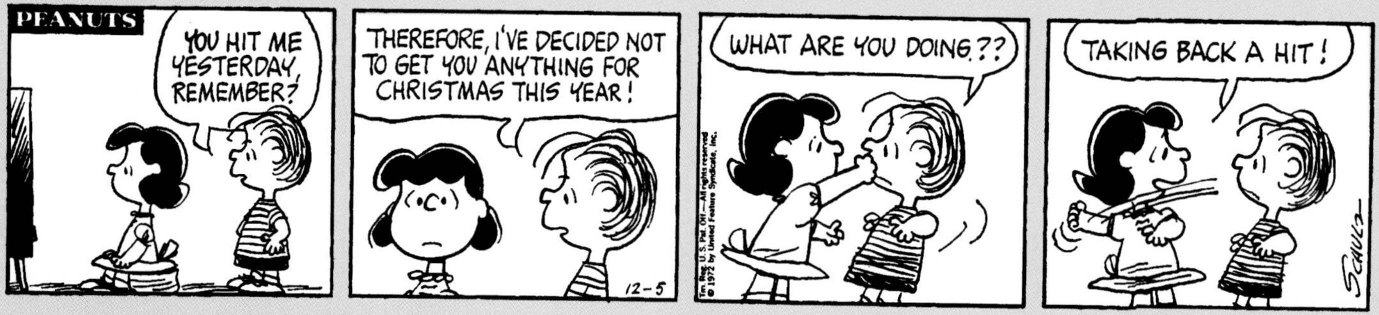
PEANUTS
YOU HIT ME YESTERDAY, REMEMBER?
THEREFORE, I'VE DECIDED NOT TO GET YOU ANYTHING FOR CHRISTMAS THIS YEAR!
12-5
WHAT ARE YOU DOING??
Tm. Reg. U.S. Pat. Off.—All rights reserved © 1972 by United Feature Syndicate, Inc.
TAKING BACK A HIT!
SCHULZ

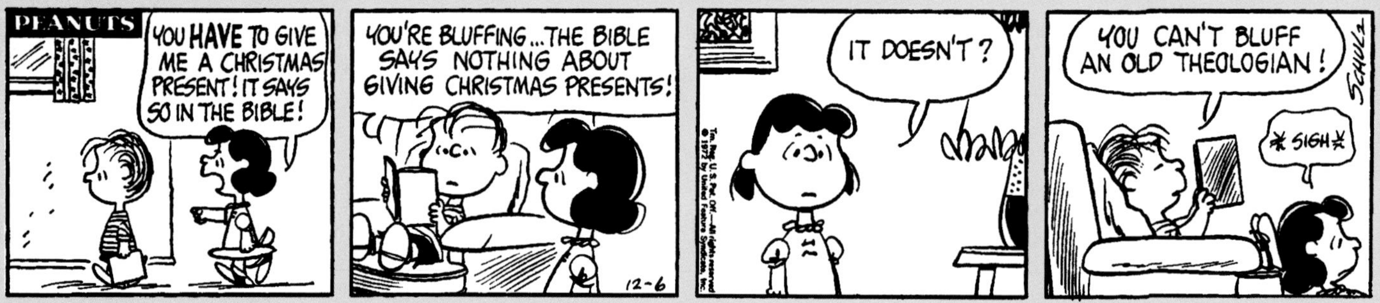
PEANUTS
YOU HAVE TO GIVE ME A CHRISTMAS PRESENT! IT SAYS SO IN THE BIBLE!
YOU'RE BLUFFING...THE BIBLE SAYS NOTHING ABOUT GIVING CHRISTMAS PRESENTS!
12-6
IT DOESN'T?
Tm. Reg. U.S. Pat. Off.—All rights reserved © 1972 by United Feature Syndicate, Inc.
YOU CAN'T BLUFF AN OLD THEOLOGIAN!
SIGH
SCHULZ

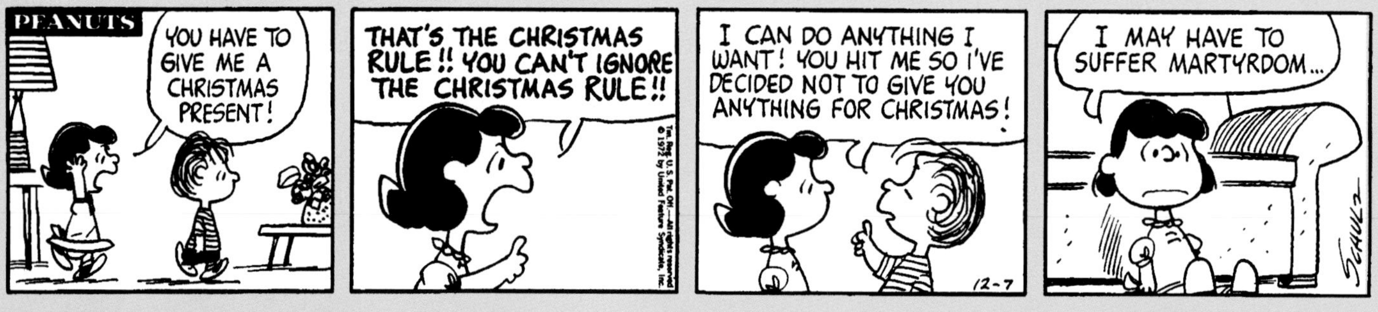
PEANUTS
YOU HAVE TO GIVE ME A CHRISTMAS PRESENT!
THAT'S THE CHRISTMAS RULE!! YOU CAN'T IGNORE THE CHRISTMAS RULE!!
Tm. Reg. U.S. Pat. Off.—All rights reserved © 1972 by United Feature Syndicate, Inc.
I CAN DO ANYTHING I WANT! YOU HIT ME SO I'VE DECIDED NOT TO GIVE YOU ANYTHING FOR CHRISTMAS!
12-7
I MAY HAVE TO SUFFER MARTYRDOM...
SCHULZ

I'M WRITING TO SANTA CLAUS..WHICH SHOULD I ASK FOR, A BICYCLE OR A DOG?

PEANUTS
HERE IT IS!! I FOUND IT!
I FOUND THE WORD "SISTER" IN THE BIBLE!
THERE IT IS, RIGHT THERE! SEE? THERE'S THE WORD "SISTER" RIGHT THERE IN THE BIBLE!
SO?
12-8
THAT PROVES YOU HAVE TO GIVE ME A CHRISTMAS PRESENT!!!
OH, GOOD GRIEF!
SCHULZ

PEANUTS
I DON'T THINK I'LL TELL WOODSTOCK ABOUT SANTA CLAUS...
12-14
HE'LL NEVER GET ANY PRESENTS ANYWAY
SANTA CLAUS NEVER BRINGS PRESENTS TO TINY, NONDESCRIPT, NOBODY BIRDS
IT'S KIND OF SAD AT CHRISTMASTIME TO BE A NOBODY BIRD...
SCHULZ

PEANUTS
WHAT I REALLY SHOULD DO IS INVITE WOODSTOCK BACK TO THE DAISY HILL PUPPY FARM FOR CHRISTMAS
12-15
HE'D LIKE THAT...IT'S FUN TO GO HOME FOR CHRISTMAS...
BUT HOW CAN YOU GO HOME FOR CHRISTMAS WHEN YOUR HOME HAS BEEN REPLACED BY A SIX-STORY PARKING GARAGE?
GEE, THAT'S SAD!
SCHULZ

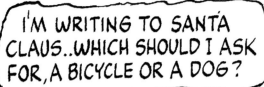

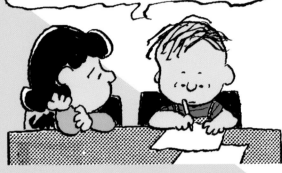

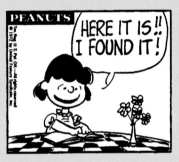

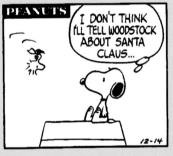

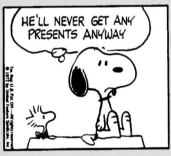

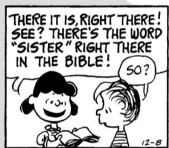

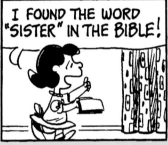

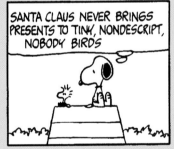

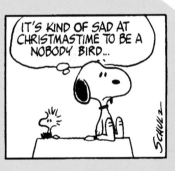

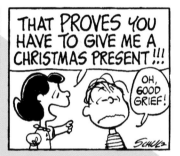

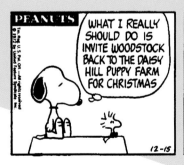

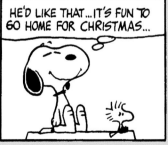

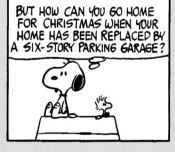

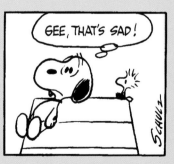

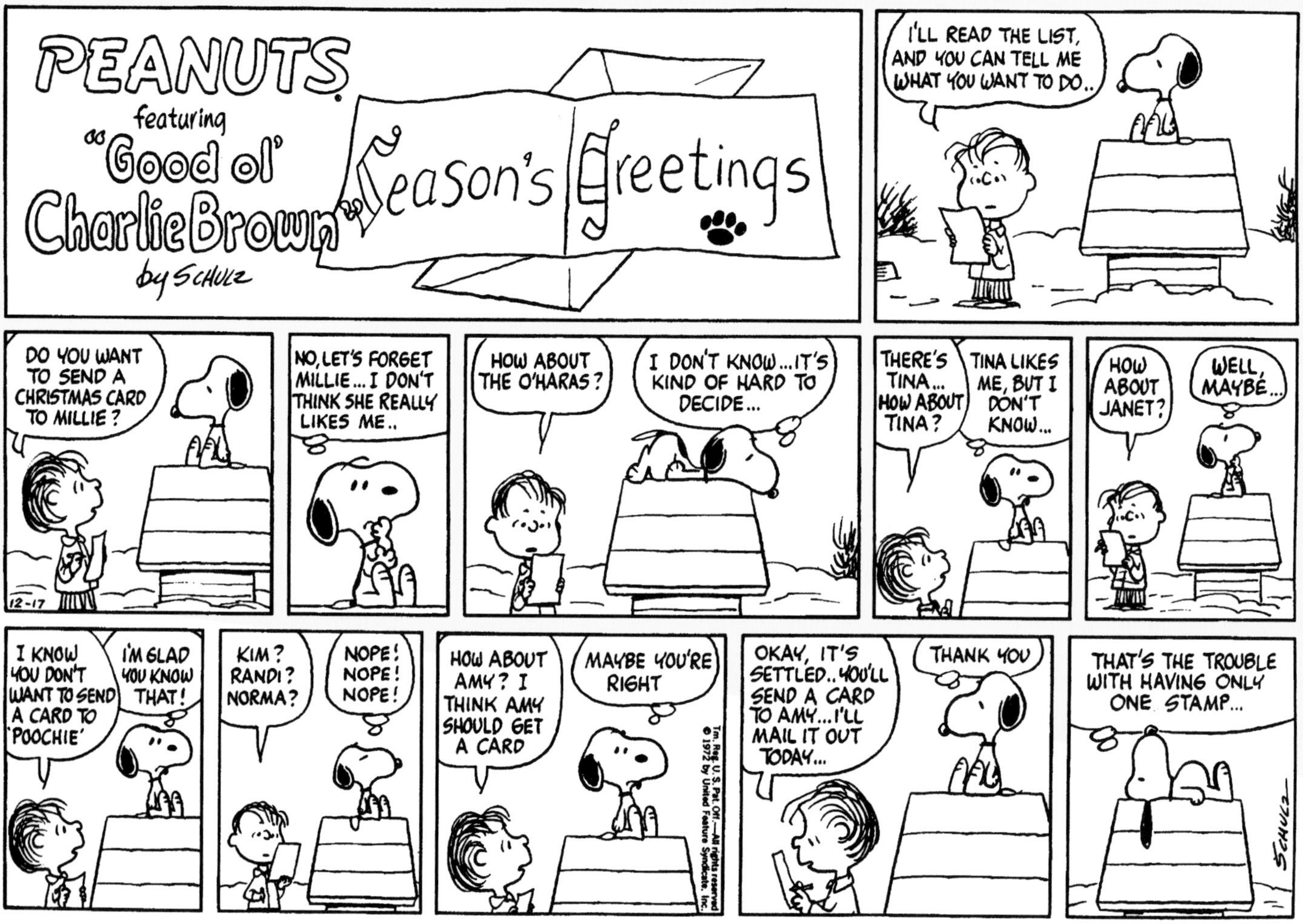
PEANUTS
featuring "Good ol' CharlieBrown"
by SCHULZ
Season's Greetings
I'LL READ THE LIST, AND YOU CAN TELL ME WHAT YOU WANT TO DO..
DO YOU WANT TO SEND A CHRISTMAS CARD TO MILLIE?
12-17
NO, LET'S FORGET MILLIE... I DON'T THINK SHE REALLY LIKES ME..
HOW ABOUT THE O'HARAS?
I DON'T KNOW... IT'S KIND OF HARD TO DECIDE...
THERE'S TINA... HOW ABOUT TINA?
TINA LIKES ME, BUT I DON'T KNOW...
HOW ABOUT JANET?
WELL, MAYBE...
I KNOW YOU DON'T WANT TO SEND A CARD TO 'POOCHIE'
I'M GLAD YOU KNOW THAT!
KIM? RANDI? NORMA?
NOPE! NOPE! NOPE!
HOW ABOUT AMY? I THINK AMY SHOULD GET A CARD
MAYBE YOU'RE RIGHT
Tm. Reg. U.S. Pat. Off.—All rights reserved © 1972 by United Feature Syndicate, Inc.
OKAY, IT'S SETTLED.. YOU'LL SEND A CARD TO AMY... I'LL MAIL IT OUT TODAY...
THANK YOU
THAT'S THE TROUBLE WITH HAVING ONLY ONE STAMP...
SCHULZ

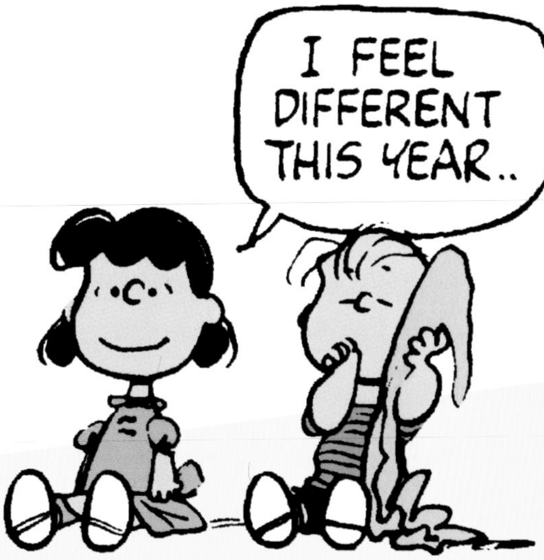
I FEEL DIFFERENT THIS YEAR..

PEANUTS
I LOVE THE HOLIDAY SEASON!
I LIKE TO SEE PEOPLE BUYING PRESENTS AND DECORATING THEIR HOMES...I LIKE CHRISTMAS TREES, TOO
12-18
EVERYONE SHOULD HAVE A CHRISTMAS TREE... EVEN WOODSTOCK..
Tm. Reg. U.S. Pat. Off.—All rights reserved © 1972 by United Feature Syndicate, Inc.
SCHULZ

PEANUTS
12-22
Tm. Reg. U.S. Pat. Off.—All rights reserved © 1972 by United Feature Syndicate, Inc.
THE WORLD IS FILLED WITH COMEDIANS!
SCHULZ

PEANUTS
I CAN SEE MYSELF!
12-23
Tm. Reg. U.S. Pat. Off.—All rights reserved © 1972 by United Feature Syndicate, Inc.
I'D LOOK FUNNY WITH A BIG NOSE..
SCHULZ

BECAUSE I SAID SO, THAT'S WHY!

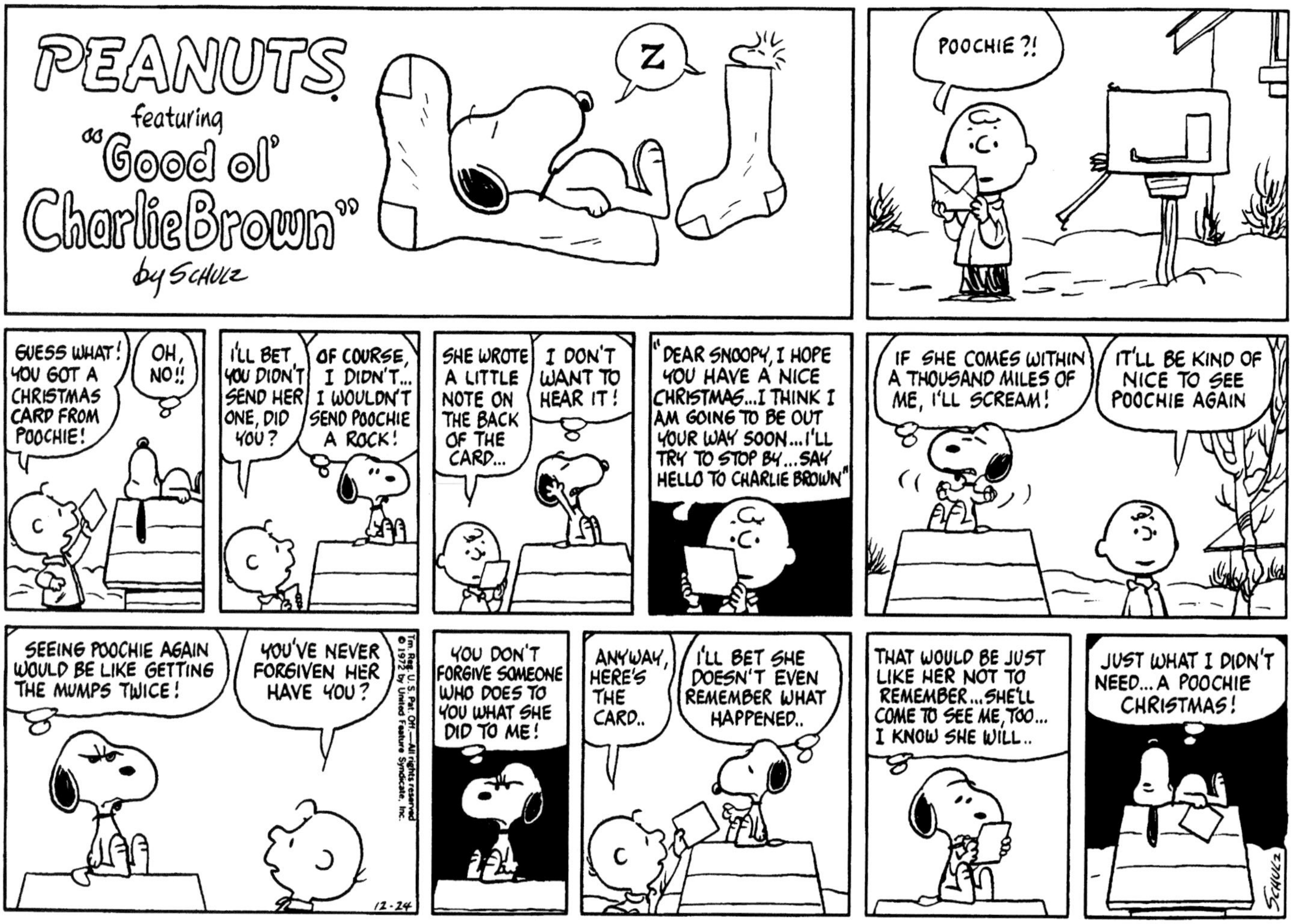
PEANUTS
featuring
"Good ol' CharlieBrown"
by SCHULZ
Z
POOCHIE ?!
GUESS WHAT! YOU GOT A CHRISTMAS CARD FROM POOCHIE!
OH, NO!!
I'LL BET YOU DIDN'T SEND HER ONE, DID YOU?
OF COURSE, I DIDN'T... I WOULDN'T SEND POOCHIE A ROCK!
SHE WROTE A LITTLE NOTE ON THE BACK OF THE CARD...
I DON'T WANT TO HEAR IT!
"DEAR SNOOPY, I HOPE YOU HAVE A NICE CHRISTMAS...I THINK I AM GOING TO BE OUT YOUR WAY SOON...I'LL TRY TO STOP BY...SAY HELLO TO CHARLIE BROWN"
IF SHE COMES WITHIN A THOUSAND MILES OF ME, I'LL SCREAM!
IT'LL BE KIND OF NICE TO SEE POOCHIE AGAIN
SEEING POOCHIE AGAIN WOULD BE LIKE GETTING THE MUMPS TWICE!
YOU'VE NEVER FORGIVEN HER HAVE YOU?
Tm. Reg. U.S. Pat. Off.—All rights reserved © 1972 by United Feature Syndicate, Inc.
12-24
YOU DON'T FORGIVE SOMEONE WHO DOES TO YOU WHAT SHE DID TO ME!
ANYWAY, HERE'S THE CARD..
I'LL BET SHE DOESN'T EVEN REMEMBER WHAT HAPPENED..
THAT WOULD BE JUST LIKE HER NOT TO REMEMBER...SHE'LL COME TO SEE ME, TOO... I KNOW SHE WILL..
JUST WHAT I DIDN'T NEED...A POOCHIE CHRISTMAS!
SCHULZ

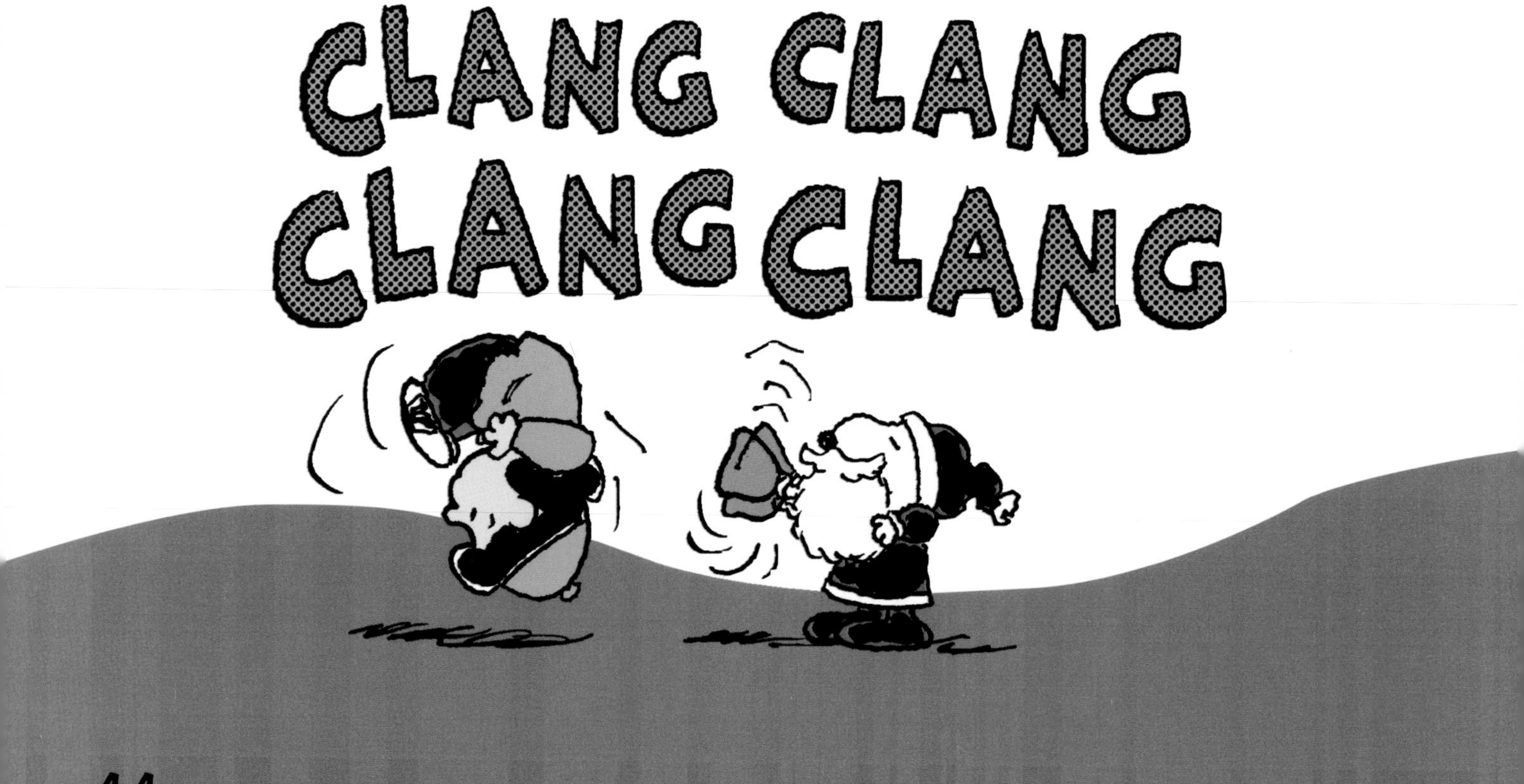
CLANG CLANG
CLANG CLANG

PEANUTS
12-25
*
Tm. Reg. U.S. Pat. Off.—All rights reserved © 1972 by United Feature Syndicate, Inc.
* Merry Christmas
SCHULZ

PEANUTS
I JUST WANTED TO THANK YOU AGAIN FOR THE STRING OF PEARLS YOU GAVE ME FOR CHRISTMAS...
12-26
Tm. Reg. U.S. Pat. Off.—All rights reserved © 1972 by United Feature Syndicate, Inc.
I DID NOT GIVE YOU A STRING OF PEARLS FOR CHRISTMAS..
I'LL SAY YOU DIDN'T!
SCHULZ

PEANUTS
RING!
Tm. Reg. U.S. Pat. Off.—All rights reserved © 1972 by United Feature Syndicate, Inc.
HI! I JUST STOPPED BY TO THANK YOU AGAIN FOR THE MINK STOLE YOU GAVE ME FOR CHRISTMAS
12-27
I DID NOT GIVE YOU A MINK STOLE FOR CHRISTMAS!
I'LL SAY YOU DIDN'T!
SCHULZ

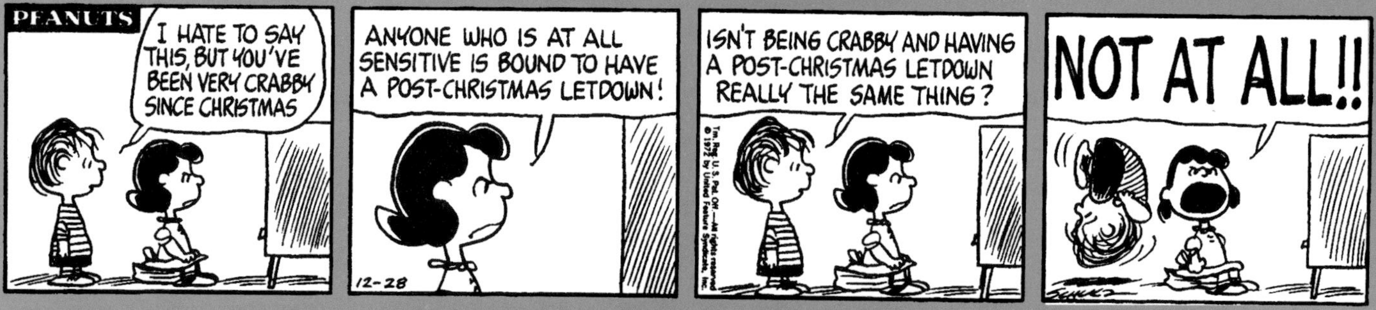
PEANUTS
I HATE TO SAY THIS, BUT YOU'VE BEEN VERY CRABBY SINCE CHRISTMAS
ANYONE WHO IS AT ALL SENSITIVE IS BOUND TO HAVE A POST-CHRISTMAS LETDOWN!
12-28
ISN'T BEING CRABBY AND HAVING A POST-CHRISTMAS LETDOWN REALLY THE SAME THING?
NOT AT ALL!!

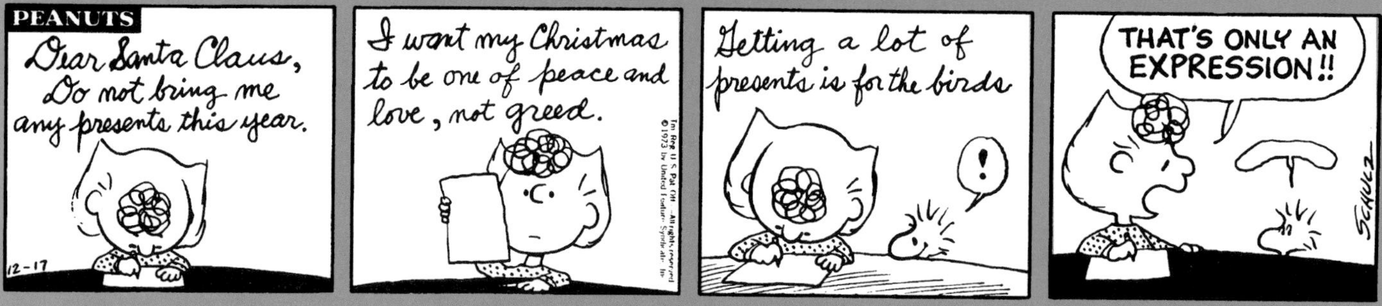
PEANUTS
Dear Santa Claus, Do not bring me any presents this year.
12-17
I want my Christmas to be one of peace and love, not greed.
Getting a lot of presents is for the birds
!
THAT'S ONLY AN EXPRESSION!!

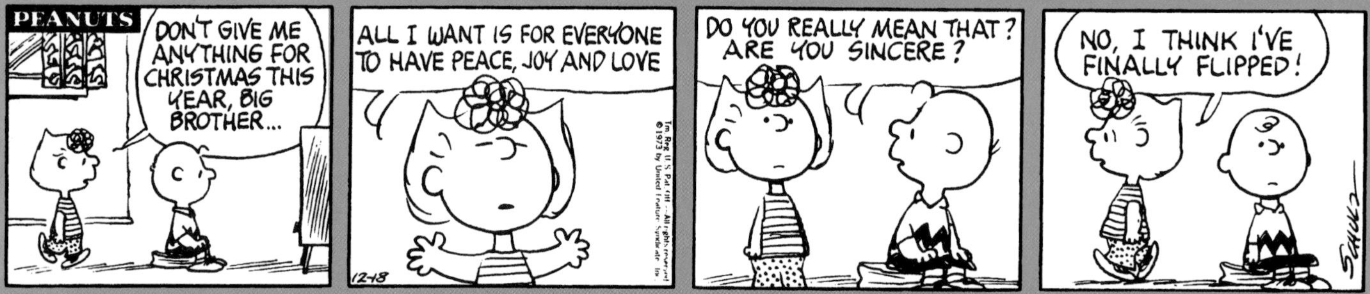
PEANUTS
DON'T GIVE ME ANYTHING FOR CHRISTMAS THIS YEAR, BIG BROTHER...
ALL I WANT IS FOR EVERYONE TO HAVE PEACE, JOY AND LOVE
12-18
DO YOU REALLY MEAN THAT? ARE YOU SINCERE?
NO, I THINK I'VE FINALLY FLIPPED!

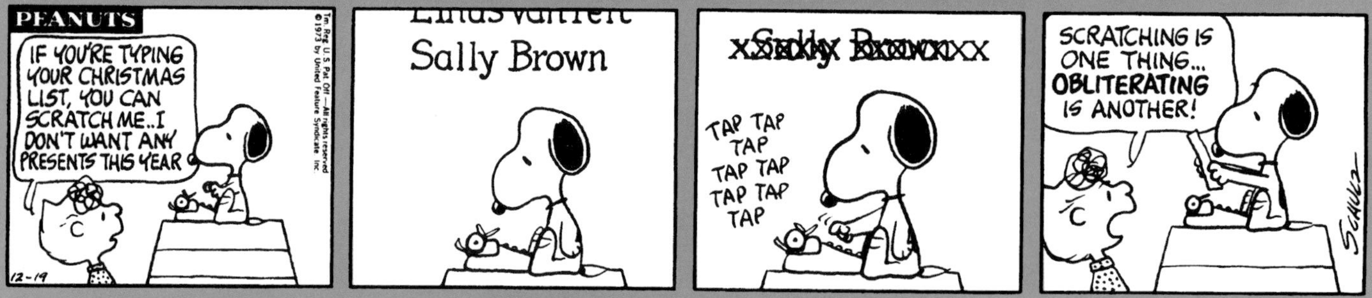
PEANUTS
IF YOU'RE TYPING YOUR CHRISTMAS LIST, YOU CAN SCRATCH ME..I DON'T WANT ANY PRESENTS THIS YEAR
12-19
Sally Brown
TAP TAP TAP TAP TAP TAP TAP TAP
SCRATCHING IS ONE THING... OBLITERATING IS ANOTHER!

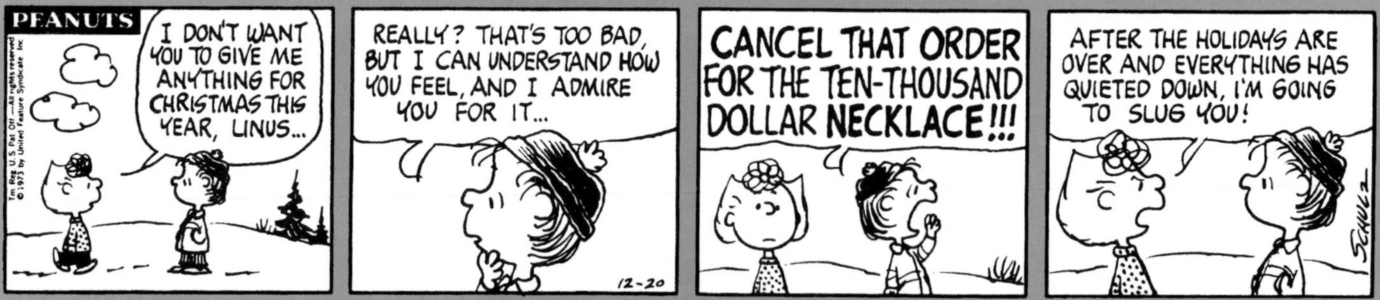
PEANUTS
I DON'T WANT YOU TO GIVE ME ANYTHING FOR CHRISTMAS THIS YEAR, LINUS...
REALLY? THAT'S TOO BAD, BUT I CAN UNDERSTAND HOW YOU FEEL, AND I ADMIRE YOU FOR IT...
12-20
CANCEL THAT ORDER FOR THE TEN-THOUSAND DOLLAR NECKLACE!!!
AFTER THE HOLIDAYS ARE OVER AND EVERYTHING HAS QUIETED DOWN, I'M GOING TO SLUG YOU!

PEANUTS
EVERYONE SHOULD BE LIKE ME...I'VE ASKED FOR NOTHING FOR CHRISTMAS...
I AM TOTALLY UNSELFISH! IF EVERYONE WAS LIKE ME, THIS WOULD BE A BETTER WORLD...
MAYBE SOMEONE WILL START A NEW MOVEMENT WHERE EVERYONE WILL TRY TO BE LIKE **ME**!
Tm Reg U.S. Pat Off—All rights reserved © 1973 by United Feature Syndicate Inc.
12-21
I COULD BE THE HEAD **ME**!!
SCHULZ

PEANUTS
THE WHOLE THING IS CRAZY!
TAKE CHRISTMAS STOCKINGS, FOR INSTANCE...
WHAT IF YOU HANG UP YOUR STOCKING AND SANTA CLAUS DOESN'T EVEN SEE IT ?!
SOME OF US DON'T TAKE ANY CHANCES
Tm Reg U.S. Pat Off—All rights reserved © 1973 by United Feature Syndicate Inc.
12-22
SCHULZ

LOOK, GRAMMA SENT US A CHRISTMAS CARD WITH A DOLLAR IN IT..

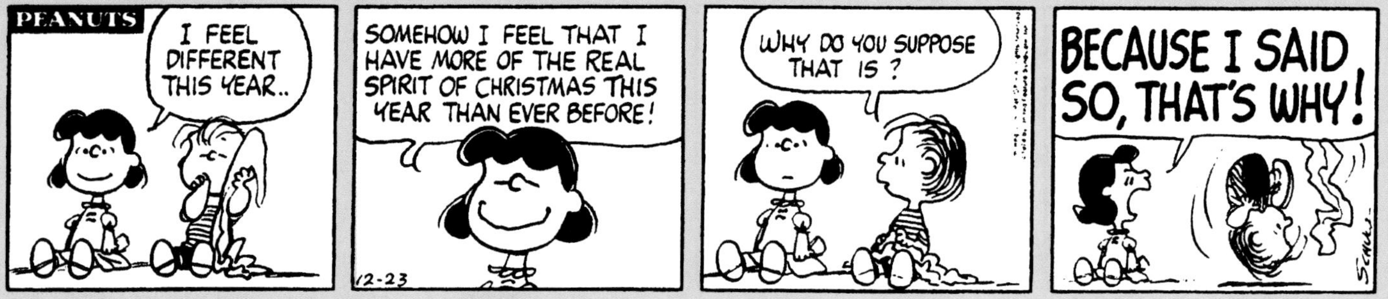
PEANUTS
I FEEL DIFFERENT THIS YEAR..
SOMEHOW I FEEL THAT I HAVE MORE OF THE REAL SPIRIT OF CHRISTMAS THIS YEAR THAN EVER BEFORE!
12-23
WHY DO YOU SUPPOSE THAT IS ?
BECAUSE I SAID SO, THAT'S WHY!
SCHULZ

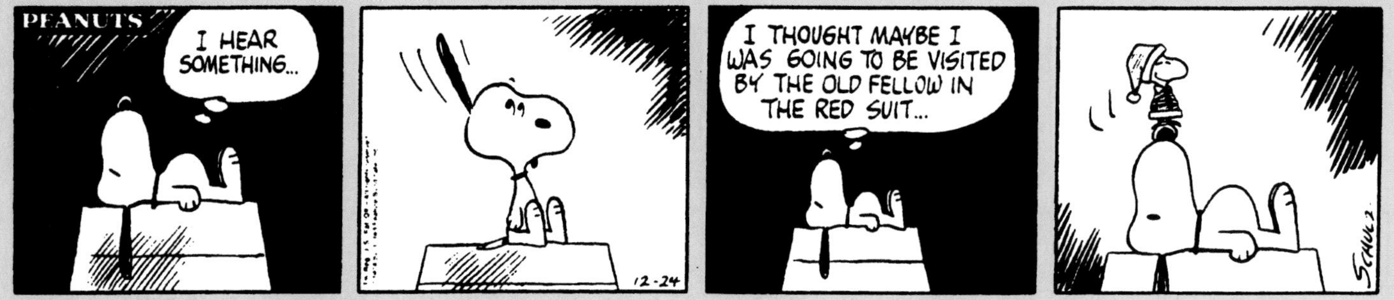
PEANUTS
I HEAR SOMETHING...
12-24
I THOUGHT MAYBE I WAS GOING TO BE VISITED BY THE OLD FELLOW IN THE RED SUIT...
SCHULZ

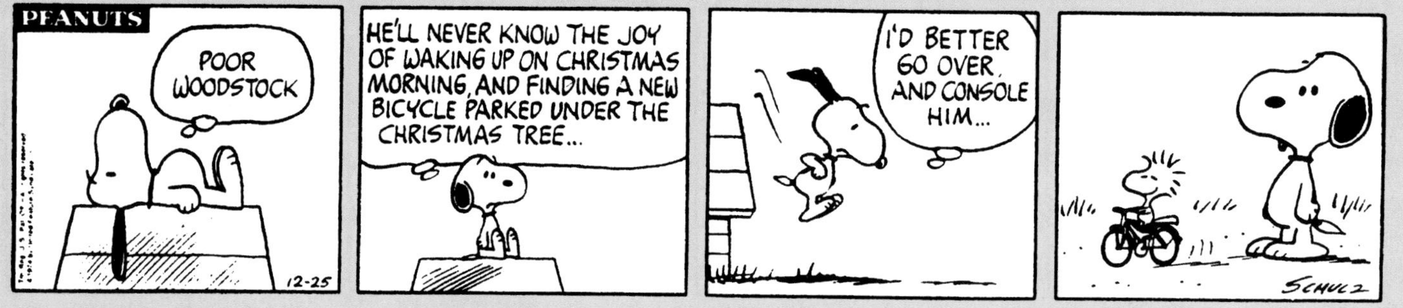
PEANUTS
POOR WOODSTOCK
12-25
HE'LL NEVER KNOW THE JOY OF WAKING UP ON CHRISTMAS MORNING, AND FINDING A NEW BICYCLE PARKED UNDER THE CHRISTMAS TREE...
I'D BETTER GO OVER AND CONSOLE HIM...
SCHULZ

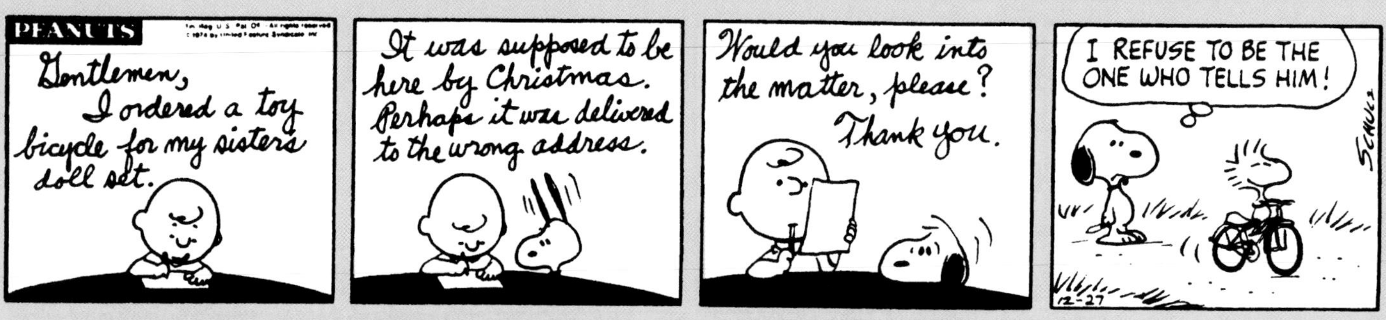
PEANUTS
Gentlemen,
I ordered a toy bicycle for my sister's doll set.
It was supposed to be here by Christmas. Perhaps it was delivered to the wrong address.
Would you look into the matter, please?
Thank you.
I REFUSE TO BE THE ONE WHO TELLS HIM!
SCHULZ
12-27

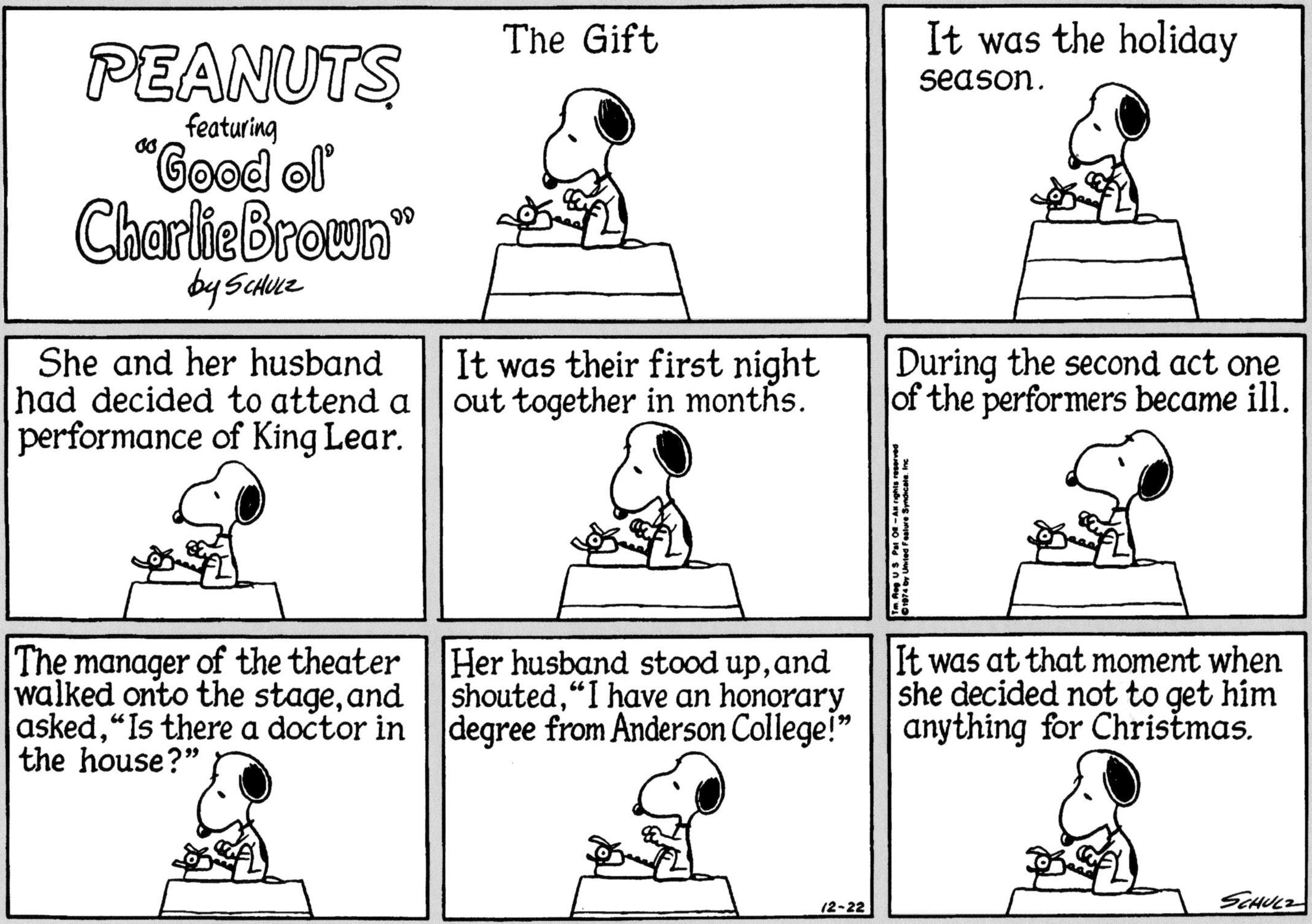
PEANUTS
featuring
"Good ol' CharlieBrown"
by SCHULZ
The Gift
It was the holiday season.
She and her husband had decided to attend a performance of King Lear.
It was their first night out together in months.
During the second act one of the performers became ill.
Tm. Reg U.S. Pat Off — All rights reserved
©1974 by United Feature Syndicate, Inc.
The manager of the theater walked onto the stage, and asked, "Is there a doctor in the house?"
Her husband stood up, and shouted, "I have an honorary degree from Anderson College!"
12-22
It was at that moment when she decided not to get him anything for Christmas.
SCHULZ

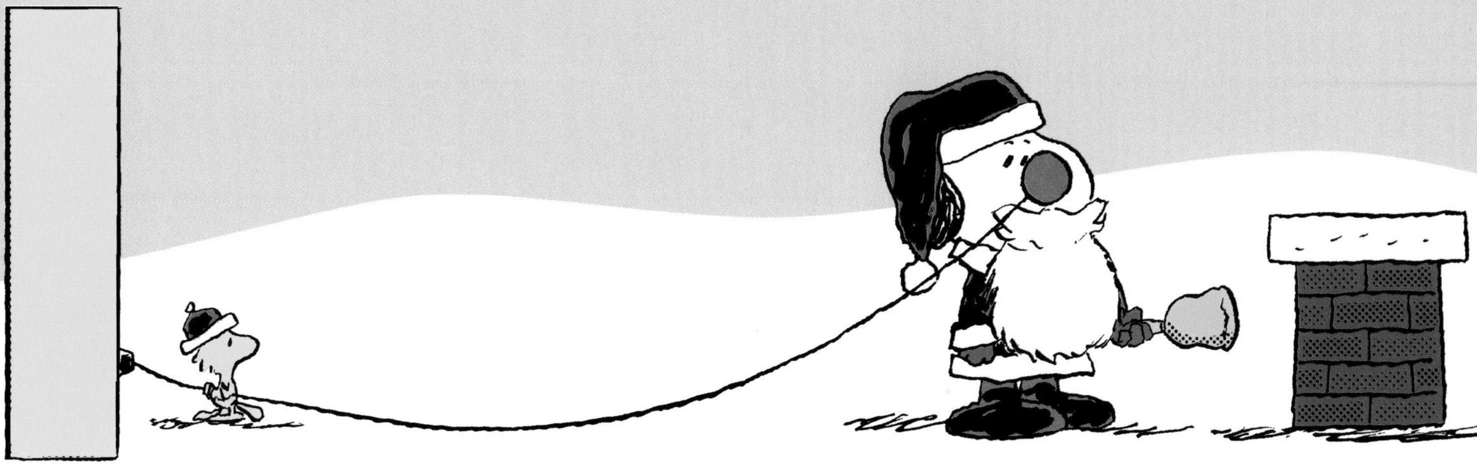

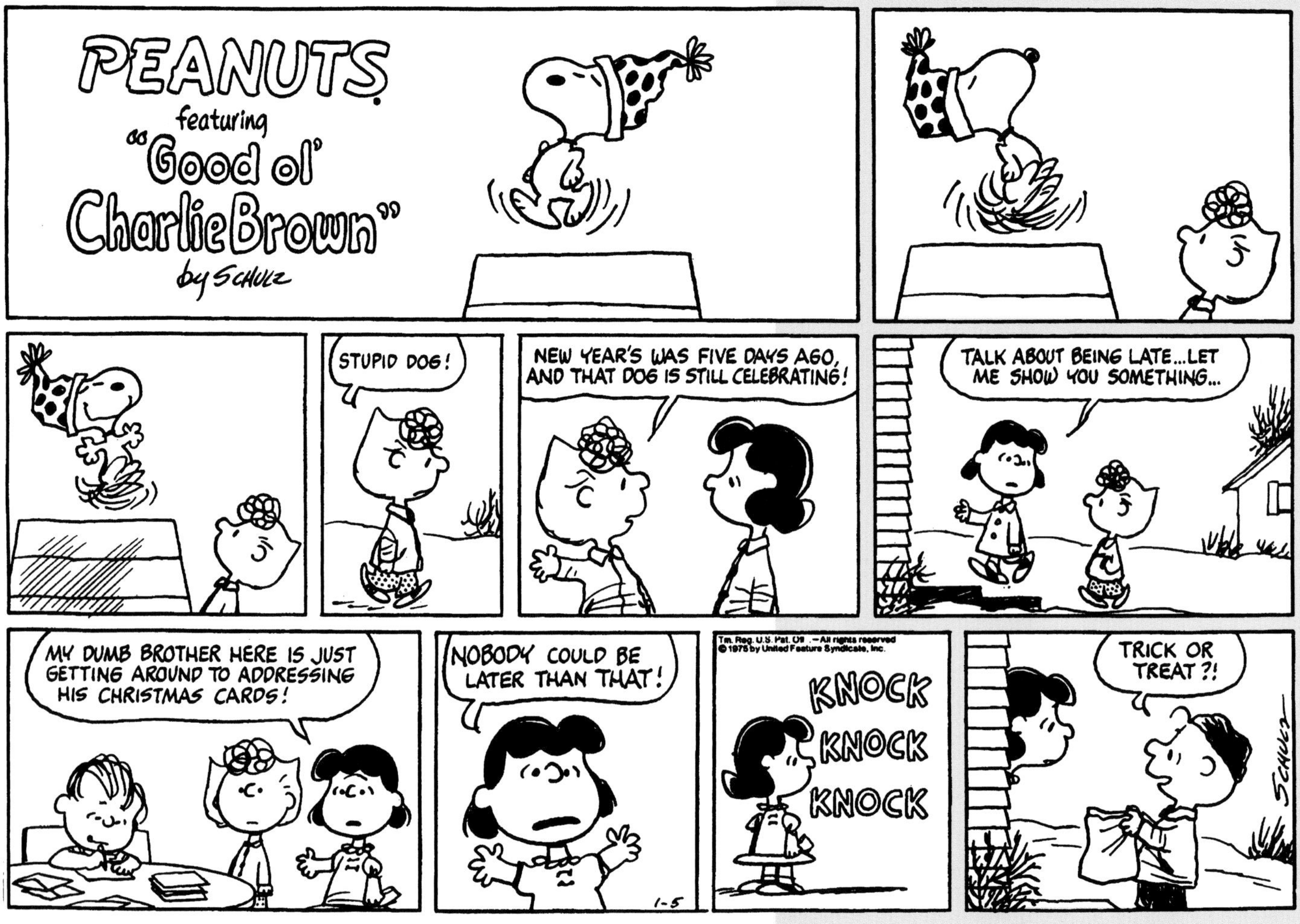
PEANUTS
featuring
"Good ol' CharlieBrown"
by SCHULZ
STUPID DOG!
NEW YEAR'S WAS FIVE DAYS AGO, AND THAT DOG IS STILL CELEBRATING!
TALK ABOUT BEING LATE...LET ME SHOW YOU SOMETHING...
MY DUMB BROTHER HERE IS JUST GETTING AROUND TO ADDRESSING HIS CHRISTMAS CARDS!
NOBODY COULD BE LATER THAN THAT!
1-5
Tm. Reg. U.S. Pat. Off. —All rights reserved
© 1975 by United Feature Syndicate, Inc.
KNOCK
KNOCK
KNOCK
TRICK OR TREAT?!
SCHULZ

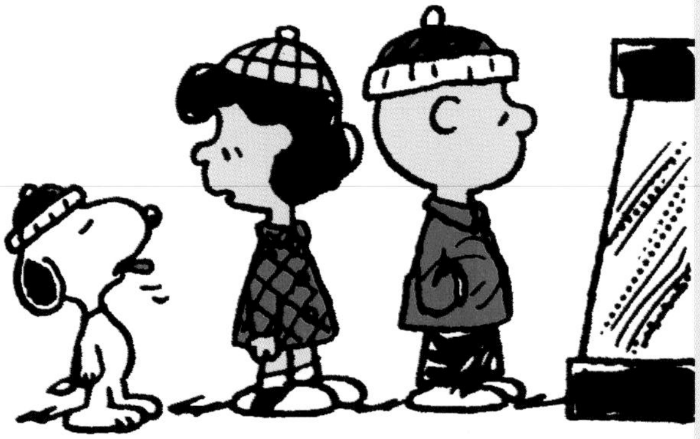

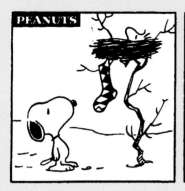

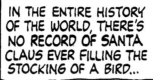

PEANUTS
IN THE ENTIRE HISTORY OF THE WORLD, THERE'S NO RECORD OF SANTA CLAUS EVER FILLING THE STOCKING OF A BIRD...
12-22
BUT THAT DOESN'T DISCOURAGE WOODSTOCK..
Tm. Reg U S Pat Off.—All rights reserved ©1975 by United Feature Syndicate, Inc.
HE FEELS THE ODDS ARE WITH HIM!
SCHULZ

PEANUTS
THE ORANGE WAS A GOOD IDEA, WASN'T IT?
12-23
I FIGURE IF YOU PUT THE ORANGE IN WOODSTOCK'S CHRISTMAS STOCKING, IT WILL MAKE HIM VERY HAPPY
I'M GLAD YOU AGREE THAT THE ORANGE IS A GOOD IDEA
THE ORANGE WAS A GREAT IDEA...EXCEPT I ATE IT!
SCHULZ
Tm. Reg U.S. Pat Off.—All rights reserved ©1975 by United Feature Syndicate, Inc.

PEANUTS
LOOK AT THIS PICTURE OF SANTA CLAUS.. TALK ABOUT FAT CITY!
I CAN'T BELIEVE HE CAN CRAWL UP AND DOWN ALL THOSE CHIMNEYS WITHOUT LOSING A LITTLE WEIGHT...
DO YOU KNOW WHAT'S GONNA HAPPEN? ONE OF THESE TIMES HE'S GONNA HAVE A CORONARY RIGHT IN SOME POOR LITTLE KID'S LIVING ROOM!
12-24
DON'T WORRY ABOUT IT... MERRY CHRISTMAS
IT COULD BE **OUR** LIVING ROOM!
SCHULZ
©1975 by United Feature Syndicate, Inc.

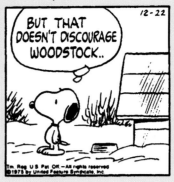

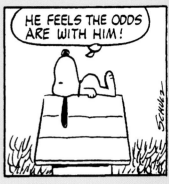

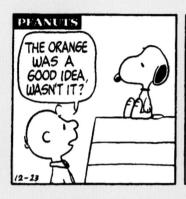

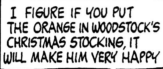

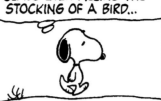

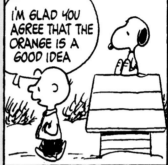

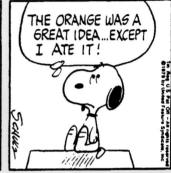

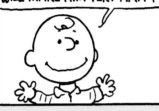

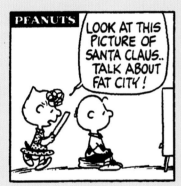

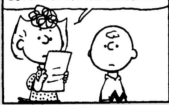

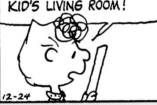

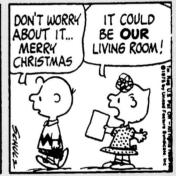

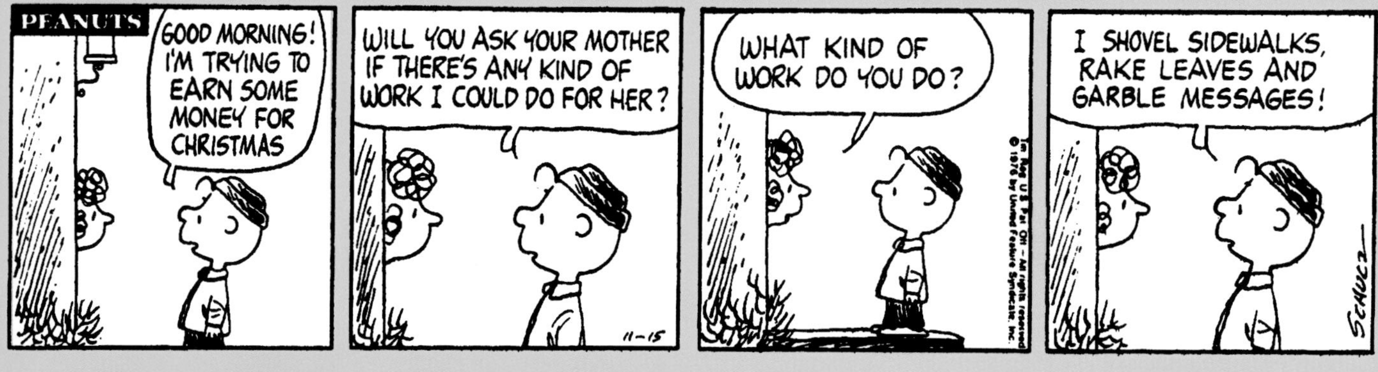
PEANUTS
GOOD MORNING! I'M TRYING TO EARN SOME MONEY FOR CHRISTMAS
WILL YOU ASK YOUR MOTHER IF THERE'S ANY KIND OF WORK I COULD DO FOR HER?
11-15
WHAT KIND OF WORK DO YOU DO?
I SHOVEL SIDEWALKS, RAKE LEAVES AND GARBLE MESSAGES!
SCHULZ

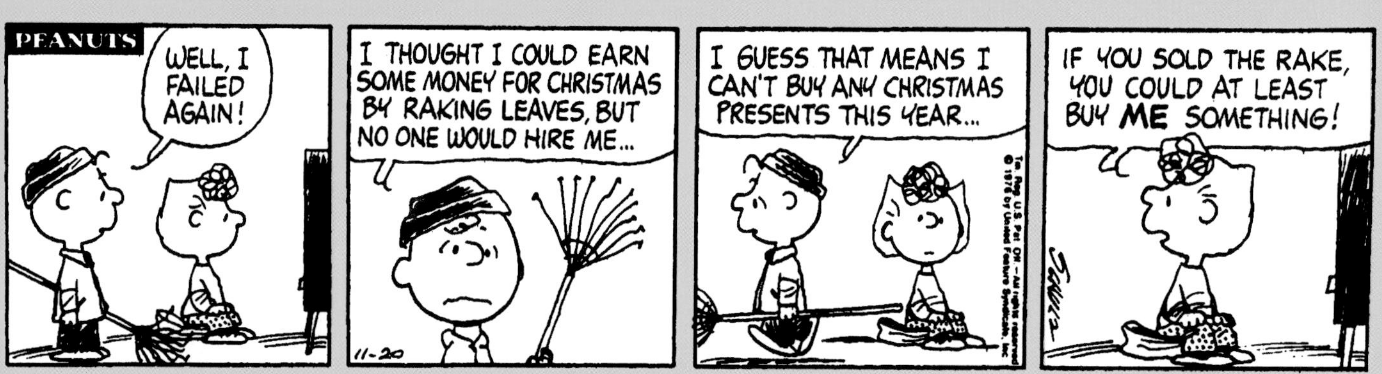
PEANUTS
WELL, I FAILED AGAIN!
I THOUGHT I COULD EARN SOME MONEY FOR CHRISTMAS BY RAKING LEAVES, BUT NO ONE WOULD HIRE ME...
11-20
I GUESS THAT MEANS I CAN'T BUY ANY CHRISTMAS PRESENTS THIS YEAR...
IF YOU SOLD THE RAKE, YOU COULD AT LEAST BUY **ME** SOMETHING!
SCHULZ

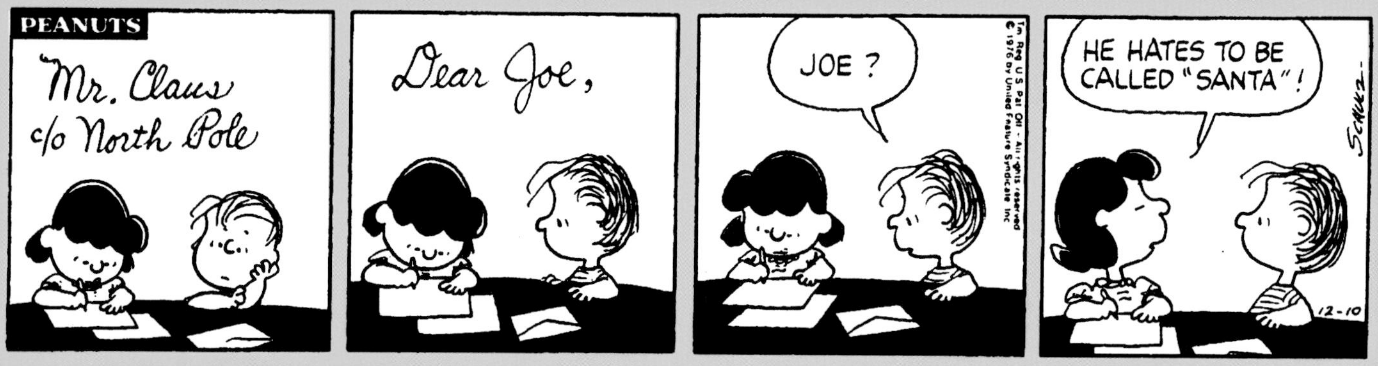
PEANUTS
Mr. Claus c/o North Pole
Dear Joe,
JOE?
HE HATES TO BE CALLED "SANTA"!
SCHULZ
12-10

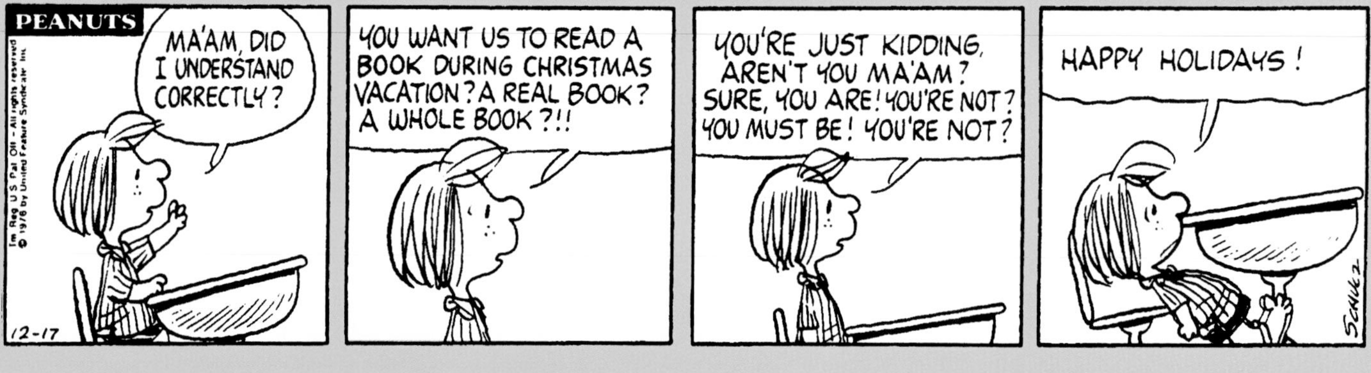
PEANUTS
MA'AM, DID I UNDERSTAND CORRECTLY?
12-17
YOU WANT US TO READ A BOOK DURING CHRISTMAS VACATION? A REAL BOOK? A WHOLE BOOK?!!
YOU'RE JUST KIDDING, AREN'T YOU MA'AM? SURE, YOU ARE! YOU'RE NOT? YOU MUST BE! YOU'RE NOT?
HAPPY HOLIDAYS!
SCHULZ

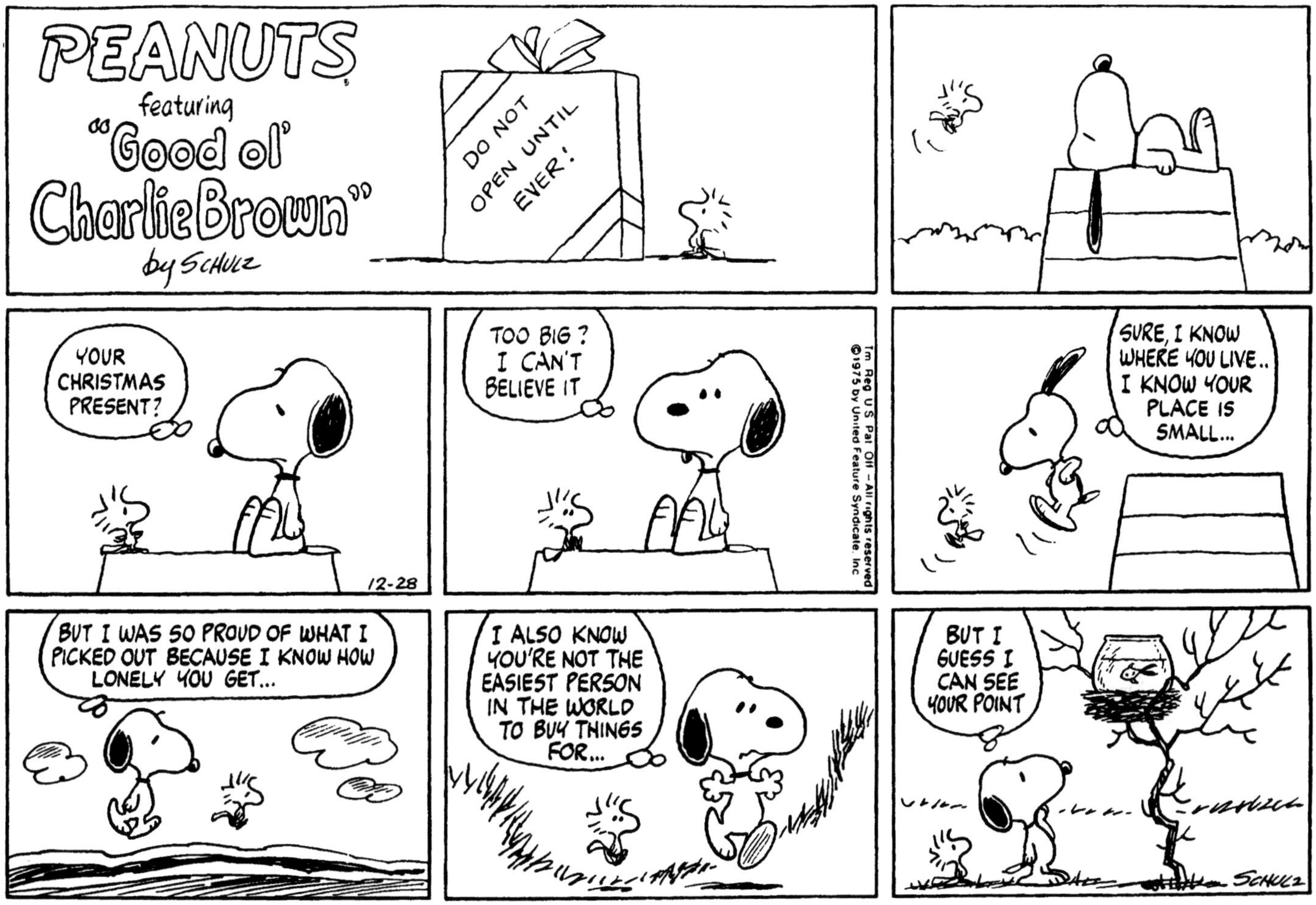
PEANUTS
featuring "Good ol' CharlieBrown"
by SCHULZ
DO NOT OPEN UNTIL EVER!
YOUR CHRISTMAS PRESENT?
12-28
TOO BIG? I CAN'T BELIEVE IT
Tm Reg U S Pat Off — All rights reserved ©1975 by United Feature Syndicate, Inc
SURE, I KNOW WHERE YOU LIVE.. I KNOW YOUR PLACE IS SMALL...
BUT I WAS SO PROUD OF WHAT I PICKED OUT BECAUSE I KNOW HOW LONELY YOU GET...
I ALSO KNOW YOU'RE NOT THE EASIEST PERSON IN THE WORLD TO BUY THINGS FOR...
BUT I GUESS I CAN SEE YOUR POINT
SCHULZ

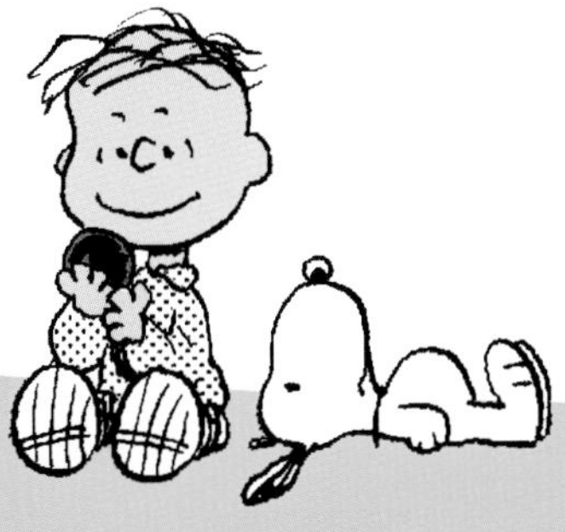

Dear Snooty Claus,

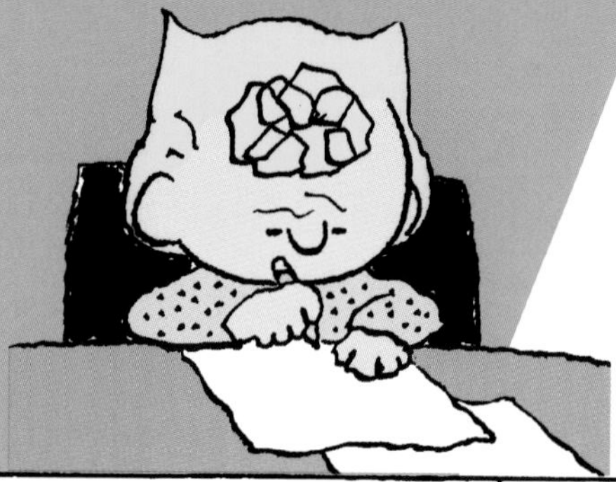

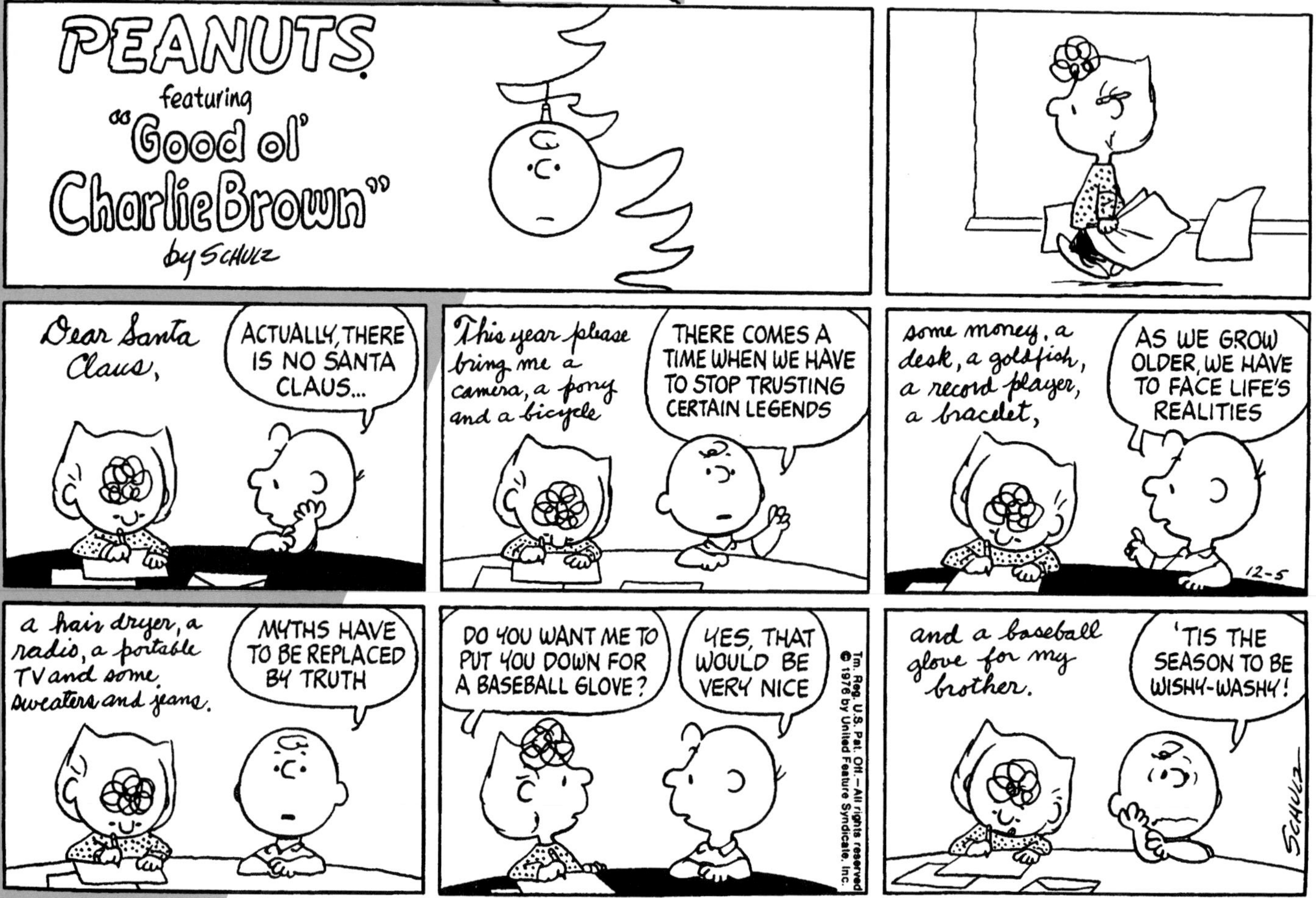
PEANUTS
featuring
"Good ol' CharlieBrown"
by SCHULZ
Dear Santa Claus,
ACTUALLY, THERE IS NO SANTA CLAUS...
This year please bring me a camera, a pony and a bicycle
THERE COMES A TIME WHEN WE HAVE TO STOP TRUSTING CERTAIN LEGENDS
some money, a desk, a goldfish, a record player, a bracelet,
AS WE GROW OLDER, WE HAVE TO FACE LIFE'S REALITIES
12-5
a hair dryer, a radio, a portable TV and some sweaters and jeans.
MYTHS HAVE TO BE REPLACED BY TRUTH
DO YOU WANT ME TO PUT YOU DOWN FOR A BASEBALL GLOVE?
YES, THAT WOULD BE VERY NICE
Tm. Reg. U.S. Pat. Off.—All rights reserved © 1976 by United Feature Syndicate, Inc.
and a baseball glove for my brother.
'TIS THE SEASON TO BE WISHY-WASHY!
SCHULZ

PEANUTS

GUESS WHAT, CHUCK! DISASTER TIME!

OUR TEACHER WANTS US TO READ A BOOK DURING CHRISTMAS VACATION... GOT ANY SUGGESTIONS?

12-20

ON WHAT BOOK TO READ?

NO, ON HOW TO GET OUT OF IT!

PEANUTS

YOU KNOW, I MAY HAVE BEEN WRONG ABOUT THOSE CHRISTMAS STOCKINGS...

IF YOU WANT TO HANG UP A CHRISTMAS STOCKING, LITTLE FRIEND, I THINK YOU SHOULD!

HANG UP AS MANY AS YOU WANT! MERRY CHRISTMAS!!

12-24

PEANUTS

HERE COMES WOODSTOCK...

12-25

HE DOESN'T KNOW I GOT HIM SOMETHING FOR CHRISTMAS

I'M GONNA SURPRISE HIM, AND HANG THIS LITTLE CANDY CANE RIGHT ON HIS NOSE...

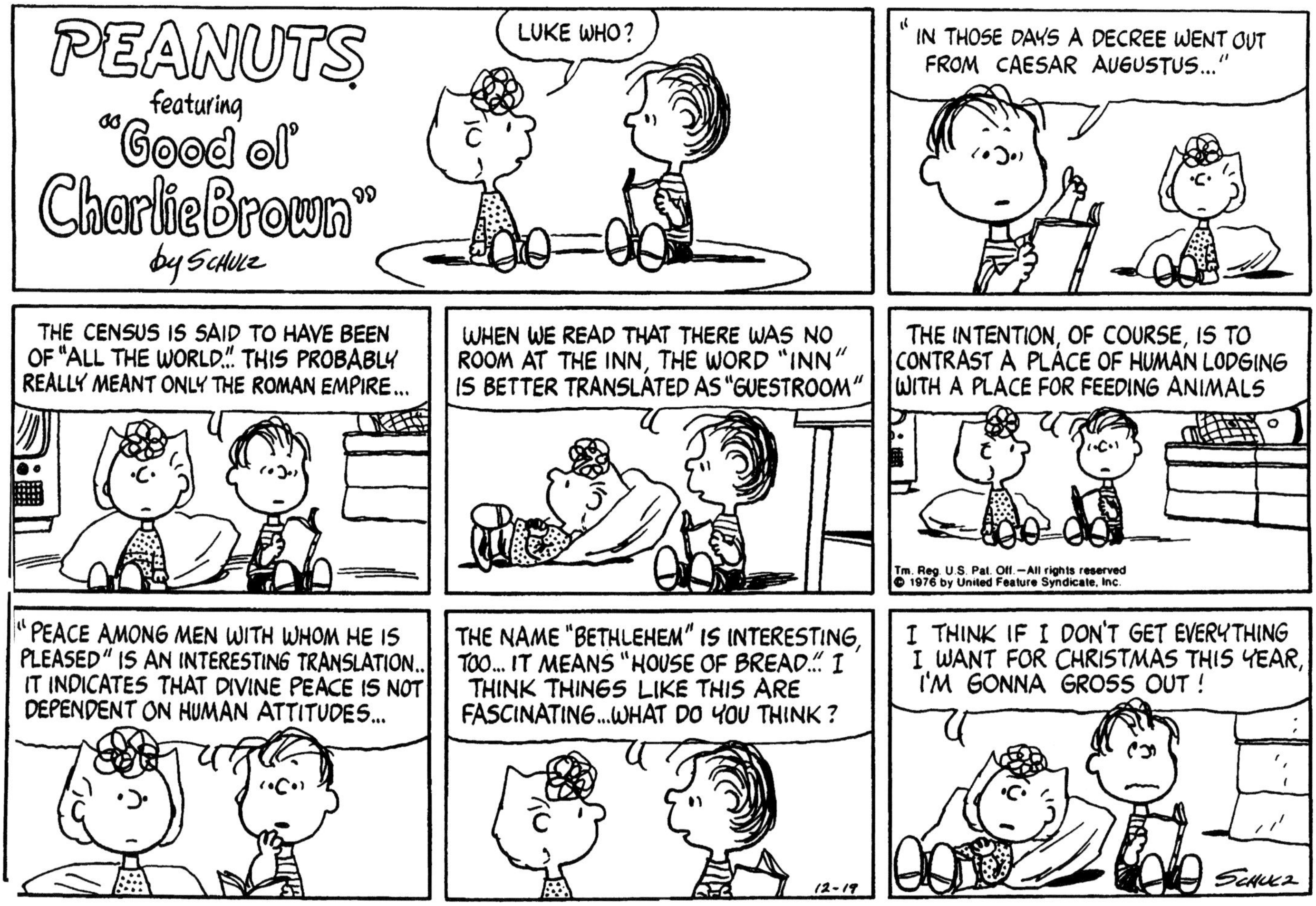
PEANUTS
featuring
"Good ol' CharlieBrown"
by SCHULZ
LUKE WHO?
"IN THOSE DAYS A DECREE WENT OUT FROM CAESAR AUGUSTUS..."
THE CENSUS IS SAID TO HAVE BEEN OF "ALL THE WORLD." THIS PROBABLY REALLY MEANT ONLY THE ROMAN EMPIRE...
WHEN WE READ THAT THERE WAS NO ROOM AT THE INN, THE WORD "INN" IS BETTER TRANSLATED AS "GUESTROOM"
THE INTENTION, OF COURSE, IS TO CONTRAST A PLACE OF HUMAN LODGING WITH A PLACE FOR FEEDING ANIMALS
Tm. Reg. U.S. Pat. Off.—All rights reserved
© 1976 by United Feature Syndicate, Inc.
"PEACE AMONG MEN WITH WHOM HE IS PLEASED" IS AN INTERESTING TRANSLATION.. IT INDICATES THAT DIVINE PEACE IS NOT DEPENDENT ON HUMAN ATTITUDES...
THE NAME "BETHLEHEM" IS INTERESTING, TOO... IT MEANS "HOUSE OF BREAD." I THINK THINGS LIKE THIS ARE FASCINATING...WHAT DO YOU THINK?
12-19
I THINK IF I DON'T GET EVERYTHING I WANT FOR CHRISTMAS THIS YEAR, I'M GONNA GROSS OUT!
SCHULZ

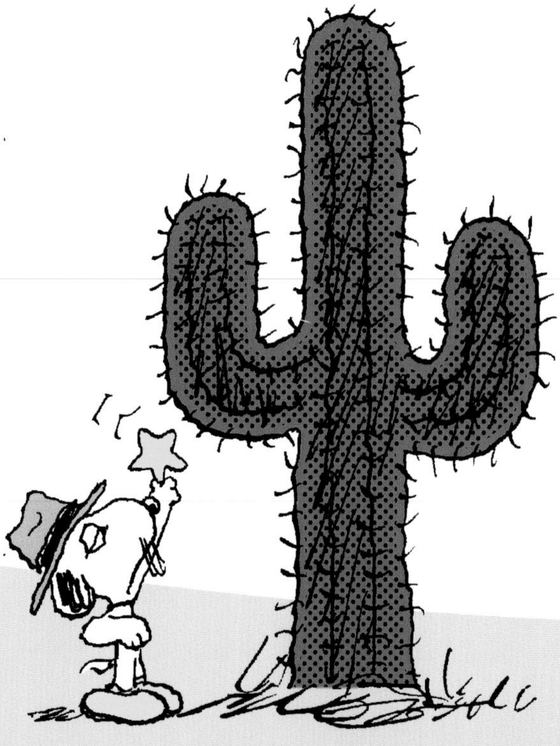

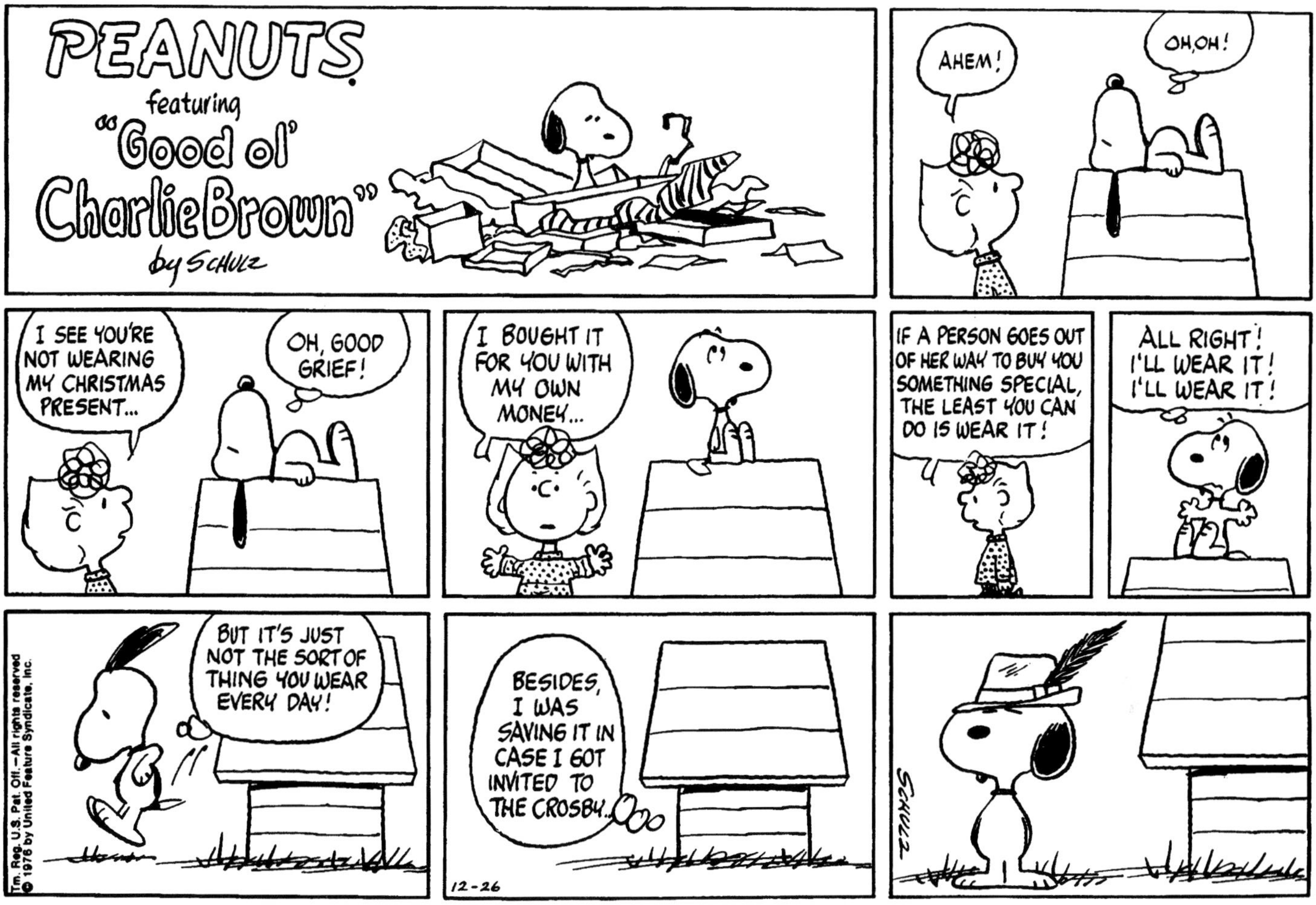
PEANUTS
featuring
"Good ol' CharlieBrown"
by SCHULZ
AHEM!
OH,OH!
I SEE YOU'RE NOT WEARING MY CHRISTMAS PRESENT...
OH, GOOD GRIEF!
I BOUGHT IT FOR YOU WITH MY OWN MONEY...
IF A PERSON GOES OUT OF HER WAY TO BUY YOU SOMETHING SPECIAL, THE LEAST YOU CAN DO IS WEAR IT!
ALL RIGHT! I'LL WEAR IT! I'LL WEAR IT!
Tm. Reg. U.S. Pat. Off.—All rights reserved
© 1976 by United Feature Syndicate, Inc.
BUT IT'S JUST NOT THE SORT OF THING YOU WEAR EVERY DAY!
BESIDES, I WAS SAVING IT IN CASE I GOT INVITED TO THE CROSBY..
12-26
SCHULZ

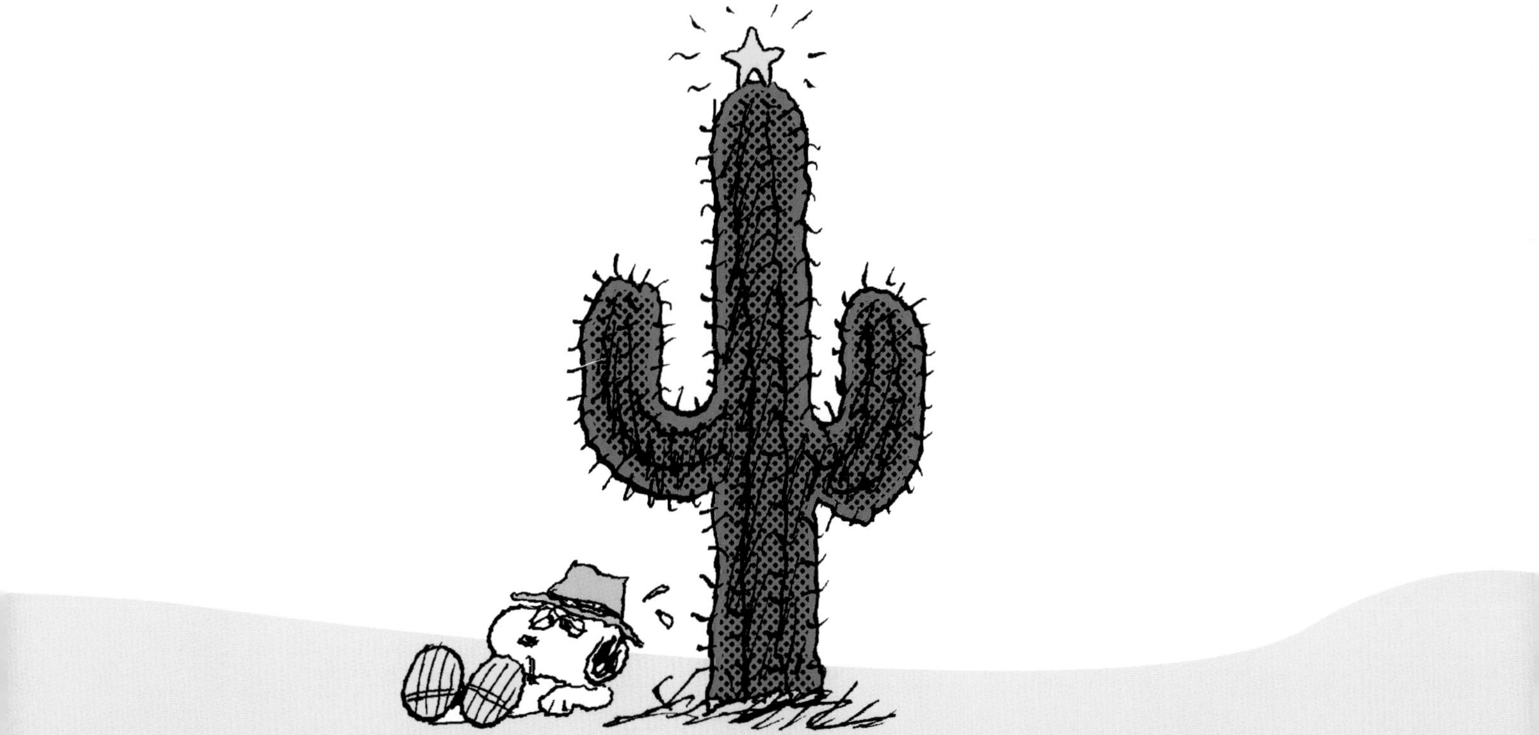

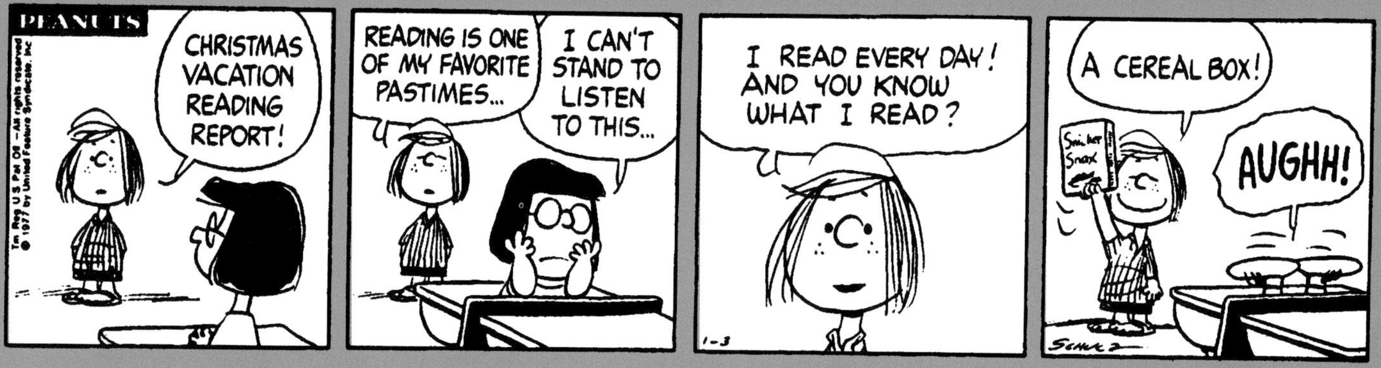
PEANUTS
CHRISTMAS VACATION READING REPORT!
READING IS ONE OF MY FAVORITE PASTIMES...
I CAN'T STAND TO LISTEN TO THIS...
I READ EVERY DAY! AND YOU KNOW WHAT I READ?
A CEREAL BOX!
AUGHH!

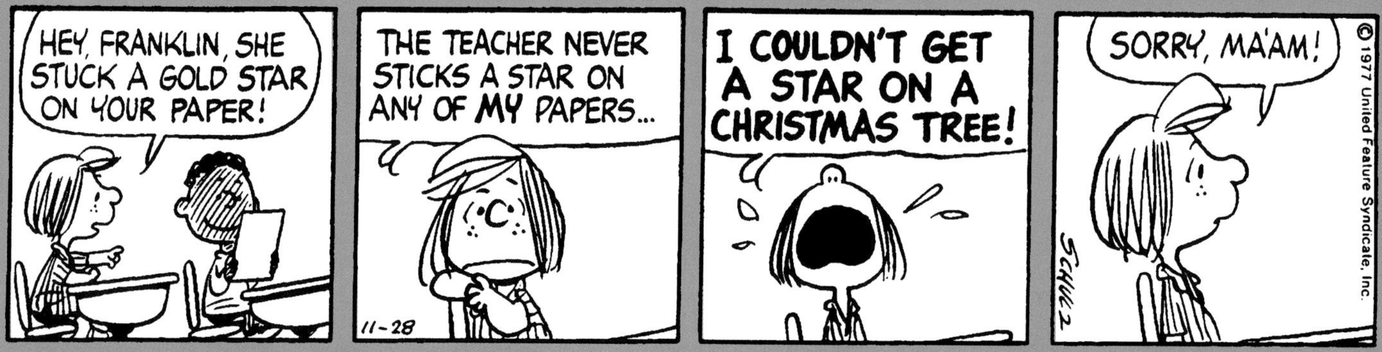
HEY, FRANKLIN, SHE STUCK A GOLD STAR ON YOUR PAPER!
THE TEACHER NEVER STICKS A STAR ON ANY OF **MY** PAPERS...
I COULDN'T GET A STAR ON A CHRISTMAS TREE!
SORRY, MA'AM!
© 1977 United Feature Syndicate, Inc.

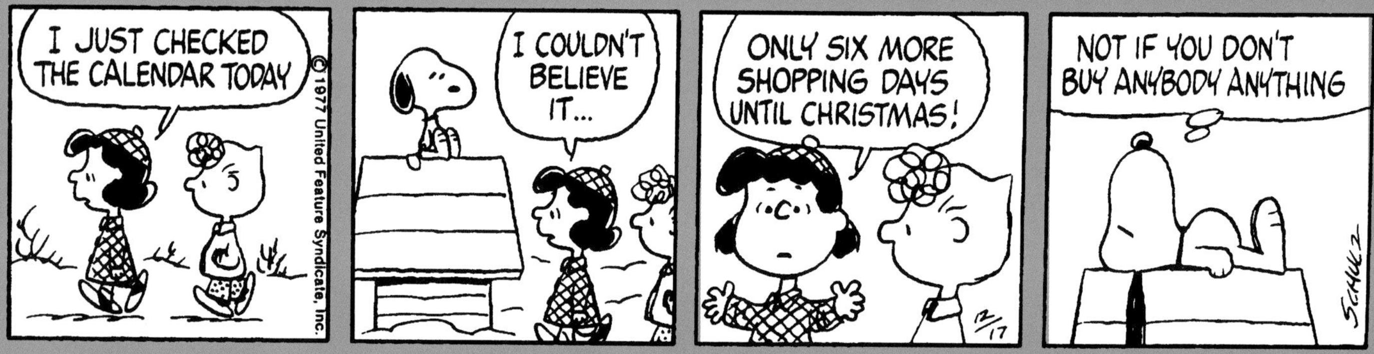
I JUST CHECKED THE CALENDAR TODAY
© 1977 United Feature Syndicate, Inc.
I COULDN'T BELIEVE IT...
ONLY SIX MORE SHOPPING DAYS UNTIL CHRISTMAS!
NOT IF YOU DON'T BUY ANYBODY ANYTHING

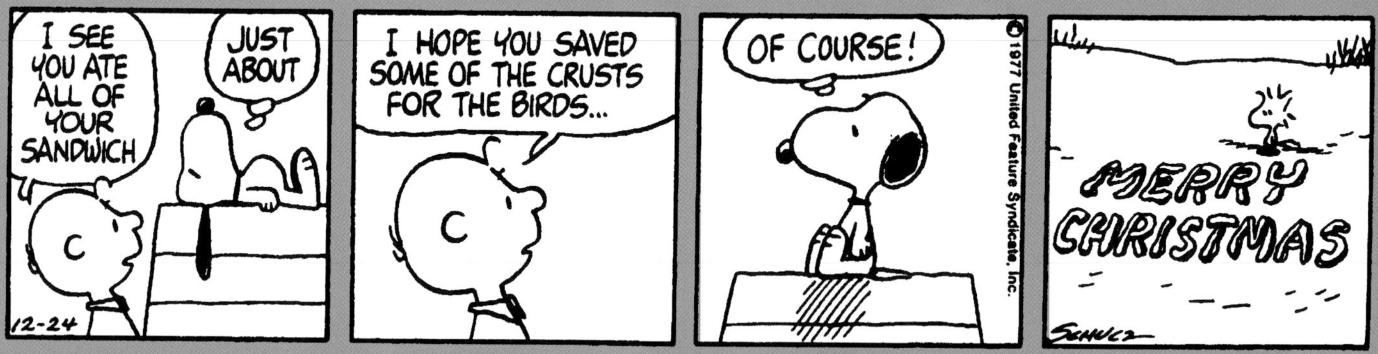
I SEE YOU ATE ALL OF YOUR SANDWICH
JUST ABOUT
I HOPE YOU SAVED SOME OF THE CRUSTS FOR THE BIRDS...
OF COURSE!
© 1977 United Feature Syndicate, Inc.
MERRY CHRISTMAS

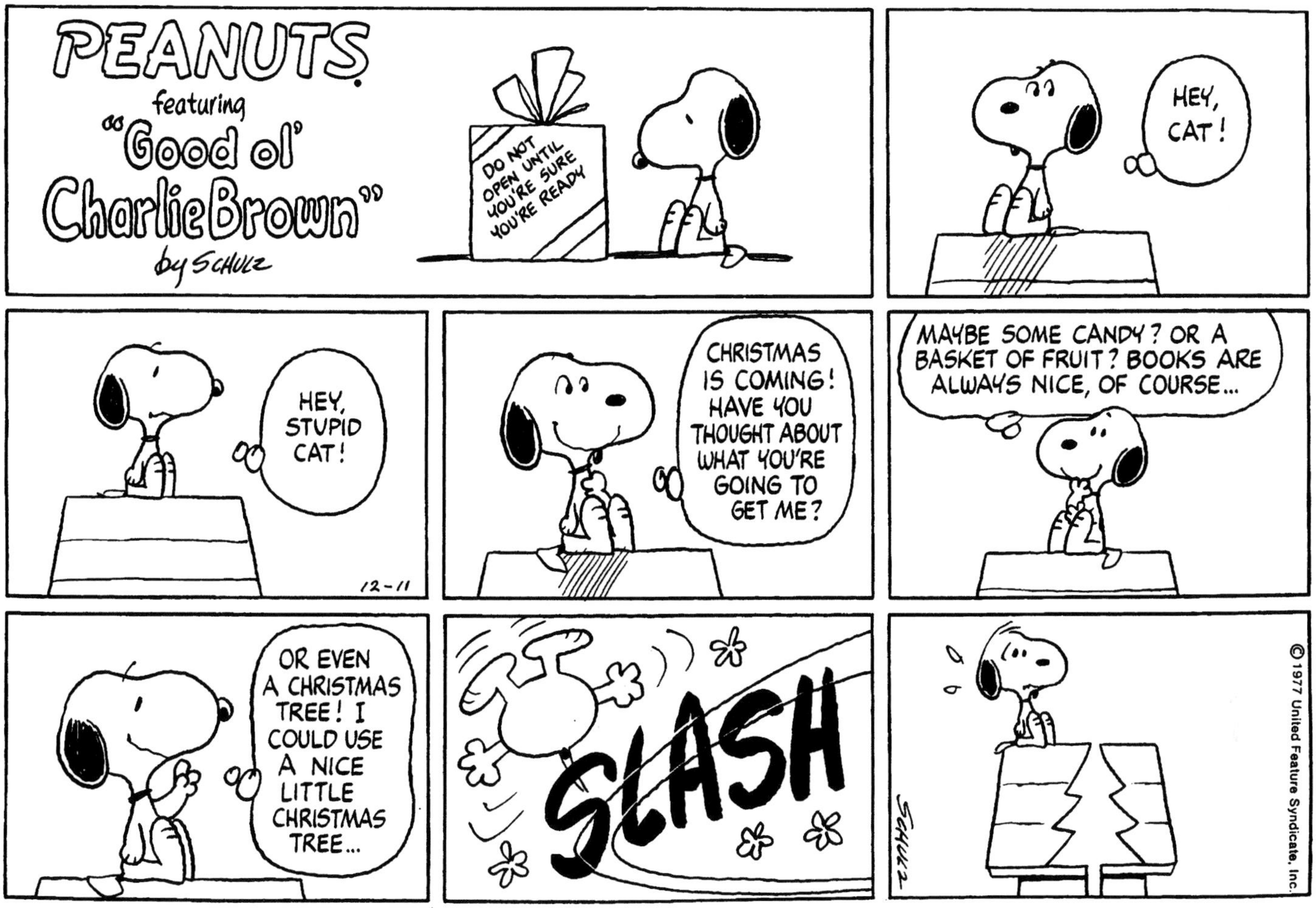
PEANUTS
featuring
"Good ol' Charlie Brown"
by SCHULZ
DO NOT OPEN UNTIL YOU'RE SURE YOU'RE READY
HEY, CAT!
HEY, STUPID CAT!
12-11
CHRISTMAS IS COMING! HAVE YOU THOUGHT ABOUT WHAT YOU'RE GOING TO GET ME?
MAYBE SOME CANDY? OR A BASKET OF FRUIT? BOOKS ARE ALWAYS NICE, OF COURSE...
OR EVEN A CHRISTMAS TREE! I COULD USE A NICE LITTLE CHRISTMAS TREE...
SLASH
SCHULZ
© 1977 United Feature Syndicate, Inc.

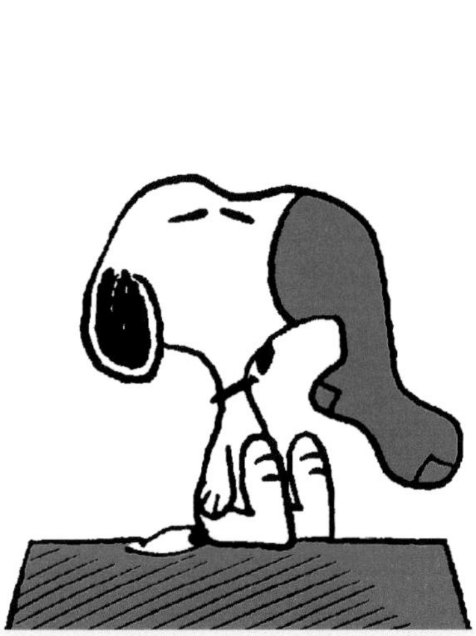

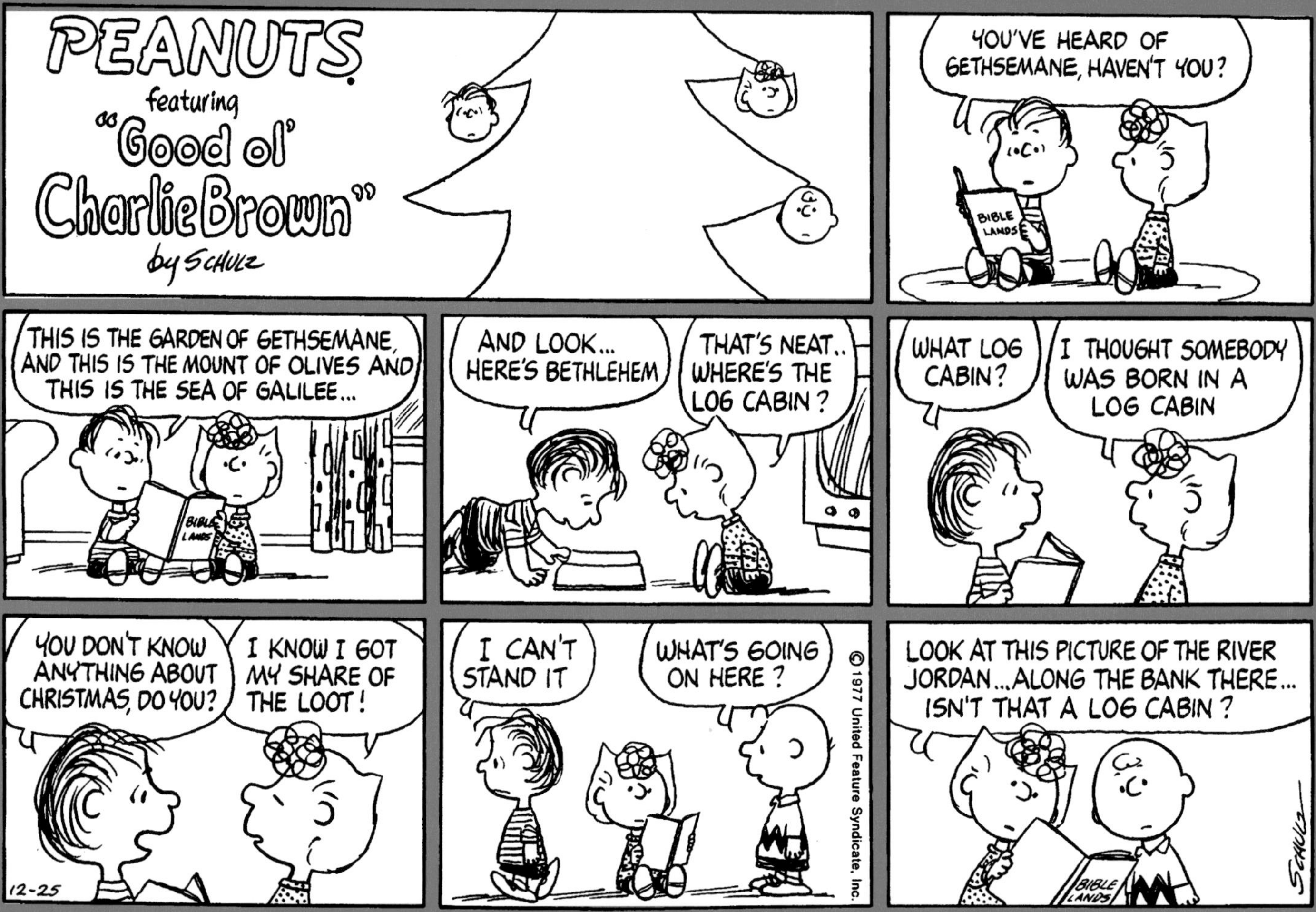
PEANUTS
featuring
"Good ol' CharlieBrown"
by SCHULZ
YOU'VE HEARD OF GETHSEMANE, HAVEN'T YOU?
BIBLE LANDS
THIS IS THE GARDEN OF GETHSEMANE, AND THIS IS THE MOUNT OF OLIVES AND THIS IS THE SEA OF GALILEE...
AND LOOK... HERE'S BETHLEHEM
THAT'S NEAT.. WHERE'S THE LOG CABIN?
WHAT LOG CABIN?
I THOUGHT SOMEBODY WAS BORN IN A LOG CABIN
YOU DON'T KNOW ANYTHING ABOUT CHRISTMAS, DO YOU?
I KNOW I GOT MY SHARE OF THE LOOT!
12-25
I CAN'T STAND IT
WHAT'S GOING ON HERE?
© 1977 United Feature Syndicate, Inc.
LOOK AT THIS PICTURE OF THE RIVER JORDAN...ALONG THE BANK THERE... ISN'T THAT A LOG CABIN?
BIBLE LANDS
SCHULZ

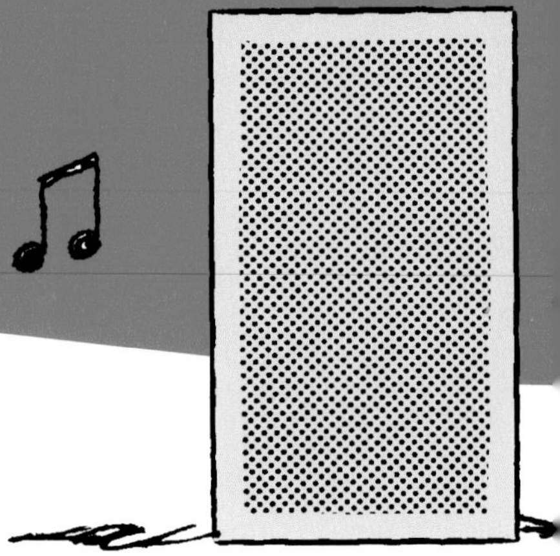

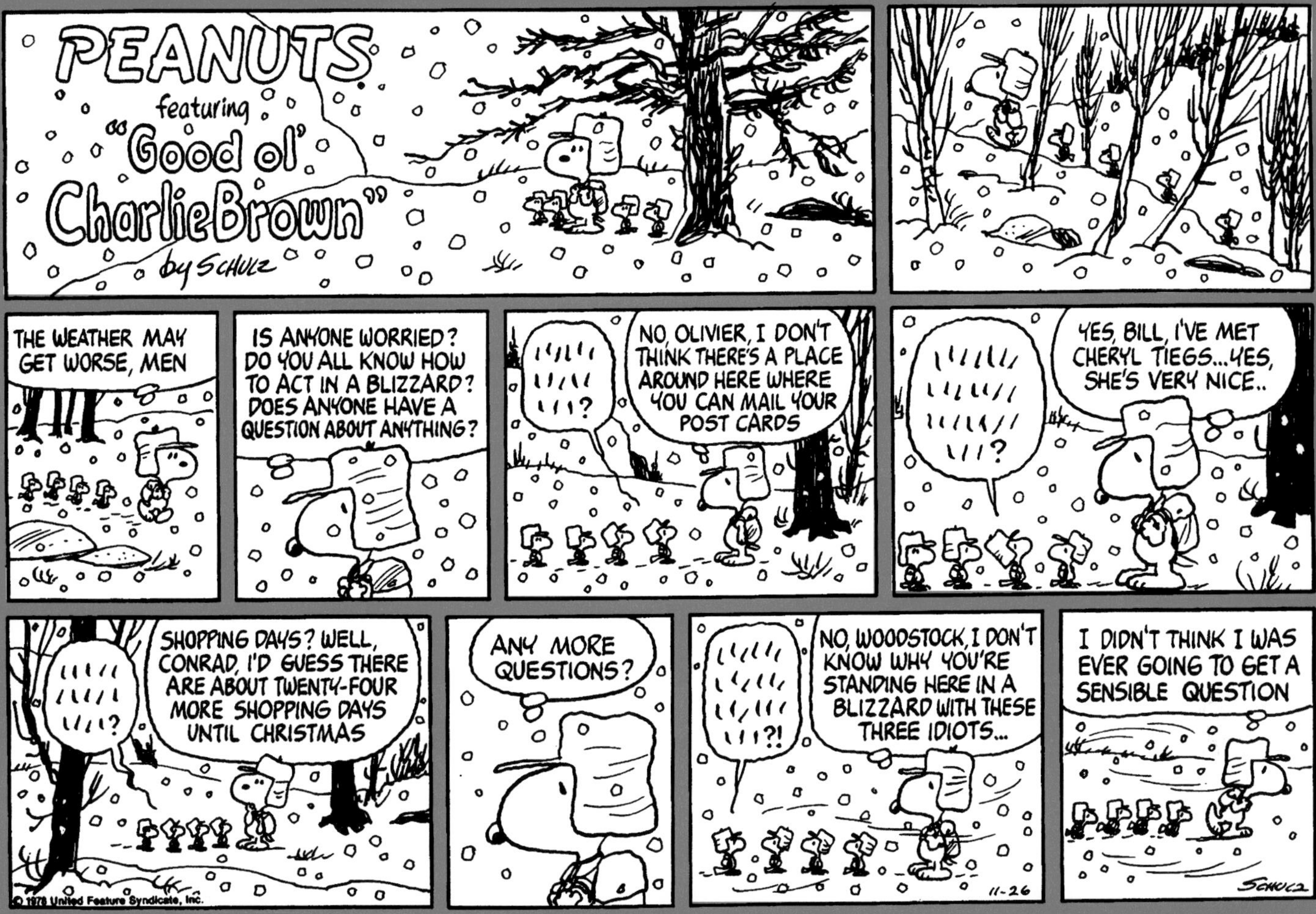
PEANUTS
featuring "Good ol' Charlie Brown"
by SCHULZ
THE WEATHER MAY GET WORSE, MEN
IS ANYONE WORRIED? DO YOU ALL KNOW HOW TO ACT IN A BLIZZARD? DOES ANYONE HAVE A QUESTION ABOUT ANYTHING?
NO, OLIVIER, I DON'T THINK THERE'S A PLACE AROUND HERE WHERE YOU CAN MAIL YOUR POST CARDS
YES, BILL, I'VE MET CHERYL TIEGS...YES, SHE'S VERY NICE..
SHOPPING DAYS? WELL, CONRAD, I'D GUESS THERE ARE ABOUT TWENTY-FOUR MORE SHOPPING DAYS UNTIL CHRISTMAS
© 1978 United Feature Syndicate, Inc.
ANY MORE QUESTIONS?
NO, WOODSTOCK, I DON'T KNOW WHY YOU'RE STANDING HERE IN A BLIZZARD WITH THESE THREE IDIOTS...
11-26
I DIDN'T THINK I WAS EVER GOING TO GET A SENSIBLE QUESTION
SCHULZ

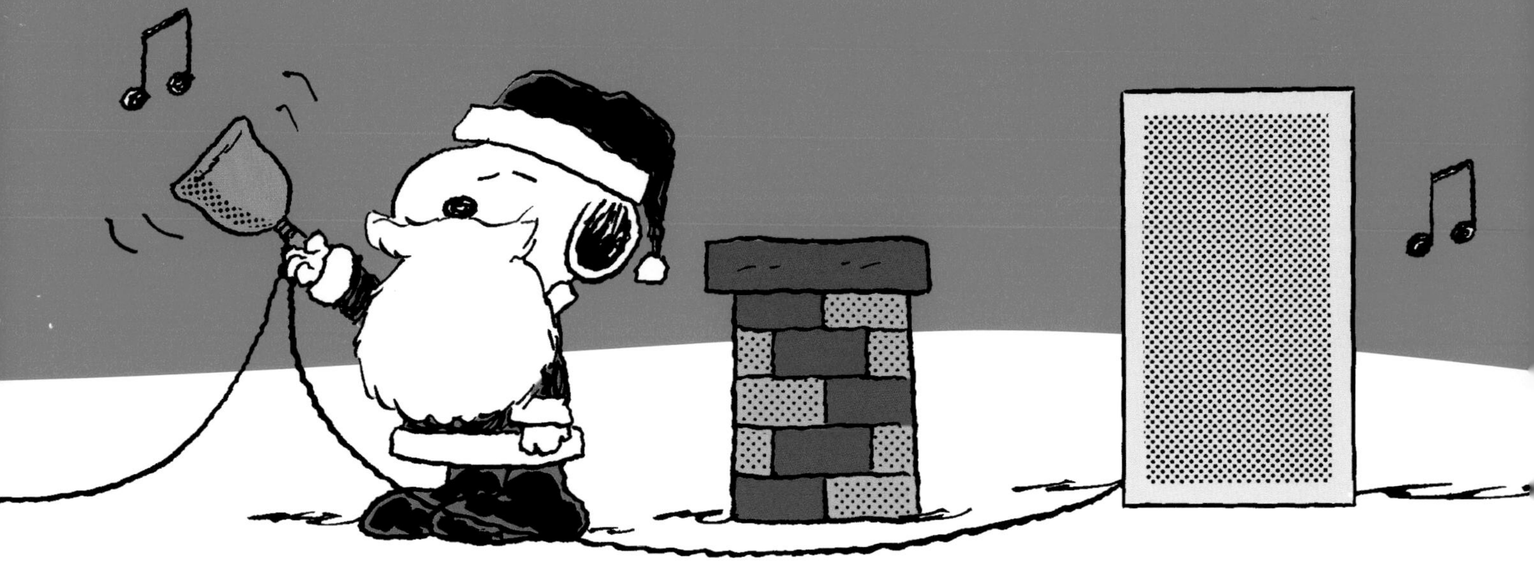

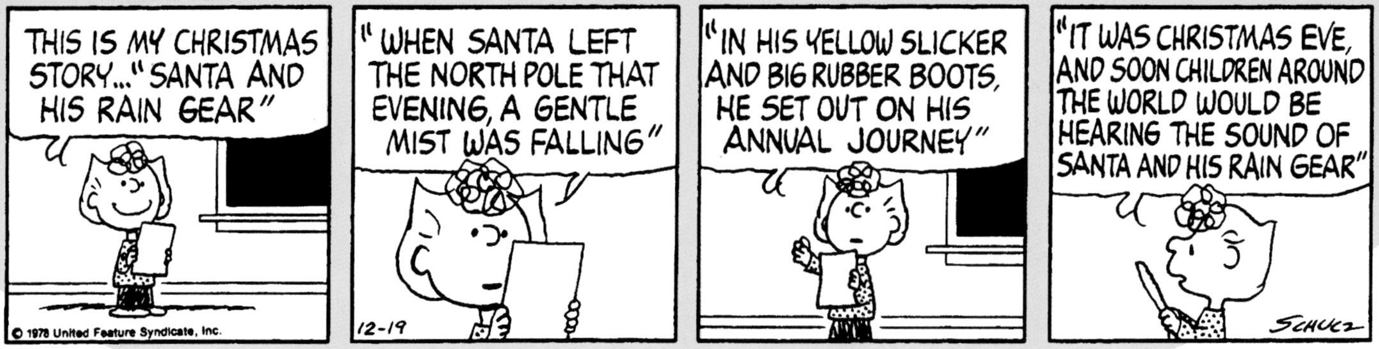
THIS IS MY CHRISTMAS STORY..."SANTA AND HIS RAIN GEAR"
© 1978 United Feature Syndicate, Inc.
"WHEN SANTA LEFT THE NORTH POLE THAT EVENING, A GENTLE MIST WAS FALLING"
12-19
"IN HIS YELLOW SLICKER AND BIG RUBBER BOOTS, HE SET OUT ON HIS ANNUAL JOURNEY"
"IT WAS CHRISTMAS EVE, AND SOON CHILDREN AROUND THE WORLD WOULD BE HEARING THE SOUND OF SANTA AND HIS RAIN GEAR"
SCHULZ

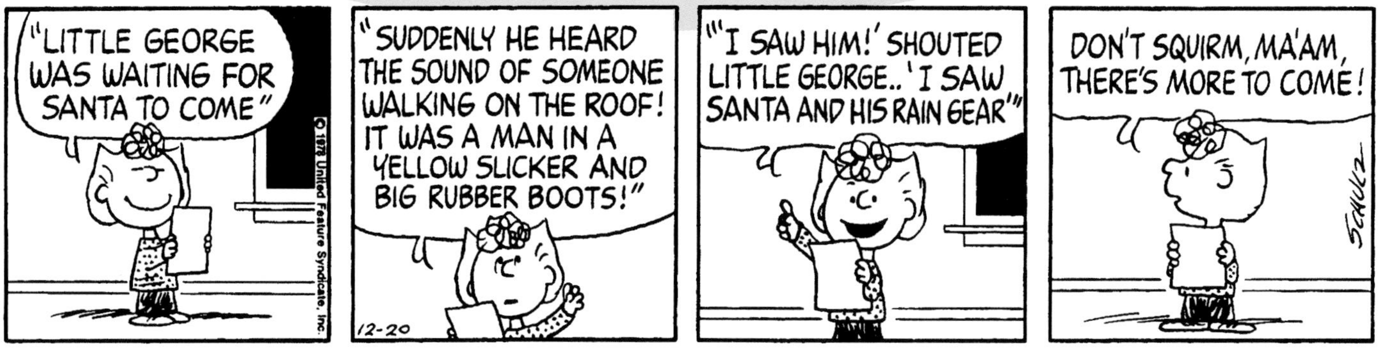
"LITTLE GEORGE WAS WAITING FOR SANTA TO COME"
© 1978 United Feature Syndicate, Inc.
"SUDDENLY HE HEARD THE SOUND OF SOMEONE WALKING ON THE ROOF! IT WAS A MAN IN A YELLOW SLICKER AND BIG RUBBER BOOTS!"
12-20
"'I SAW HIM!' SHOUTED LITTLE GEORGE..'I SAW SANTA AND HIS RAIN GEAR'"
DON'T SQUIRM, MA'AM, THERE'S MORE TO COME!
SCHULZ

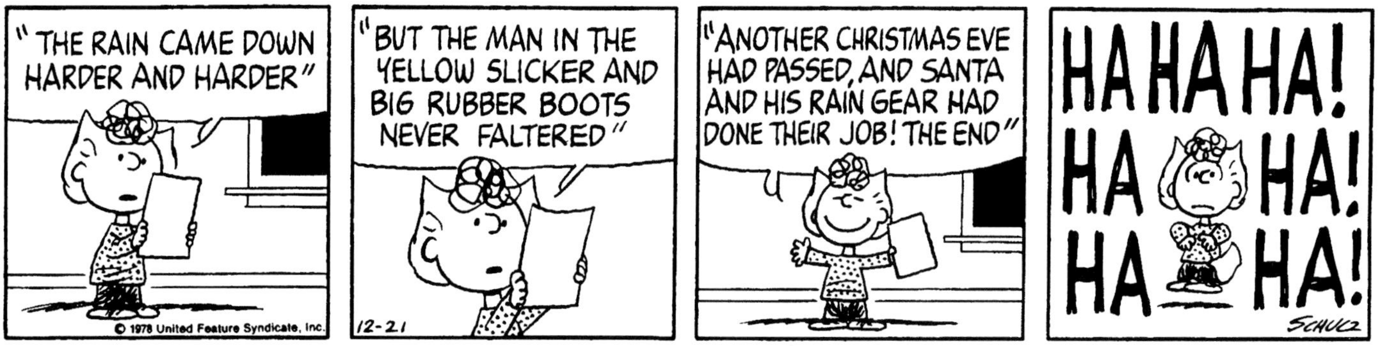
"THE RAIN CAME DOWN HARDER AND HARDER"
© 1978 United Feature Syndicate, Inc.
"BUT THE MAN IN THE YELLOW SLICKER AND BIG RUBBER BOOTS NEVER FALTERED"
12-21
"ANOTHER CHRISTMAS EVE HAD PASSED, AND SANTA AND HIS RAIN GEAR HAD DONE THEIR JOB! THE END"
HA HA HA! HA HA! HA HA!
SCHULZ

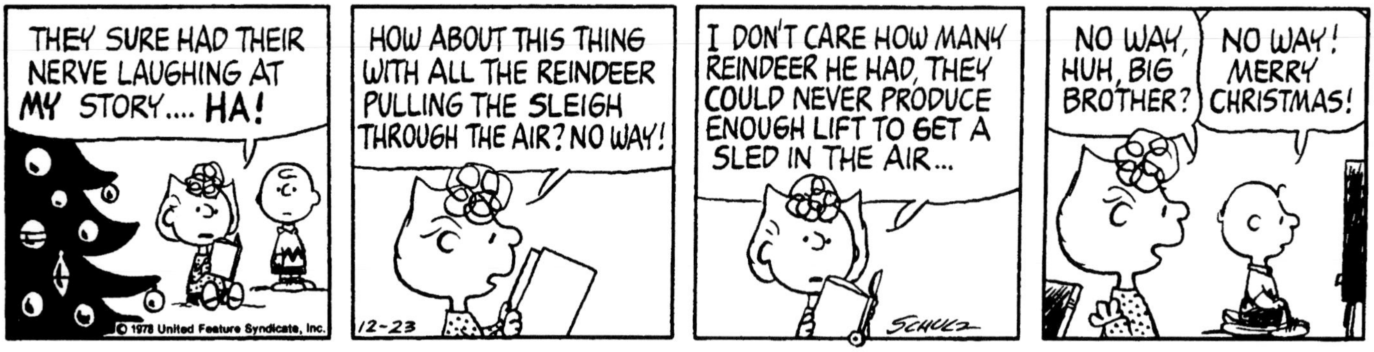
THEY SURE HAD THEIR NERVE LAUGHING AT MY STORY.... HA!
© 1978 United Feature Syndicate, Inc.
HOW ABOUT THIS THING WITH ALL THE REINDEER PULLING THE SLEIGH THROUGH THE AIR? NO WAY!
12-23
I DON'T CARE HOW MANY REINDEER HE HAD, THEY COULD NEVER PRODUCE ENOUGH LIFT TO GET A SLED IN THE AIR...
SCHULZ
NO WAY, HUH, BIG BROTHER?
NO WAY! MERRY CHRISTMAS!

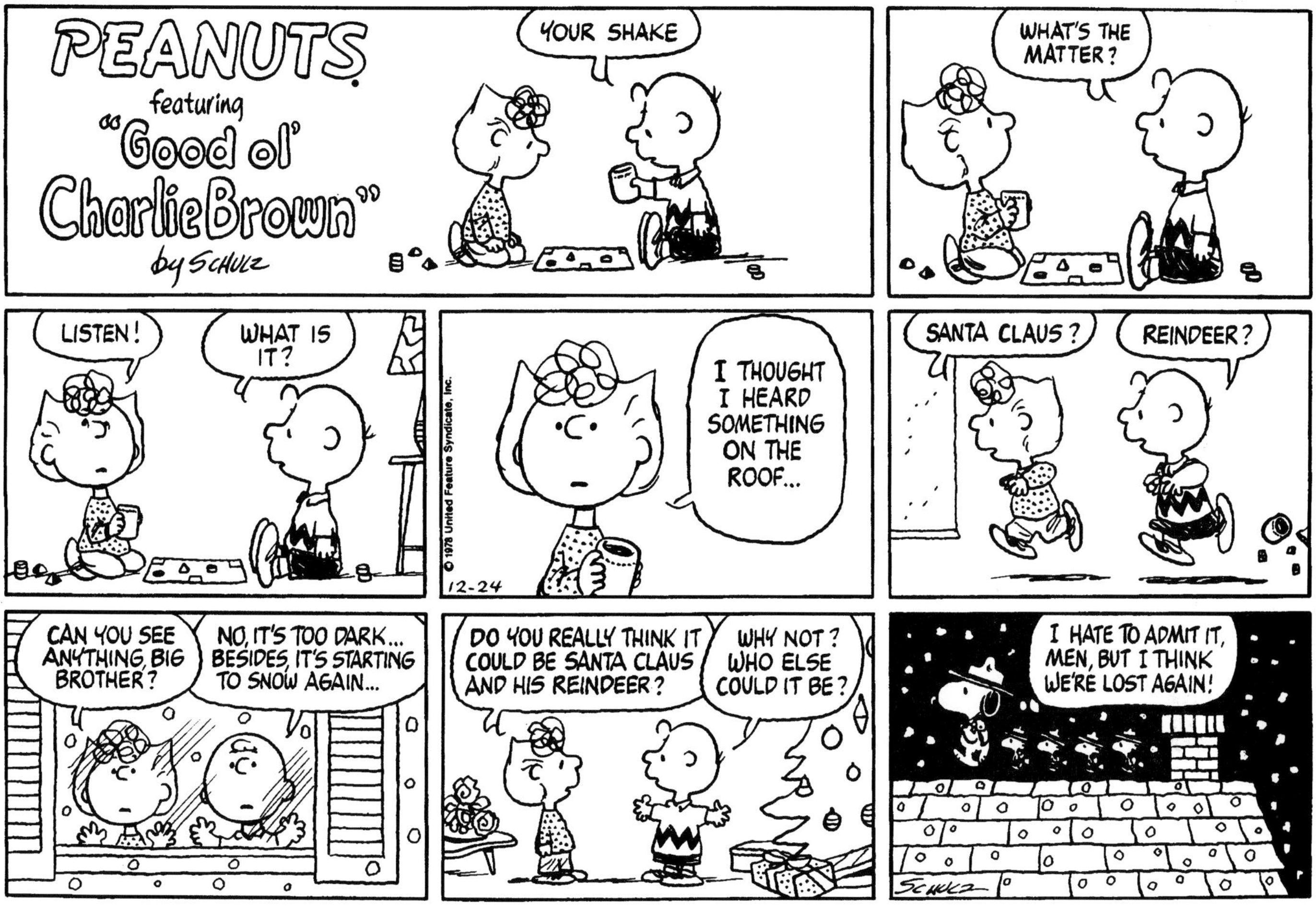
PEANUTS
featuring "Good ol' CharlieBrown"
by SCHULZ
YOUR SHAKE
WHAT'S THE MATTER?
LISTEN!
WHAT IS IT?
I THOUGHT I HEARD SOMETHING ON THE ROOF...
© 1978 United Feature Syndicate, Inc.
12-24
SANTA CLAUS?
REINDEER?
CAN YOU SEE ANYTHING, BIG BROTHER?
NO, IT'S TOO DARK... BESIDES, IT'S STARTING TO SNOW AGAIN...
DO YOU REALLY THINK IT COULD BE SANTA CLAUS AND HIS REINDEER?
WHY NOT? WHO ELSE COULD IT BE?
I HATE TO ADMIT IT, MEN, BUT I THINK WE'RE LOST AGAIN!
SCHULZ

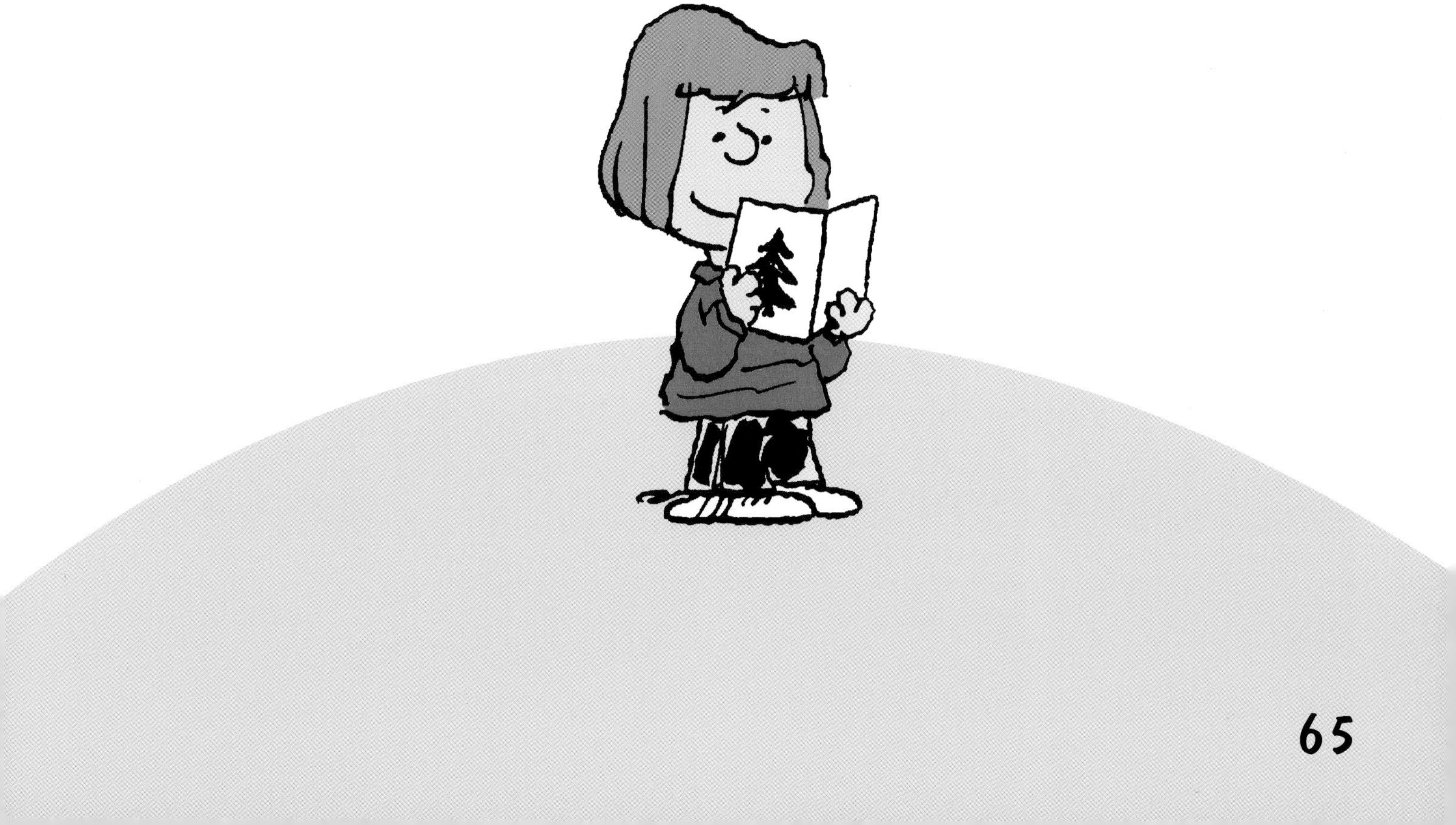

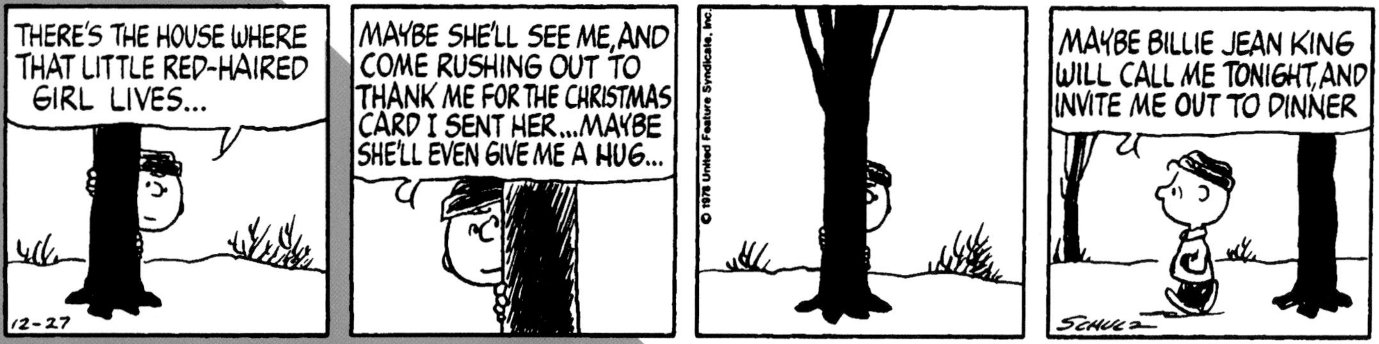
THERE'S THE HOUSE WHERE THAT LITTLE RED-HAIRED GIRL LIVES...
MAYBE SHE'LL SEE ME, AND COME RUSHING OUT TO THANK ME FOR THE CHRISTMAS CARD I SENT HER...MAYBE SHE'LL EVEN GIVE ME A HUG...
MAYBE BILLIE JEAN KING WILL CALL ME TONIGHT, AND INVITE ME OUT TO DINNER
© 1978 United Feature Syndicate, Inc.

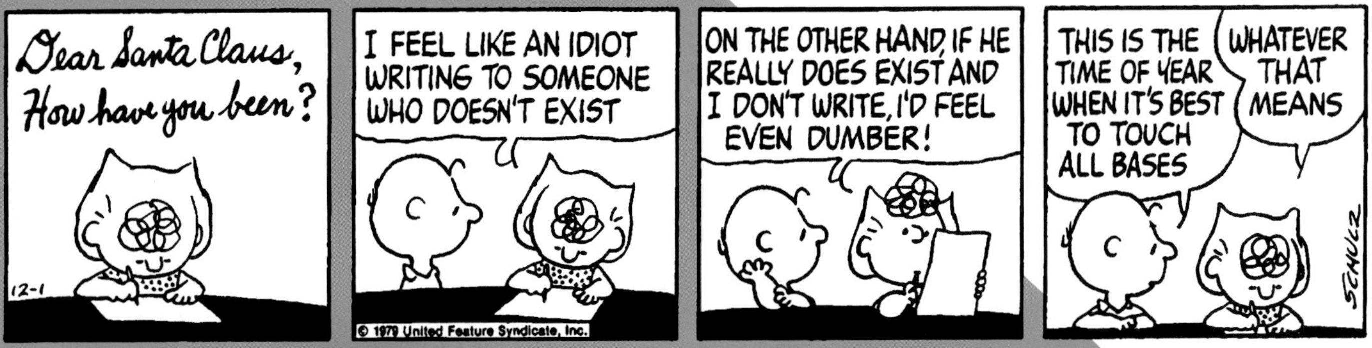
Dear Santa Claus,
How have you been?
I FEEL LIKE AN IDIOT WRITING TO SOMEONE WHO DOESN'T EXIST
ON THE OTHER HAND, IF HE REALLY DOES EXIST AND I DON'T WRITE, I'D FEEL EVEN DUMBER!
THIS IS THE TIME OF YEAR WHEN IT'S BEST TO TOUCH ALL BASES
WHATEVER THAT MEANS
© 1979 United Feature Syndicate, Inc.

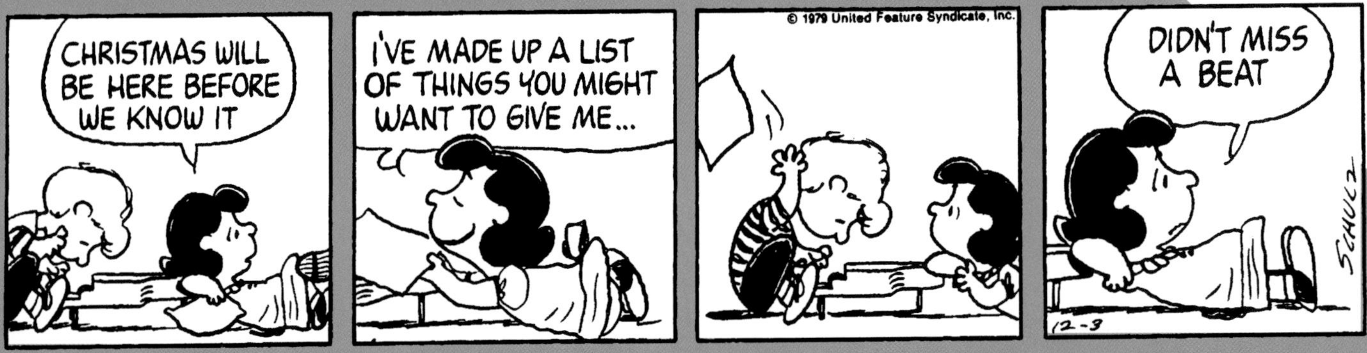
CHRISTMAS WILL BE HERE BEFORE WE KNOW IT
I'VE MADE UP A LIST OF THINGS YOU MIGHT WANT TO GIVE ME...
DIDN'T MISS A BEAT
© 1979 United Feature Syndicate, Inc.

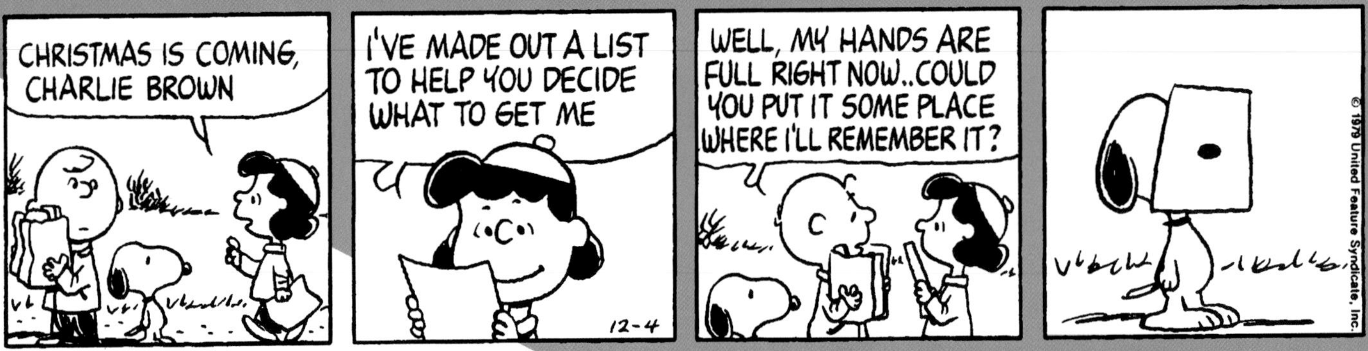
CHRISTMAS IS COMING, CHARLIE BROWN
I'VE MADE OUT A LIST TO HELP YOU DECIDE WHAT TO GET ME
WELL, MY HANDS ARE FULL RIGHT NOW..COULD YOU PUT IT SOME PLACE WHERE I'LL REMEMBER IT?
© 1979 United Feature Syndicate, Inc.

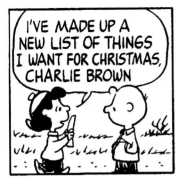

I'VE MADE UP A NEW LIST OF THINGS I WANT FOR CHRISTMAS, CHARLIE BROWN
I HATE TO ADMIT IT, BUT I CAN'T EVEN REMEMBER WHERE WE PUT THE OTHER LIST
12-6
DON'T WORRY, I KNOW JUST WHERE IT IS...
© 1978 United Feature Syndicate, Inc.
JOE SPINDLE!
SCHULZ

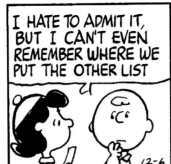

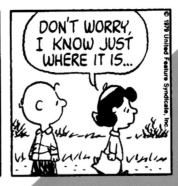

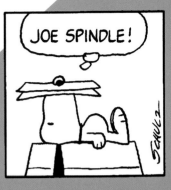

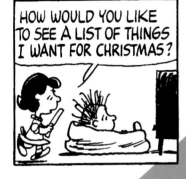

HOW WOULD YOU LIKE TO SEE A LIST OF THINGS I WANT FOR CHRISTMAS?
ABSOLUTELY NOT! I WANT MY GIFT TO YOU THIS YEAR TO BE A COMPLETE AND DELIGHTFUL SURPRISE
WHAT A LOVELY GENEROUS THOUGHT...
SNIF
12-8
© 1978 United Feature Syndicate, Inc.
OFF THE OL' HOOKEROO!
SCHULZ

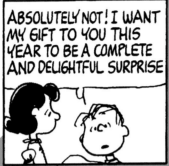

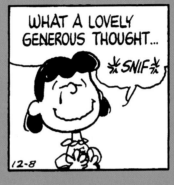

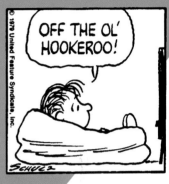

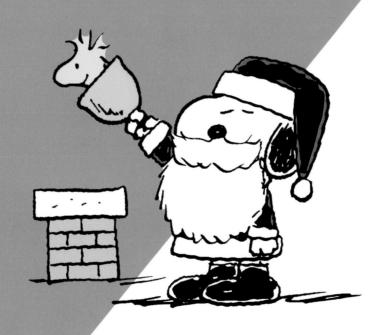

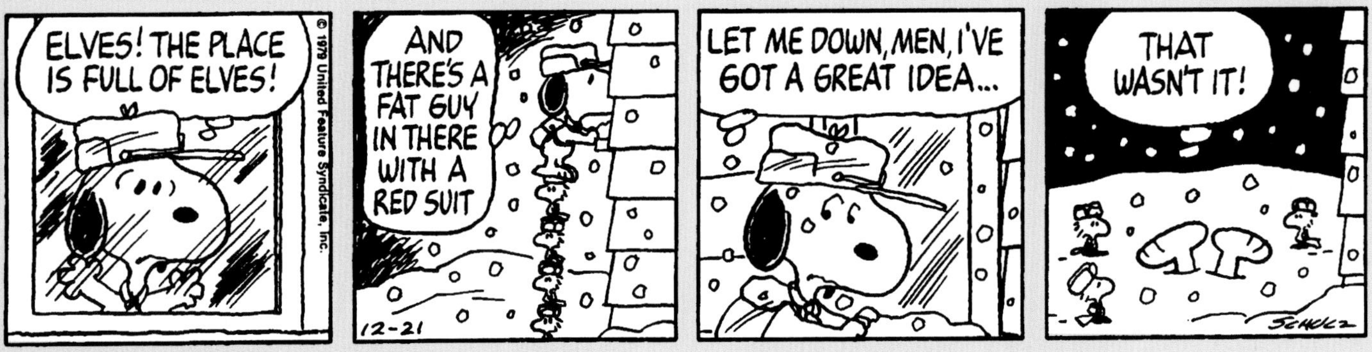
ELVES! THE PLACE IS FULL OF ELVES!
© 1979 United Feature Syndicate, Inc.
AND THERE'S A FAT GUY IN THERE WITH A RED SUIT
12-21
LET ME DOWN, MEN, I'VE GOT A GREAT IDEA...
THAT WASN'T IT!

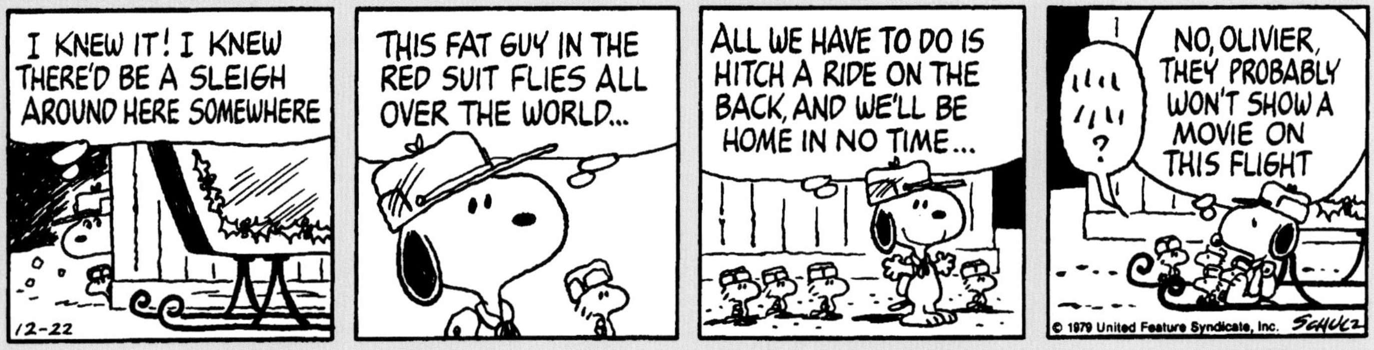
I KNEW IT! I KNEW THERE'D BE A SLEIGH AROUND HERE SOMEWHERE
12-22
THIS FAT GUY IN THE RED SUIT FLIES ALL OVER THE WORLD...
ALL WE HAVE TO DO IS HITCH A RIDE ON THE BACK, AND WE'LL BE HOME IN NO TIME...
NO, OLIVIER, THEY PROBABLY WON'T SHOW A MOVIE ON THIS FLIGHT
© 1979 United Feature Syndicate, Inc.

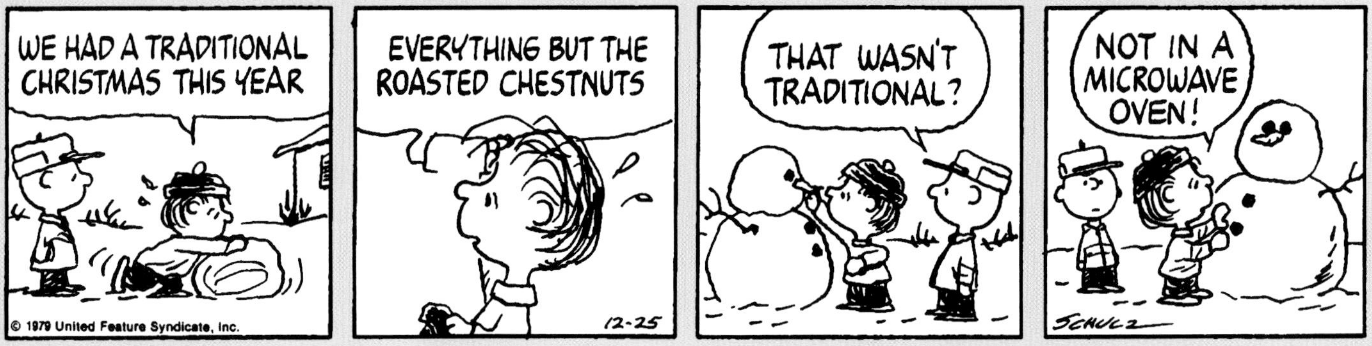
WE HAD A TRADITIONAL CHRISTMAS THIS YEAR
© 1979 United Feature Syndicate, Inc.
EVERYTHING BUT THE ROASTED CHESTNUTS
12-25
THAT WASN'T TRADITIONAL?
NOT IN A MICROWAVE OVEN!

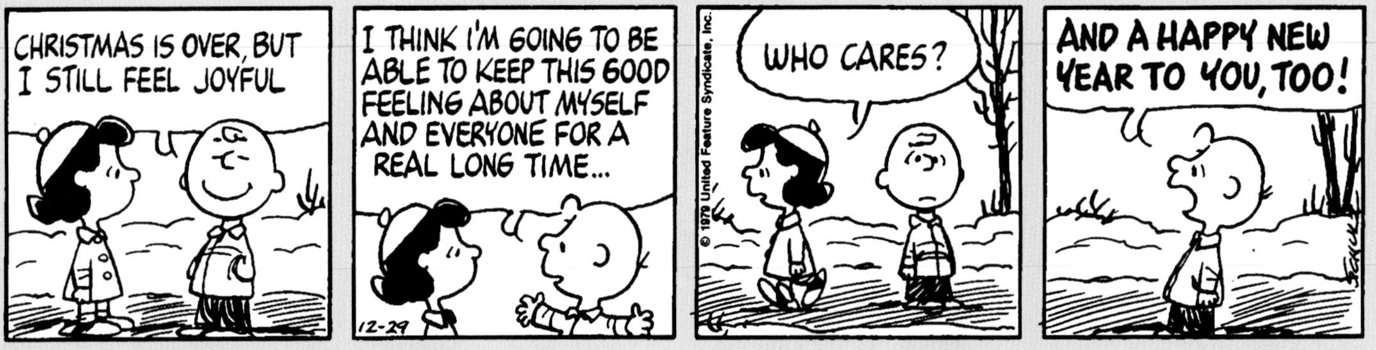
CHRISTMAS IS OVER, BUT I STILL FEEL JOYFUL
I THINK I'M GOING TO BE ABLE TO KEEP THIS GOOD FEELING ABOUT MYSELF AND EVERYONE FOR A REAL LONG TIME...
12-29
© 1979 United Feature Syndicate, Inc.
WHO CARES?
AND A HAPPY NEW YEAR TO YOU, TOO!

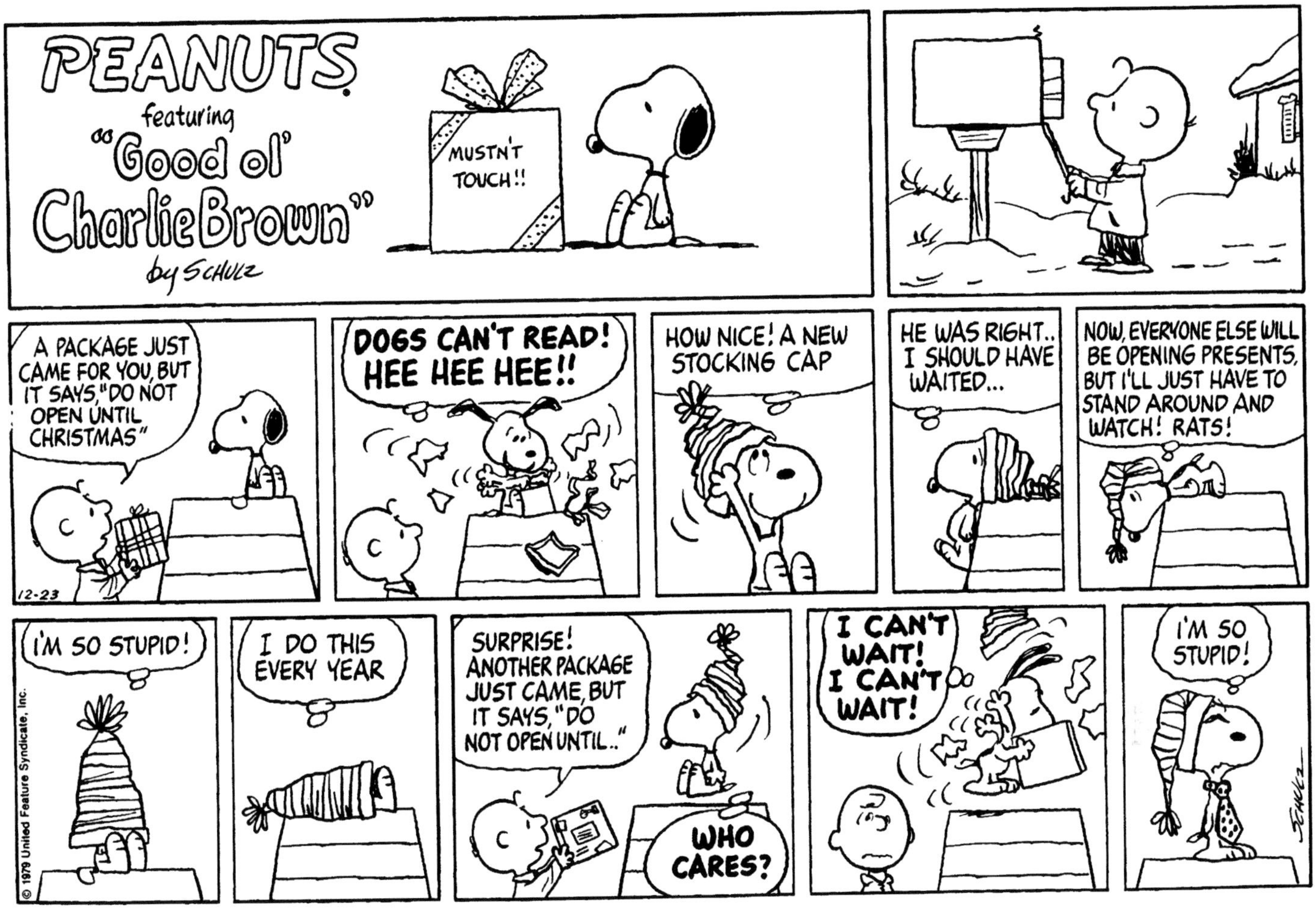

PEANUTS
featuring "Good ol' Charlie Brown"
by SCHULZ
MUSTN'T TOUCH!!
A PACKAGE JUST CAME FOR YOU, BUT IT SAYS, "DO NOT OPEN UNTIL CHRISTMAS"
DOGS CAN'T READ! HEE HEE HEE!!
HOW NICE! A NEW STOCKING CAP
HE WAS RIGHT.. I SHOULD HAVE WAITED...
NOW, EVERYONE ELSE WILL BE OPENING PRESENTS, BUT I'LL JUST HAVE TO STAND AROUND AND WATCH! RATS!
I'M SO STUPID!
I DO THIS EVERY YEAR
SURPRISE! ANOTHER PACKAGE JUST CAME, BUT IT SAYS, "DO NOT OPEN UNTIL.."
WHO CARES?
I CAN'T WAIT! I CAN'T WAIT!
I'M SO STUPID!
12-23
© 1979 United Feature Syndicate, Inc.
SCHULZ

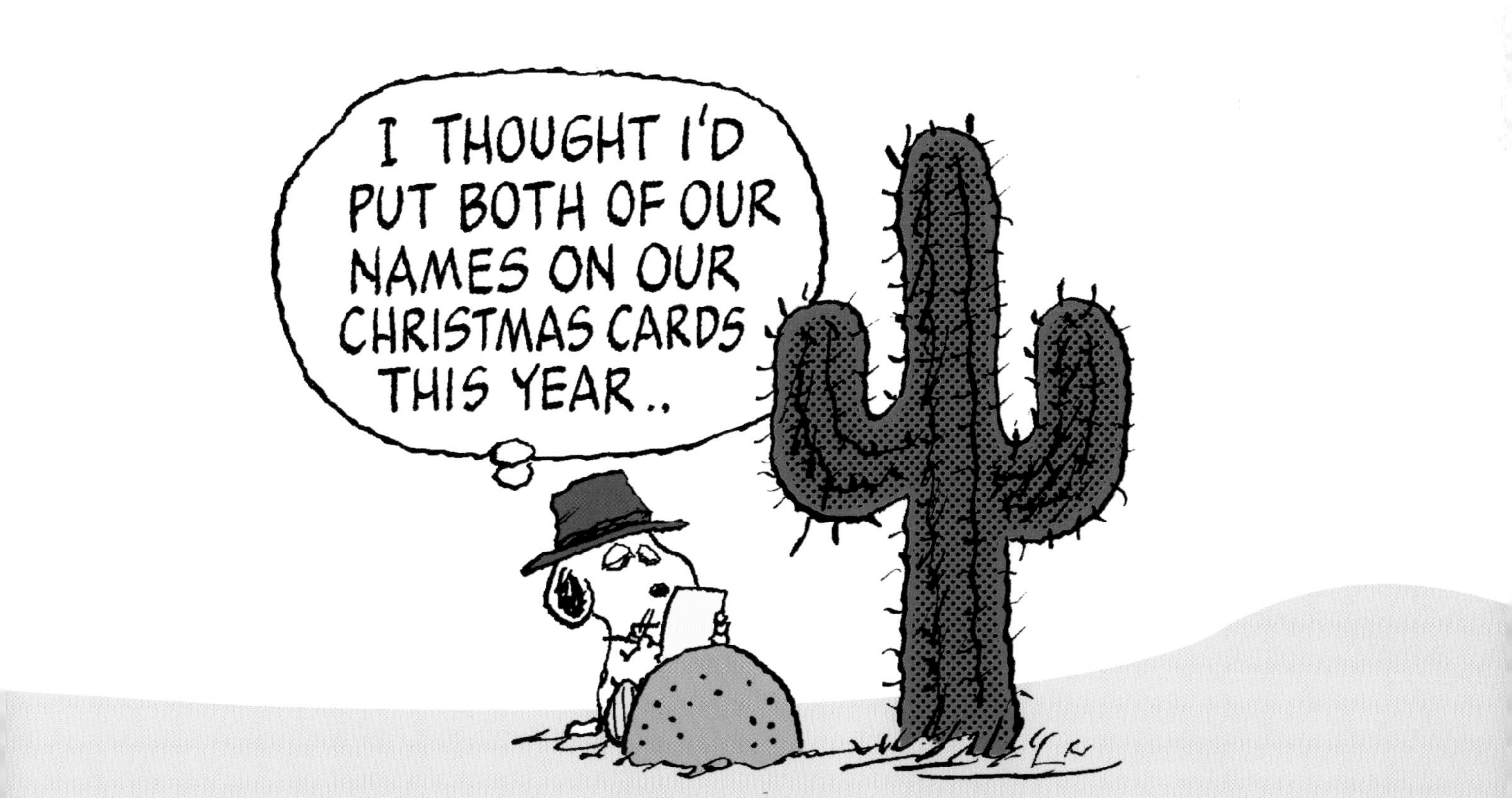

I THOUGHT I'D PUT BOTH OF OUR NAMES ON OUR CHRISTMAS CARDS THIS YEAR..

DID I SEE YOUR FAMILY TAKING DOWN YOUR CHRISTMAS TREE YESTERDAY?
ALL THE DECORATIONS AND ORNAMENTS HAVE BEEN PACKED AWAY, AND EVERYTHING CLEANED UP
1-5
HOW ABOUT YOU?
© 1980 United Feature Syndicate, Inc.
I HAVEN'T SENT OUT MY CARDS YET!
SCHULZ

ADDRESSING YOUR CHRISTMAS CARDS, HUH, BIG BROTHER?
12-1
THAT'S A GOOD IDEA
© 1980 United Feature Syndicate, Inc.
DO YOUR CHRISTMAS SMUDGING EARLY!

I want my Christmas to be one of peace and love, not greed.

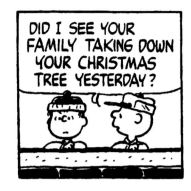

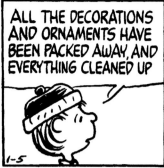

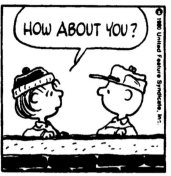

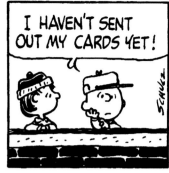

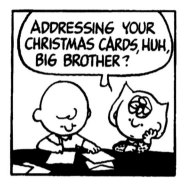

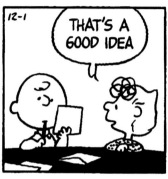

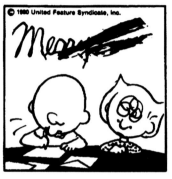

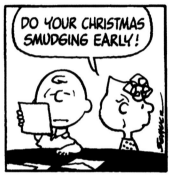

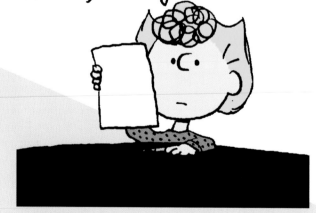

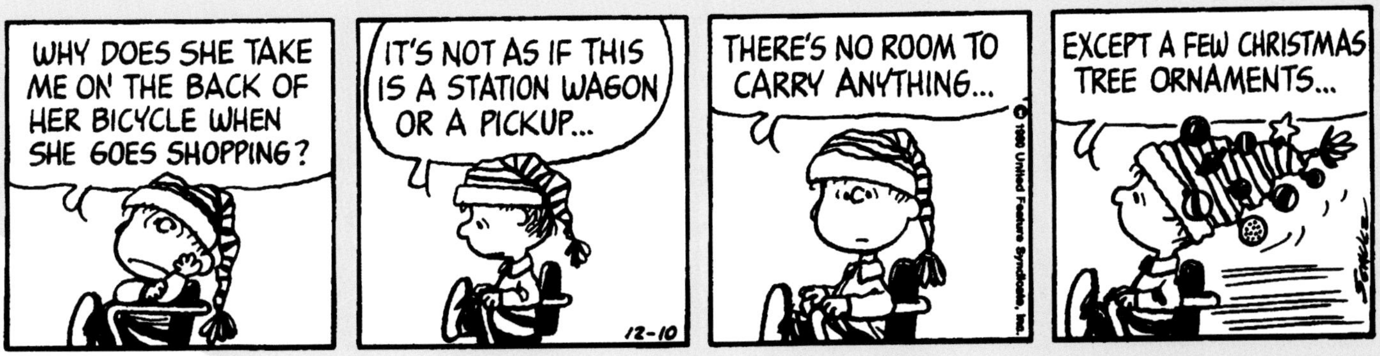
WHY DOES SHE TAKE ME ON THE BACK OF HER BICYCLE WHEN SHE GOES SHOPPING?
IT'S NOT AS IF THIS IS A STATION WAGON OR A PICKUP...
12-10
THERE'S NO ROOM TO CARRY ANYTHING...
© 1980 United Feature Syndicate, Inc.
EXCEPT A FEW CHRISTMAS TREE ORNAMENTS...

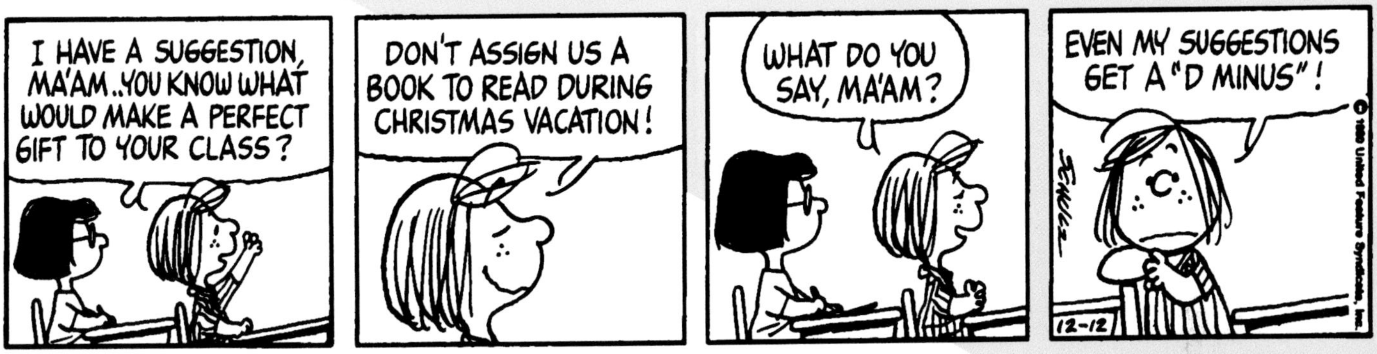
I HAVE A SUGGESTION, MA'AM..YOU KNOW WHAT WOULD MAKE A PERFECT GIFT TO YOUR CLASS?
DON'T ASSIGN US A BOOK TO READ DURING CHRISTMAS VACATION!
WHAT DO YOU SAY, MA'AM?
EVEN MY SUGGESTIONS GET A "D MINUS"!
© 1980 United Feature Syndicate, Inc.
12-12

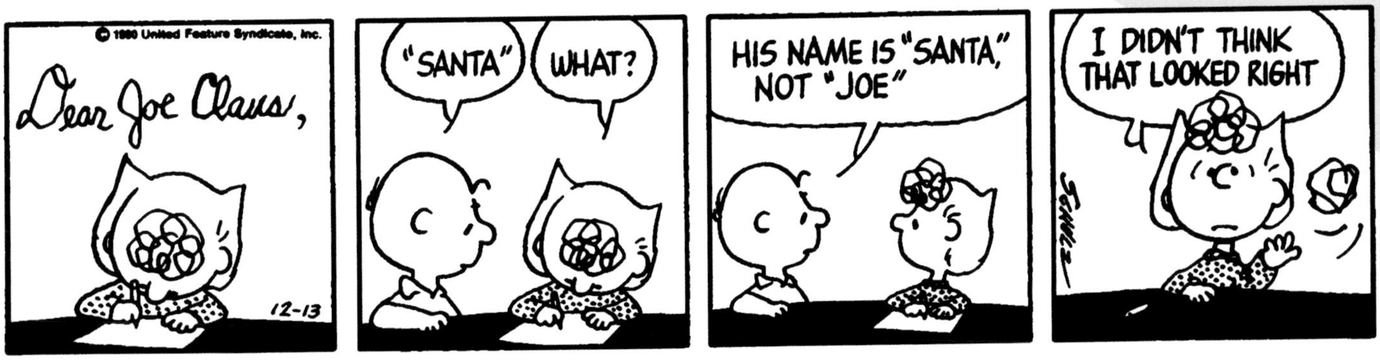
© 1980 United Feature Syndicate, Inc.
Dear Joe Claus,
12-13
"SANTA"
WHAT?
HIS NAME IS "SANTA," NOT "JOE"
I DIDN'T THINK THAT LOOKED RIGHT

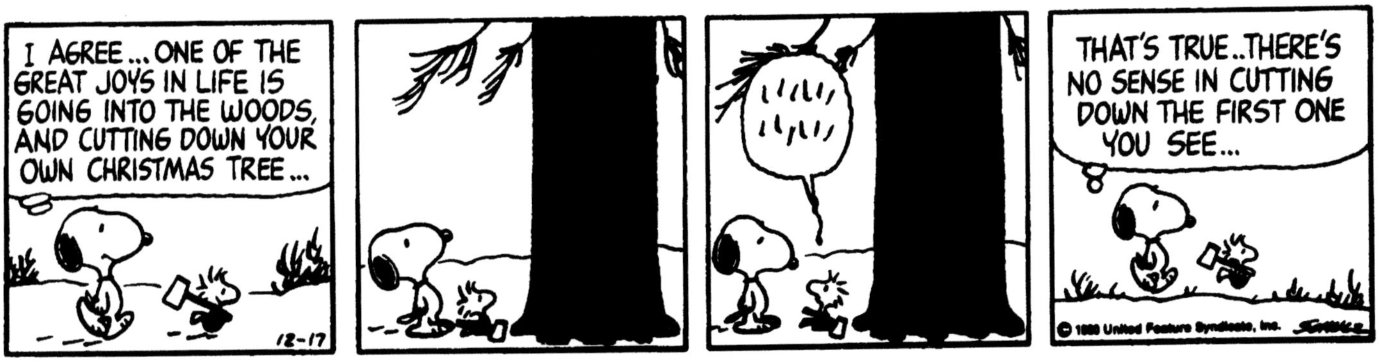
I AGREE... ONE OF THE GREAT JOYS IN LIFE IS GOING INTO THE WOODS, AND CUTTING DOWN YOUR OWN CHRISTMAS TREE...
12-17
THAT'S TRUE..THERE'S NO SENSE IN CUTTING DOWN THE FIRST ONE YOU SEE...
© 1980 United Feature Syndicate, Inc.

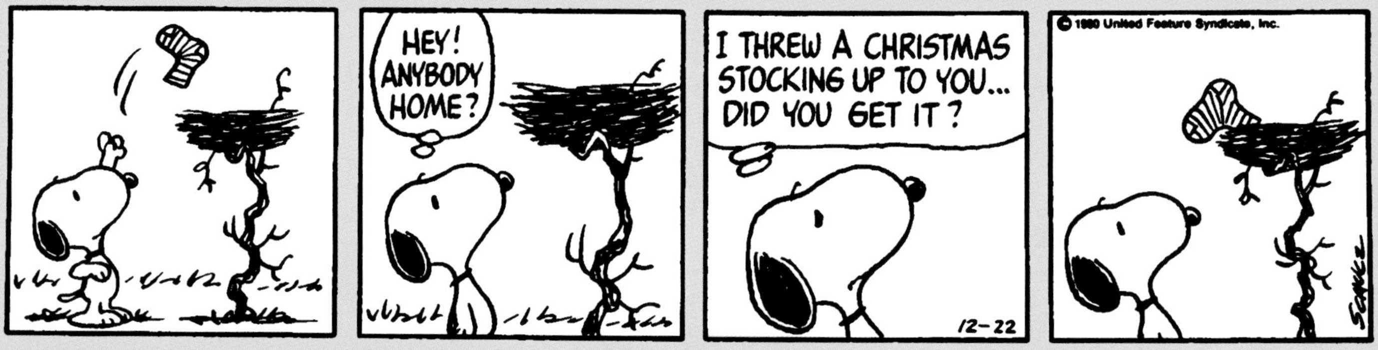
© 1980 United Feature Syndicate, Inc.
HEY! ANYBODY HOME?
I THREW A CHRISTMAS STOCKING UP TO YOU... DID YOU GET IT?
12-22

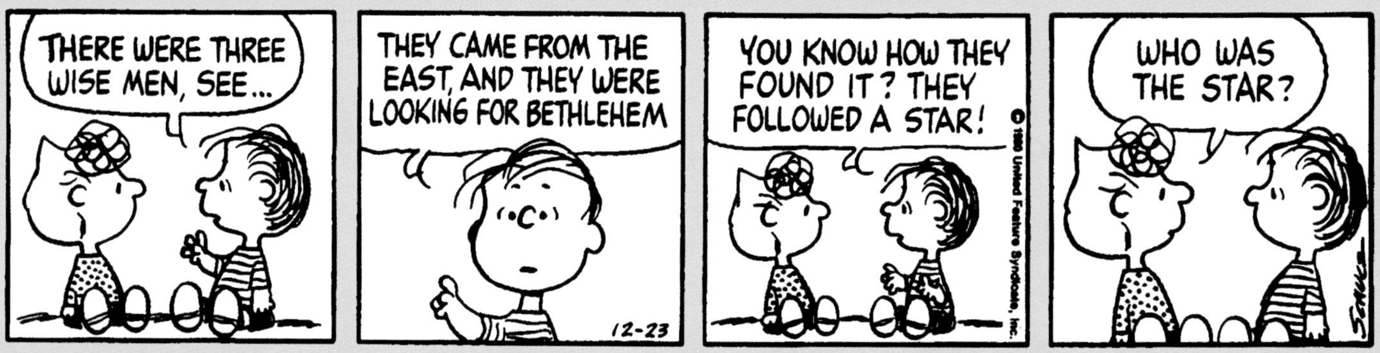
THERE WERE THREE WISE MEN, SEE...
THEY CAME FROM THE EAST, AND THEY WERE LOOKING FOR BETHLEHEM
12-23
YOU KNOW HOW THEY FOUND IT? THEY FOLLOWED A STAR!
© 1980 United Feature Syndicate, Inc.
WHO WAS THE STAR?

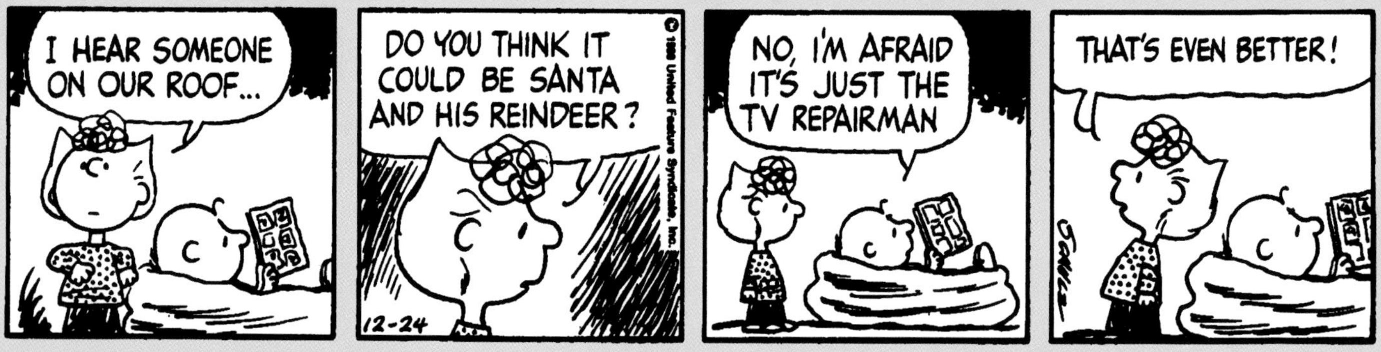
I HEAR SOMEONE ON OUR ROOF...
DO YOU THINK IT COULD BE SANTA AND HIS REINDEER?
© 1980 United Feature Syndicate, Inc.
12-24
NO, I'M AFRAID IT'S JUST THE TV REPAIRMAN
THAT'S EVEN BETTER!

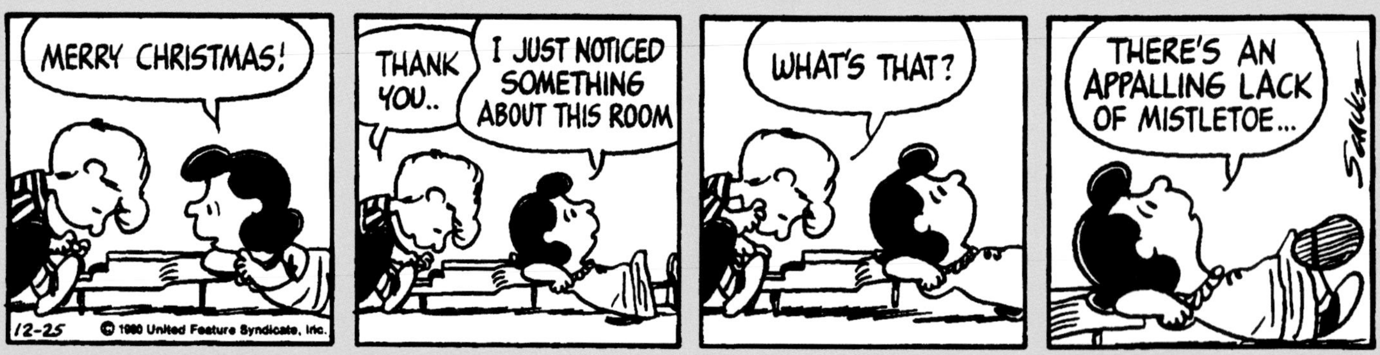
MERRY CHRISTMAS!
12-25
© 1980 United Feature Syndicate, Inc.
THANK YOU..
I JUST NOTICED SOMETHING ABOUT THIS ROOM
WHAT'S THAT?
THERE'S AN APPALLING LACK OF MISTLETOE...

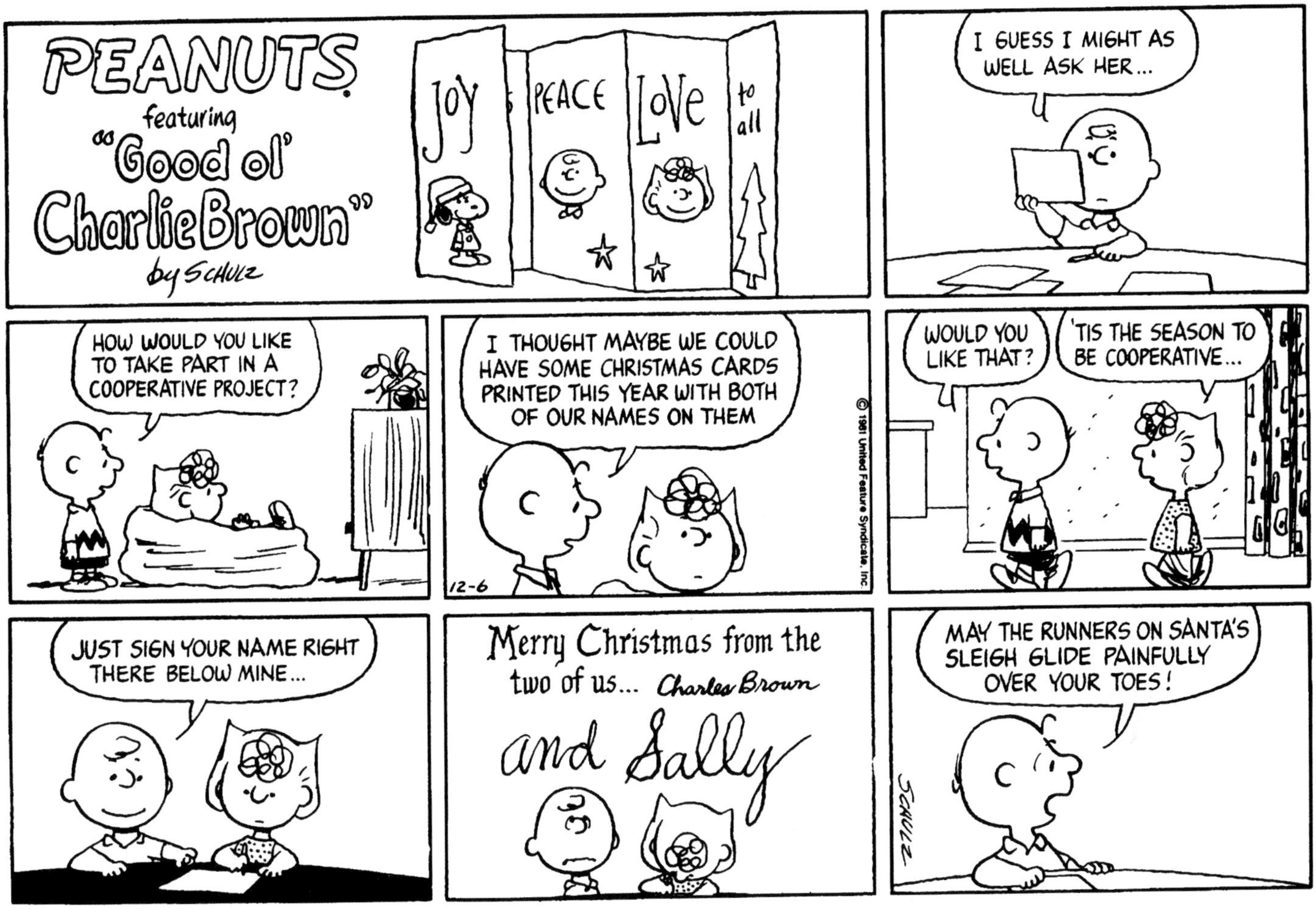
PEANUTS
featuring
"Good ol' Charlie Brown"
by SCHULZ
JOY
PEACE
LOVE
to all
I GUESS I MIGHT AS WELL ASK HER...
HOW WOULD YOU LIKE TO TAKE PART IN A COOPERATIVE PROJECT?
I THOUGHT MAYBE WE COULD HAVE SOME CHRISTMAS CARDS PRINTED THIS YEAR WITH BOTH OF OUR NAMES ON THEM
12-6
© 1981 United Feature Syndicate, Inc.
WOULD YOU LIKE THAT?
'TIS THE SEASON TO BE COOPERATIVE...
JUST SIGN YOUR NAME RIGHT THERE BELOW MINE...
Merry Christmas from the two of us... Charles Brown
and Sally
MAY THE RUNNERS ON SANTA'S SLEIGH GLIDE PAINFULLY OVER YOUR TOES!
SCHULZ

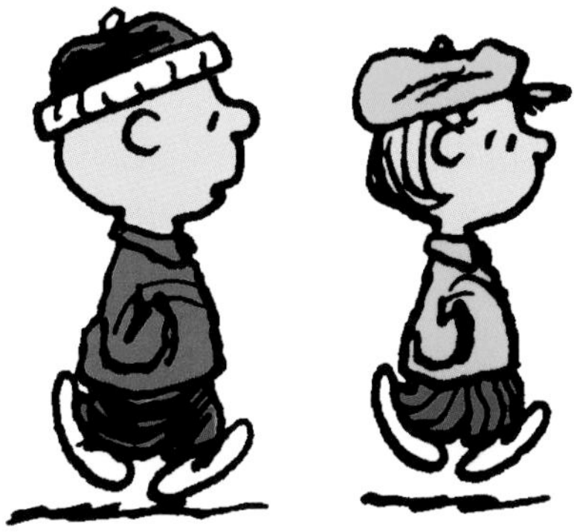

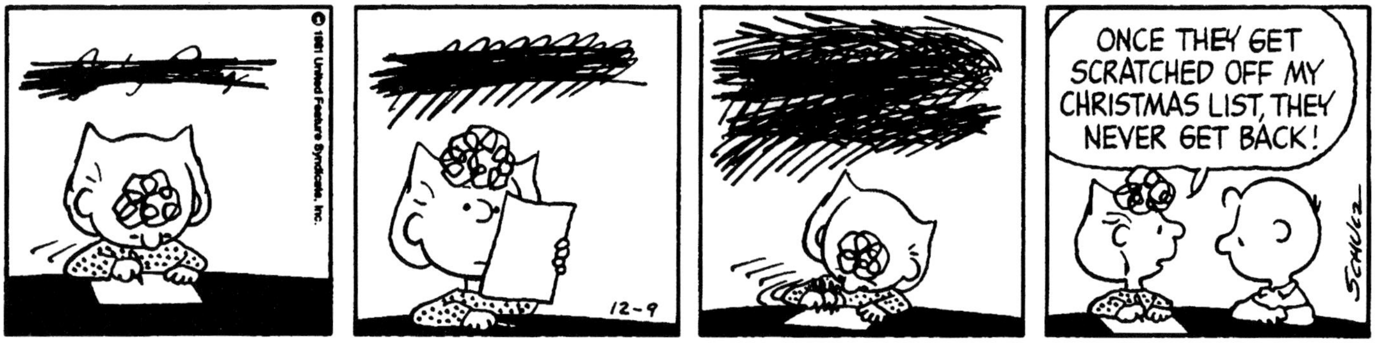

© 1981 United Feature Syndicate, Inc.
12-9
ONCE THEY GET SCRATCHED OFF MY CHRISTMAS LIST, THEY NEVER GET BACK!
SCHULZ

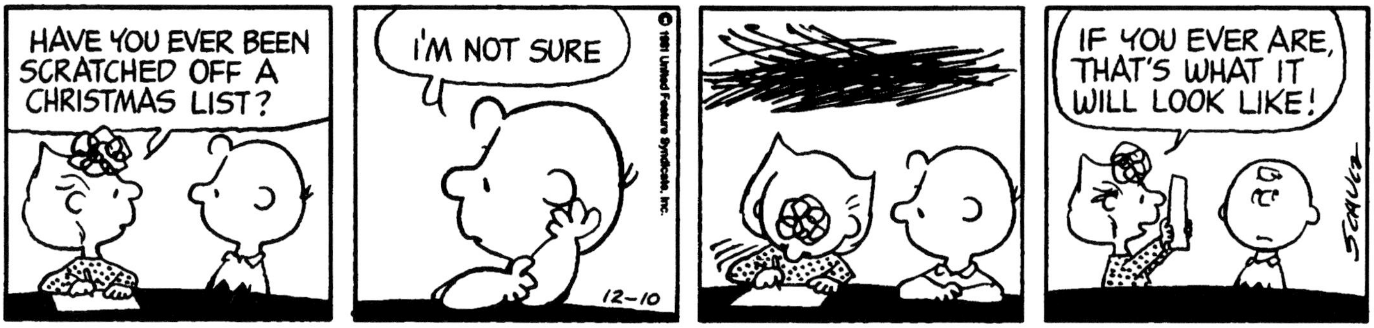

HAVE YOU EVER BEEN SCRATCHED OFF A CHRISTMAS LIST?
I'M NOT SURE
© 1981 United Feature Syndicate, Inc.
12-10
IF YOU EVER ARE, THAT'S WHAT IT WILL LOOK LIKE!
SCHULZ

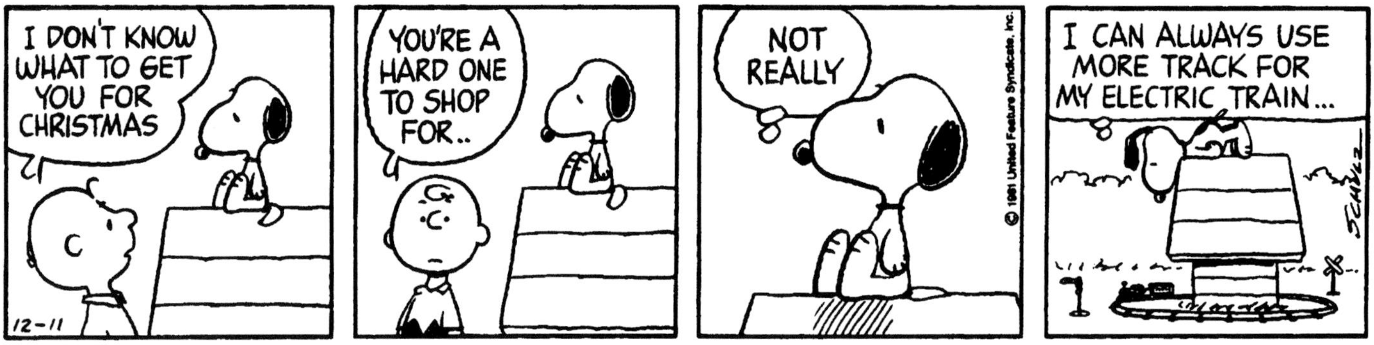

I DON'T KNOW WHAT TO GET YOU FOR CHRISTMAS
12-11
YOU'RE A HARD ONE TO SHOP FOR..
NOT REALLY
© 1981 United Feature Syndicate, Inc.
I CAN ALWAYS USE MORE TRACK FOR MY ELECTRIC TRAIN...
SCHULZ

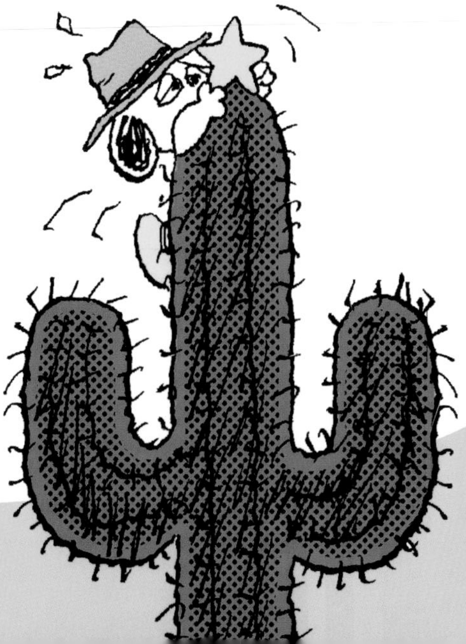

TELL ME WHAT YOU THINK OF THIS...
IT'S MY OWN COMPOSITION
12-18
© 1981 United Feature Syndicate, Inc.
THAT'S NICE...I LIKE CHRISTMAS MUSIC..
SCHULZ

I THINK I'M ACTUALLY AFRAID TO BE HAPPY... EVERY TIME I'M HAPPY SOMETHING BAD HAPPENS
THAT'S NONSENSE, CHARLES...
© 1981 United Feature Syndicate, Inc.
ANYWAY, HAVE A VERY MERRY CHRISTMAS..
12-24
NOW YOU DID IT!
SCHULZ

MERRY CHRISTMAS!
12-25
© 1980 United Feature Syndicate, Inc.
THANK YOU..
I JUST NOTICED SOMETHING ABOUT THIS ROOM
WHAT'S THAT?
THERE'S AN APPALLING LACK OF MISTLETOE...
SCHULZ

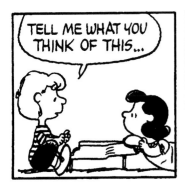

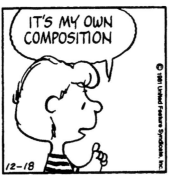

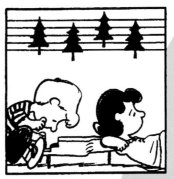

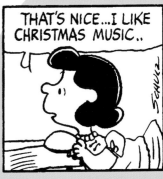

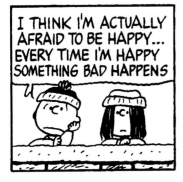

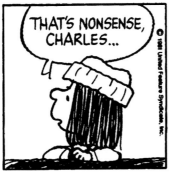

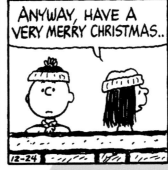

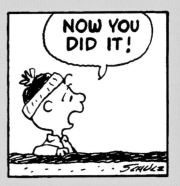

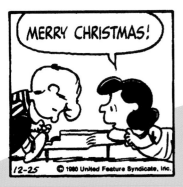

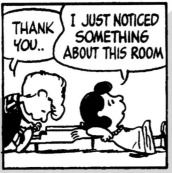

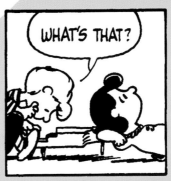

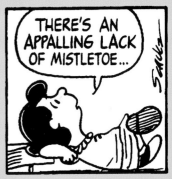

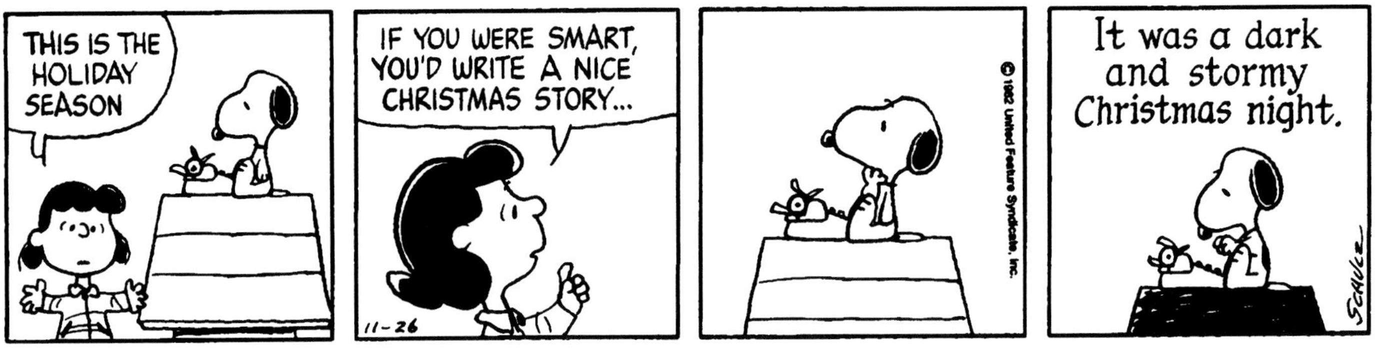
THIS IS THE HOLIDAY SEASON
IF YOU WERE SMART, YOU'D WRITE A NICE CHRISTMAS STORY...
11-26
© 1982 United Feature Syndicate, Inc.
It was a dark and stormy Christmas night.
SCHULZ

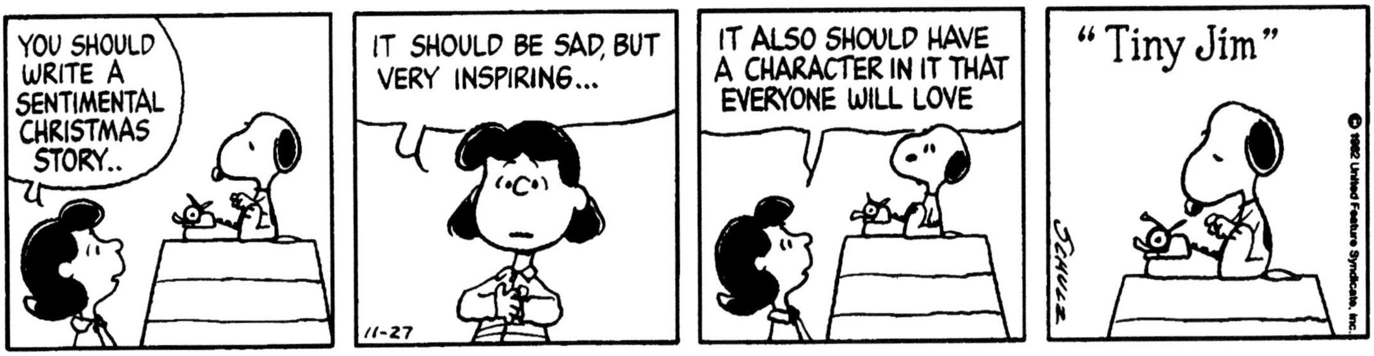
YOU SHOULD WRITE A SENTIMENTAL CHRISTMAS STORY..
IT SHOULD BE SAD, BUT VERY INSPIRING...
11-27
IT ALSO SHOULD HAVE A CHARACTER IN IT THAT EVERYONE WILL LOVE
"Tiny Jim"
SCHULZ
© 1982 United Feature Syndicate, Inc.

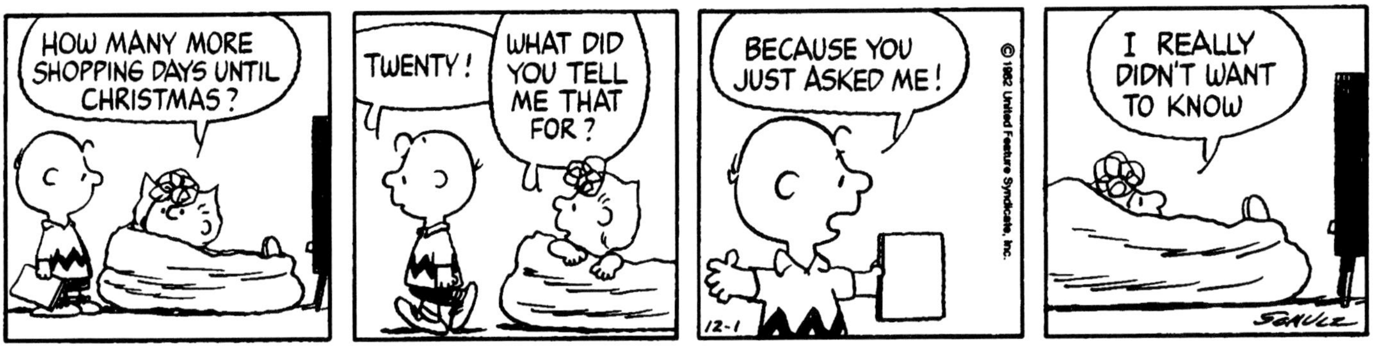
HOW MANY MORE SHOPPING DAYS UNTIL CHRISTMAS?
TWENTY!
WHAT DID YOU TELL ME THAT FOR?
BECAUSE YOU JUST ASKED ME!
12-1
© 1982 United Feature Syndicate, Inc.
I REALLY DIDN'T WANT TO KNOW
SCHULZ

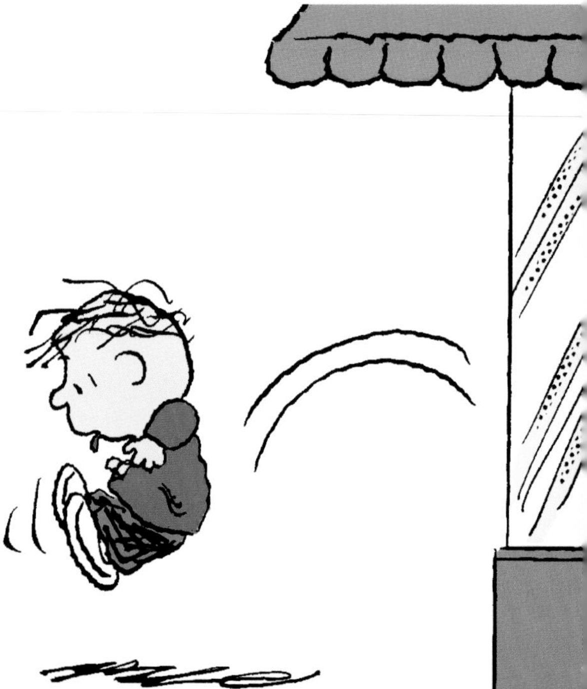

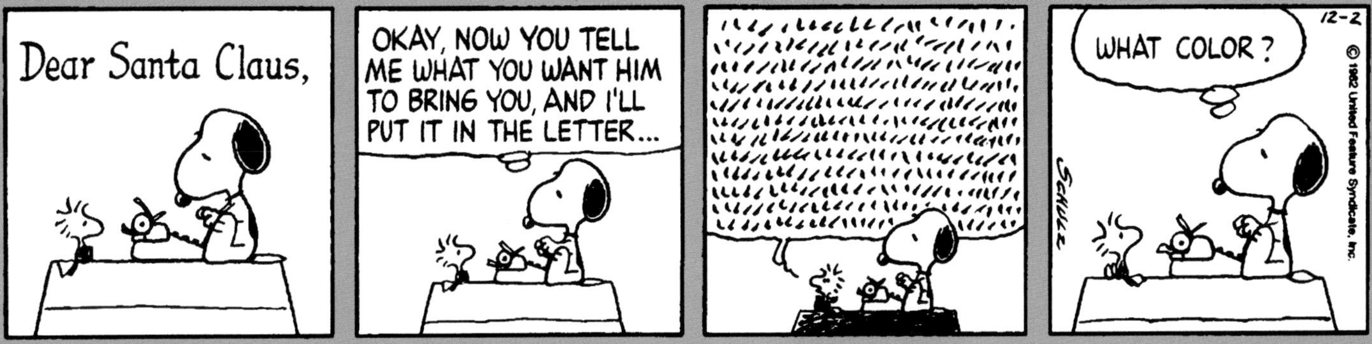
Dear Santa Claus,
OKAY, NOW YOU TELL ME WHAT YOU WANT HIM TO BRING YOU, AND I'LL PUT IT IN THE LETTER...
WHAT COLOR?
12-2
© 1982 United Feature Syndicate, Inc.

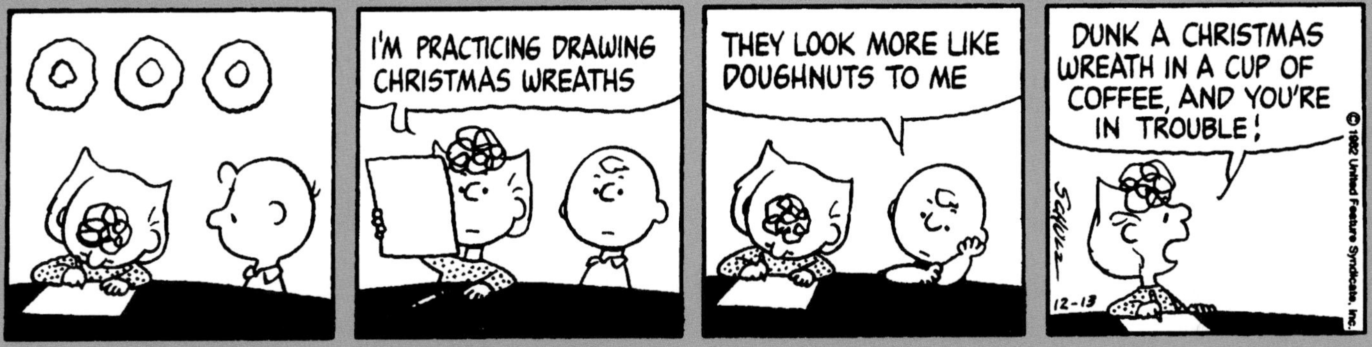
I'M PRACTICING DRAWING CHRISTMAS WREATHS
THEY LOOK MORE LIKE DOUGHNUTS TO ME
DUNK A CHRISTMAS WREATH IN A CUP OF COFFEE, AND YOU'RE IN TROUBLE!
12-13
© 1982 United Feature Syndicate, Inc.

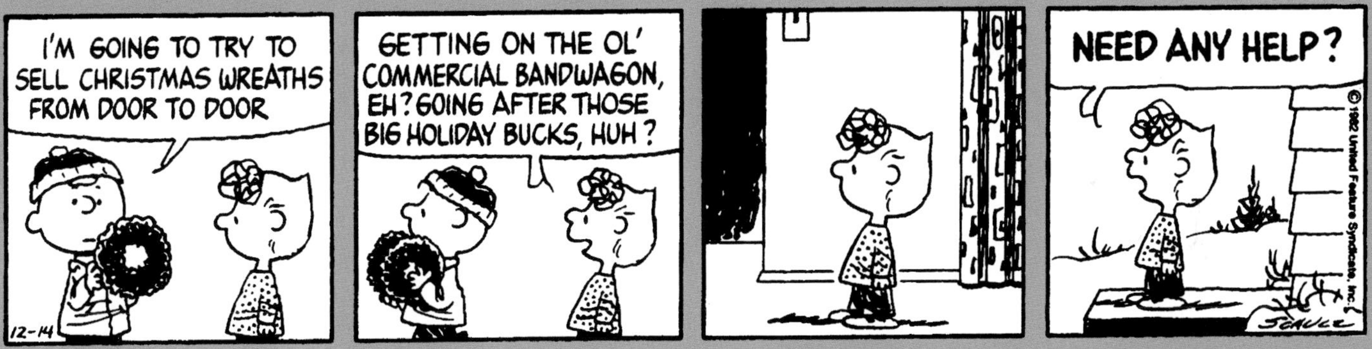
I'M GOING TO TRY TO SELL CHRISTMAS WREATHS FROM DOOR TO DOOR
12-14
GETTING ON THE OL' COMMERCIAL BANDWAGON, EH? GOING AFTER THOSE BIG HOLIDAY BUCKS, HUH?
NEED ANY HELP?
© 1982 United Feature Syndicate, Inc.

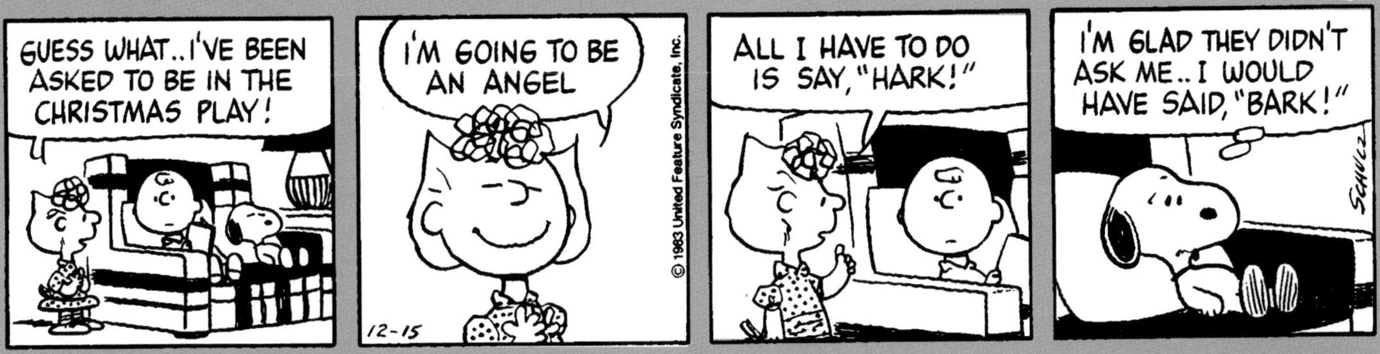
GUESS WHAT.. I'VE BEEN ASKED TO BE IN THE CHRISTMAS PLAY!
I'M GOING TO BE AN ANGEL
12-15
© 1983 United Feature Syndicate, Inc.
ALL I HAVE TO DO IS SAY, "HARK!"
I'M GLAD THEY DIDN'T ASK ME.. I WOULD HAVE SAID, "BARK!"

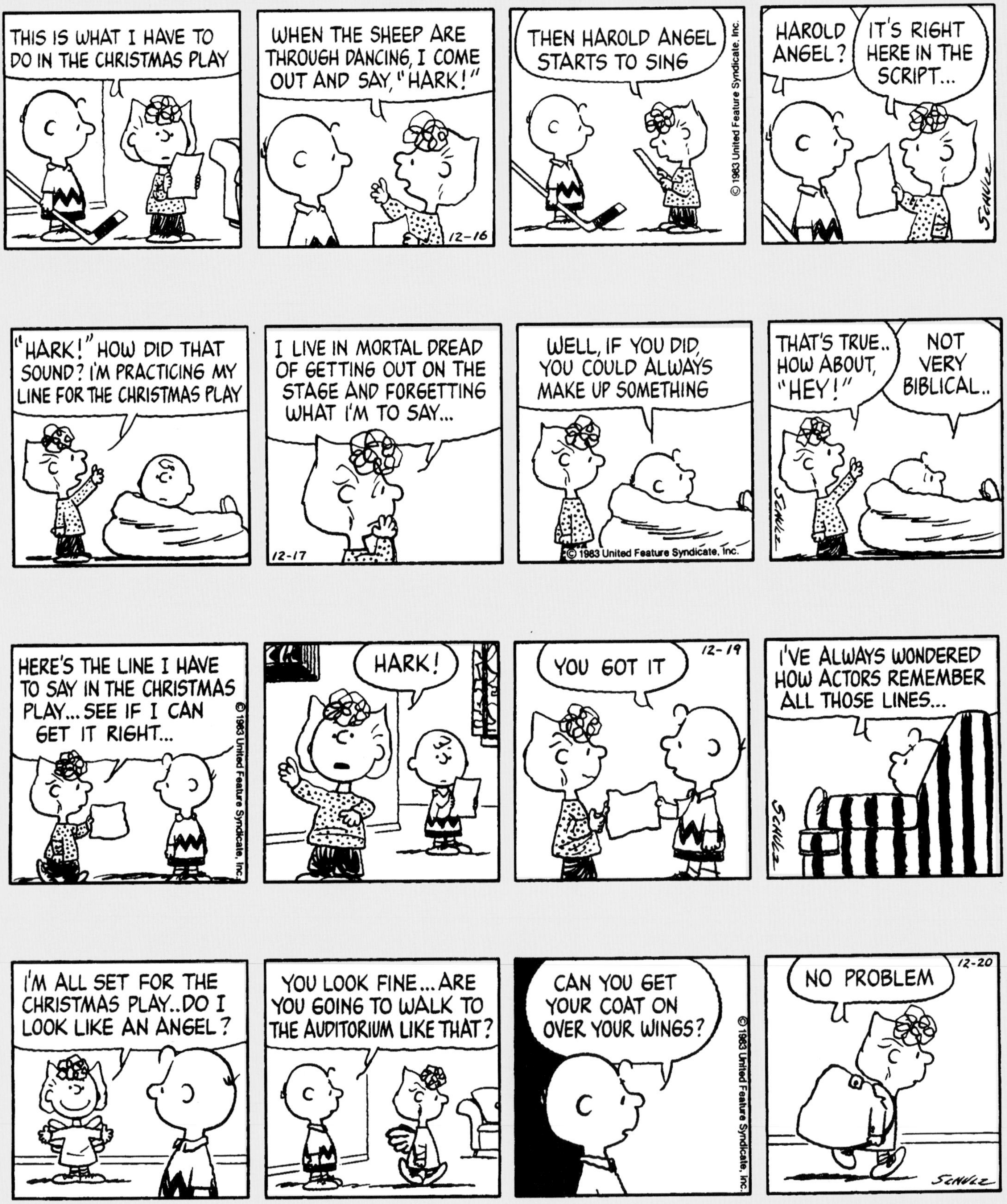
THIS IS WHAT I HAVE TO DO IN THE CHRISTMAS PLAY
WHEN THE SHEEP ARE THROUGH DANCING, I COME OUT AND SAY, "HARK!"
12-16
THEN HAROLD ANGEL STARTS TO SING
© 1983 United Feature Syndicate, Inc.
HAROLD ANGEL?
IT'S RIGHT HERE IN THE SCRIPT...
SCHULZ
"HARK!" HOW DID THAT SOUND? I'M PRACTICING MY LINE FOR THE CHRISTMAS PLAY
I LIVE IN MORTAL DREAD OF GETTING OUT ON THE STAGE AND FORGETTING WHAT I'M TO SAY...
12-17
WELL, IF YOU DID, YOU COULD ALWAYS MAKE UP SOMETHING
© 1983 United Feature Syndicate, Inc.
THAT'S TRUE.. HOW ABOUT, "HEY!"
NOT VERY BIBLICAL..
SCHULZ
HERE'S THE LINE I HAVE TO SAY IN THE CHRISTMAS PLAY... SEE IF I CAN GET IT RIGHT...
© 1983 United Feature Syndicate, Inc.
HARK!
YOU GOT IT
12-19
I'VE ALWAYS WONDERED HOW ACTORS REMEMBER ALL THOSE LINES...
SCHULZ
I'M ALL SET FOR THE CHRISTMAS PLAY..DO I LOOK LIKE AN ANGEL?
YOU LOOK FINE... ARE YOU GOING TO WALK TO THE AUDITORIUM LIKE THAT?
CAN YOU GET YOUR COAT ON OVER YOUR WINGS?
© 1983 United Feature Syndicate, Inc.
NO PROBLEM
12-20
SCHULZ

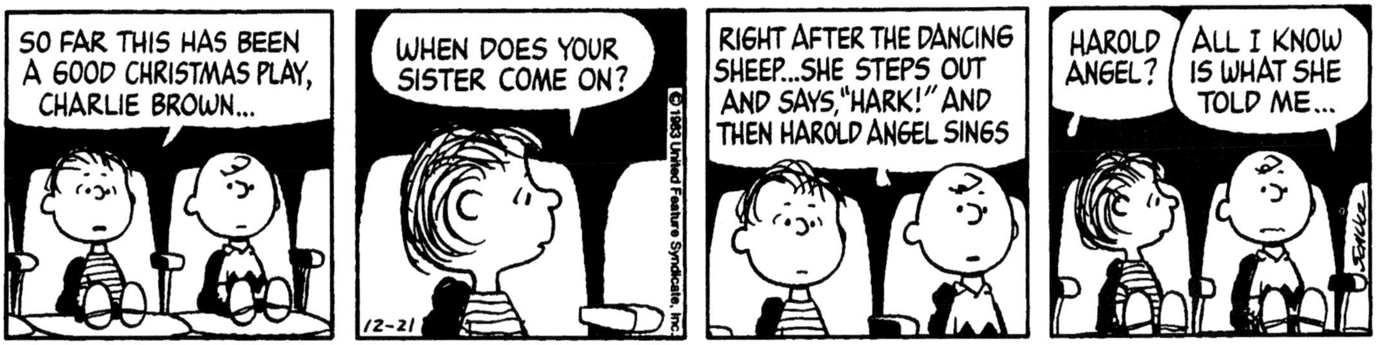
SO FAR THIS HAS BEEN A GOOD CHRISTMAS PLAY, CHARLIE BROWN...
WHEN DOES YOUR SISTER COME ON?
12-21
© 1983 United Feature Syndicate, Inc.
RIGHT AFTER THE DANCING SHEEP...SHE STEPS OUT AND SAYS, "HARK!" AND THEN HAROLD ANGEL SINGS
HAROLD ANGEL?
ALL I KNOW IS WHAT SHE TOLD ME...
SCHULZ

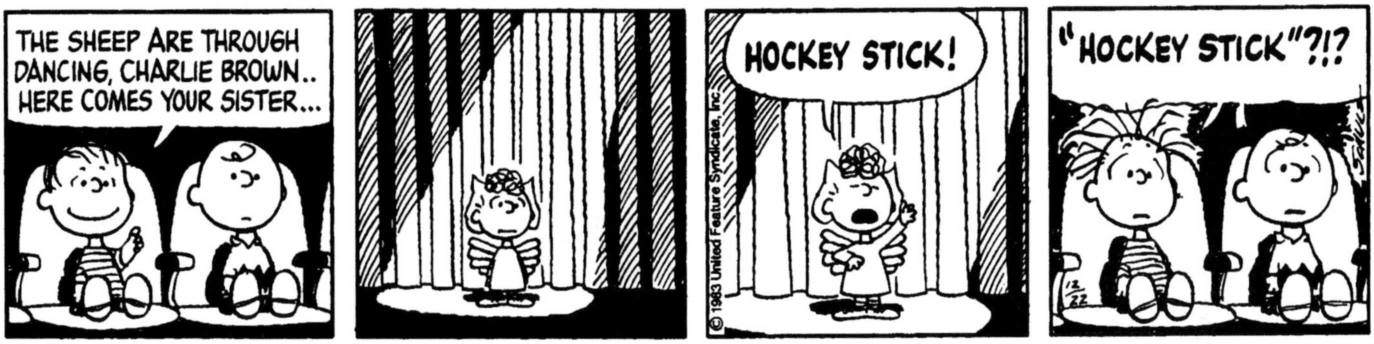
THE SHEEP ARE THROUGH DANCING, CHARLIE BROWN.. HERE COMES YOUR SISTER...
HOCKEY STICK!
© 1983 United Feature Syndicate, Inc.
"HOCKEY STICK"?!?
SCHULZ
12/22

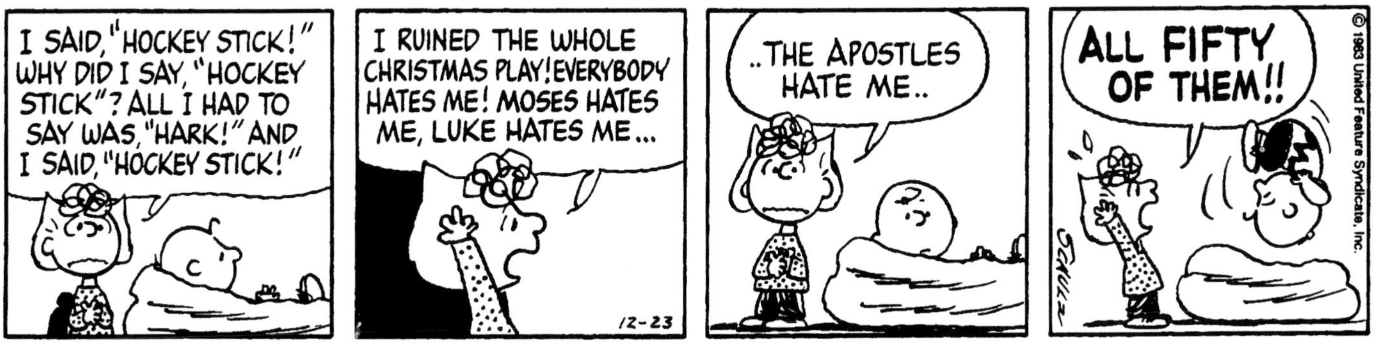
I SAID, "HOCKEY STICK!" WHY DID I SAY, "HOCKEY STICK"? ALL I HAD TO SAY WAS, "HARK!" AND I SAID, "HOCKEY STICK!"
I RUINED THE WHOLE CHRISTMAS PLAY! EVERYBODY HATES ME! MOSES HATES ME, LUKE HATES ME...
12-23
..THE APOSTLES HATE ME..
ALL FIFTY OF THEM!!
SCHULZ
© 1983 United Feature Syndicate, Inc.

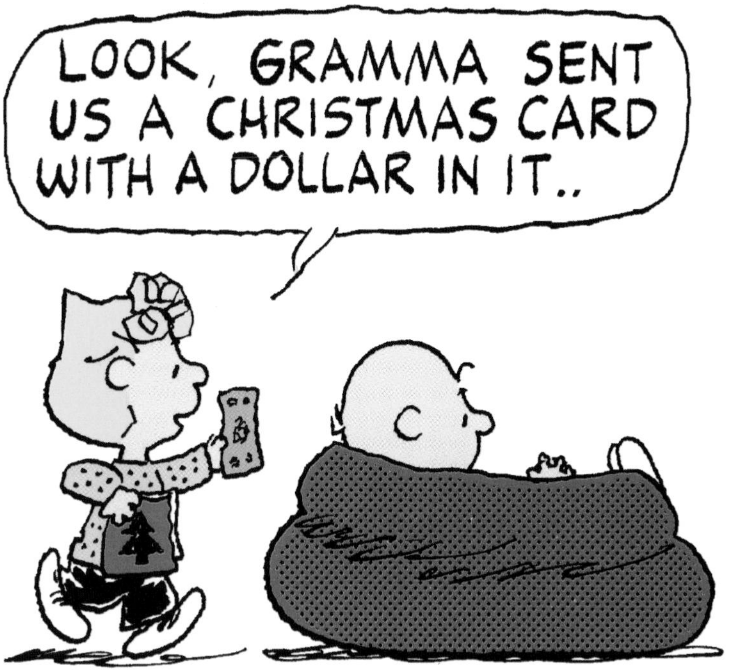
LOOK, GRAMMA SENT US A CHRISTMAS CARD WITH A DOLLAR IN IT..

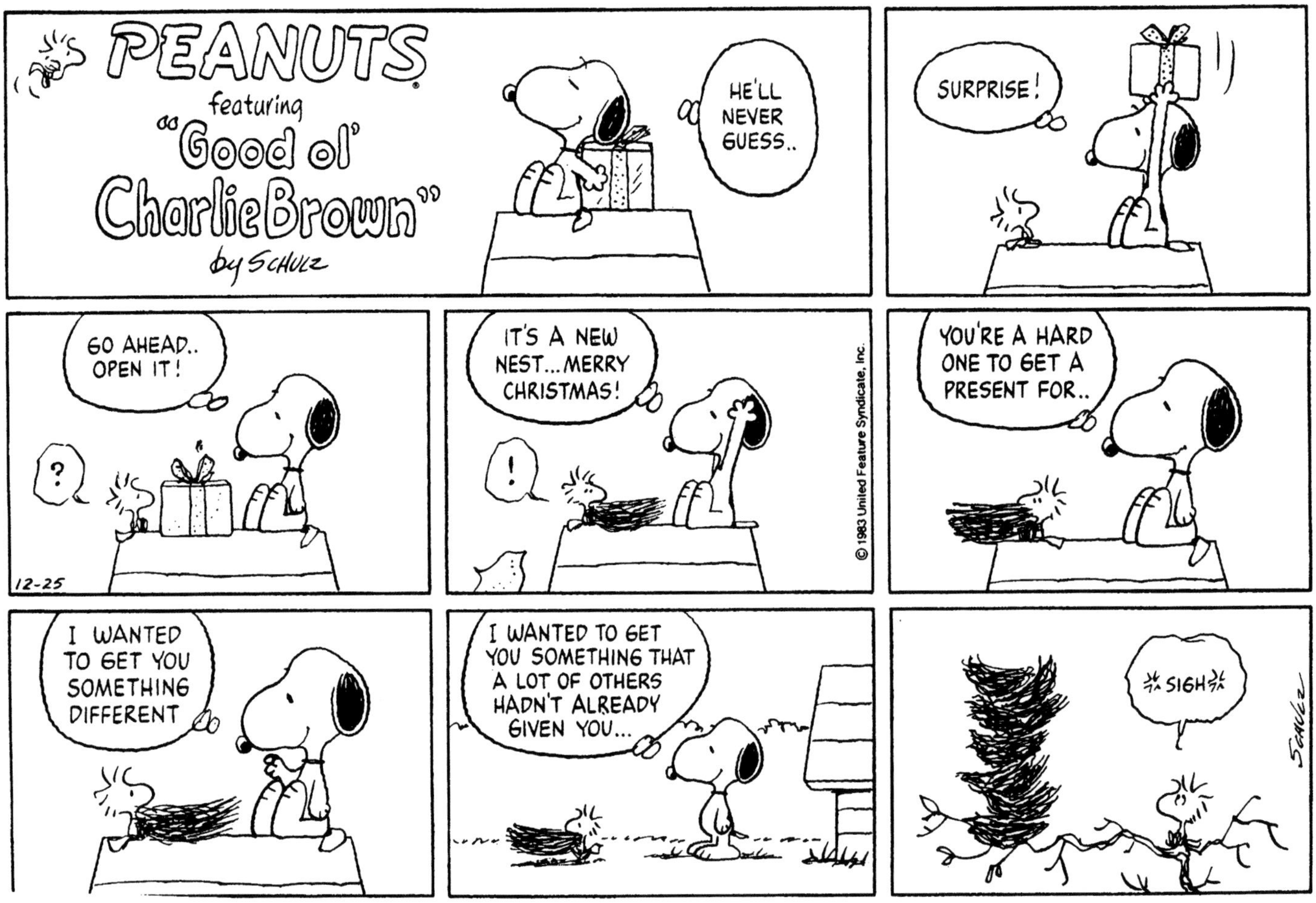
PEANUTS
featuring "Good ol' CharlieBrown"
by SCHULZ
HE'LL NEVER GUESS..
SURPRISE!
GO AHEAD.. OPEN IT!
?
12-25
IT'S A NEW NEST...MERRY CHRISTMAS!
!
© 1983 United Feature Syndicate, Inc.
YOU'RE A HARD ONE TO GET A PRESENT FOR..
I WANTED TO GET YOU SOMETHING DIFFERENT
I WANTED TO GET YOU SOMETHING THAT A LOT OF OTHERS HADN'T ALREADY GIVEN YOU...
SIGH
SCHULZ

"Twas the month before Christmas"

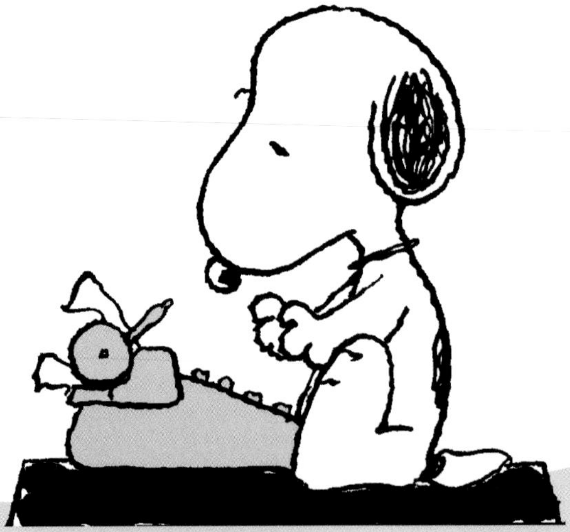

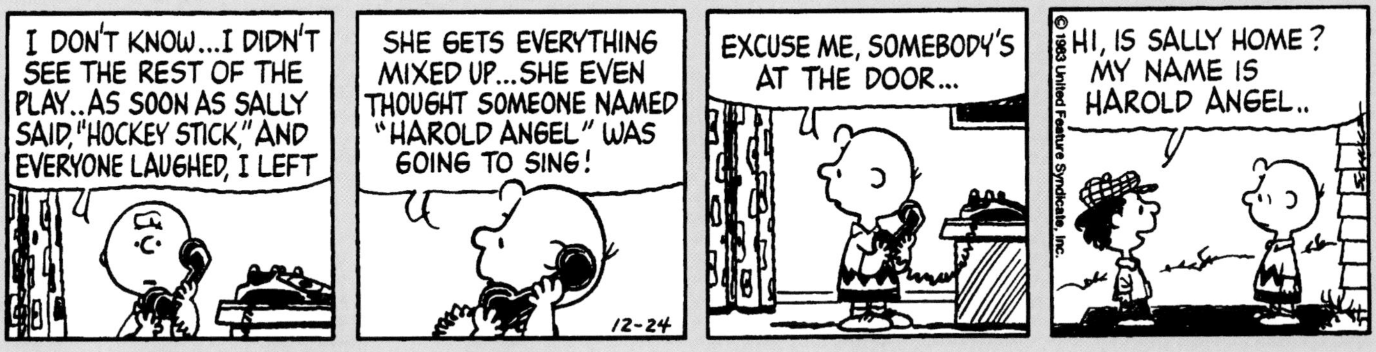
I DON'T KNOW...I DIDN'T SEE THE REST OF THE PLAY..AS SOON AS SALLY SAID, "HOCKEY STICK," AND EVERYONE LAUGHED, I LEFT
SHE GETS EVERYTHING MIXED UP...SHE EVEN THOUGHT SOMEONE NAMED "HAROLD ANGEL" WAS GOING TO SING!
12-24
EXCUSE ME, SOMEBODY'S AT THE DOOR...
© 1983 United Feature Syndicate, Inc.
HI, IS SALLY HOME? MY NAME IS HAROLD ANGEL..
SCHULZ

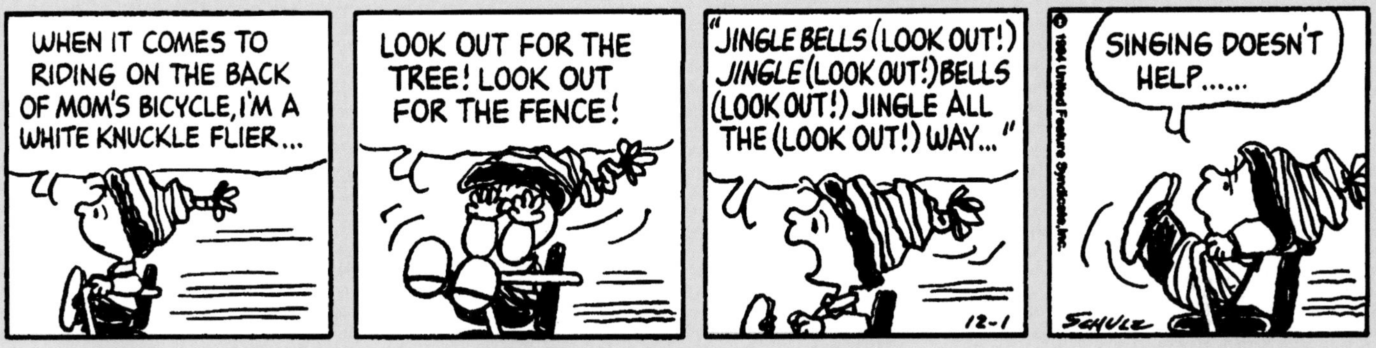
WHEN IT COMES TO RIDING ON THE BACK OF MOM'S BICYCLE, I'M A WHITE KNUCKLE FLIER...
LOOK OUT FOR THE TREE! LOOK OUT FOR THE FENCE!
"JINGLE BELLS (LOOK OUT!) JINGLE (LOOK OUT!) BELLS (LOOK OUT!) JINGLE ALL THE (LOOK OUT!) WAY..."
12-1
© 1984 United Feature Syndicate, Inc.
SINGING DOESN'T HELP......
SCHULZ

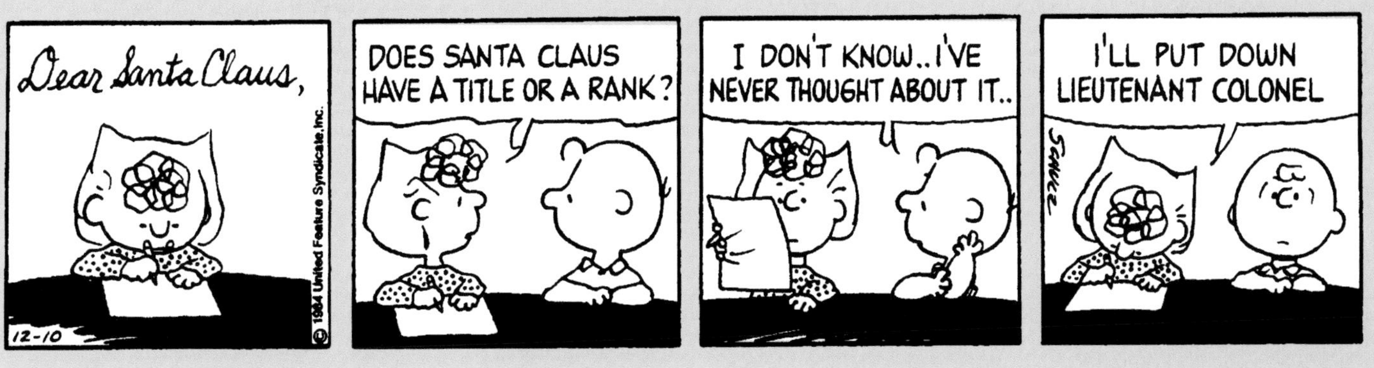
Dear Santa Claus,
12-10
© 1984 United Feature Syndicate, Inc.
DOES SANTA CLAUS HAVE A TITLE OR A RANK?
I DON'T KNOW..I'VE NEVER THOUGHT ABOUT IT..
I'LL PUT DOWN LIEUTENANT COLONEL
SCHULZ

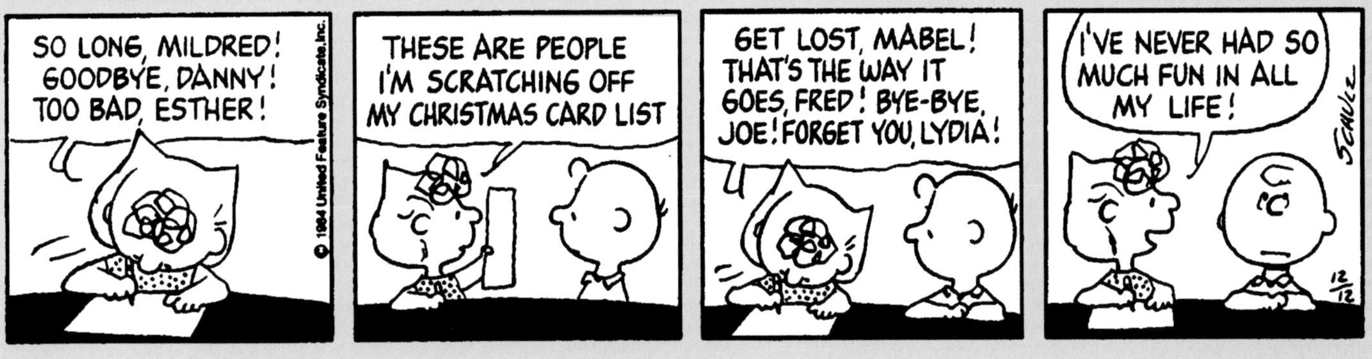
SO LONG, MILDRED! GOODBYE, DANNY! TOO BAD, ESTHER!
© 1984 United Feature Syndicate, Inc.
THESE ARE PEOPLE I'M SCRATCHING OFF MY CHRISTMAS CARD LIST
GET LOST, MABEL! THAT'S THE WAY IT GOES, FRED! BYE-BYE, JOE! FORGET YOU, LYDIA!
I'VE NEVER HAD SO MUCH FUN IN ALL MY LIFE!
SCHULZ
12/12

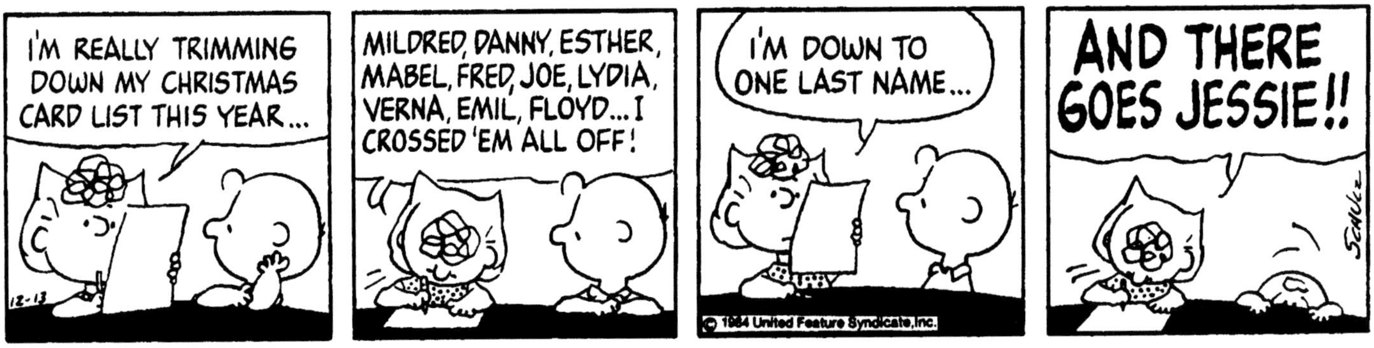
I'M REALLY TRIMMING DOWN MY CHRISTMAS CARD LIST THIS YEAR...
12-13
MILDRED, DANNY, ESTHER, MABEL, FRED, JOE, LYDIA, VERNA, EMIL, FLOYD... I CROSSED 'EM ALL OFF!
I'M DOWN TO ONE LAST NAME...
© 1984 United Feature Syndicate, Inc.
AND THERE GOES JESSIE!!
SCHULZ

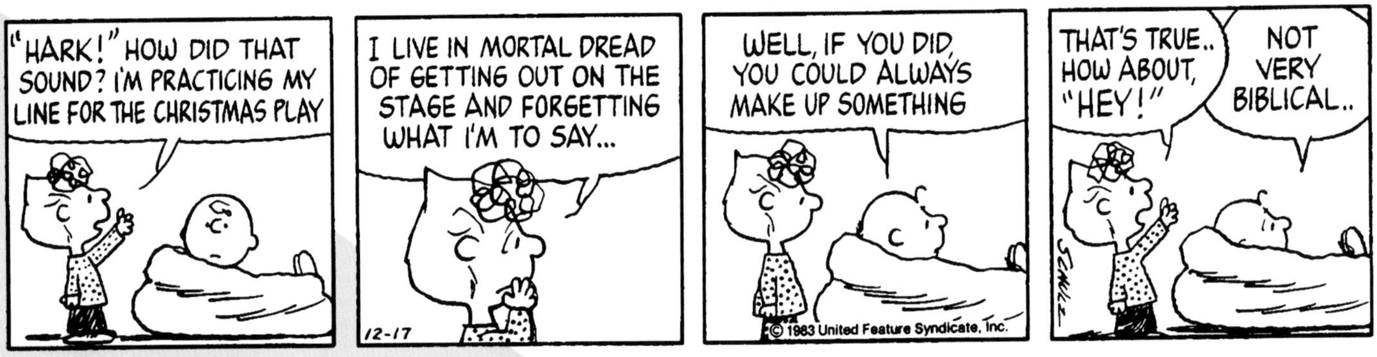
"HARK!" HOW DID THAT SOUND? I'M PRACTICING MY LINE FOR THE CHRISTMAS PLAY
I LIVE IN MORTAL DREAD OF GETTING OUT ON THE STAGE AND FORGETTING WHAT I'M TO SAY...
12-17
WELL, IF YOU DID, YOU COULD ALWAYS MAKE UP SOMETHING
© 1983 United Feature Syndicate, Inc.
THAT'S TRUE.. HOW ABOUT, "HEY!"
NOT VERY BIBLICAL..
SCHULZ

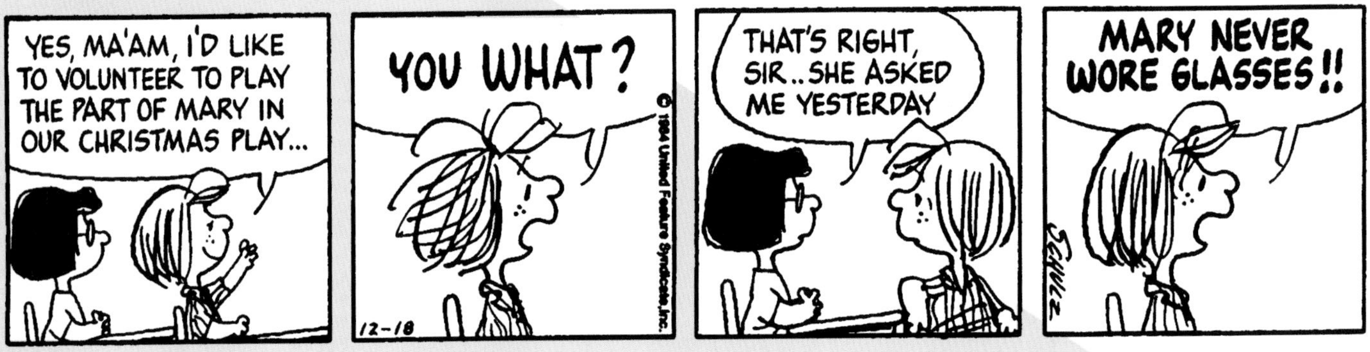
YES, MA'AM, I'D LIKE TO VOLUNTEER TO PLAY THE PART OF MARY IN OUR CHRISTMAS PLAY...
YOU WHAT?
12-18
© 1984 United Feature Syndicate, Inc.
THAT'S RIGHT, SIR.. SHE ASKED ME YESTERDAY
MARY NEVER WORE GLASSES!!
SCHULZ

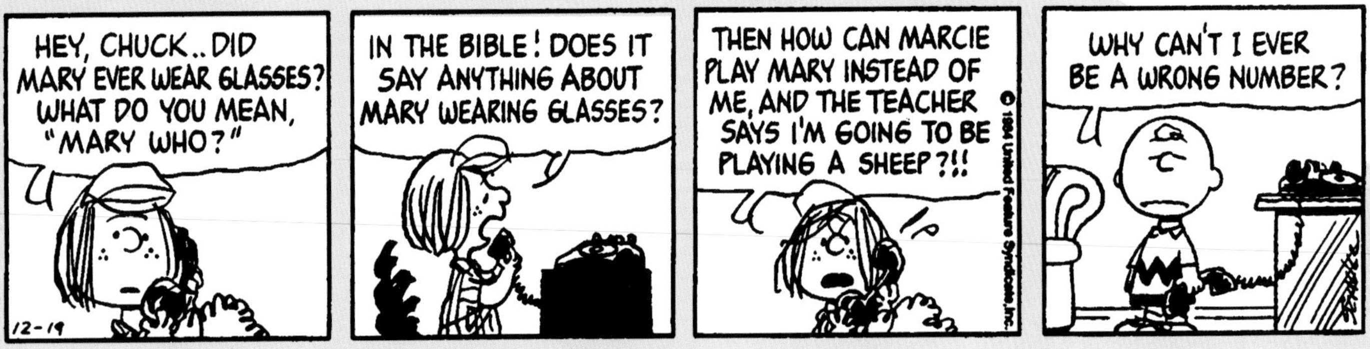
HEY, CHUCK.. DID MARY EVER WEAR GLASSES? WHAT DO YOU MEAN, "MARY WHO?"
12-19
IN THE BIBLE! DOES IT SAY ANYTHING ABOUT MARY WEARING GLASSES?
THEN HOW CAN MARCIE PLAY MARY INSTEAD OF ME, AND THE TEACHER SAYS I'M GOING TO BE PLAYING A SHEEP?!!
© 1984 United Feature Syndicate, Inc.
WHY CAN'T I EVER BE A WRONG NUMBER?
SCHULZ

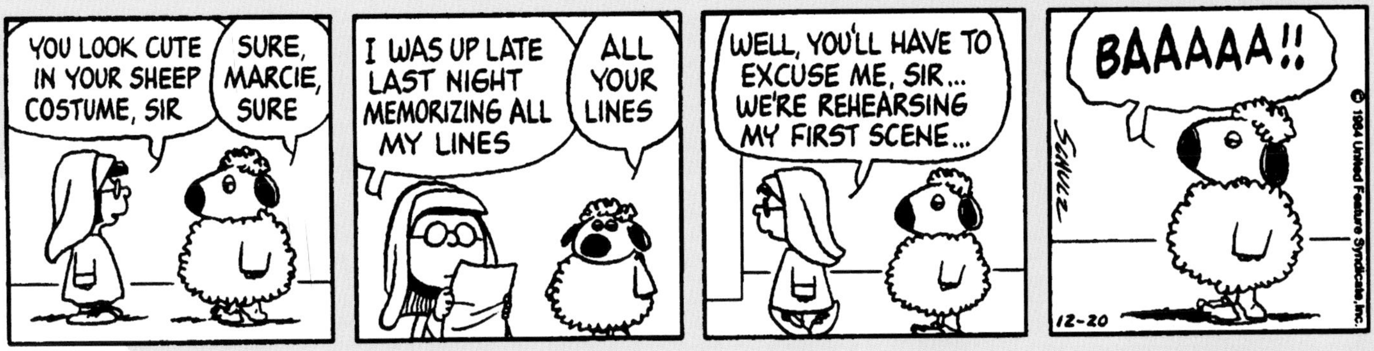
YOU LOOK CUTE IN YOUR SHEEP COSTUME, SIR
SURE, MARCIE, SURE
I WAS UP LATE LAST NIGHT MEMORIZING ALL MY LINES
ALL YOUR LINES
WELL, YOU'LL HAVE TO EXCUSE ME, SIR... WE'RE REHEARSING MY FIRST SCENE...
BAAAAA!!
SCHULZ
© 1984 United Feature Syndicate, Inc.
12-20

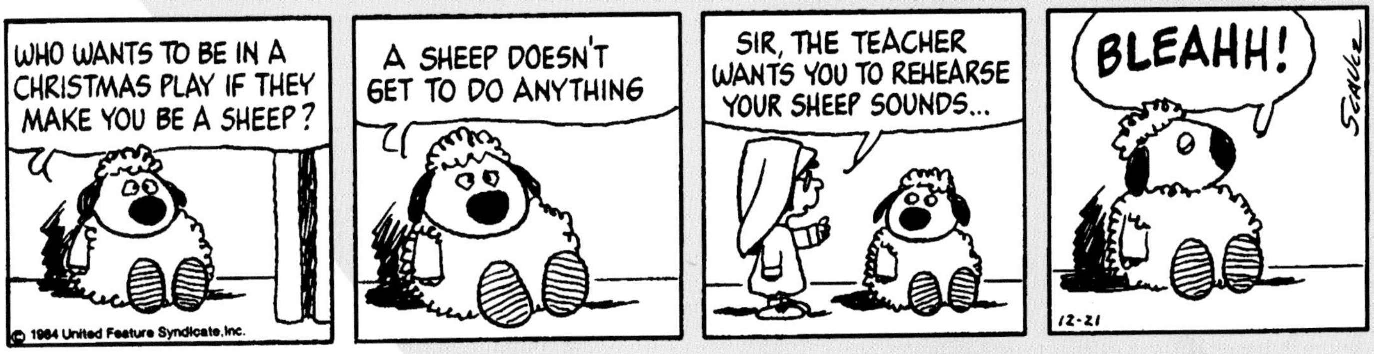
WHO WANTS TO BE IN A CHRISTMAS PLAY IF THEY MAKE YOU BE A SHEEP?
A SHEEP DOESN'T GET TO DO ANYTHING
SIR, THE TEACHER WANTS YOU TO REHEARSE YOUR SHEEP SOUNDS...
BLEAHH!
SCHULZ
© 1984 United Feature Syndicate, Inc.
12-21

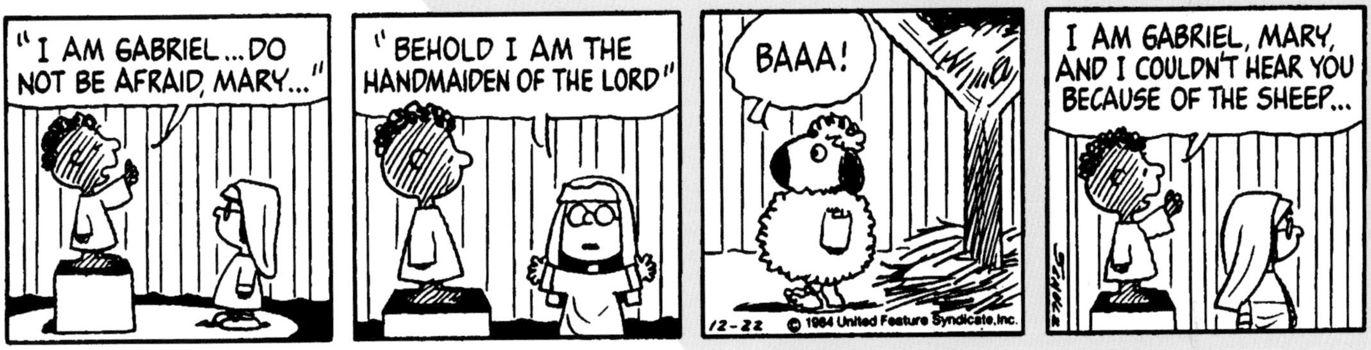
"I AM GABRIEL...DO NOT BE AFRAID, MARY..."
"BEHOLD I AM THE HANDMAIDEN OF THE LORD"
BAAA!
I AM GABRIEL, MARY, AND I COULDN'T HEAR YOU BECAUSE OF THE SHEEP...
SCHULZ
12-22
© 1984 United Feature Syndicate, Inc.

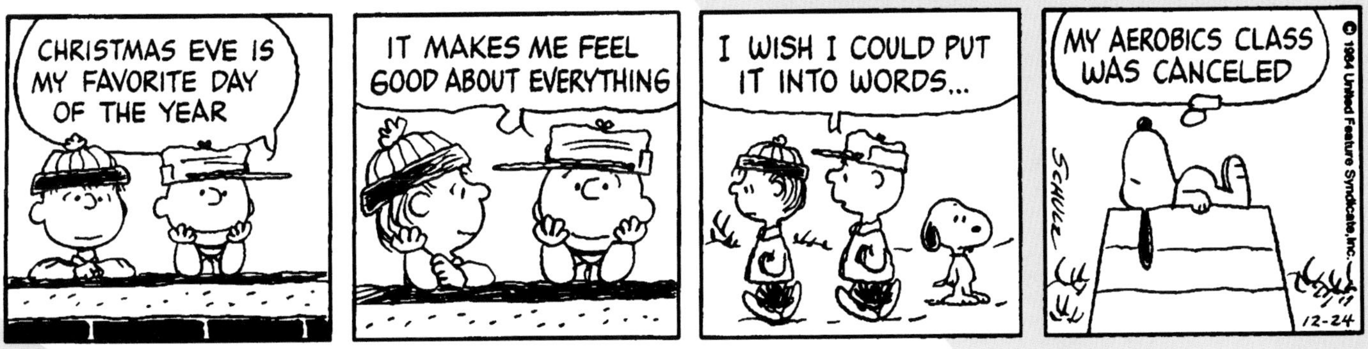
CHRISTMAS EVE IS MY FAVORITE DAY OF THE YEAR
IT MAKES ME FEEL GOOD ABOUT EVERYTHING
I WISH I COULD PUT IT INTO WORDS...
MY AEROBICS CLASS WAS CANCELED
SCHULZ
© 1984 United Feature Syndicate, Inc.
12-24

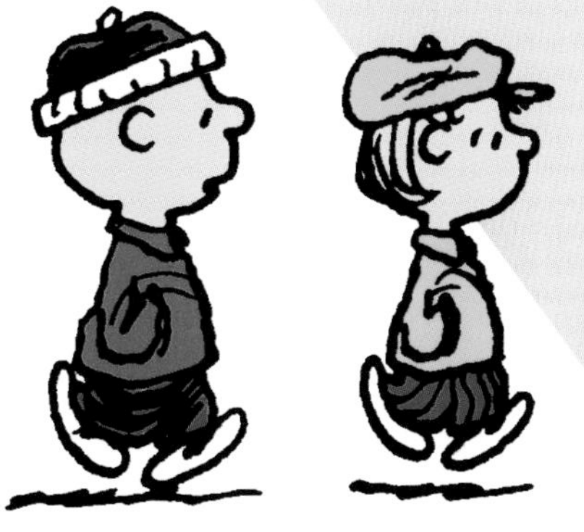

IS THAT THE SCARF YOU GOT FOR CHRISTMAS?
IT'S KIND OF LONG, ISN'T IT?
© 1984 United Feature Syndicate, Inc.
12-27
A LONG SCARF CAN BE VERY USEFUL...
SCHULZ

What I did on my Christmas Vacation. I went outside and looked at the clouds.
They formed beautiful patterns with beautiful colors. I looked at them every morning and every evening.
Which is all I did on my Christmas Vacation.
© 1984 United Feature Syndicate, Inc.
12-28
And what's wrong with that?
SCHULZ

I want my Christmas to be one of peace and love, not greed.

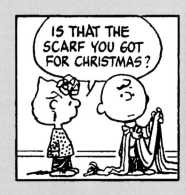

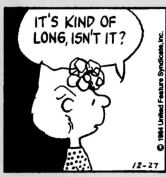

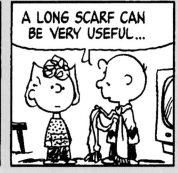

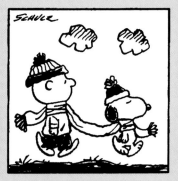

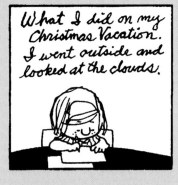

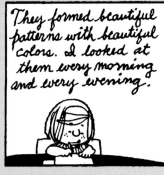

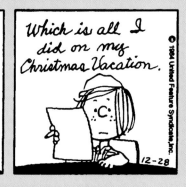

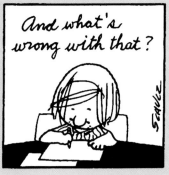

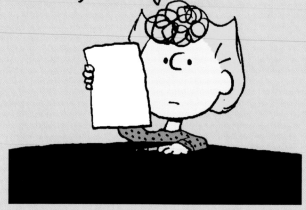

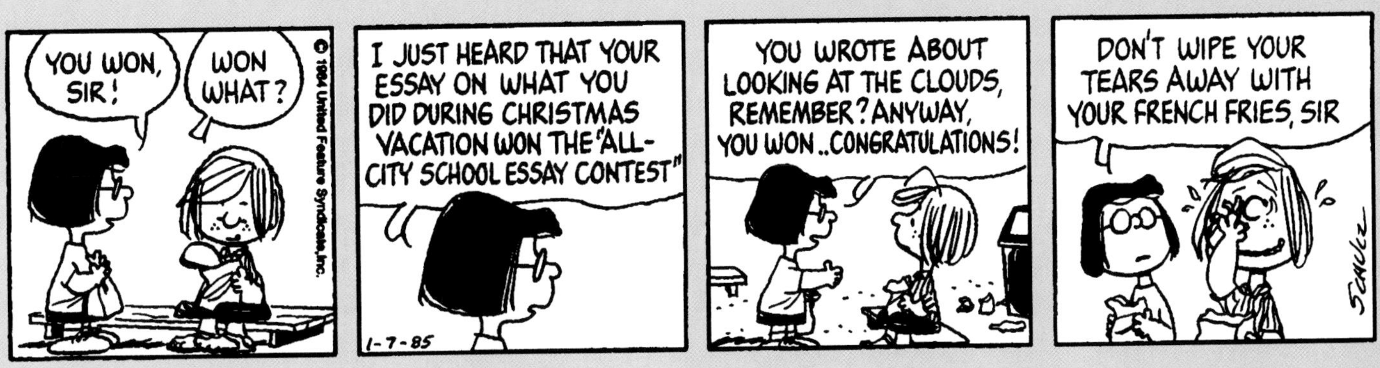
YOU WON, SIR!
WON WHAT?
© 1984 United Feature Syndicate, Inc.
I JUST HEARD THAT YOUR ESSAY ON WHAT YOU DID DURING CHRISTMAS VACATION WON THE "ALL-CITY SCHOOL ESSAY CONTEST"
1-7-85
YOU WROTE ABOUT LOOKING AT THE CLOUDS, REMEMBER? ANYWAY, YOU WON..CONGRATULATIONS!
DON'T WIPE YOUR TEARS AWAY WITH YOUR FRENCH FRIES, SIR
SCHULZ

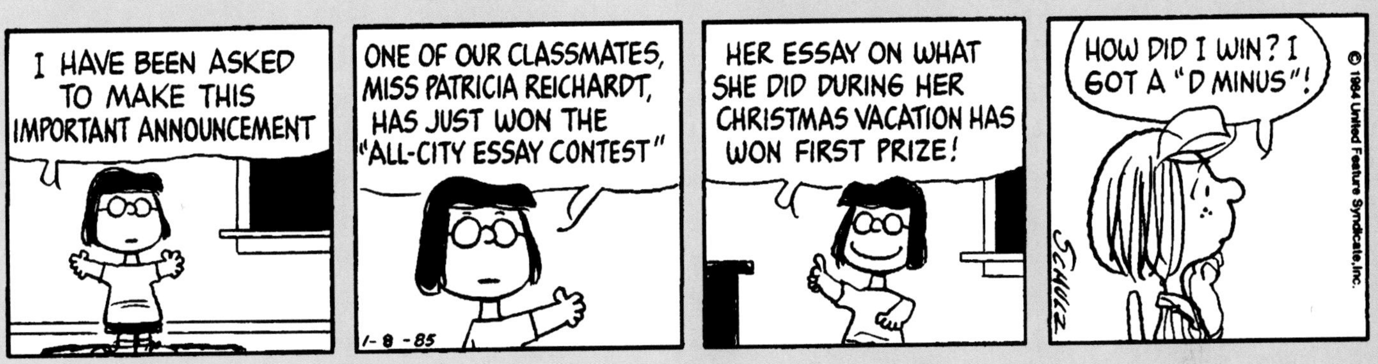
I HAVE BEEN ASKED TO MAKE THIS IMPORTANT ANNOUNCEMENT
ONE OF OUR CLASSMATES, MISS PATRICIA REICHARDT, HAS JUST WON THE "ALL-CITY ESSAY CONTEST"
1-8-85
HER ESSAY ON WHAT SHE DID DURING HER CHRISTMAS VACATION HAS WON FIRST PRIZE!
HOW DID I WIN? I GOT A "D MINUS"!
© 1984 United Feature Syndicate, Inc.
SCHULZ

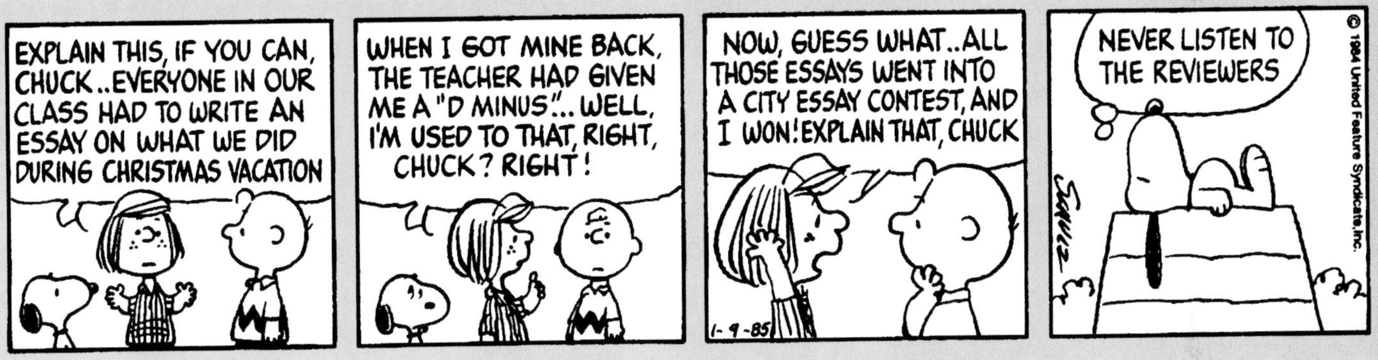
EXPLAIN THIS, IF YOU CAN, CHUCK..EVERYONE IN OUR CLASS HAD TO WRITE AN ESSAY ON WHAT WE DID DURING CHRISTMAS VACATION
WHEN I GOT MINE BACK, THE TEACHER HAD GIVEN ME A "D MINUS"... WELL, I'M USED TO THAT, RIGHT, CHUCK? RIGHT!
NOW, GUESS WHAT..ALL THOSE ESSAYS WENT INTO A CITY ESSAY CONTEST, AND I WON! EXPLAIN THAT, CHUCK
1-9-85
NEVER LISTEN TO THE REVIEWERS
© 1984 United Feature Syndicate, Inc.
SCHULZ

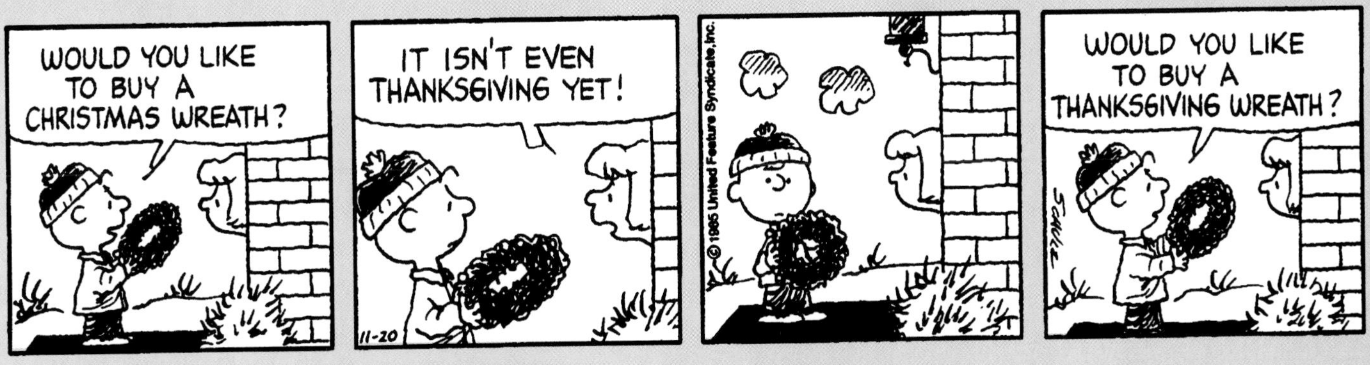
WOULD YOU LIKE TO BUY A CHRISTMAS WREATH?
IT ISN'T EVEN THANKSGIVING YET!
11-20
© 1985 United Feature Syndicate, Inc.
WOULD YOU LIKE TO BUY A THANKSGIVING WREATH?
SCHULZ

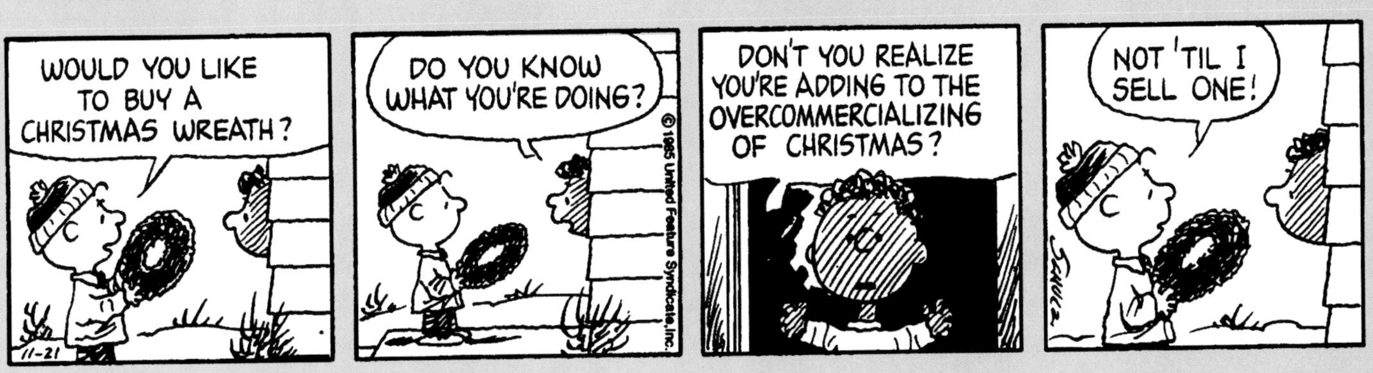
WOULD YOU LIKE TO BUY A CHRISTMAS WREATH?
11-21
DO YOU KNOW WHAT YOU'RE DOING?
© 1985 United Feature Syndicate, Inc.
DON'T YOU REALIZE YOU'RE ADDING TO THE OVERCOMMERCIALIZING OF CHRISTMAS?
NOT 'TIL I SELL ONE!
SCHULZ

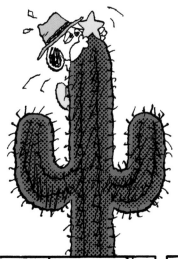

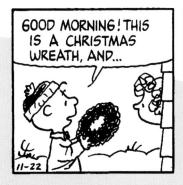

GOOD MORNING! THIS IS A CHRISTMAS WREATH, AND...
11-22
THANK YOU! I LOVE SAMPLES!
SLAM!
I GIVE UP! I CAN'T IMAGINE ANYONE ELSE HAVING AS MUCH TROUBLE AS I DO SELLING CHRISTMAS WREATHS...
© 1985 United Feature Syndicate, Inc.
SCHULZ

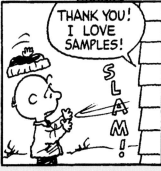

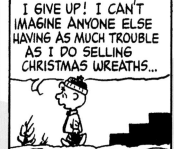

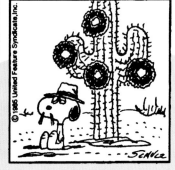

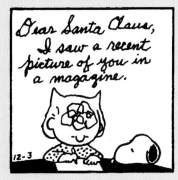

Dear Santa Claus, I saw a recent picture of you in a magazine.
12-3
You look fatter than ever.
© 1985 United Feature Syndicate, Inc.
I know how you usually fly through the air with your reindeer and sleigh.
I'll be surprised this year if you even get off the ground.
SCHULZ

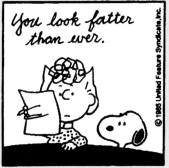

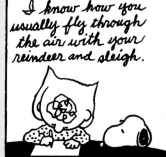

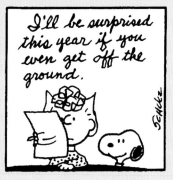

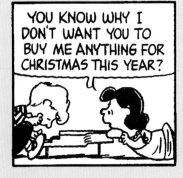

YOU KNOW WHY I DON'T WANT YOU TO BUY ME ANYTHING FOR CHRISTMAS THIS YEAR?
BECAUSE I KNOW YOU HATE ME!
© 1985 United Feature Syndicate, Inc.
12-5
I'VE NEVER SAID I HATE YOU...
THEN BUY ME SOMETHING!!

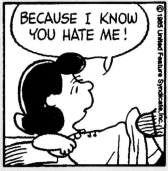

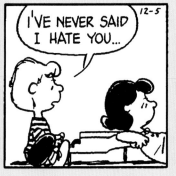

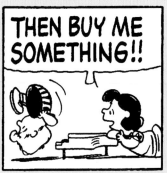

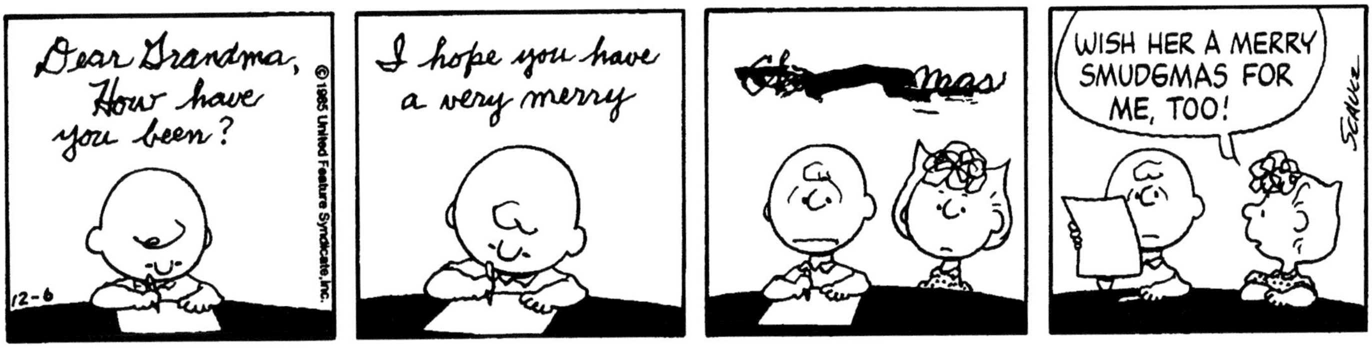
Dear Grandma,
How have you been?
© 1985 United Feature Syndicate, Inc.
12-6
I hope you have a very merry
mas
WISH HER A MERRY SMUDGMAS FOR ME, TOO!
SCHULZ

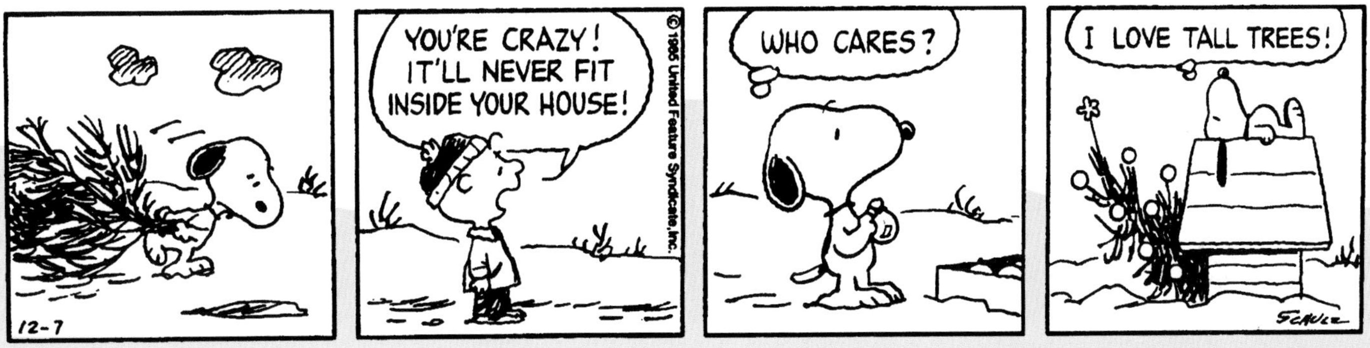
12-7
YOU'RE CRAZY! IT'LL NEVER FIT INSIDE YOUR HOUSE!
© 1985 United Feature Syndicate, Inc.
WHO CARES?
I LOVE TALL TREES!
SCHULZ

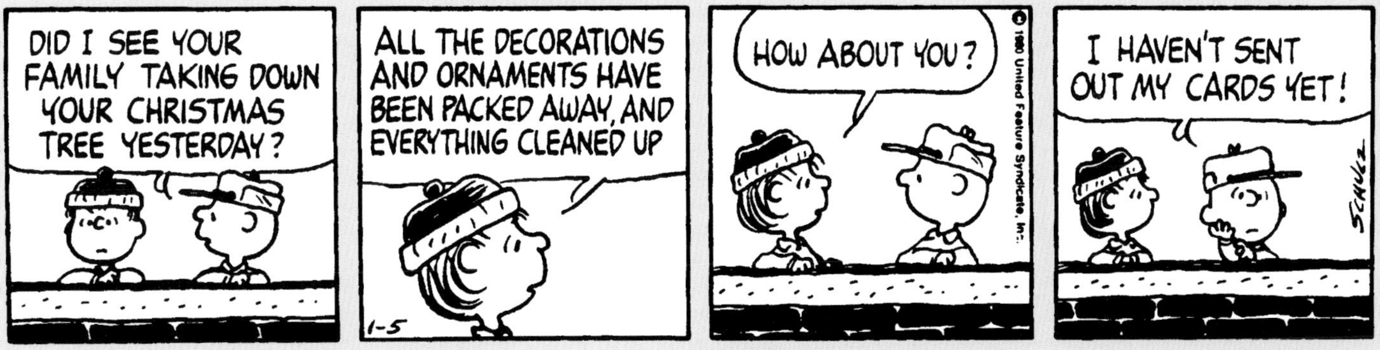
DID I SEE YOUR FAMILY TAKING DOWN YOUR CHRISTMAS TREE YESTERDAY?
ALL THE DECORATIONS AND ORNAMENTS HAVE BEEN PACKED AWAY, AND EVERYTHING CLEANED UP
1-5
HOW ABOUT YOU?
© 1986 United Feature Syndicate, Inc.
I HAVEN'T SENT OUT MY CARDS YET!
SCHULZ

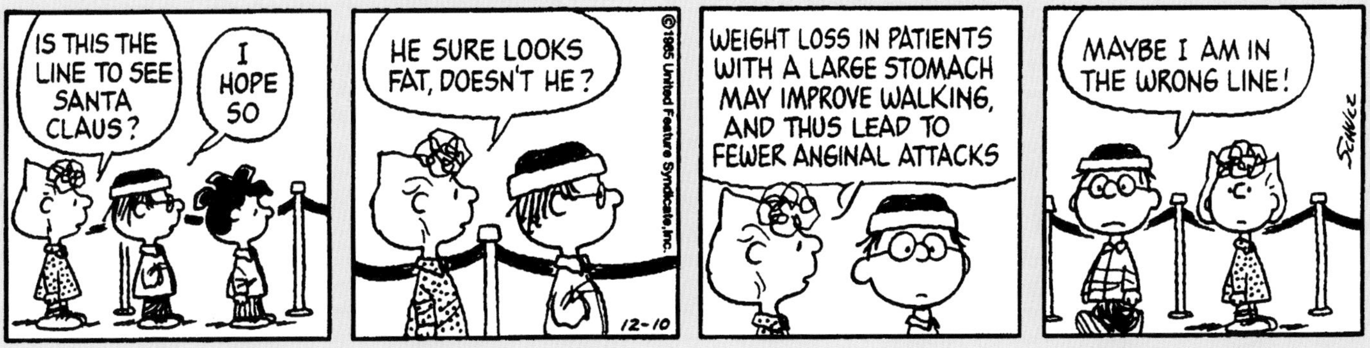
IS THIS THE LINE TO SEE SANTA CLAUS?
I HOPE SO
HE SURE LOOKS FAT, DOESN'T HE?
© 1985 United Feature Syndicate, Inc.
12-10
WEIGHT LOSS IN PATIENTS WITH A LARGE STOMACH MAY IMPROVE WALKING, AND THUS LEAD TO FEWER ANGINAL ATTACKS
MAYBE I AM IN THE WRONG LINE!
SCHULZ

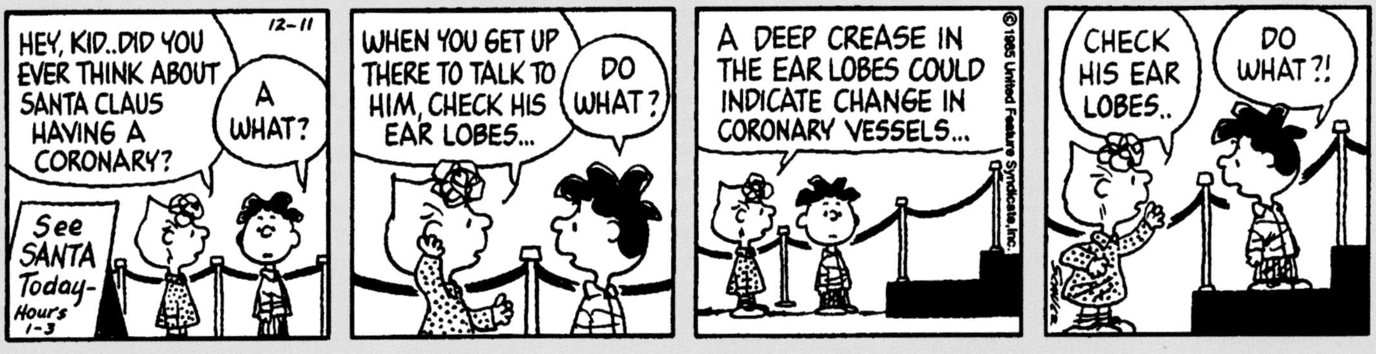
12-11
HEY, KID..DID YOU EVER THINK ABOUT SANTA CLAUS HAVING A CORONARY?
A WHAT?
See SANTA Today- Hours 1-3
WHEN YOU GET UP THERE TO TALK TO HIM, CHECK HIS EAR LOBES...
DO WHAT?
A DEEP CREASE IN THE EAR LOBES COULD INDICATE CHANGE IN CORONARY VESSELS...
© 1985 United Feature Syndicate, Inc.
CHECK HIS EAR LOBES..
DO WHAT?!
SCHULZ

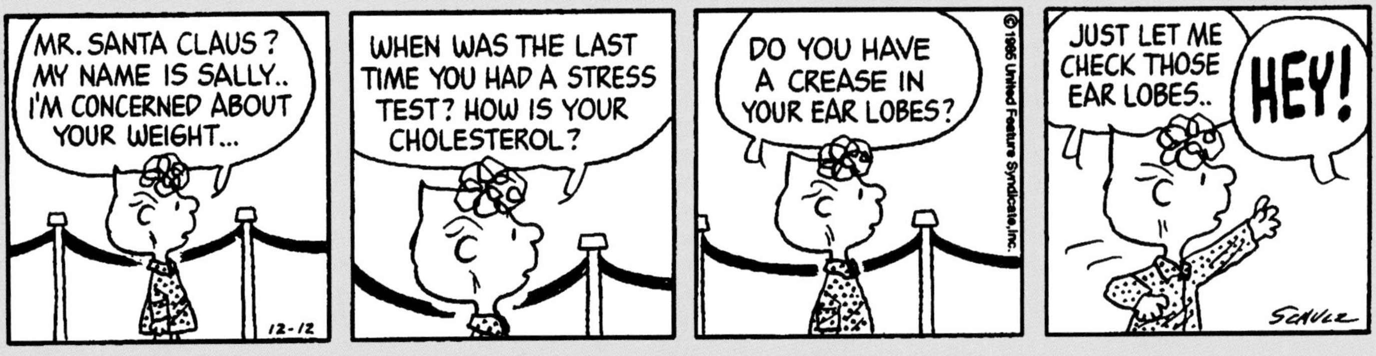
MR. SANTA CLAUS? MY NAME IS SALLY.. I'M CONCERNED ABOUT YOUR WEIGHT...
12-12
WHEN WAS THE LAST TIME YOU HAD A STRESS TEST? HOW IS YOUR CHOLESTEROL?
DO YOU HAVE A CREASE IN YOUR EAR LOBES?
© 1985 United Feature Syndicate, Inc.
JUST LET ME CHECK THOSE EAR LOBES..
HEY!
SCHULZ

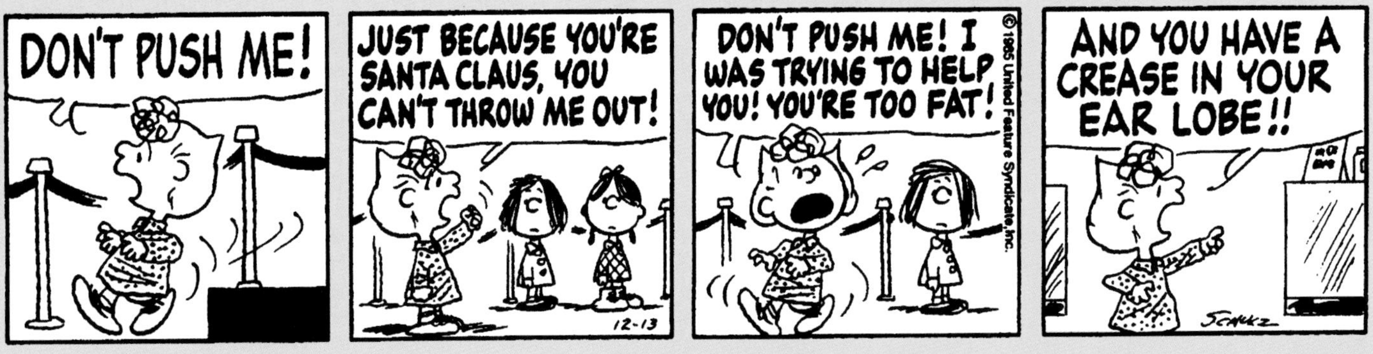
DON'T PUSH ME!
JUST BECAUSE YOU'RE SANTA CLAUS, YOU CAN'T THROW ME OUT!
12-13
DON'T PUSH ME! I WAS TRYING TO HELP YOU! YOU'RE TOO FAT!
© 1985 United Feature Syndicate, Inc.
AND YOU HAVE A CREASE IN YOUR EAR LOBE!!
SCHULZ

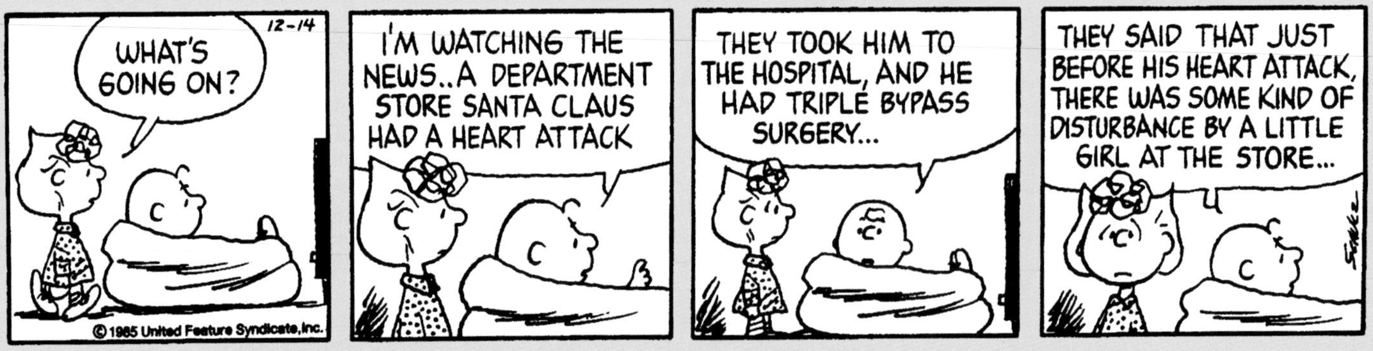
12-14
WHAT'S GOING ON?
© 1985 United Feature Syndicate, Inc.
I'M WATCHING THE NEWS..A DEPARTMENT STORE SANTA CLAUS HAD A HEART ATTACK
THEY TOOK HIM TO THE HOSPITAL, AND HE HAD TRIPLE BYPASS SURGERY...
THEY SAID THAT JUST BEFORE HIS HEART ATTACK, THERE WAS SOME KIND OF DISTURBANCE BY A LITTLE GIRL AT THE STORE...
SCHULZ

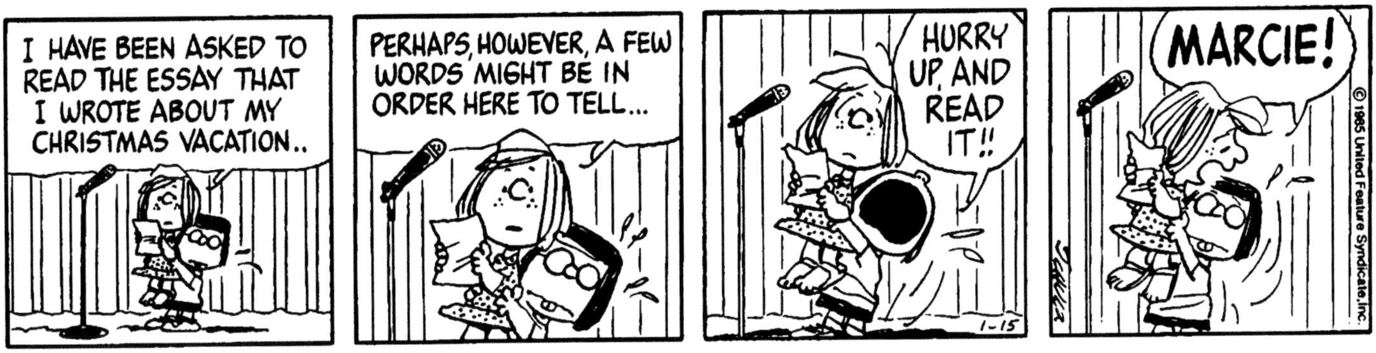
I HAVE BEEN ASKED TO READ THE ESSAY THAT I WROTE ABOUT MY CHRISTMAS VACATION..
PERHAPS, HOWEVER, A FEW WORDS MIGHT BE IN ORDER HERE TO TELL...
HURRY UP, AND READ IT!!
1-15
SCHULZ
MARCIE!
© 1985 United Feature Syndicate, Inc.

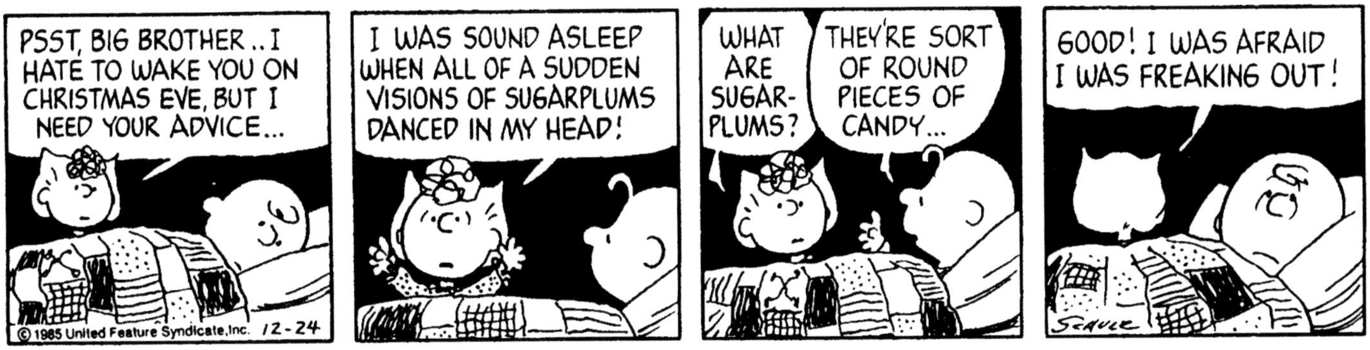
PSST, BIG BROTHER.. I HATE TO WAKE YOU ON CHRISTMAS EVE, BUT I NEED YOUR ADVICE...
© 1985 United Feature Syndicate, Inc.
12-24
I WAS SOUND ASLEEP WHEN ALL OF A SUDDEN VISIONS OF SUGARPLUMS DANCED IN MY HEAD!
WHAT ARE SUGAR-PLUMS?
THEY'RE SORT OF ROUND PIECES OF CANDY...
GOOD! I WAS AFRAID I WAS FREAKING OUT!
SCHULZ

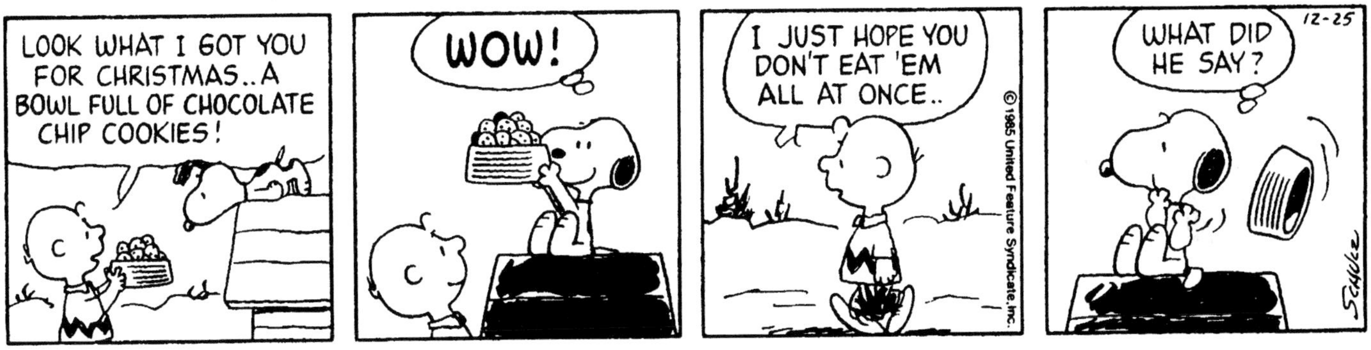
LOOK WHAT I GOT YOU FOR CHRISTMAS.. A BOWL FULL OF CHOCOLATE CHIP COOKIES!
WOW!
I JUST HOPE YOU DON'T EAT 'EM ALL AT ONCE..
© 1985 United Feature Syndicate, Inc.
12-25
WHAT DID HE SAY?
SCHULZ

Dear Snooty Claus,

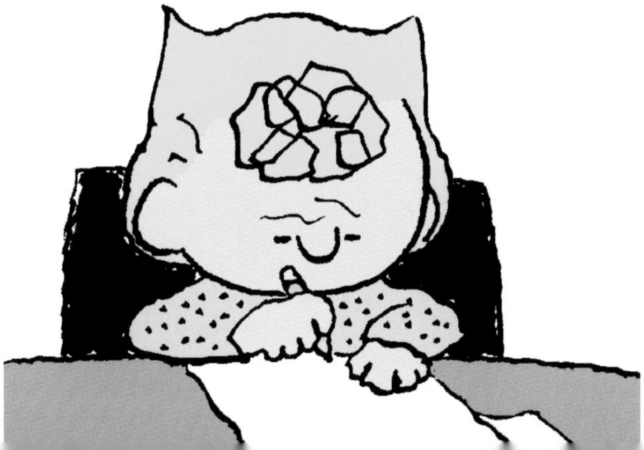

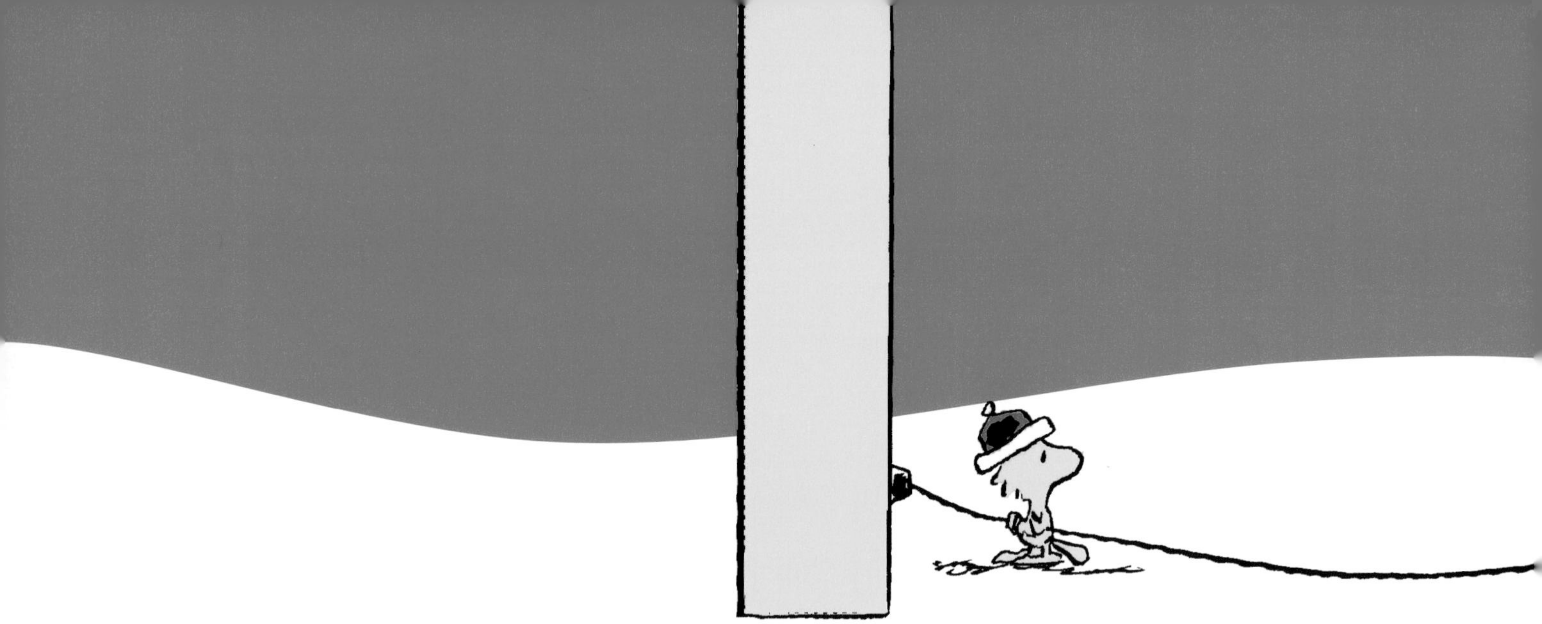

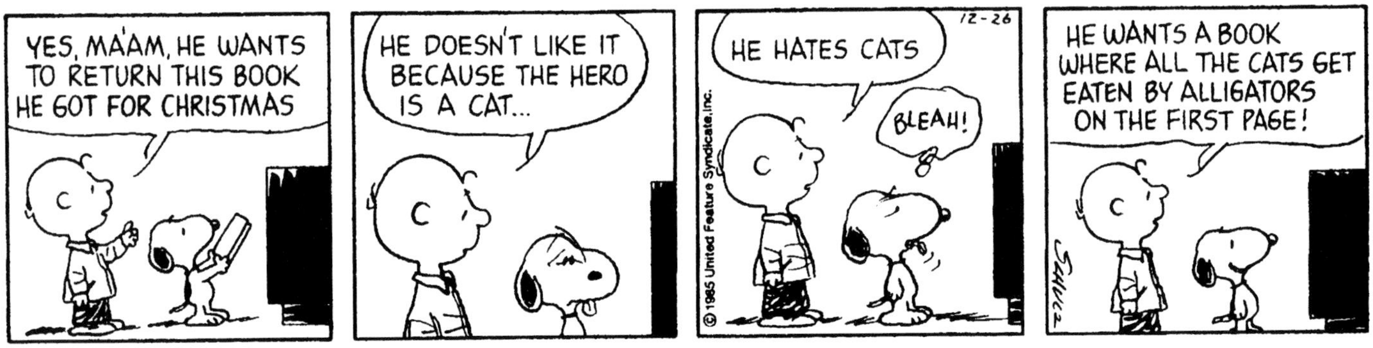
YES, MA'AM, HE WANTS TO RETURN THIS BOOK HE GOT FOR CHRISTMAS
HE DOESN'T LIKE IT BECAUSE THE HERO IS A CAT...
12-26
HE HATES CATS
BLEAH!
© 1985 United Feature Syndicate, Inc.
HE WANTS A BOOK WHERE ALL THE CATS GET EATEN BY ALLIGATORS ON THE FIRST PAGE!
SCHULZ

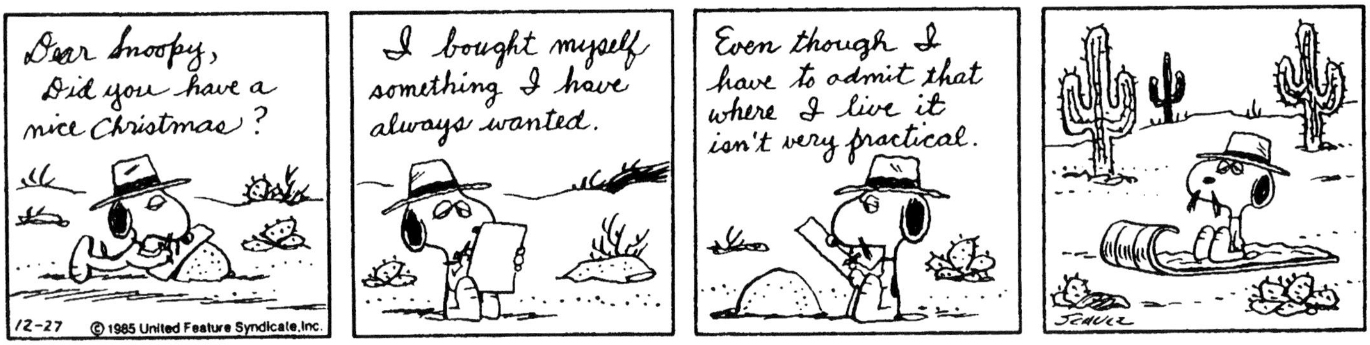
Dear Snoopy,
Did you have a nice Christmas?
12-27
© 1985 United Feature Syndicate, Inc.
I bought myself something I have always wanted.
Even though I have to admit that where I live it isn't very practical.
SCHULZ

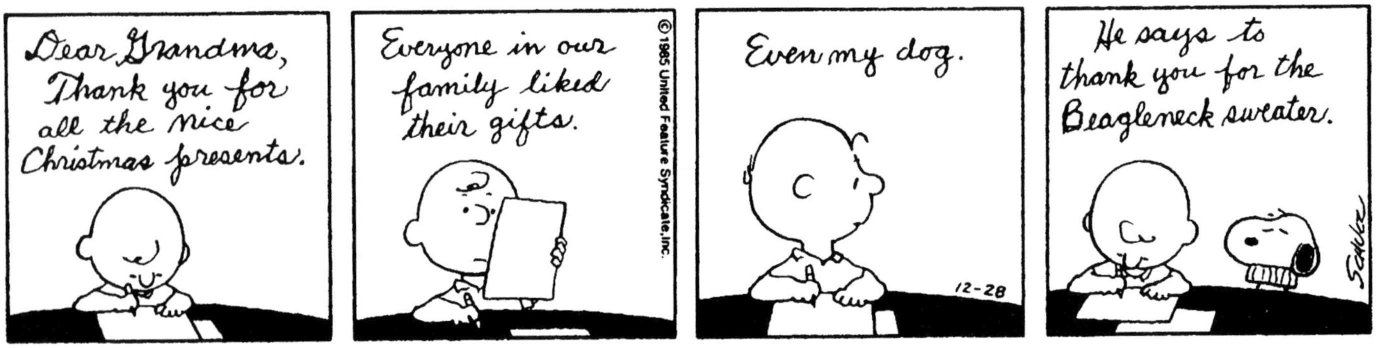
Dear Grandma,
Thank you for all the nice Christmas presents.
Everyone in our family liked their gifts.
© 1985 United Feature Syndicate, Inc.
Even my dog.
12-28
He says to thank you for the Beagleneck sweater.
SCHULZ

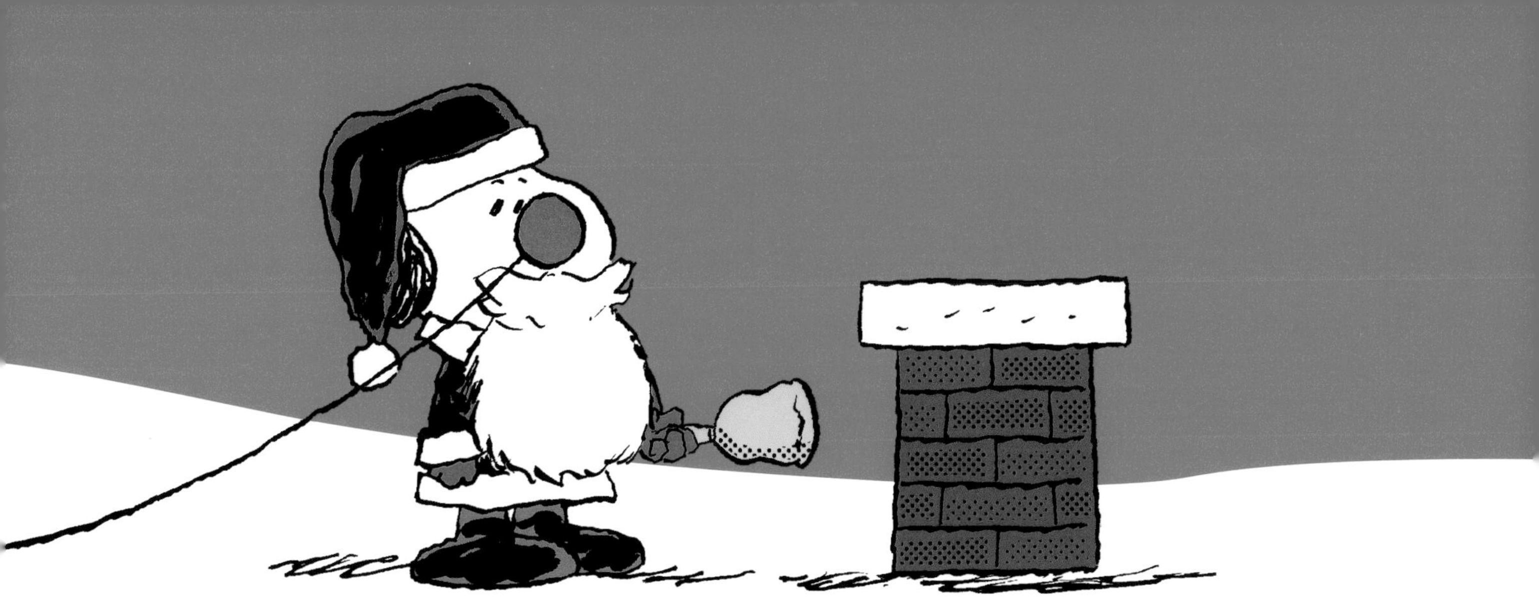

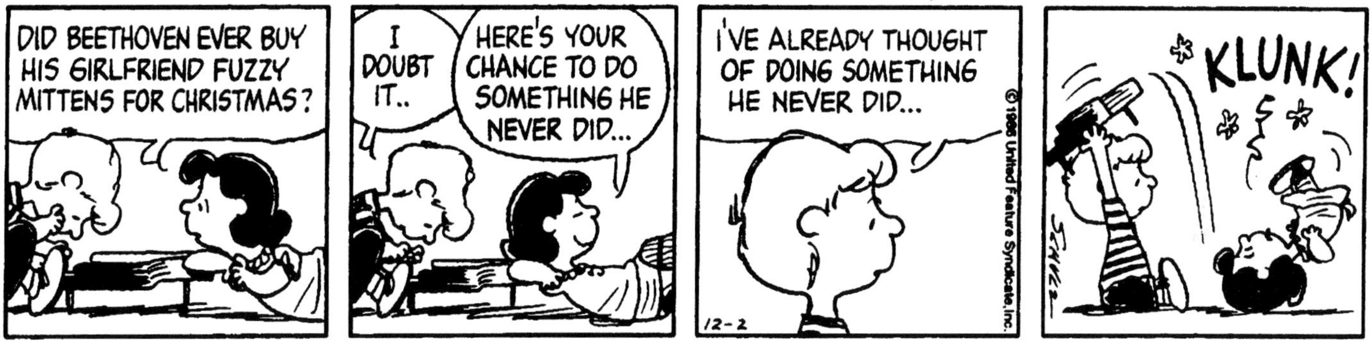
DID BEETHOVEN EVER BUY HIS GIRLFRIEND FUZZY MITTENS FOR CHRISTMAS?
I DOUBT IT..
HERE'S YOUR CHANCE TO DO SOMETHING HE NEVER DID...
I'VE ALREADY THOUGHT OF DOING SOMETHING HE NEVER DID...
KLUNK!
12-2
© 1986 United Feature Syndicate, Inc.
SCHULZ

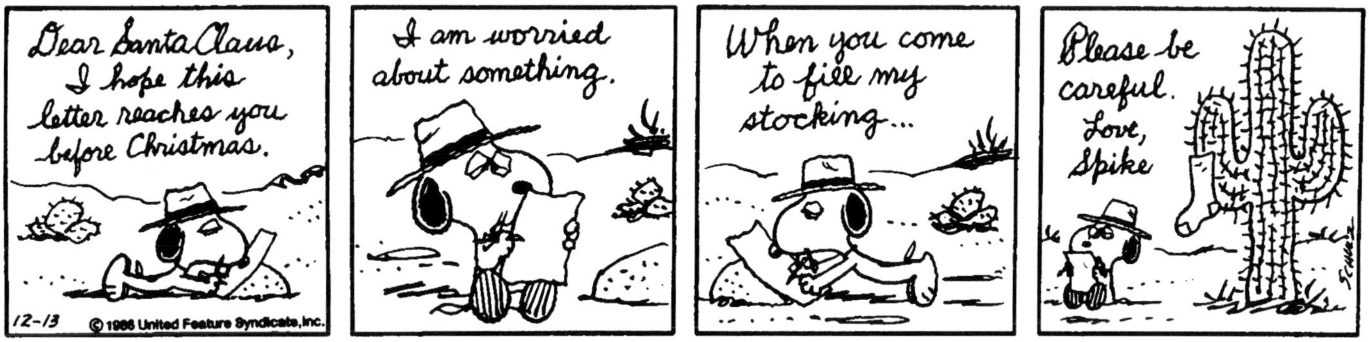
Dear Santa Claus, I hope this letter reaches you before Christmas.
I am worried about something.
When you come to fill my stocking...
Please be careful. Love, Spike
12-13
© 1986 United Feature Syndicate, Inc.
SCHULZ

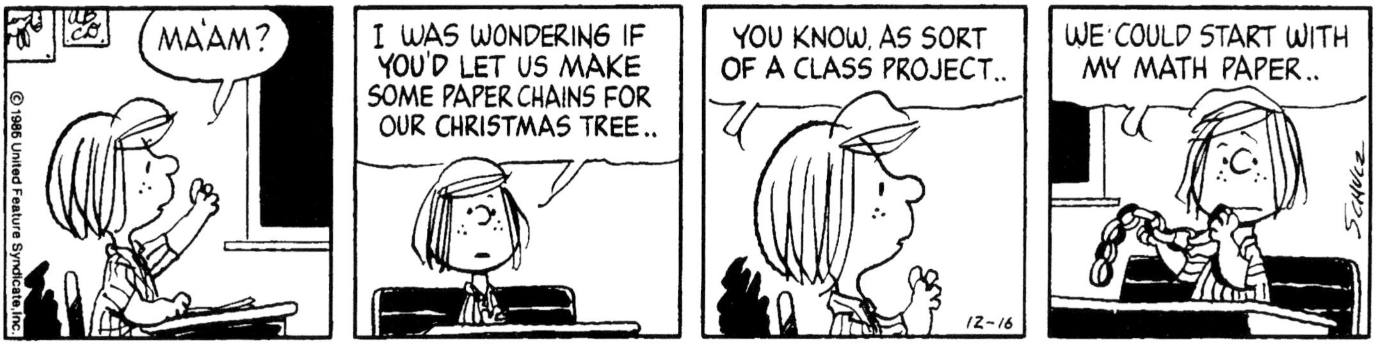
MA'AM?
I WAS WONDERING IF YOU'D LET US MAKE SOME PAPER CHAINS FOR OUR CHRISTMAS TREE..
YOU KNOW, AS SORT OF A CLASS PROJECT..
WE COULD START WITH MY MATH PAPER..
12-16
© 1986 United Feature Syndicate, Inc.
SCHULZ

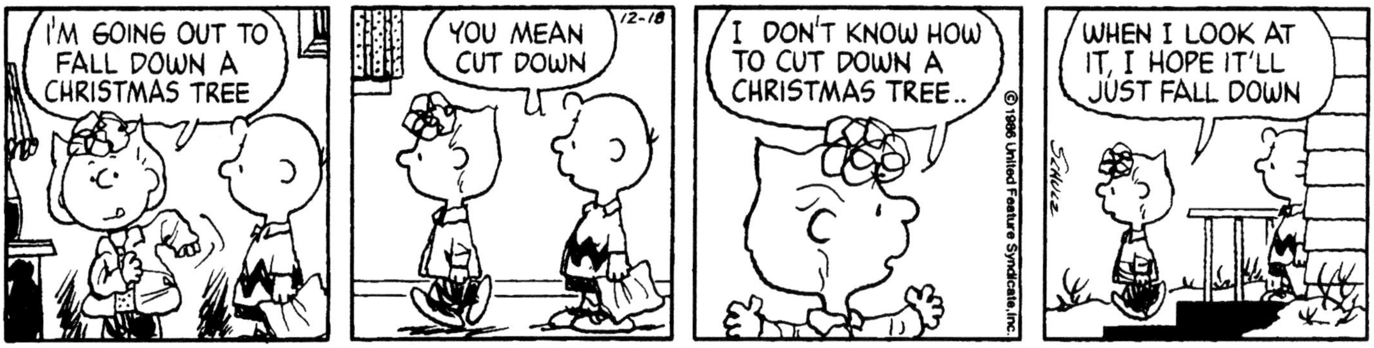
I'M GOING OUT TO FALL DOWN A CHRISTMAS TREE
12-18
YOU MEAN CUT DOWN
I DON'T KNOW HOW TO CUT DOWN A CHRISTMAS TREE..
© 1986 United Feature Syndicate, Inc.
WHEN I LOOK AT IT, I HOPE IT'LL JUST FALL DOWN
SCHULZ

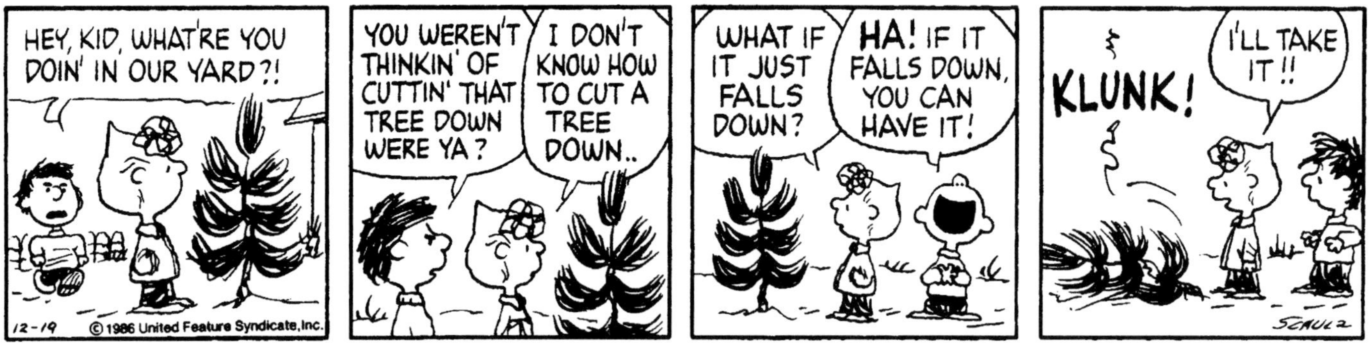
HEY, KID, WHAT'RE YOU DOIN' IN OUR YARD?!
12-19 © 1986 United Feature Syndicate, Inc.
YOU WEREN'T THINKIN' OF CUTTIN' THAT TREE DOWN WERE YA?
I DON'T KNOW HOW TO CUT A TREE DOWN..
WHAT IF IT JUST FALLS DOWN?
HA! IF IT FALLS DOWN, YOU CAN HAVE IT!
KLUNK!
I'LL TAKE IT!!
SCHULZ

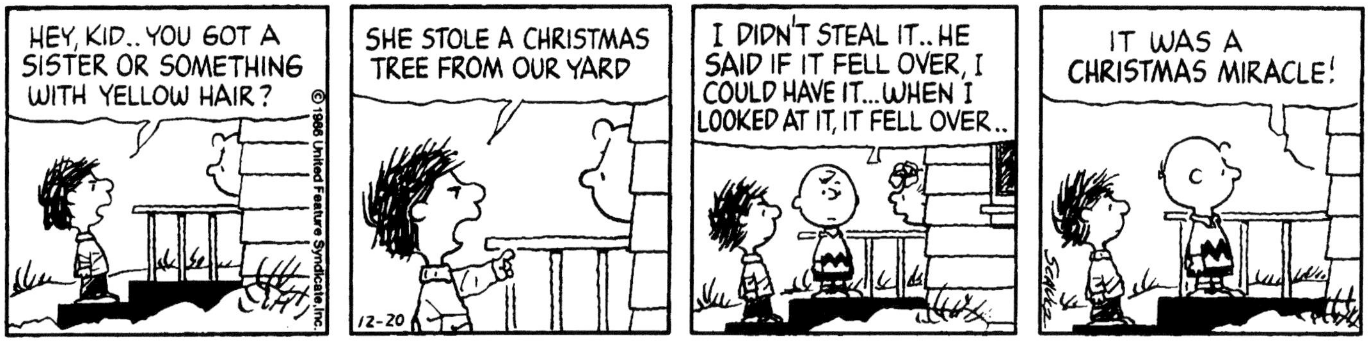
HEY, KID.. YOU GOT A SISTER OR SOMETHING WITH YELLOW HAIR?
© 1986 United Feature Syndicate, Inc.
SHE STOLE A CHRISTMAS TREE FROM OUR YARD
12-20
I DIDN'T STEAL IT.. HE SAID IF IT FELL OVER, I COULD HAVE IT... WHEN I LOOKED AT IT, IT FELL OVER..
IT WAS A CHRISTMAS MIRACLE!
SCHULZ

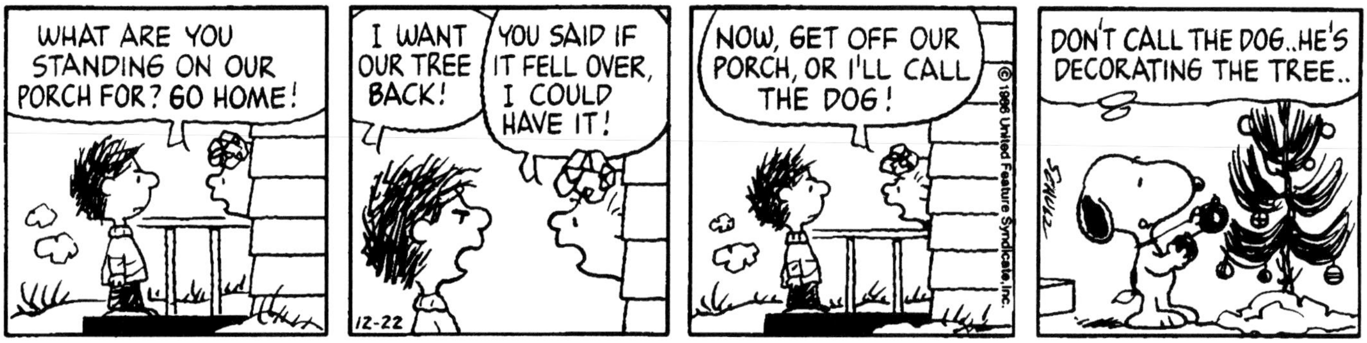
WHAT ARE YOU STANDING ON OUR PORCH FOR? GO HOME!
I WANT OUR TREE BACK!
YOU SAID IF IT FELL OVER, I COULD HAVE IT!
12-22
NOW, GET OFF OUR PORCH, OR I'LL CALL THE DOG!
© 1986 United Feature Syndicate, Inc.
DON'T CALL THE DOG..HE'S DECORATING THE TREE..
SCHULZ

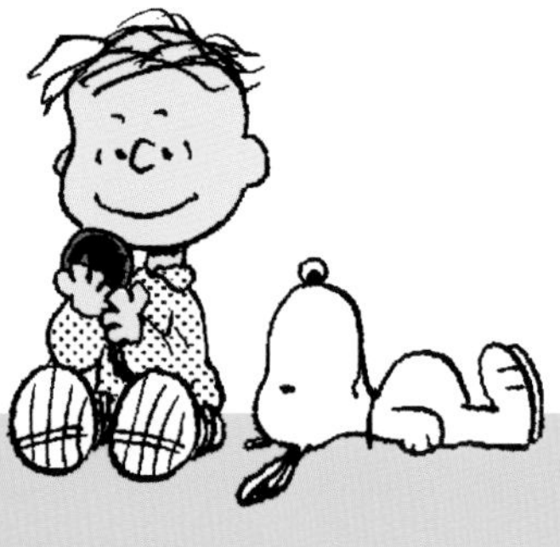

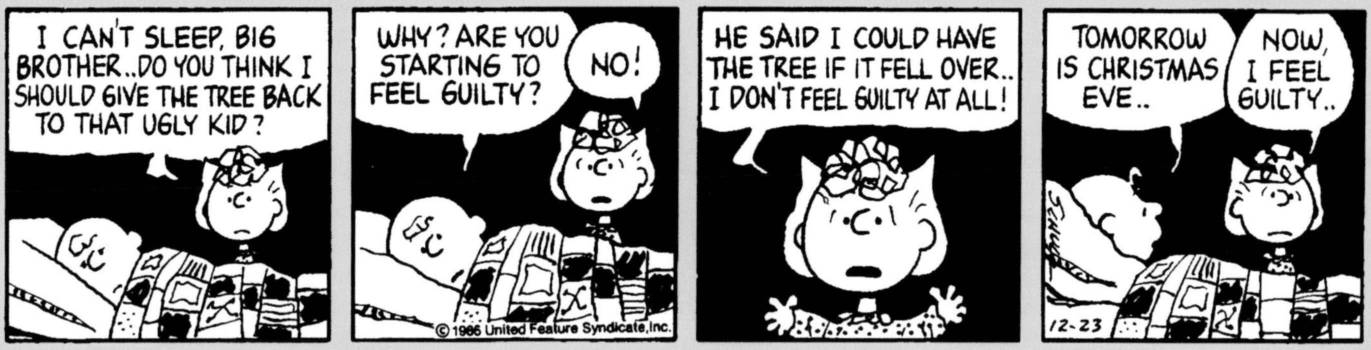
I CAN'T SLEEP, BIG BROTHER..DO YOU THINK I SHOULD GIVE THE TREE BACK TO THAT UGLY KID?
WHY? ARE YOU STARTING TO FEEL GUILTY?
NO!
© 1986 United Feature Syndicate, Inc.
HE SAID I COULD HAVE THE TREE IF IT FELL OVER.. I DON'T FEEL GUILTY AT ALL!
TOMORROW IS CHRISTMAS EVE..
NOW, I FEEL GUILTY..
12-23

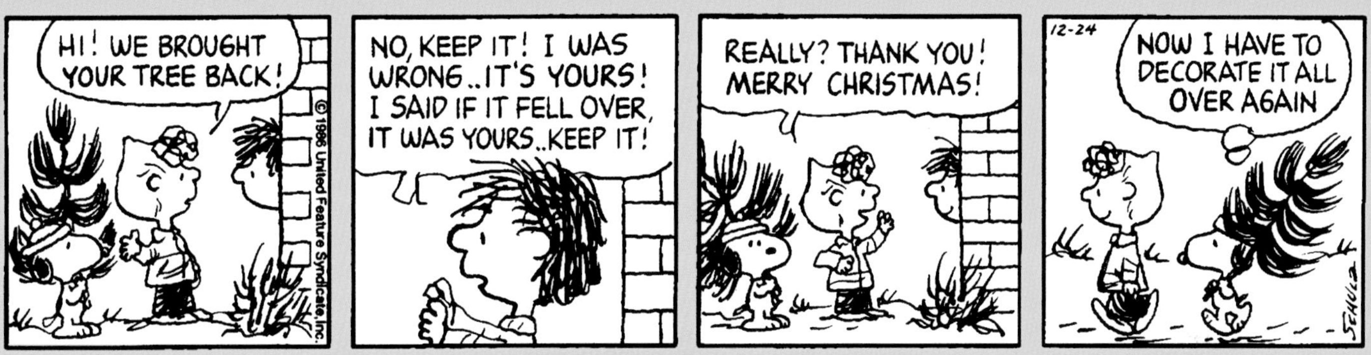
HI! WE BROUGHT YOUR TREE BACK!
© 1986 United Feature Syndicate, Inc.
NO, KEEP IT! I WAS WRONG..IT'S YOURS! I SAID IF IT FELL OVER, IT WAS YOURS..KEEP IT!
REALLY? THANK YOU! MERRY CHRISTMAS!
12-24
NOW I HAVE TO DECORATE IT ALL OVER AGAIN

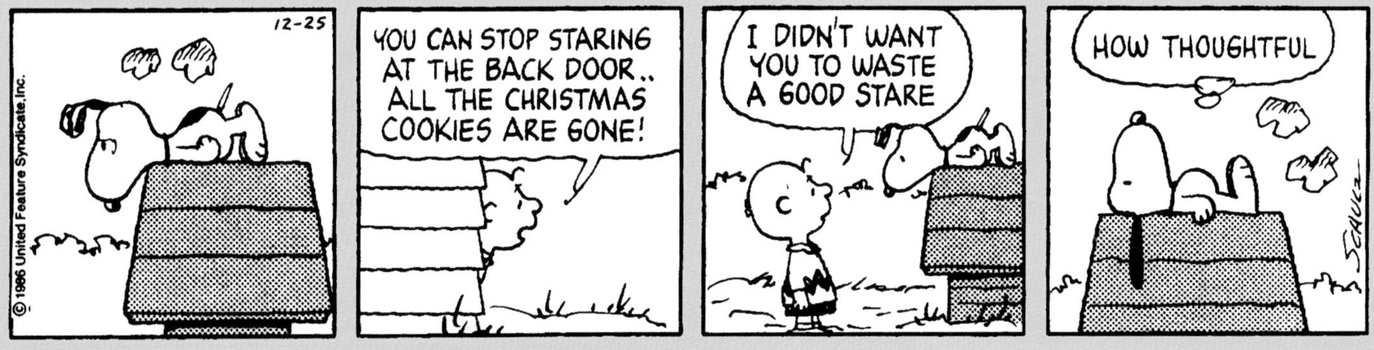
12-25
© 1986 United Feature Syndicate, Inc.
YOU CAN STOP STARING AT THE BACK DOOR.. ALL THE CHRISTMAS COOKIES ARE GONE!
I DIDN'T WANT YOU TO WASTE A GOOD STARE
HOW THOUGHTFUL

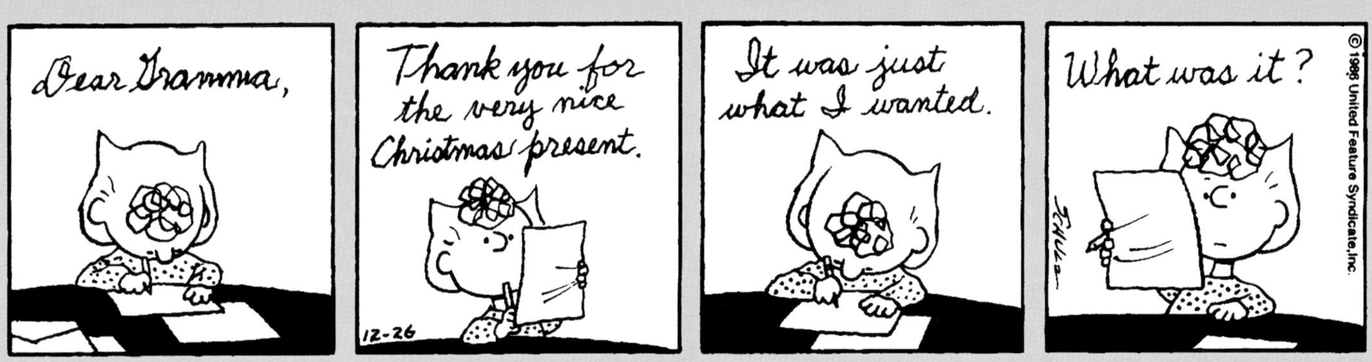
Dear Gramma,
Thank you for the very nice Christmas present.
12-26
It was just what I wanted.
What was it?
© 1986 United Feature Syndicate, Inc.

I'M MAKING OUT MY CHRISTMAS LIST..
HOW DO YOU SPELL YOUR NAME?
© 1987 United Feature Syndicate, Inc.
12-10
I'M YOUR BROTHER, AND YOU DON'T EVEN KNOW HOW TO SPELL MY NAME?!
I'LL PUT DOWN "SAM"... I KNOW HOW TO SPELL THAT..

I'M GONNA SCRATCH ANNIE OFF MY CHRISTMAS CARD LIST
ANNIE DIDN'T SEND ME A CARD LAST YEAR SO WHY SHOULD I SEND HER A CARD THIS YEAR?
YOU DON'T KNOW ANYONE NAMED ANNIE..
© 1987 United Feature Syndicate, Inc.
12-12
THAT'S NO EXCUSE!

I FEEL DIFFERENT THIS YEAR..

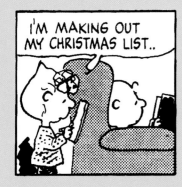

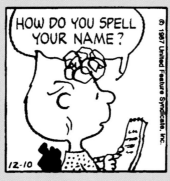

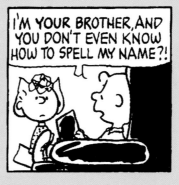

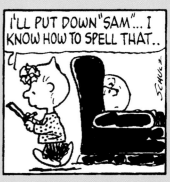

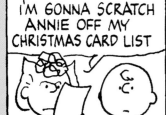

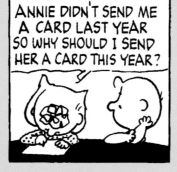

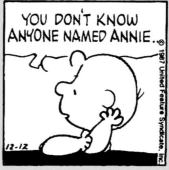

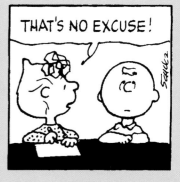

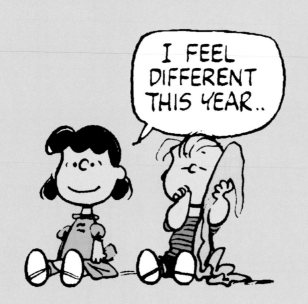

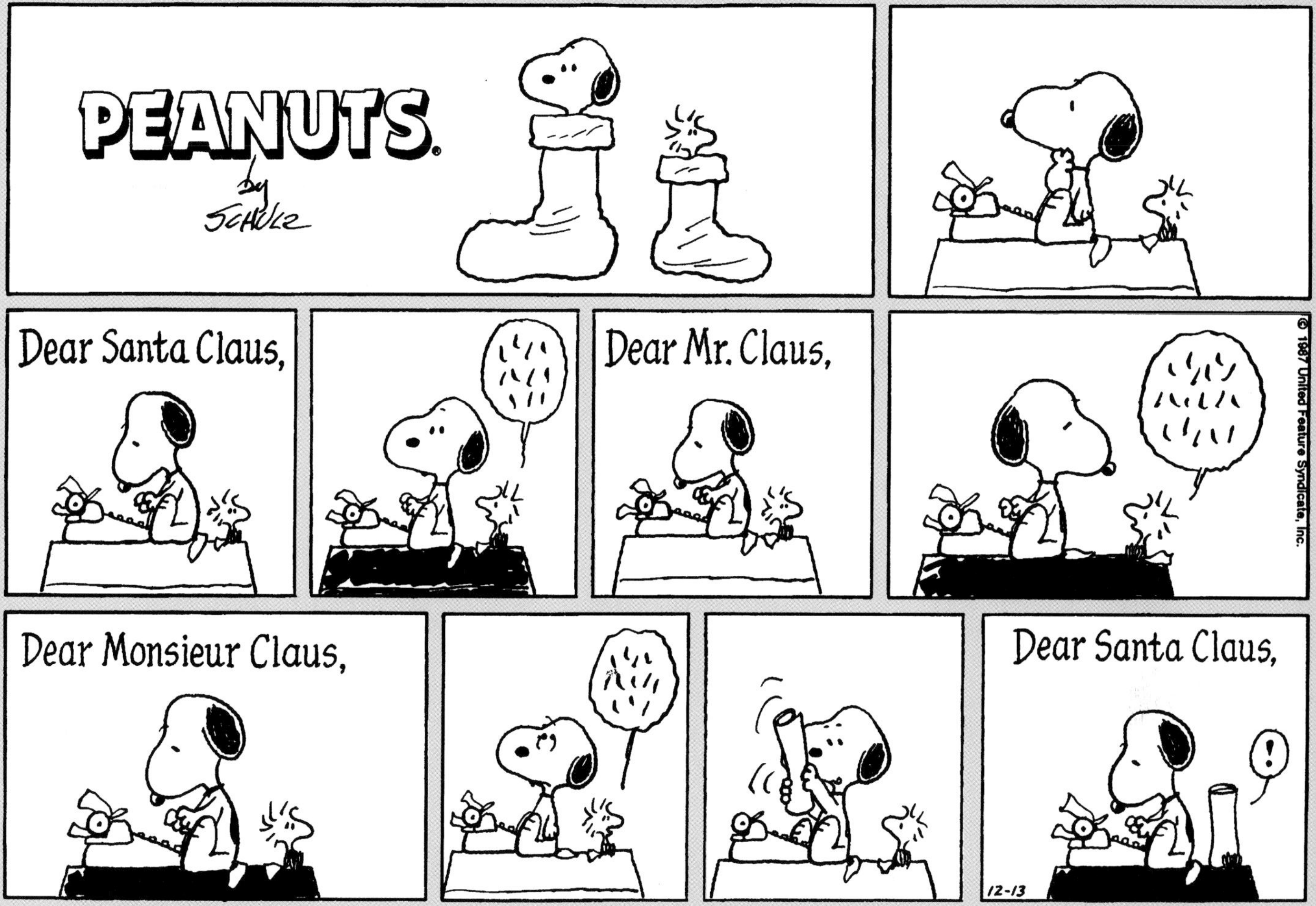
PEANUTS
by SCHULZ
Dear Santa Claus,
Dear Mr. Claus,
© 1987 United Feature Syndicate, Inc.
Dear Monsieur Claus,
Dear Santa Claus,
!
12-13

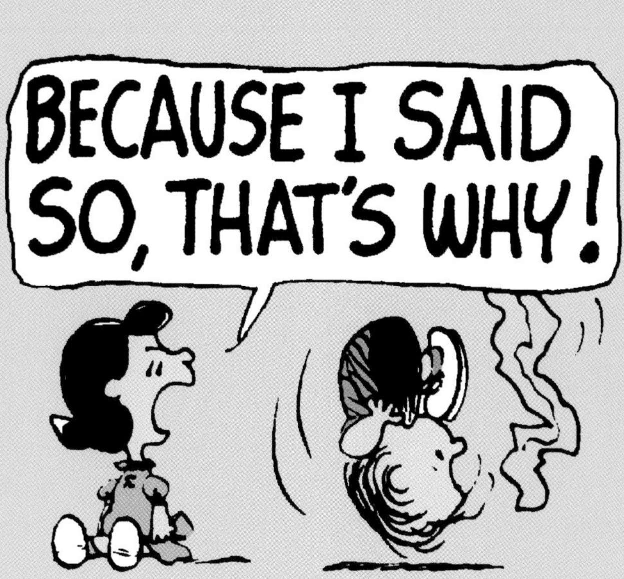
BECAUSE I SAID SO, THAT'S WHY!

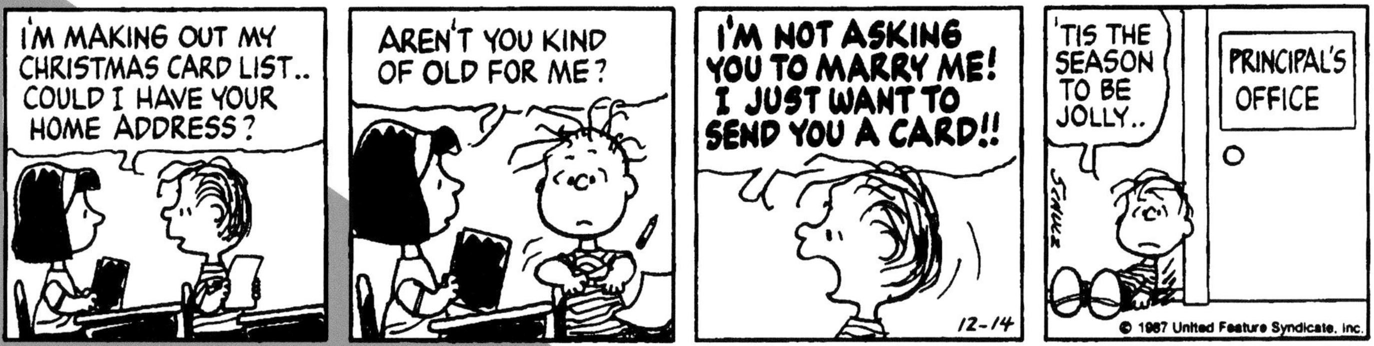
I'M MAKING OUT MY CHRISTMAS CARD LIST.. COULD I HAVE YOUR HOME ADDRESS?
AREN'T YOU KIND OF OLD FOR ME?
I'M NOT ASKING YOU TO MARRY ME! I JUST WANT TO SEND YOU A CARD!!
12-14
'TIS THE SEASON TO BE JOLLY..
PRINCIPAL'S OFFICE
SCHULZ
© 1987 United Feature Syndicate, Inc.

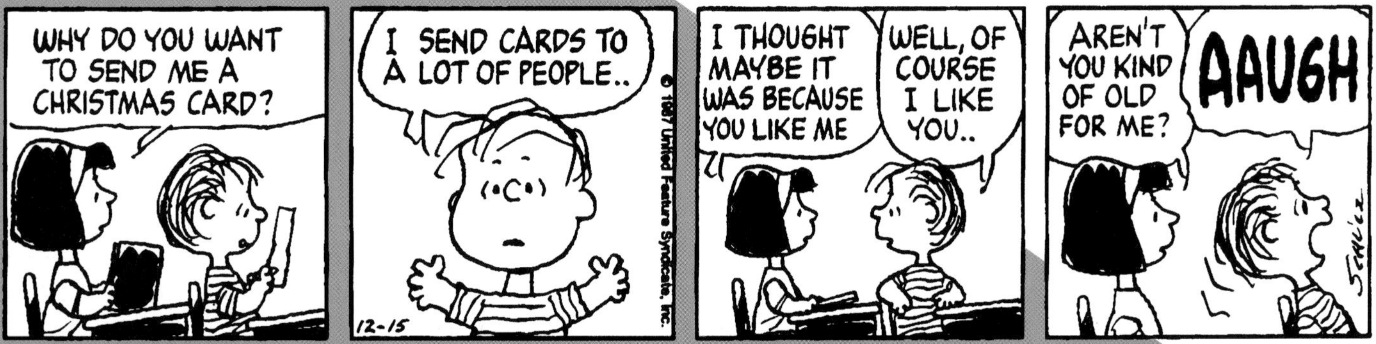
WHY DO YOU WANT TO SEND ME A CHRISTMAS CARD?
I SEND CARDS TO A LOT OF PEOPLE..
© 1987 United Feature Syndicate, Inc.
12-15
I THOUGHT MAYBE IT WAS BECAUSE YOU LIKE ME
WELL, OF COURSE I LIKE YOU..
AREN'T YOU KIND OF OLD FOR ME?
AAUGH
SCHULZ

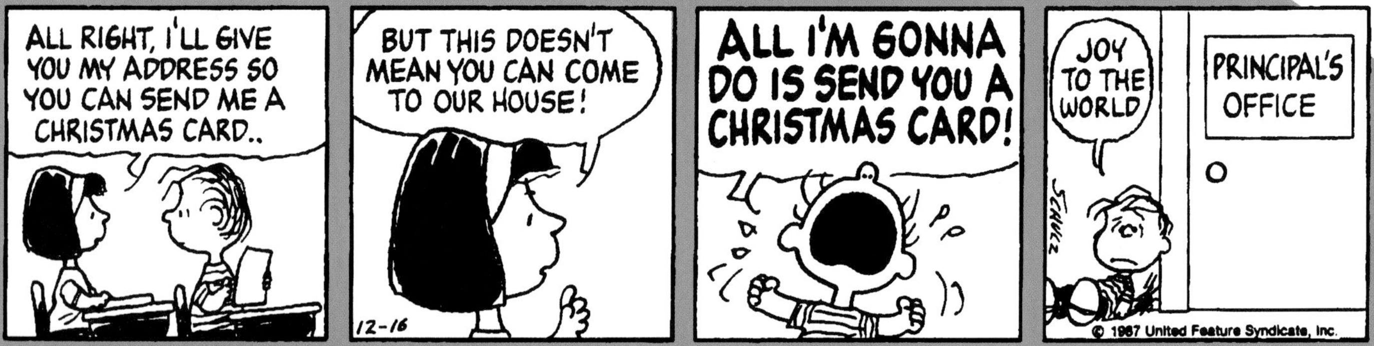
ALL RIGHT, I'LL GIVE YOU MY ADDRESS SO YOU CAN SEND ME A CHRISTMAS CARD..
BUT THIS DOESN'T MEAN YOU CAN COME TO OUR HOUSE!
12-16
ALL I'M GONNA DO IS SEND YOU A CHRISTMAS CARD!
JOY TO THE WORLD
PRINCIPAL'S OFFICE
SCHULZ
© 1987 United Feature Syndicate, Inc.

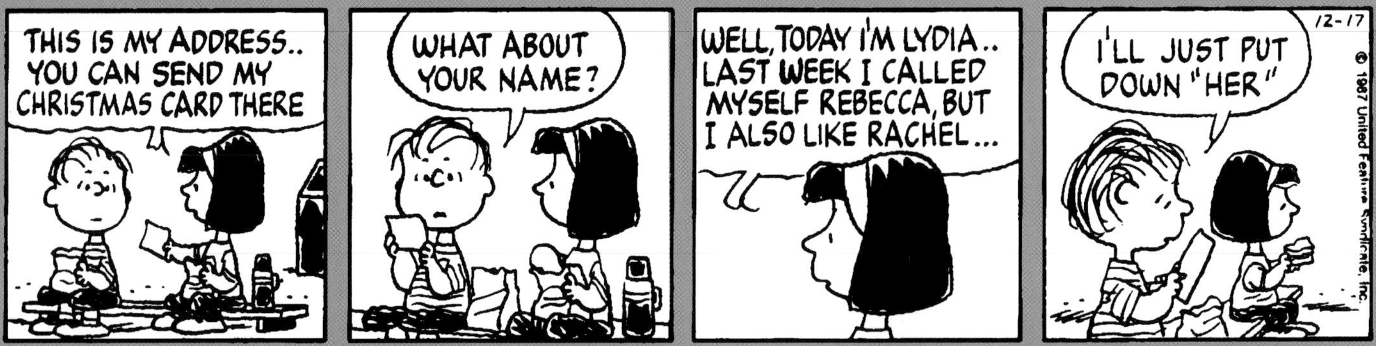
THIS IS MY ADDRESS.. YOU CAN SEND MY CHRISTMAS CARD THERE
WHAT ABOUT YOUR NAME?
WELL, TODAY I'M LYDIA.. LAST WEEK I CALLED MYSELF REBECCA, BUT I ALSO LIKE RACHEL...
12-17
I'LL JUST PUT DOWN "HER"
© 1987 United Feature Syndicate, Inc.

Dear Grandma,
How have you been?
By the way, thanks for
the Christmas present.

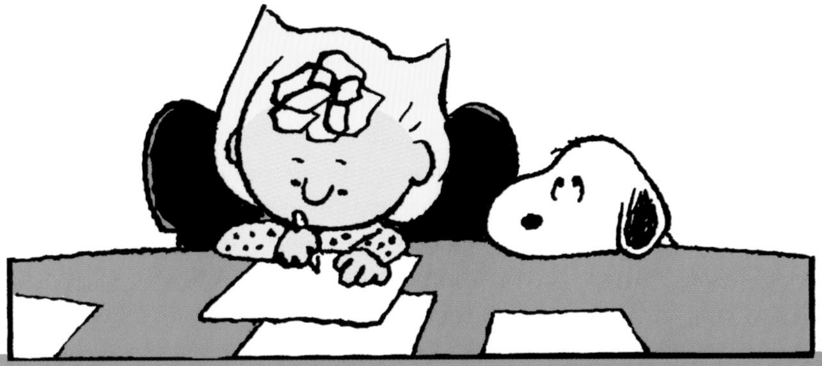

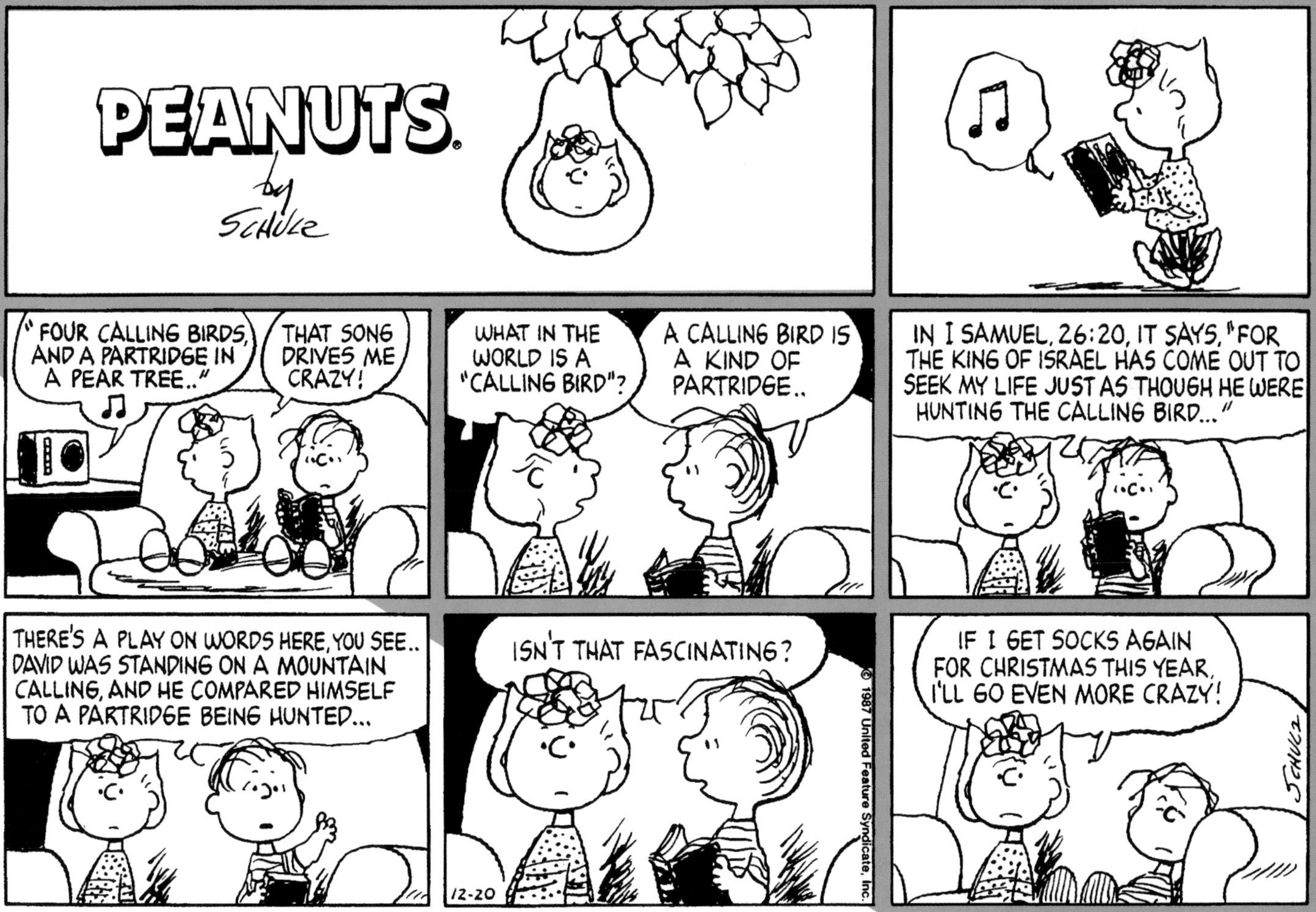
PEANUTS
by SCHULZ
"FOUR CALLING BIRDS, AND A PARTRIDGE IN A PEAR TREE.."
THAT SONG DRIVES ME CRAZY!
WHAT IN THE WORLD IS A "CALLING BIRD"?
A CALLING BIRD IS A KIND OF PARTRIDGE..
IN I SAMUEL, 26:20, IT SAYS, "FOR THE KING OF ISRAEL HAS COME OUT TO SEEK MY LIFE JUST AS THOUGH HE WERE HUNTING THE CALLING BIRD..."
THERE'S A PLAY ON WORDS HERE, YOU SEE.. DAVID WAS STANDING ON A MOUNTAIN CALLING, AND HE COMPARED HIMSELF TO A PARTRIDGE BEING HUNTED...
ISN'T THAT FASCINATING?
12-20
© 1987 United Feature Syndicate, Inc.
IF I GET SOCKS AGAIN FOR CHRISTMAS THIS YEAR, I'LL GO EVEN MORE CRAZY!
SCHULZ

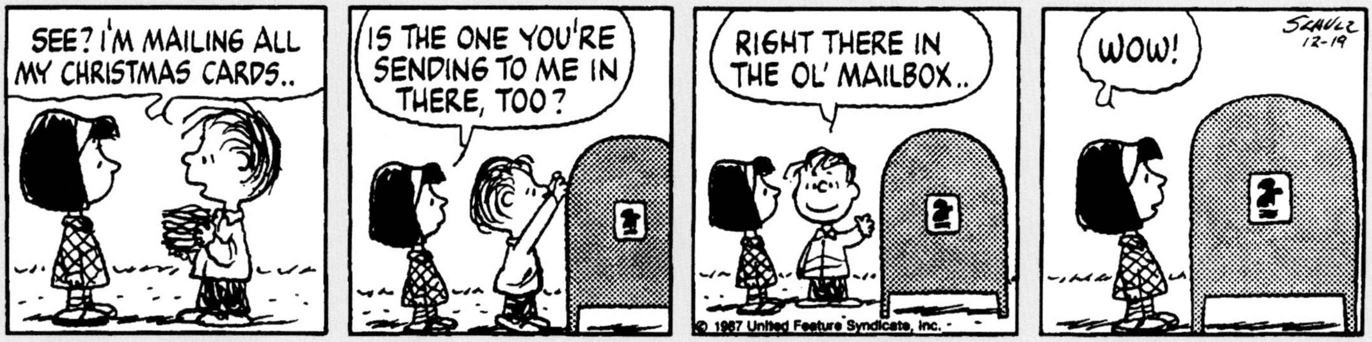
SEE? I'M MAILING ALL MY CHRISTMAS CARDS..
IS THE ONE YOU'RE SENDING TO ME IN THERE, TOO?
RIGHT THERE IN THE OL' MAILBOX..
© 1987 United Feature Syndicate, Inc.
WOW!
12-19

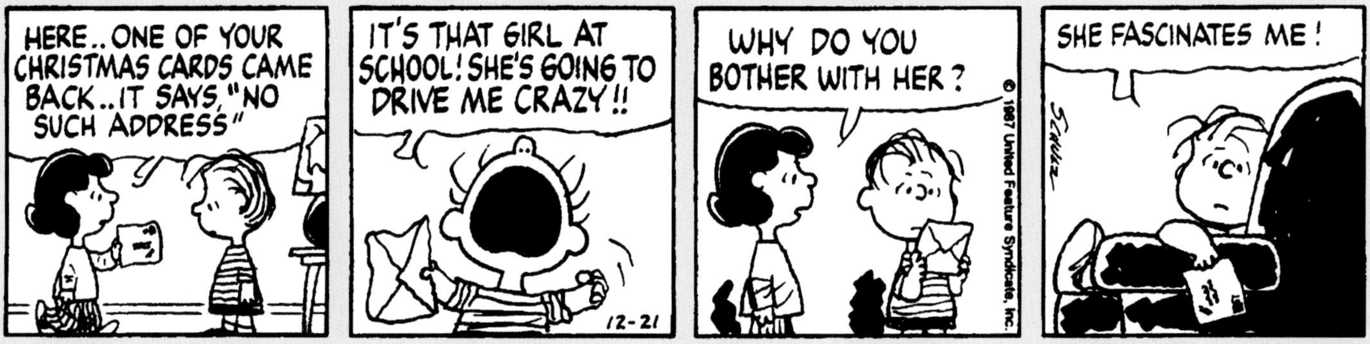
HERE..ONE OF YOUR CHRISTMAS CARDS CAME BACK..IT SAYS, "NO SUCH ADDRESS"
IT'S THAT GIRL AT SCHOOL! SHE'S GOING TO DRIVE ME CRAZY!!
12-21
WHY DO YOU BOTHER WITH HER?
© 1987 United Feature Syndicate, Inc.
SHE FASCINATES ME!

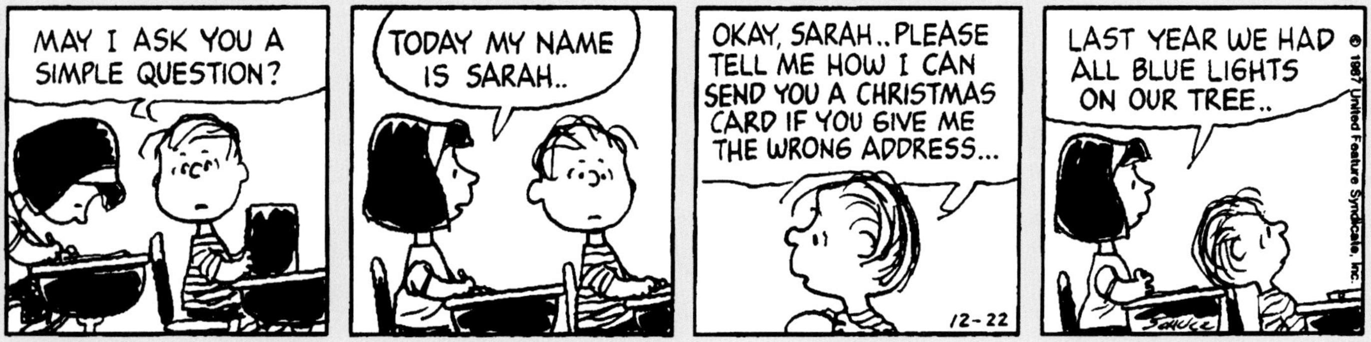
MAY I ASK YOU A SIMPLE QUESTION?
TODAY MY NAME IS SARAH..
OKAY, SARAH..PLEASE TELL ME HOW I CAN SEND YOU A CHRISTMAS CARD IF YOU GIVE ME THE WRONG ADDRESS...
12-22
LAST YEAR WE HAD ALL BLUE LIGHTS ON OUR TREE..
© 1987 United Feature Syndicate, Inc.

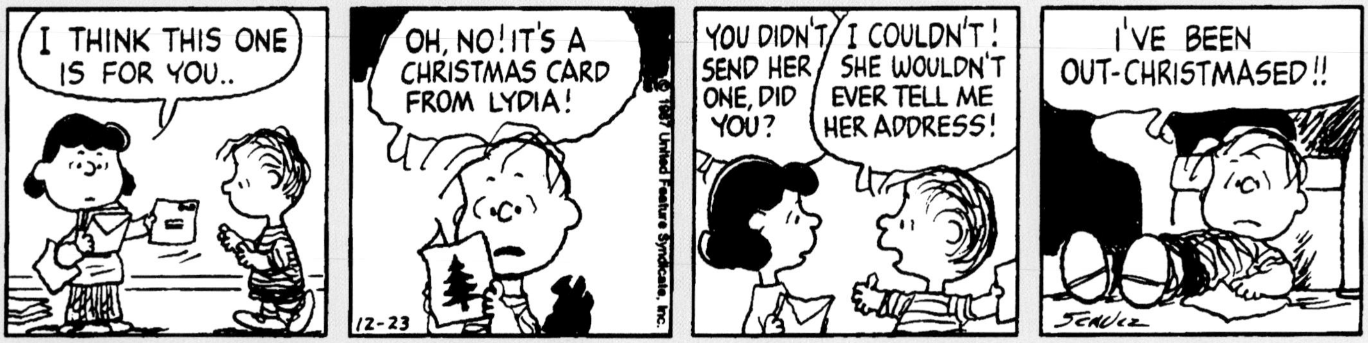
I THINK THIS ONE IS FOR YOU..
OH, NO! IT'S A CHRISTMAS CARD FROM LYDIA!
© 1987 United Feature Syndicate, Inc.
12-23
YOU DIDN'T SEND HER ONE, DID YOU?
I COULDN'T! SHE WOULDN'T EVER TELL ME HER ADDRESS!
I'VE BEEN OUT-CHRISTMASED!!

© 1987 United Feature Syndicate, Inc.
12-25

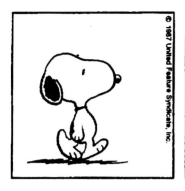

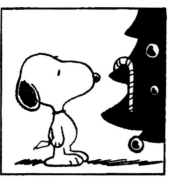

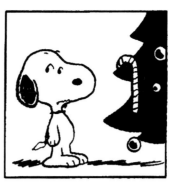

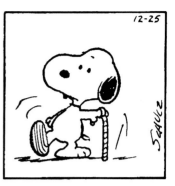

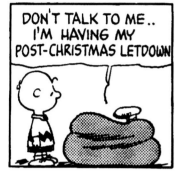

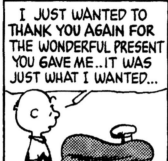

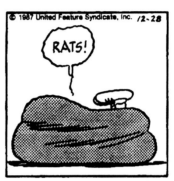

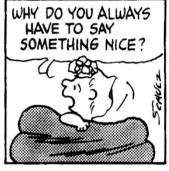

DON'T TALK TO ME.. I'M HAVING MY POST-CHRISTMAS LETDOWN
I JUST WANTED TO THANK YOU AGAIN FOR THE WONDERFUL PRESENT YOU GAVE ME..IT WAS JUST WHAT I WANTED...
© 1987 United Feature Syndicate, Inc. 12-28
RATS!
WHY DO YOU ALWAYS HAVE TO SAY SOMETHING NICE?

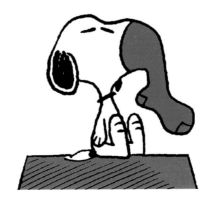

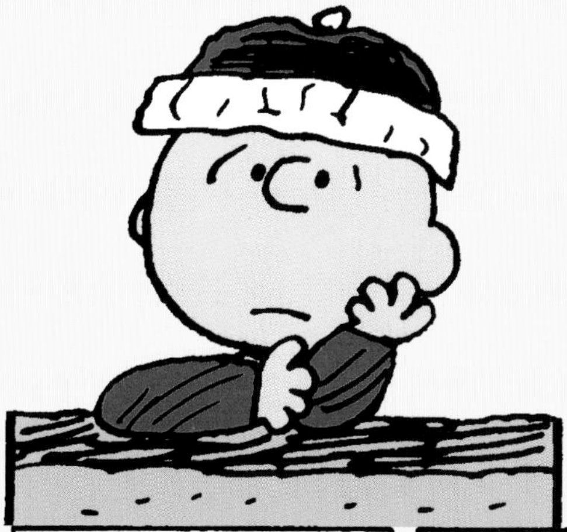

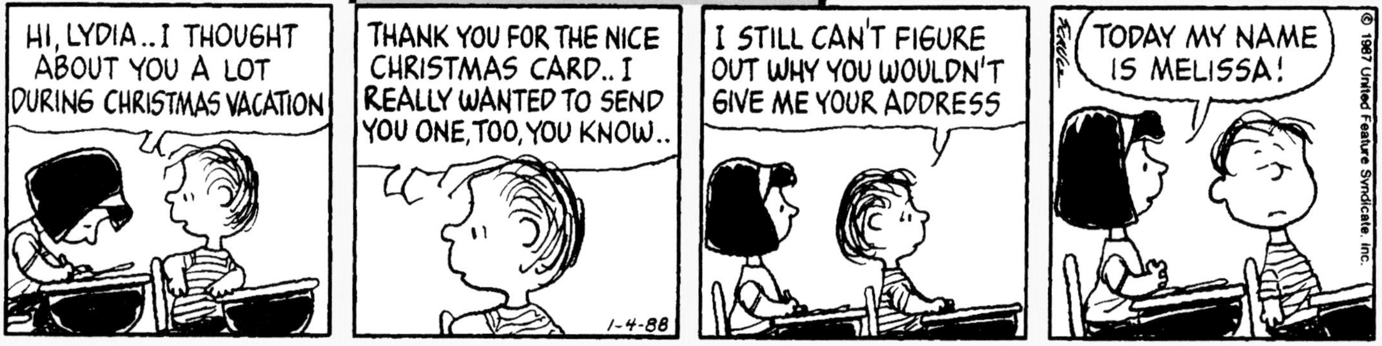

HI, LYDIA..I THOUGHT ABOUT YOU A LOT DURING CHRISTMAS VACATION
THANK YOU FOR THE NICE CHRISTMAS CARD..I REALLY WANTED TO SEND YOU ONE, TOO, YOU KNOW..
1-4-88
I STILL CAN'T FIGURE OUT WHY YOU WOULDN'T GIVE ME YOUR ADDRESS
TODAY MY NAME IS MELISSA!
© 1987 United Feature Syndicate, Inc.

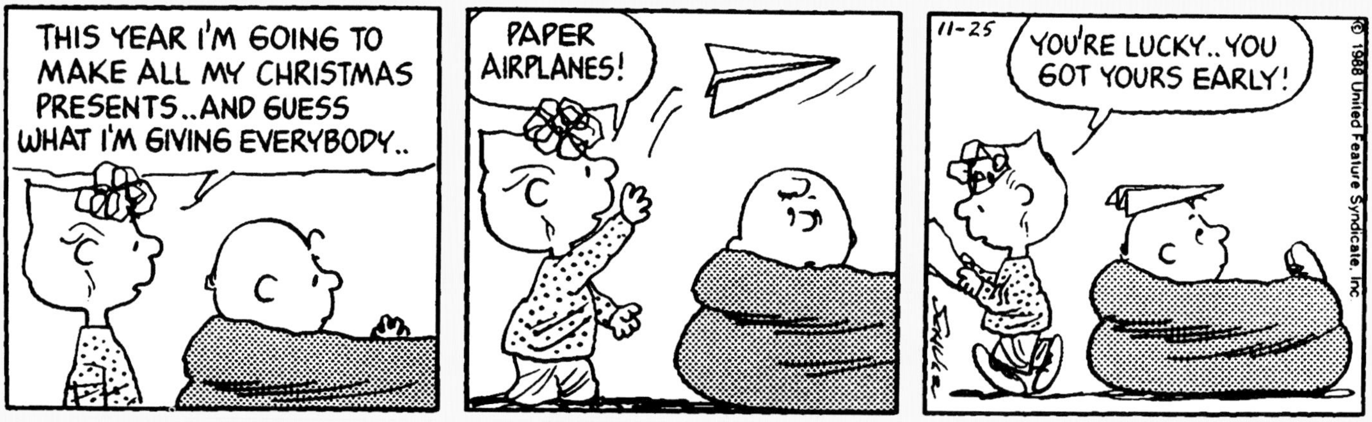

THIS YEAR I'M GOING TO MAKE ALL MY CHRISTMAS PRESENTS..AND GUESS WHAT I'M GIVING EVERYBODY..
PAPER AIRPLANES!
11-25
YOU'RE LUCKY..YOU GOT YOURS EARLY!
© 1988 United Feature Syndicate, Inc.

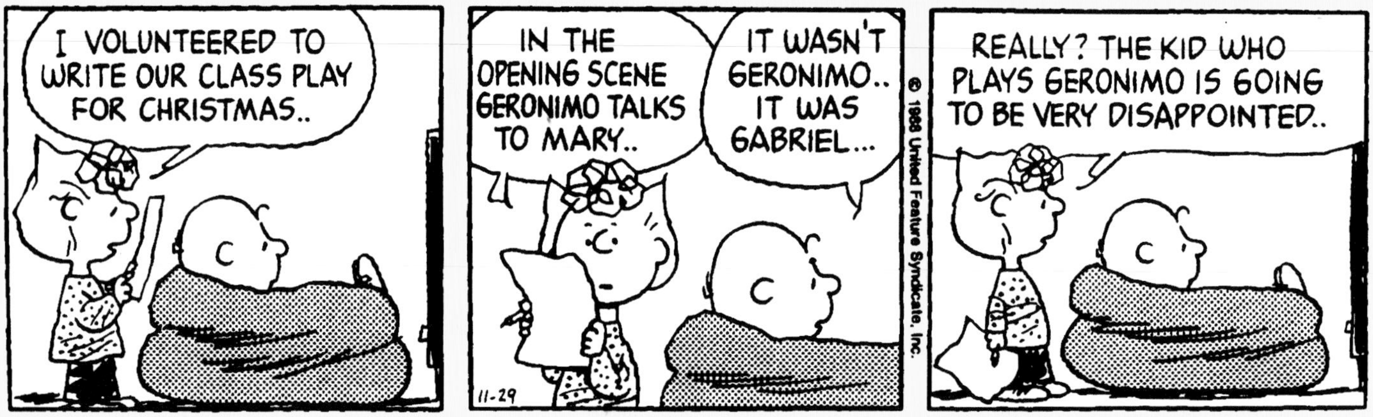

I VOLUNTEERED TO WRITE OUR CLASS PLAY FOR CHRISTMAS..
IN THE OPENING SCENE GERONIMO TALKS TO MARY..
IT WASN'T GERONIMO.. IT WAS GABRIEL...
© 1988 United Feature Syndicate, Inc.
11-29
REALLY? THE KID WHO PLAYS GERONIMO IS GOING TO BE VERY DISAPPOINTED..

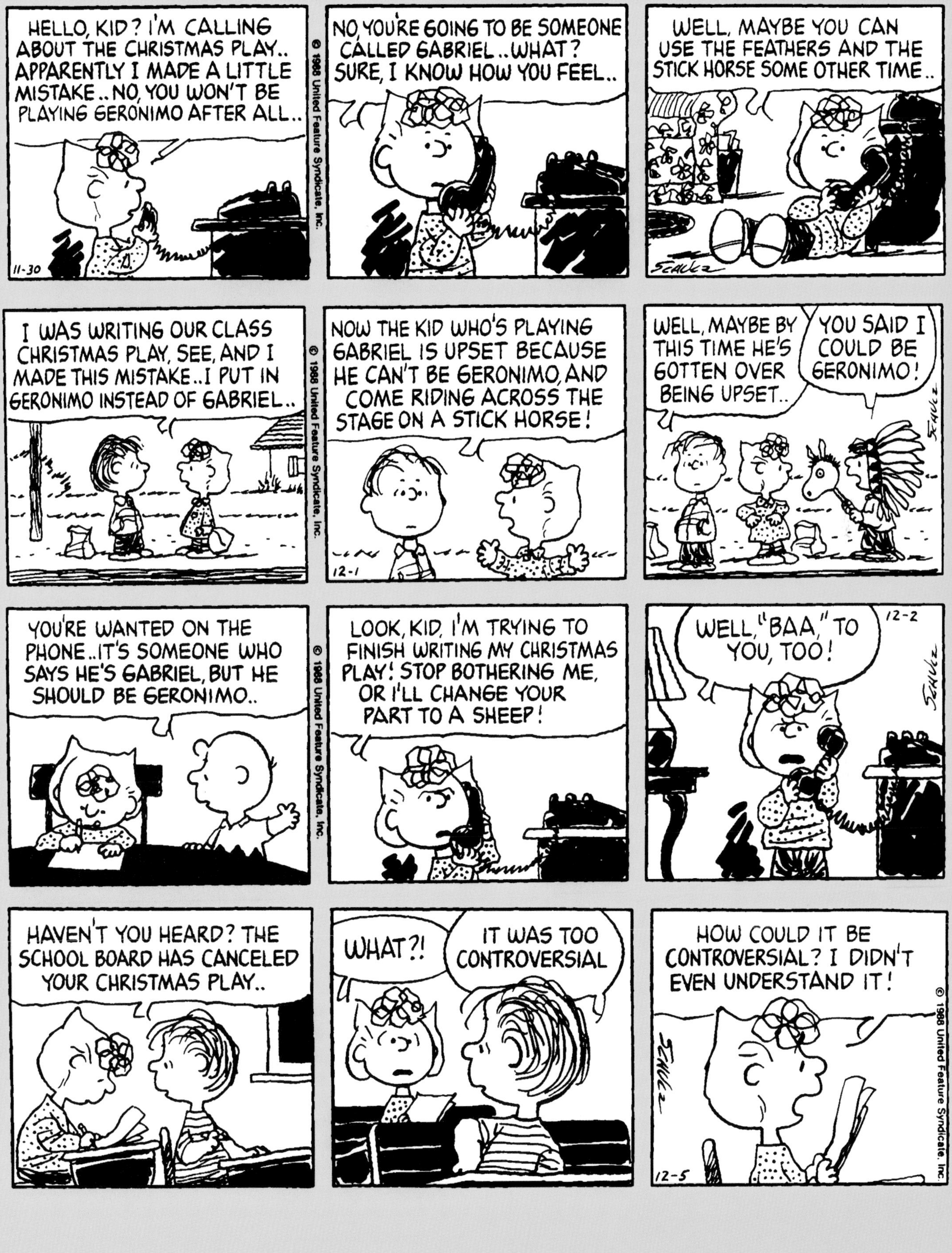
HELLO, KID? I'M CALLING ABOUT THE CHRISTMAS PLAY.. APPARENTLY I MADE A LITTLE MISTAKE..NO, YOU WON'T BE PLAYING GERONIMO AFTER ALL..
NO, YOU'RE GOING TO BE SOMEONE CALLED GABRIEL..WHAT? SURE, I KNOW HOW YOU FEEL..
WELL, MAYBE YOU CAN USE THE FEATHERS AND THE STICK HORSE SOME OTHER TIME..
© 1988 United Feature Syndicate, Inc.
I WAS WRITING OUR CLASS CHRISTMAS PLAY, SEE, AND I MADE THIS MISTAKE..I PUT IN GERONIMO INSTEAD OF GABRIEL..
NOW THE KID WHO'S PLAYING GABRIEL IS UPSET BECAUSE HE CAN'T BE GERONIMO, AND COME RIDING ACROSS THE STAGE ON A STICK HORSE!
WELL, MAYBE BY THIS TIME HE'S GOTTEN OVER BEING UPSET..
YOU SAID I COULD BE GERONIMO!
© 1988 United Feature Syndicate, Inc.
YOU'RE WANTED ON THE PHONE..IT'S SOMEONE WHO SAYS HE'S GABRIEL, BUT HE SHOULD BE GERONIMO..
LOOK, KID, I'M TRYING TO FINISH WRITING MY CHRISTMAS PLAY! STOP BOTHERING ME, OR I'LL CHANGE YOUR PART TO A SHEEP!
WELL, "BAA," TO YOU, TOO!
© 1988 United Feature Syndicate, Inc.
HAVEN'T YOU HEARD? THE SCHOOL BOARD HAS CANCELED YOUR CHRISTMAS PLAY..
WHAT?!
IT WAS TOO CONTROVERSIAL
HOW COULD IT BE CONTROVERSIAL? I DIDN'T EVEN UNDERSTAND IT!
© 1988 United Feature Syndicate, Inc.

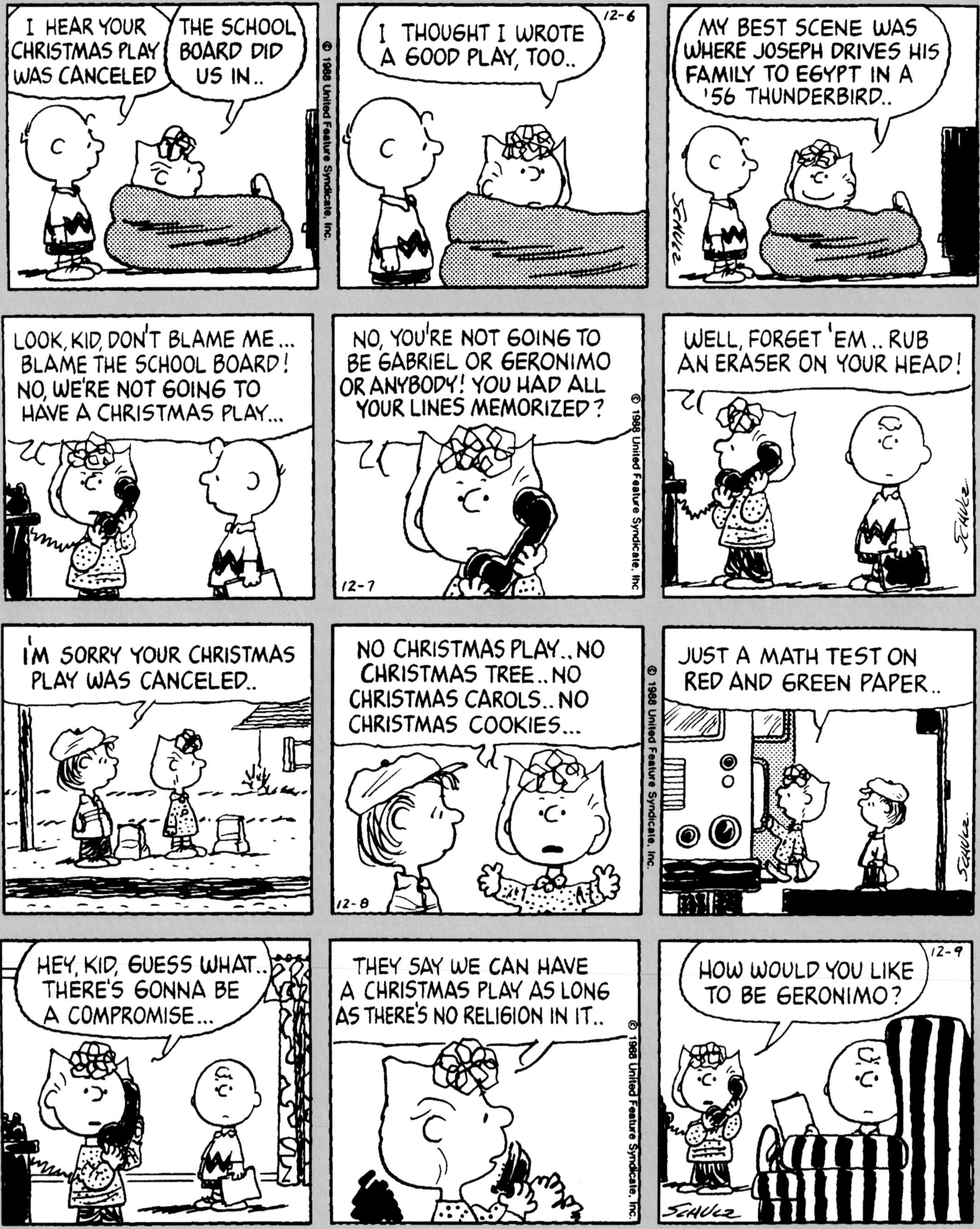
I HEAR YOUR CHRISTMAS PLAY WAS CANCELED
THE SCHOOL BOARD DID US IN..
© 1988 United Feature Syndicate, Inc.
12-6
I THOUGHT I WROTE A GOOD PLAY, TOO..
MY BEST SCENE WAS WHERE JOSEPH DRIVES HIS FAMILY TO EGYPT IN A '56 THUNDERBIRD..
SCHULZ
LOOK, KID, DON'T BLAME ME... BLAME THE SCHOOL BOARD! NO, WE'RE NOT GOING TO HAVE A CHRISTMAS PLAY...
NO, YOU'RE NOT GOING TO BE GABRIEL OR GERONIMO OR ANYBODY! YOU HAD ALL YOUR LINES MEMORIZED?
12-7
© 1988 United Feature Syndicate, Inc.
WELL, FORGET 'EM.. RUB AN ERASER ON YOUR HEAD!
SCHULZ
I'M SORRY YOUR CHRISTMAS PLAY WAS CANCELED..
NO CHRISTMAS PLAY.. NO CHRISTMAS TREE.. NO CHRISTMAS CAROLS.. NO CHRISTMAS COOKIES...
12-8
© 1988 United Feature Syndicate, Inc.
JUST A MATH TEST ON RED AND GREEN PAPER..
SCHULZ
HEY, KID, GUESS WHAT.. THERE'S GONNA BE A COMPROMISE...
THEY SAY WE CAN HAVE A CHRISTMAS PLAY AS LONG AS THERE'S NO RELIGION IN IT..
© 1988 United Feature Syndicate, Inc.
12-9
HOW WOULD YOU LIKE TO BE GERONIMO?
SCHULZ

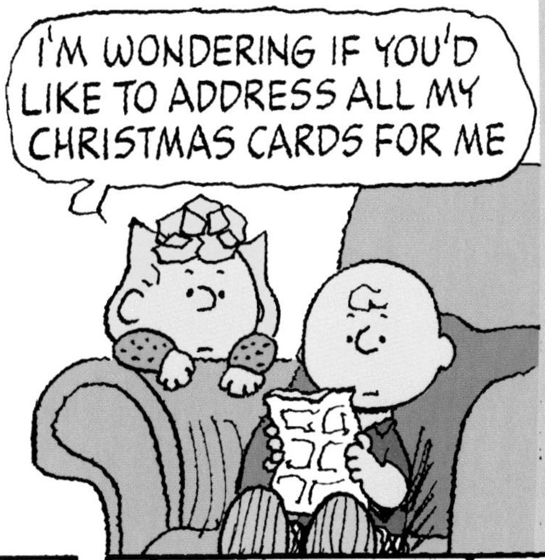
I'M WONDERING IF YOU'D LIKE TO ADDRESS ALL MY CHRISTMAS CARDS FOR ME

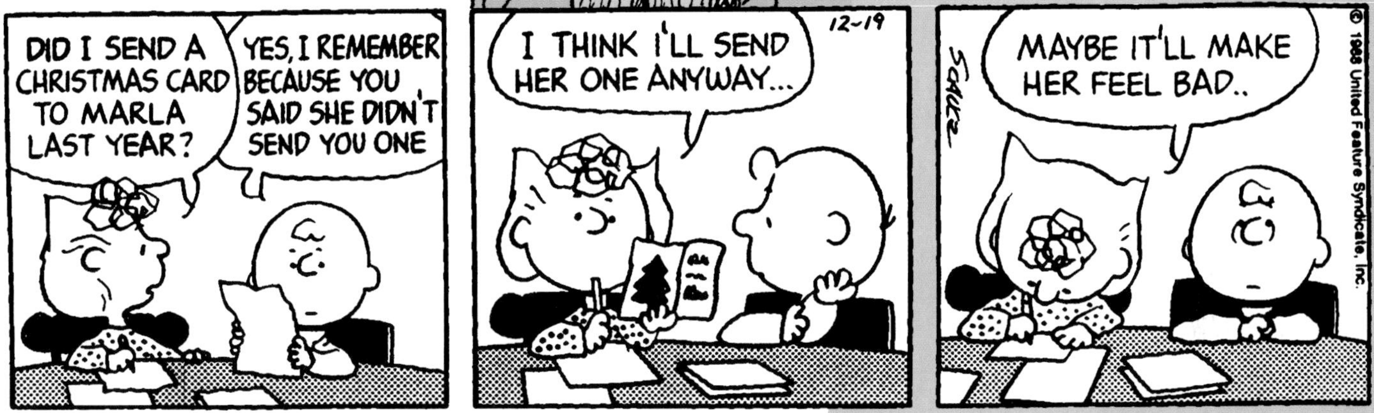
DID I SEND A CHRISTMAS CARD TO MARLA LAST YEAR?
YES, I REMEMBER BECAUSE YOU SAID SHE DIDN'T SEND YOU ONE
I THINK I'LL SEND HER ONE ANYWAY...
12-19
MAYBE IT'LL MAKE HER FEEL BAD..
SCHULZ
© 1988 United Feature Syndicate, Inc.

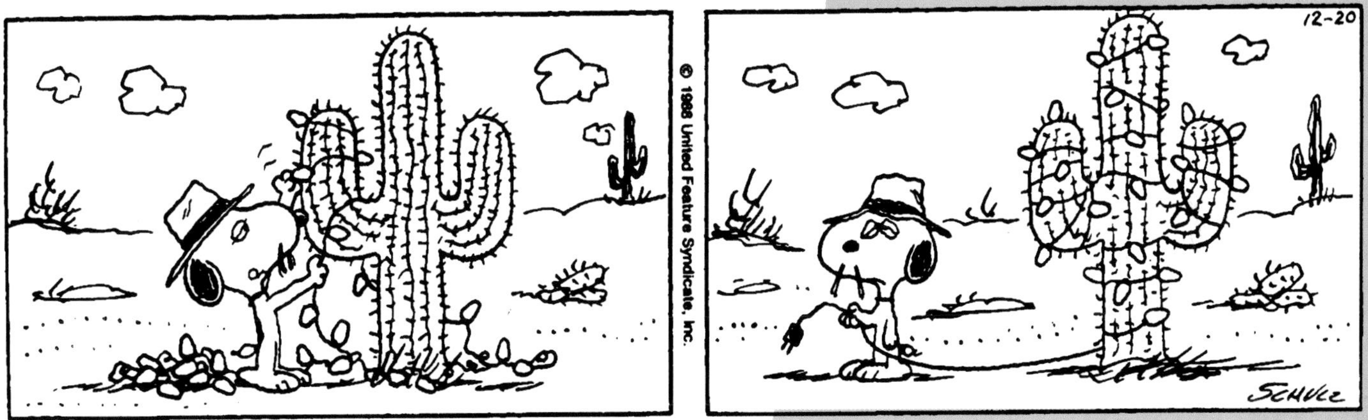
© 1988 United Feature Syndicate, Inc.
12-20
SCHULZ

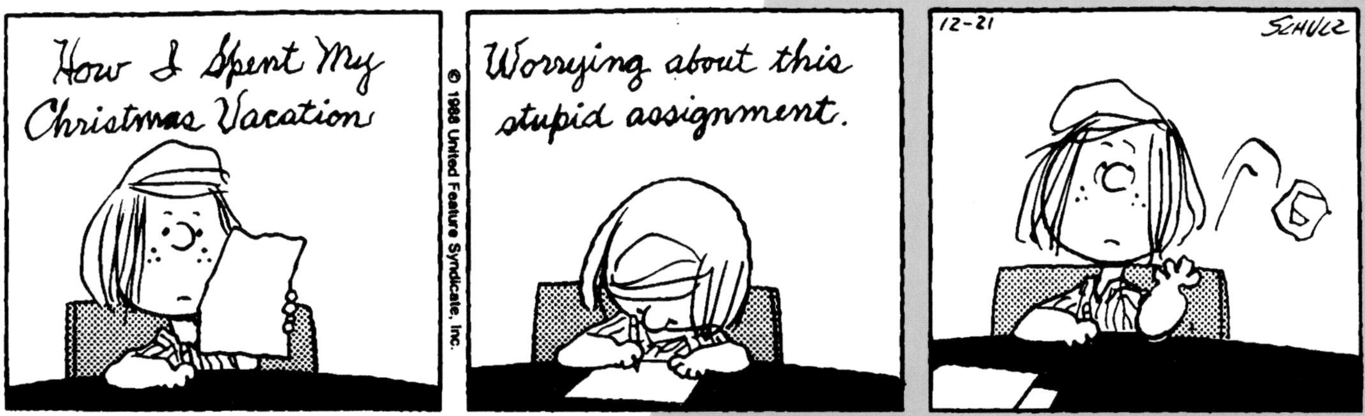
How I Spent My Christmas Vacation
© 1988 United Feature Syndicate, Inc.
Worrying about this stupid assignment.
12-21
SCHULZ

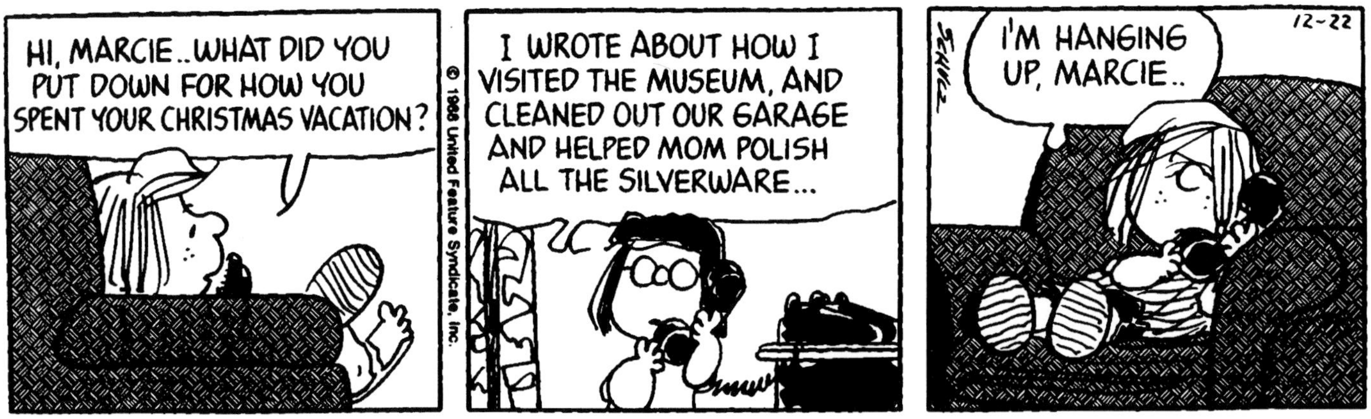
HI, MARCIE.. WHAT DID YOU PUT DOWN FOR HOW YOU SPENT YOUR CHRISTMAS VACATION?
© 1988 United Feature Syndicate, Inc.
I WROTE ABOUT HOW I VISITED THE MUSEUM, AND CLEANED OUT OUR GARAGE AND HELPED MOM POLISH ALL THE SILVERWARE...
SCHULZ
I'M HANGING UP, MARCIE..
12-22

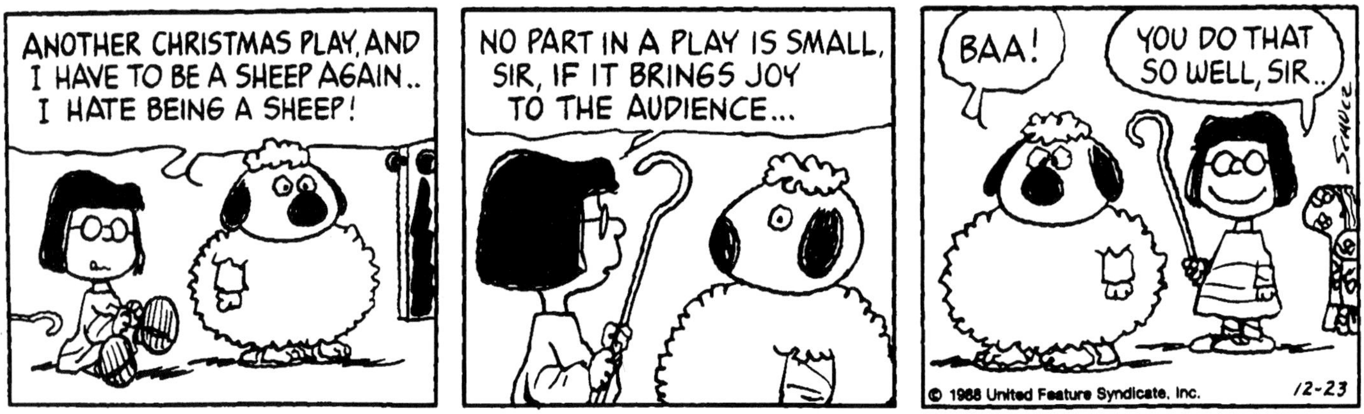
ANOTHER CHRISTMAS PLAY, AND I HAVE TO BE A SHEEP AGAIN.. I HATE BEING A SHEEP!
NO PART IN A PLAY IS SMALL, SIR, IF IT BRINGS JOY TO THE AUDIENCE...
BAA!
YOU DO THAT SO WELL, SIR..
SCHULZ
© 1988 United Feature Syndicate, Inc.
12-23

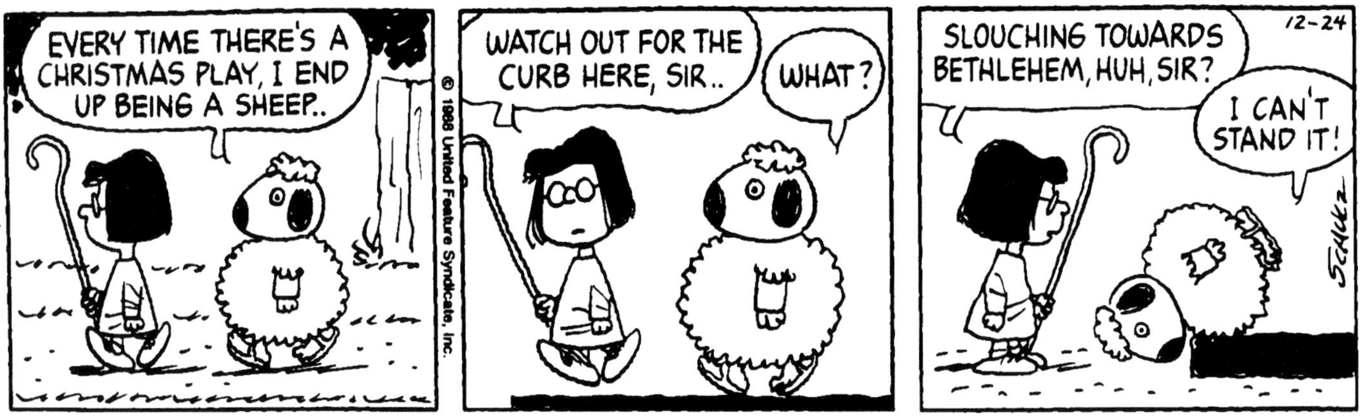
EVERY TIME THERE'S A CHRISTMAS PLAY, I END UP BEING A SHEEP..
© 1988 United Feature Syndicate, Inc.
WATCH OUT FOR THE CURB HERE, SIR..
WHAT?
12-24
SLOUCHING TOWARDS BETHLEHEM, HUH, SIR?
I CAN'T STAND IT!
SCHULZ

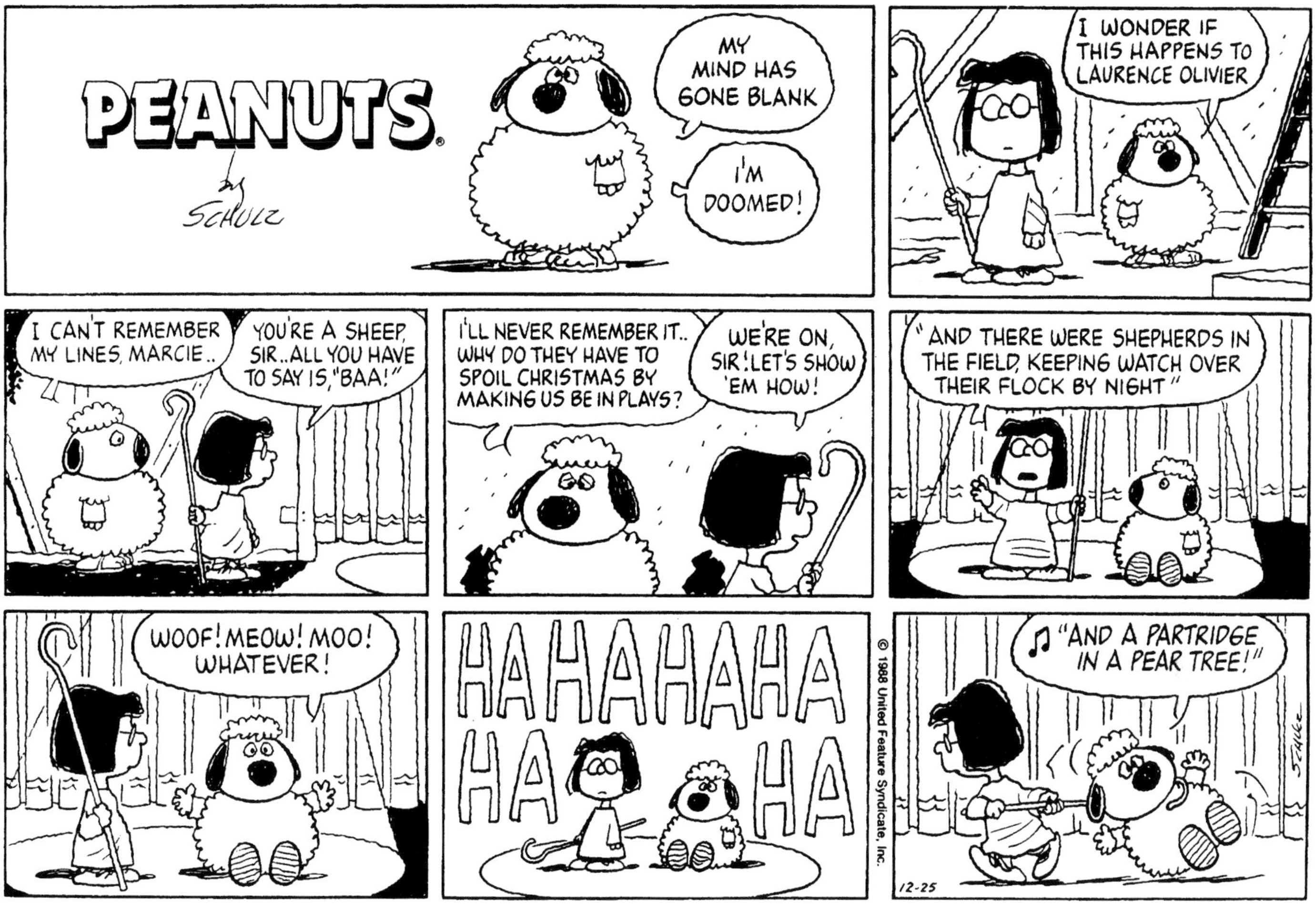
PEANUTS
by SCHULZ
MY MIND HAS GONE BLANK
I'M DOOMED!
I WONDER IF THIS HAPPENS TO LAURENCE OLIVIER
I CAN'T REMEMBER MY LINES, MARCIE..
YOU'RE A SHEEP, SIR..ALL YOU HAVE TO SAY IS, "BAA!"
I'LL NEVER REMEMBER IT.. WHY DO THEY HAVE TO SPOIL CHRISTMAS BY MAKING US BE IN PLAYS?
WE'RE ON, SIR! LET'S SHOW 'EM HOW!
"AND THERE WERE SHEPHERDS IN THE FIELD, KEEPING WATCH OVER THEIR FLOCK BY NIGHT"
WOOF! MEOW! MOO! WHATEVER!
HAHAHAHAHA HA HA
© 1988 United Feature Syndicate, Inc.
♫ "AND A PARTRIDGE IN A PEAR TREE!"
SCHULZ
12-25

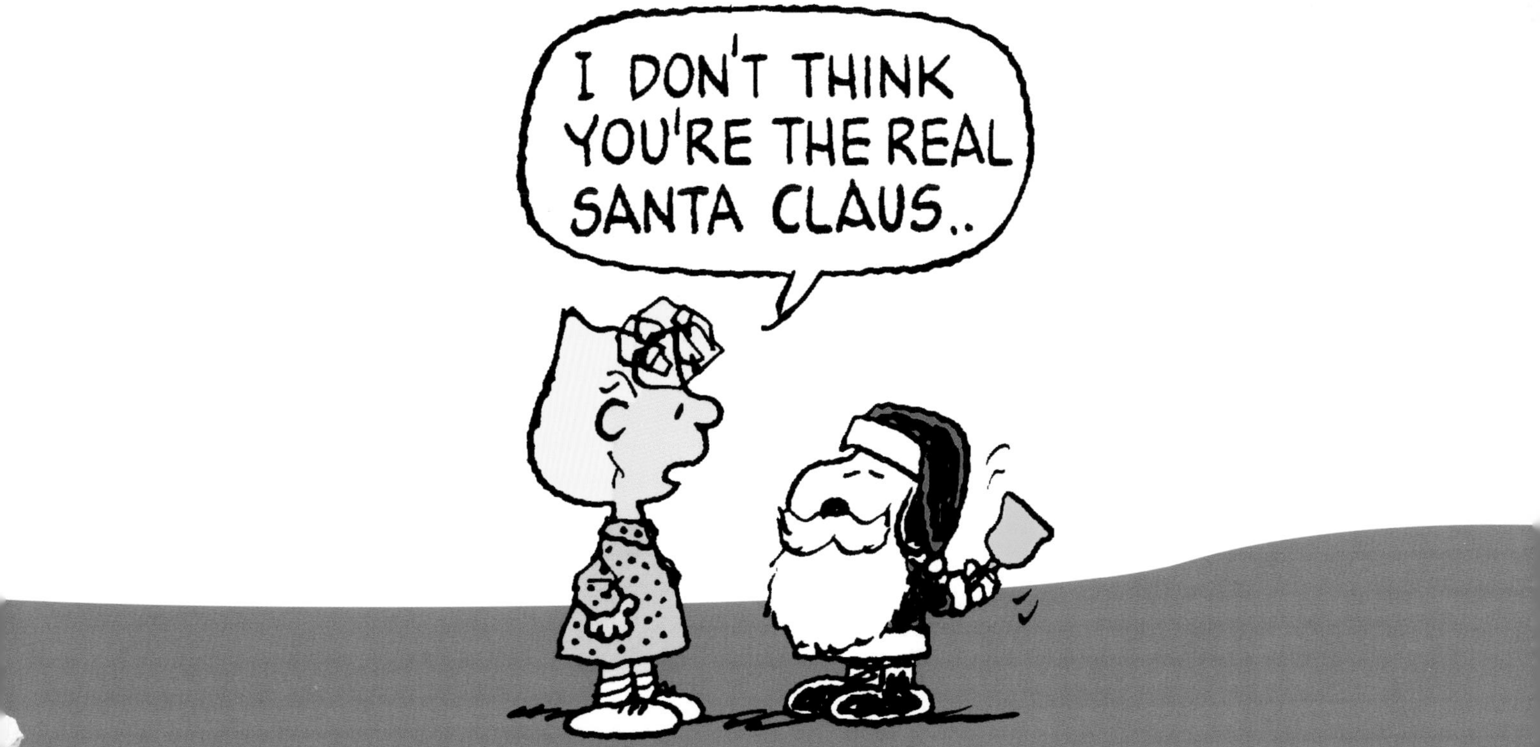
I DON'T THINK YOU'RE THE REAL SANTA CLAUS..

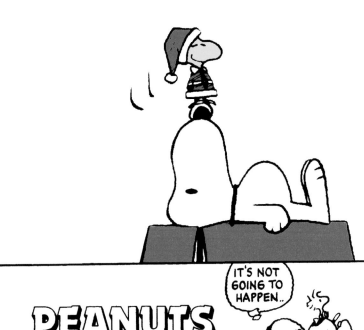

PEANUTS
by SCHULZ
IT'S NOT GOING TO HAPPEN..
NOT FOR US!
THERE'S NO USE GETTING YOUR HOPES UP..
WE'RE THE LOWEST OF THE LOW..
OLD SANTA CLAUS COULDN'T CARE LESS ABOUT CREATURES LIKE US!
WE DON'T COUNT FOR ANYTHING! THAT OLD GUY DOESN'T KNOW WE EVEN EXIST...
?
© 1989 United Feature Syndicate, Inc.
WOW! I CAN'T BELIEVE IT!
THERE'S A CARD, TOO? WHAT DOES IT SAY?
"MERRY CHRISTMAS FROM THE NEW IMPROVED SANTA CLAUS"
SCHULZ
12-24

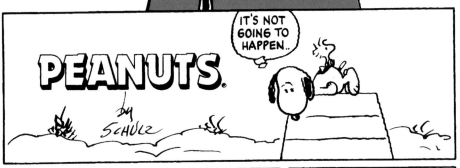

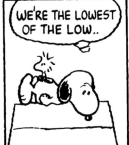

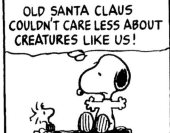

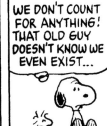

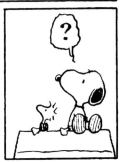

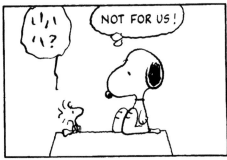

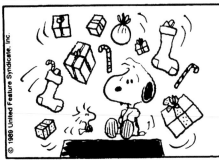

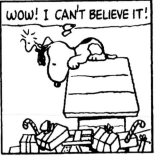

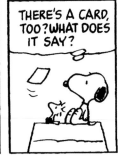

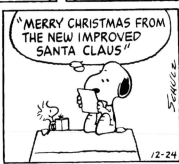

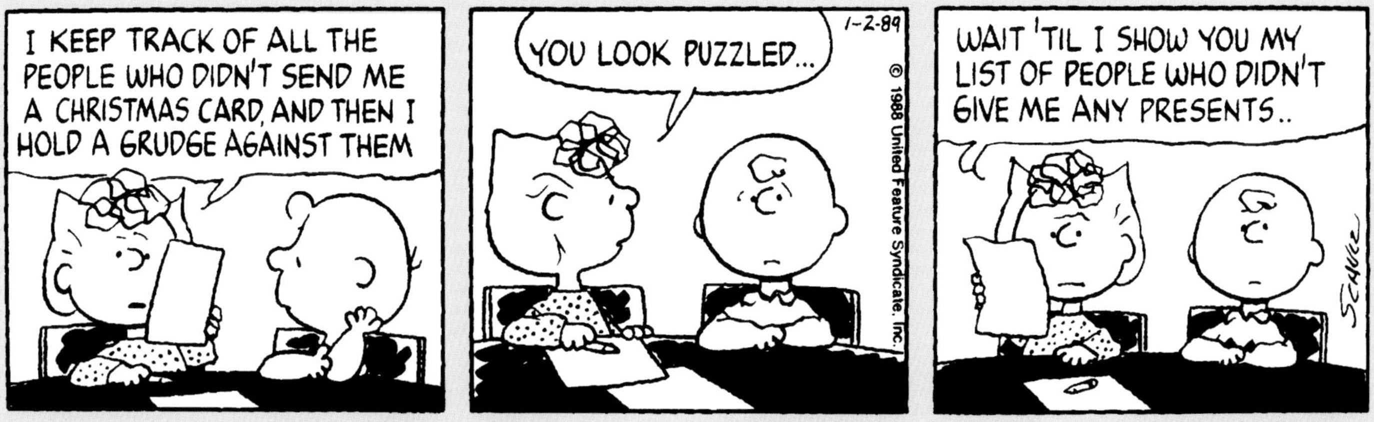
I KEEP TRACK OF ALL THE PEOPLE WHO DIDN'T SEND ME A CHRISTMAS CARD, AND THEN I HOLD A GRUDGE AGAINST THEM
YOU LOOK PUZZLED...
1-2-89
© 1988 United Feature Syndicate, Inc.
WAIT 'TIL I SHOW YOU MY LIST OF PEOPLE WHO DIDN'T GIVE ME ANY PRESENTS..
SCHULZ

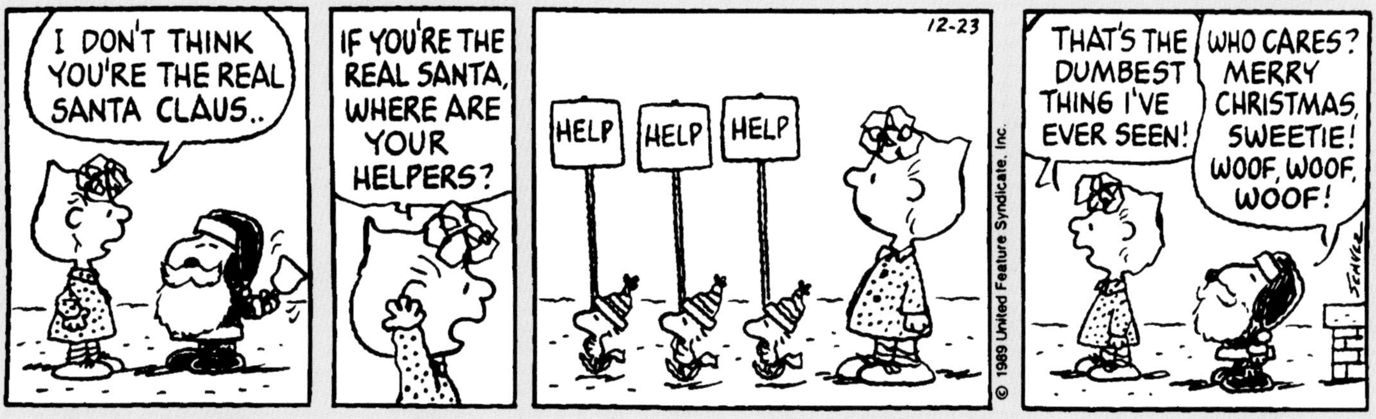
I DON'T THINK YOU'RE THE REAL SANTA CLAUS..
IF YOU'RE THE REAL SANTA, WHERE ARE YOUR HELPERS?
12-23
HELP
HELP
HELP
© 1989 United Feature Syndicate, Inc.
THAT'S THE DUMBEST THING I'VE EVER SEEN!
WHO CARES? MERRY CHRISTMAS, SWEETIE! WOOF, WOOF, WOOF!
SCHULZ

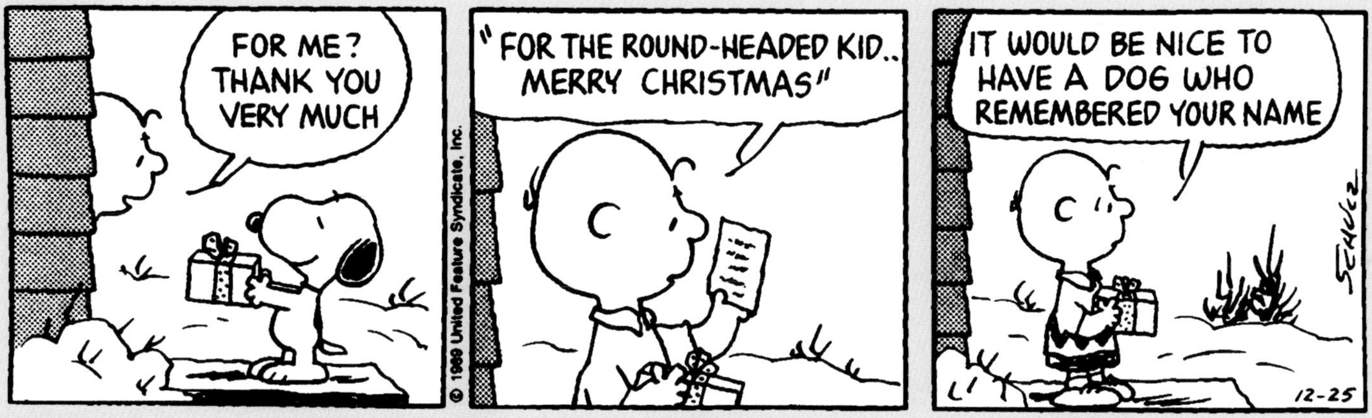
FOR ME? THANK YOU VERY MUCH
© 1989 United Feature Syndicate, Inc.
"FOR THE ROUND-HEADED KID.. MERRY CHRISTMAS"
IT WOULD BE NICE TO HAVE A DOG WHO REMEMBERED YOUR NAME
SCHULZ
12-25

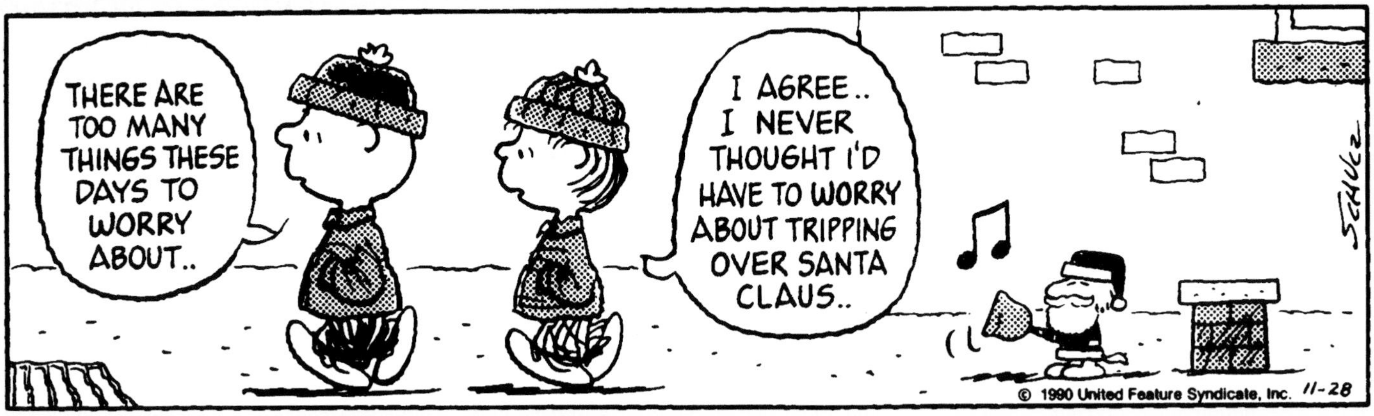
THERE ARE TOO MANY THINGS THESE DAYS TO WORRY ABOUT..
I AGREE.. I NEVER THOUGHT I'D HAVE TO WORRY ABOUT TRIPPING OVER SANTA CLAUS..
© 1990 United Feature Syndicate, Inc.
11-28

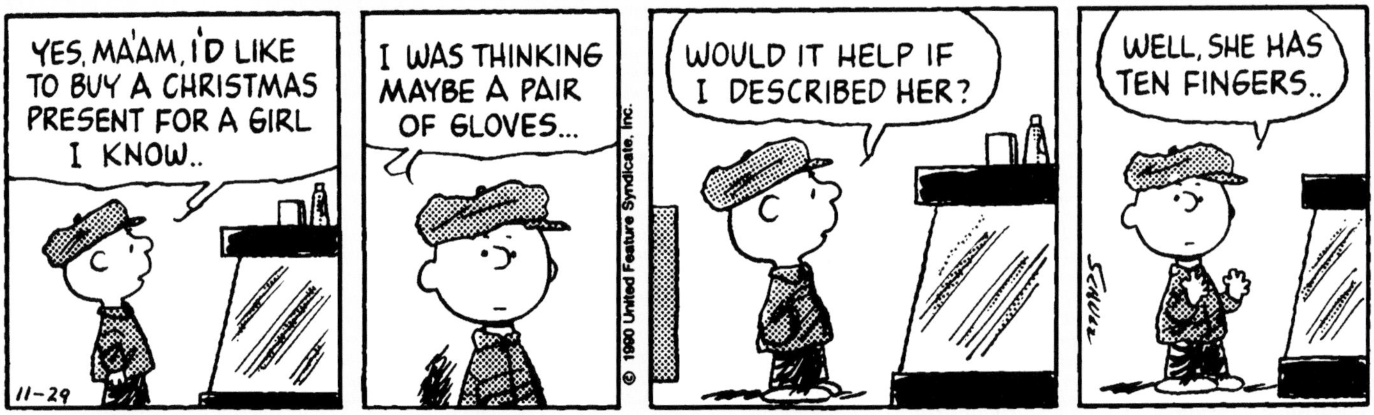
YES, MA'AM, I'D LIKE TO BUY A CHRISTMAS PRESENT FOR A GIRL I KNOW..
11-29
I WAS THINKING MAYBE A PAIR OF GLOVES...
© 1990 United Feature Syndicate, Inc.
WOULD IT HELP IF I DESCRIBED HER?
WELL, SHE HAS TEN FINGERS..

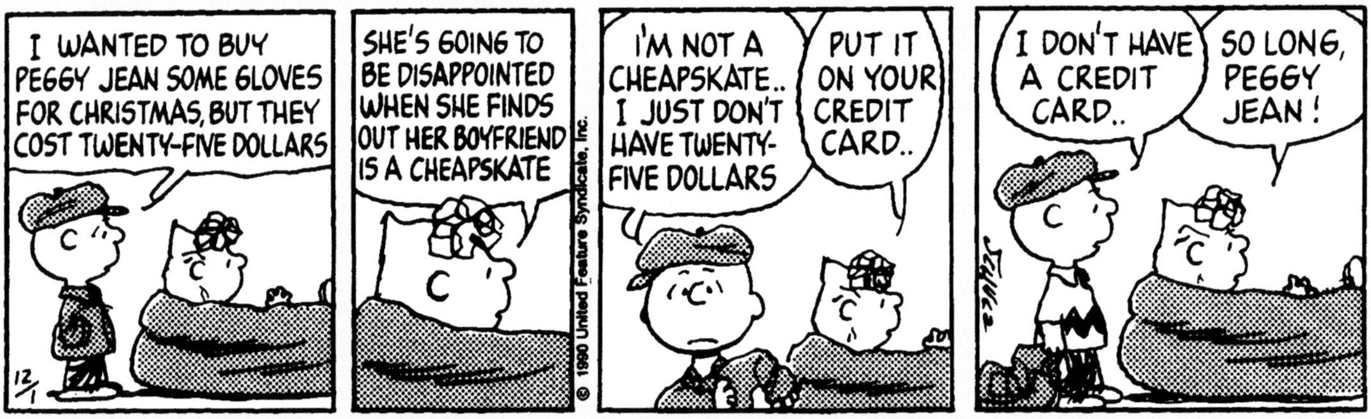
I WANTED TO BUY PEGGY JEAN SOME GLOVES FOR CHRISTMAS, BUT THEY COST TWENTY-FIVE DOLLARS
12/1
SHE'S GOING TO BE DISAPPOINTED WHEN SHE FINDS OUT HER BOYFRIEND IS A CHEAPSKATE
© 1990 United Feature Syndicate, Inc.
I'M NOT A CHEAPSKATE.. I JUST DON'T HAVE TWENTY-FIVE DOLLARS
PUT IT ON YOUR CREDIT CARD..
I DON'T HAVE A CREDIT CARD..
SO LONG, PEGGY JEAN!

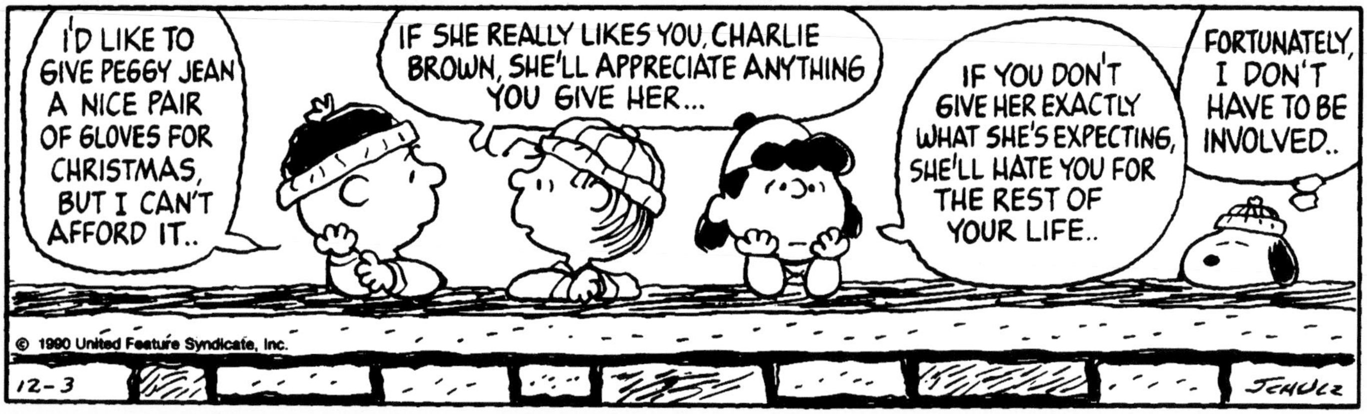
I'D LIKE TO GIVE PEGGY JEAN A NICE PAIR OF GLOVES FOR CHRISTMAS, BUT I CAN'T AFFORD IT..
IF SHE REALLY LIKES YOU, CHARLIE BROWN, SHE'LL APPRECIATE ANYTHING YOU GIVE HER...
IF YOU DON'T GIVE HER EXACTLY WHAT SHE'S EXPECTING, SHE'LL HATE YOU FOR THE REST OF YOUR LIFE..
FORTUNATELY, I DON'T HAVE TO BE INVOLVED..
© 1990 United Feature Syndicate, Inc.
12-3

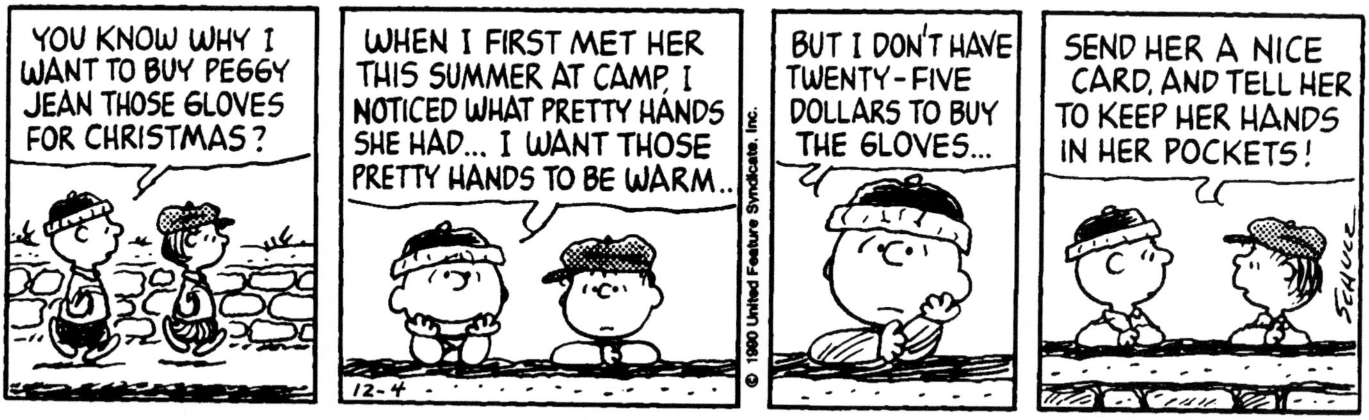
YOU KNOW WHY I WANT TO BUY PEGGY JEAN THOSE GLOVES FOR CHRISTMAS?
WHEN I FIRST MET HER THIS SUMMER AT CAMP, I NOTICED WHAT PRETTY HANDS SHE HAD... I WANT THOSE PRETTY HANDS TO BE WARM..
12-4
© 1980 United Feature Syndicate, Inc.
BUT I DON'T HAVE TWENTY-FIVE DOLLARS TO BUY THE GLOVES...
SEND HER A NICE CARD, AND TELL HER TO KEEP HER HANDS IN HER POCKETS!
SCHULZ

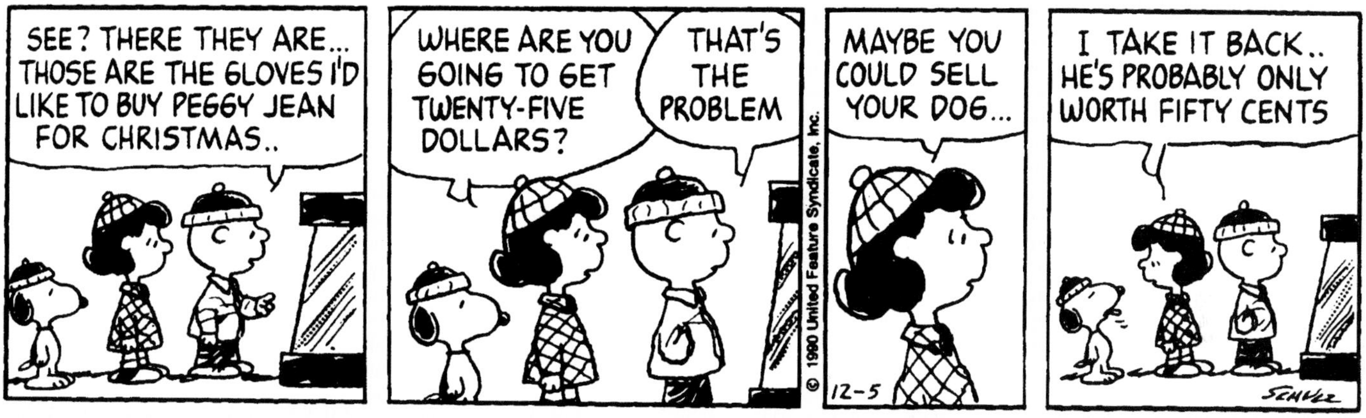
SEE? THERE THEY ARE... THOSE ARE THE GLOVES I'D LIKE TO BUY PEGGY JEAN FOR CHRISTMAS..
WHERE ARE YOU GOING TO GET TWENTY-FIVE DOLLARS?
THAT'S THE PROBLEM
© 1980 United Feature Syndicate, Inc.
MAYBE YOU COULD SELL YOUR DOG...
12-5
I TAKE IT BACK.. HE'S PROBABLY ONLY WORTH FIFTY CENTS
SCHULZ

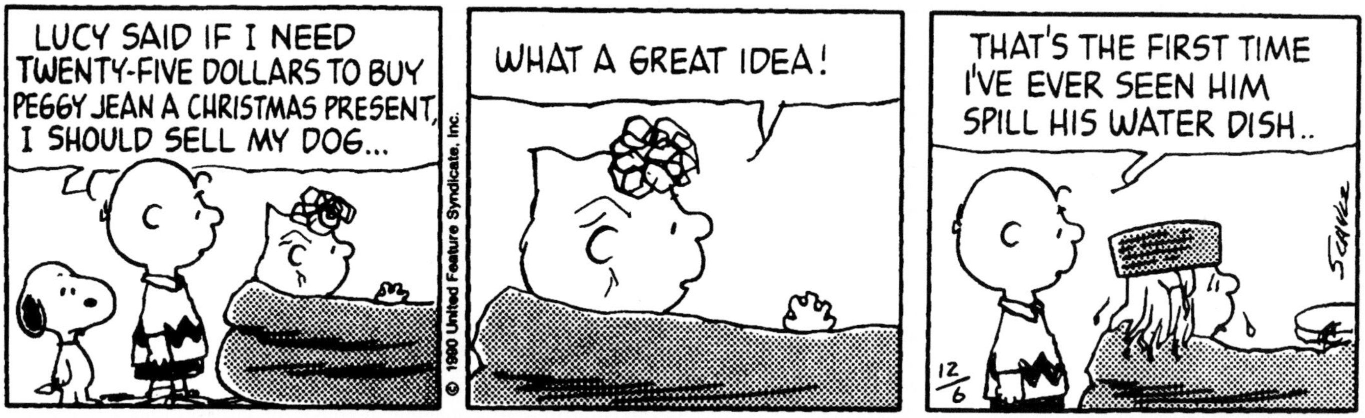
LUCY SAID IF I NEED TWENTY-FIVE DOLLARS TO BUY PEGGY JEAN A CHRISTMAS PRESENT, I SHOULD SELL MY DOG...
© 1980 United Feature Syndicate, Inc.
WHAT A GREAT IDEA!
THAT'S THE FIRST TIME I'VE EVER SEEN HIM SPILL HIS WATER DISH..
SCHULZ
12/6

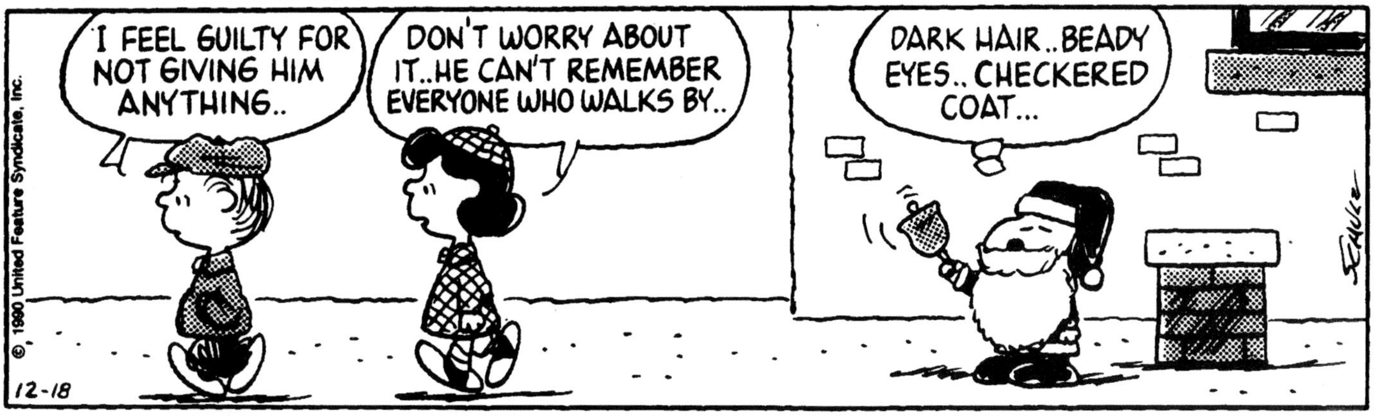
I FEEL GUILTY FOR NOT GIVING HIM ANYTHING..
DON'T WORRY ABOUT IT..HE CAN'T REMEMBER EVERYONE WHO WALKS BY..
© 1980 United Feature Syndicate, Inc.
12-18
DARK HAIR..BEADY EYES..CHECKERED COAT...
SCHULZ

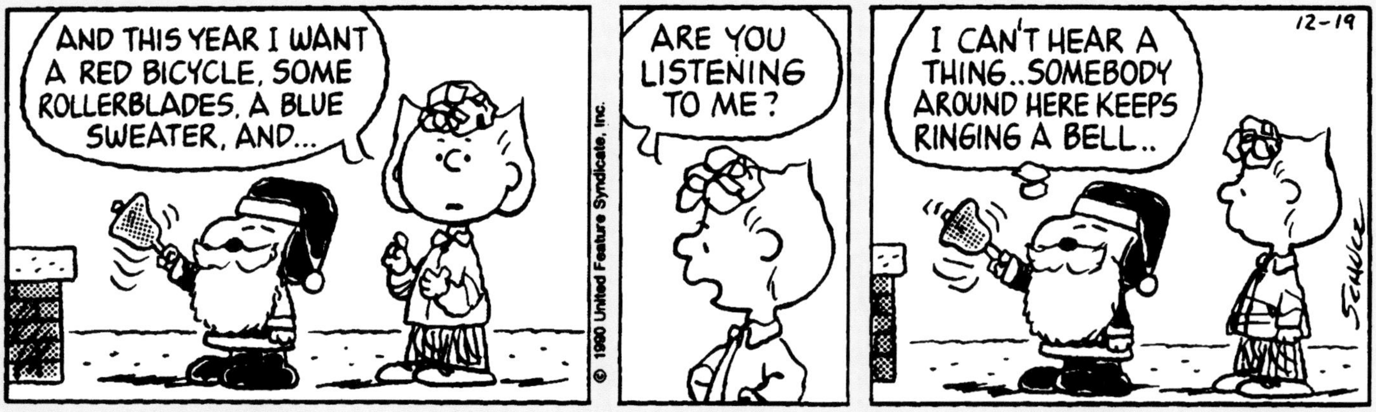
AND THIS YEAR I WANT A RED BICYCLE, SOME ROLLERBLADES, A BLUE SWEATER, AND...
© 1990 United Feature Syndicate, Inc.
ARE YOU LISTENING TO ME?
12-19
I CAN'T HEAR A THING..SOMEBODY AROUND HERE KEEPS RINGING A BELL..
SCHULZ

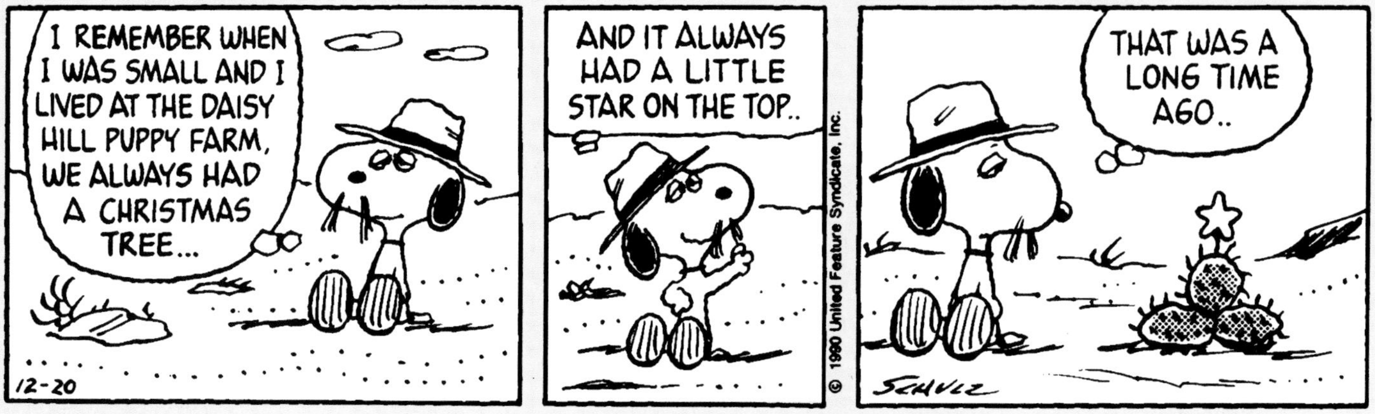
I REMEMBER WHEN I WAS SMALL AND I LIVED AT THE DAISY HILL PUPPY FARM, WE ALWAYS HAD A CHRISTMAS TREE...
12-20
AND IT ALWAYS HAD A LITTLE STAR ON THE TOP..
© 1990 United Feature Syndicate, Inc.
THAT WAS A LONG TIME AGO..
SCHULZ

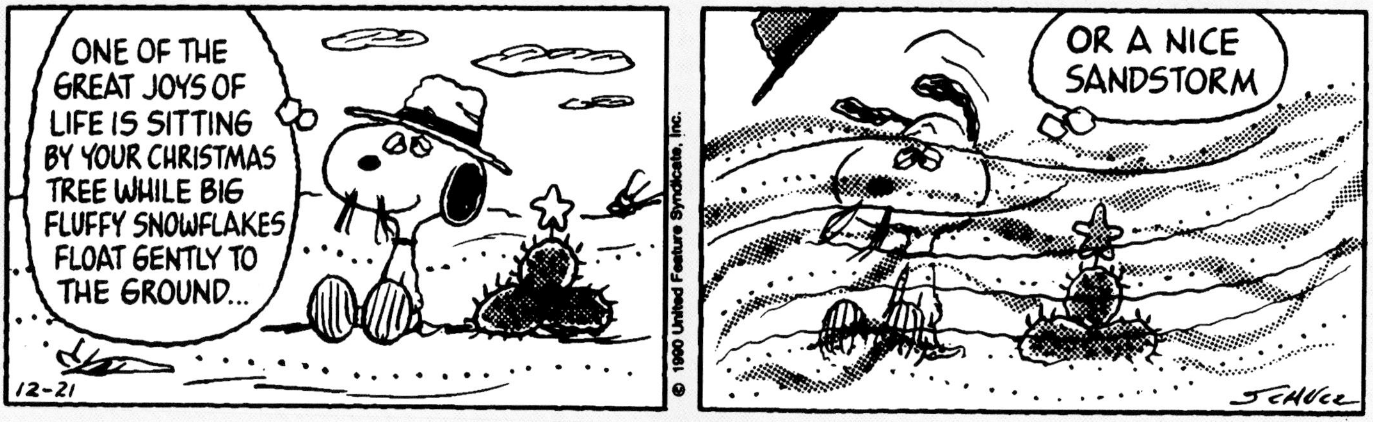
ONE OF THE GREAT JOYS OF LIFE IS SITTING BY YOUR CHRISTMAS TREE WHILE BIG FLUFFY SNOWFLAKES FLOAT GENTLY TO THE GROUND...
12-21
© 1990 United Feature Syndicate, Inc.
OR A NICE SANDSTORM
SCHULZ

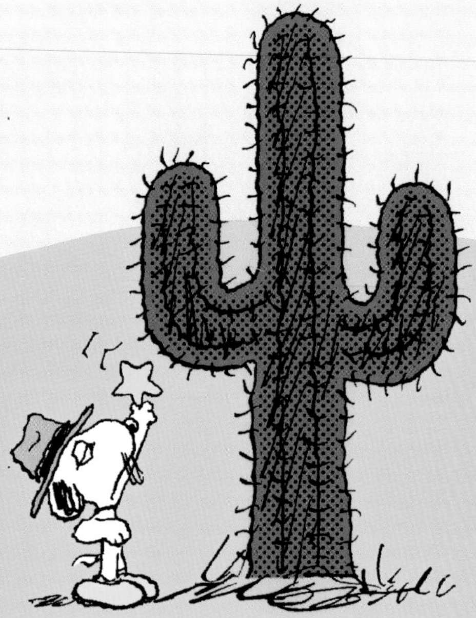

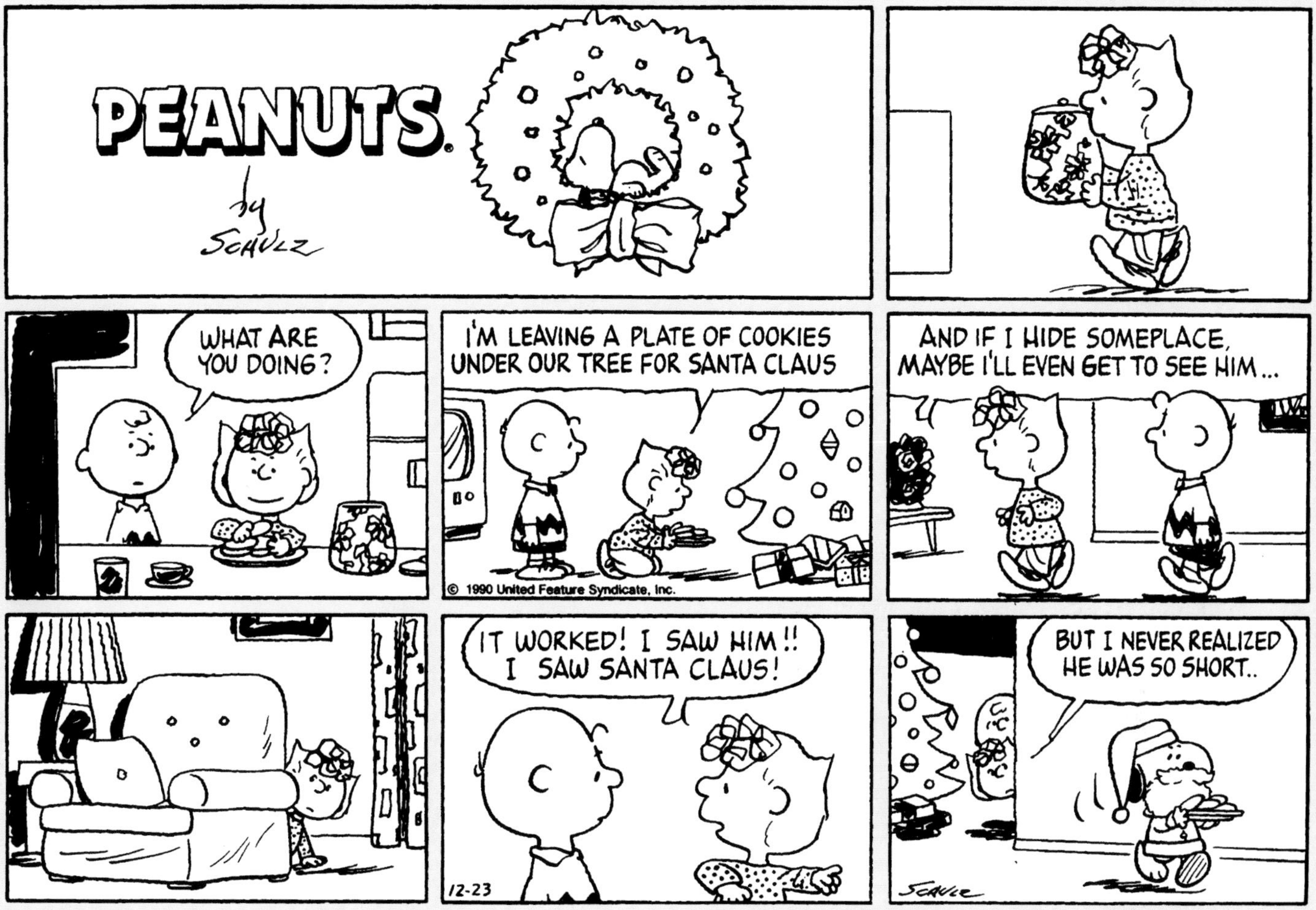
PEANUTS
by SCHULZ
WHAT ARE YOU DOING?
I'M LEAVING A PLATE OF COOKIES UNDER OUR TREE FOR SANTA CLAUS
© 1990 United Feature Syndicate, Inc.
AND IF I HIDE SOMEPLACE, MAYBE I'LL EVEN GET TO SEE HIM...
IT WORKED! I SAW HIM!! I SAW SANTA CLAUS!
12-23
BUT I NEVER REALIZED HE WAS SO SHORT..
SCHULZ

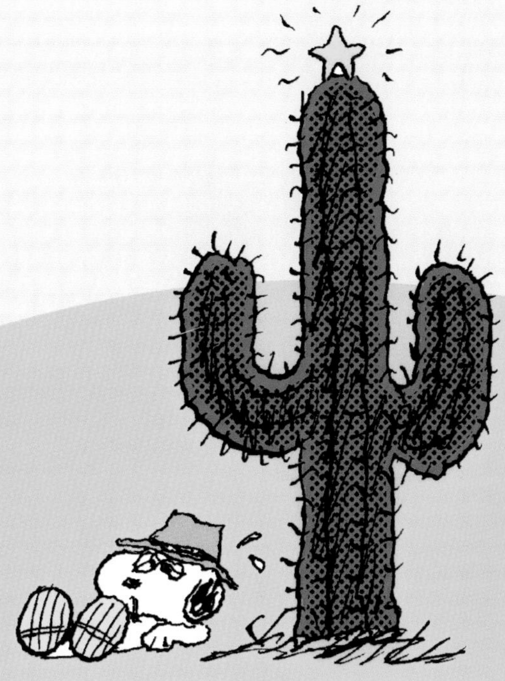

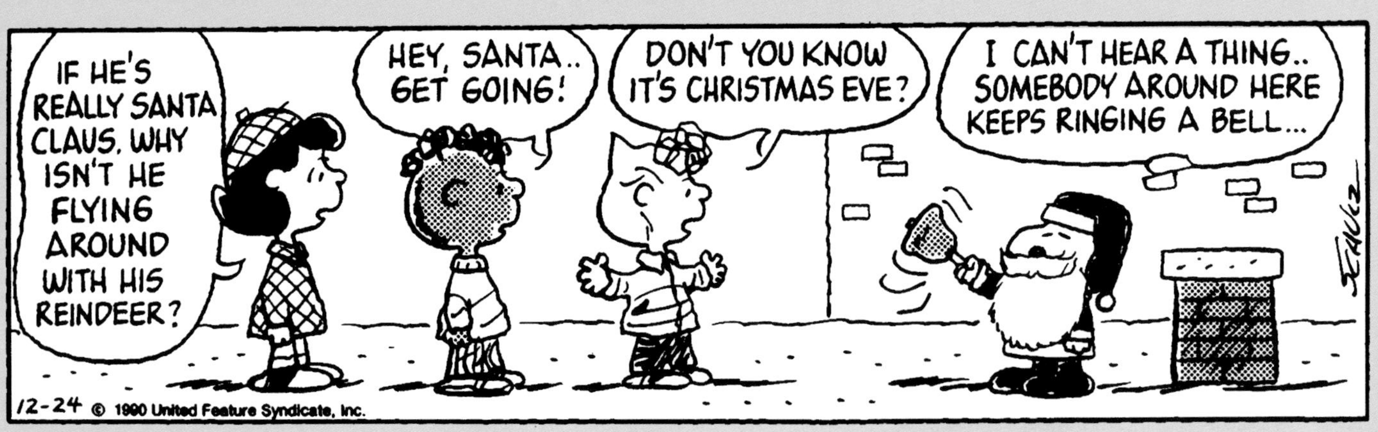
IF HE'S REALLY SANTA CLAUS, WHY ISN'T HE FLYING AROUND WITH HIS REINDEER?
HEY, SANTA.. GET GOING!
DON'T YOU KNOW IT'S CHRISTMAS EVE?
I CAN'T HEAR A THING.. SOMEBODY AROUND HERE KEEPS RINGING A BELL...
12-24 © 1990 United Feature Syndicate, Inc.

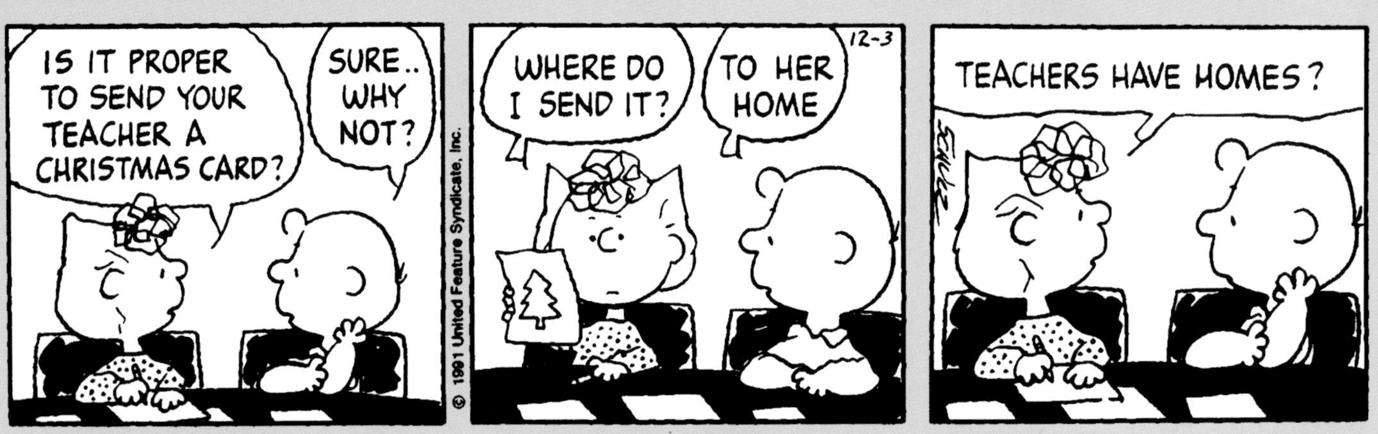
IS IT PROPER TO SEND YOUR TEACHER A CHRISTMAS CARD?
SURE.. WHY NOT?
© 1991 United Feature Syndicate, Inc.
12-3
WHERE DO I SEND IT?
TO HER HOME
TEACHERS HAVE HOMES?

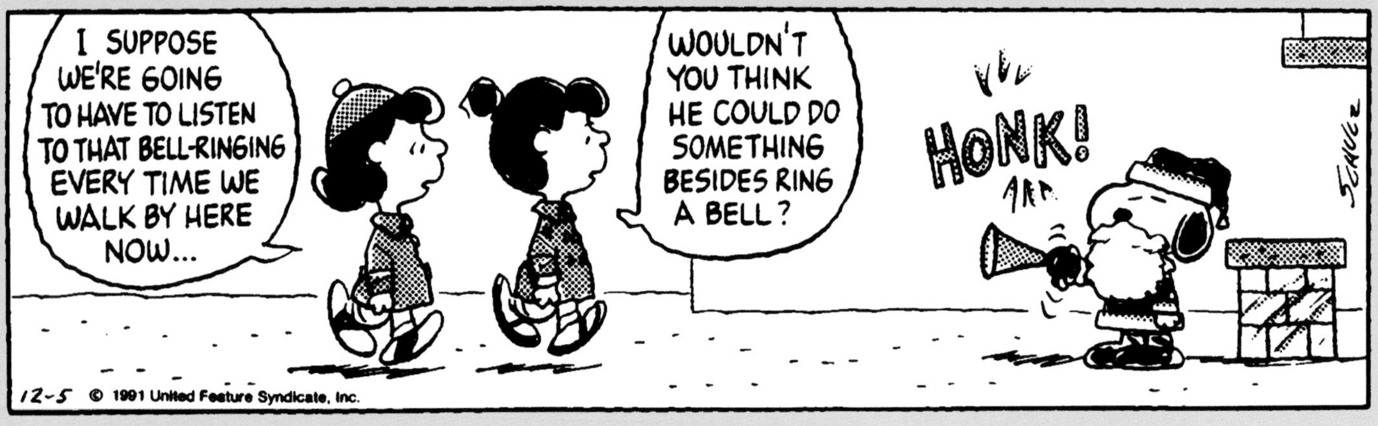
I SUPPOSE WE'RE GOING TO HAVE TO LISTEN TO THAT BELL-RINGING EVERY TIME WE WALK BY HERE NOW...
WOULDN'T YOU THINK HE COULD DO SOMETHING BESIDES RING A BELL?
HONK!
12-5 © 1991 United Feature Syndicate, Inc.

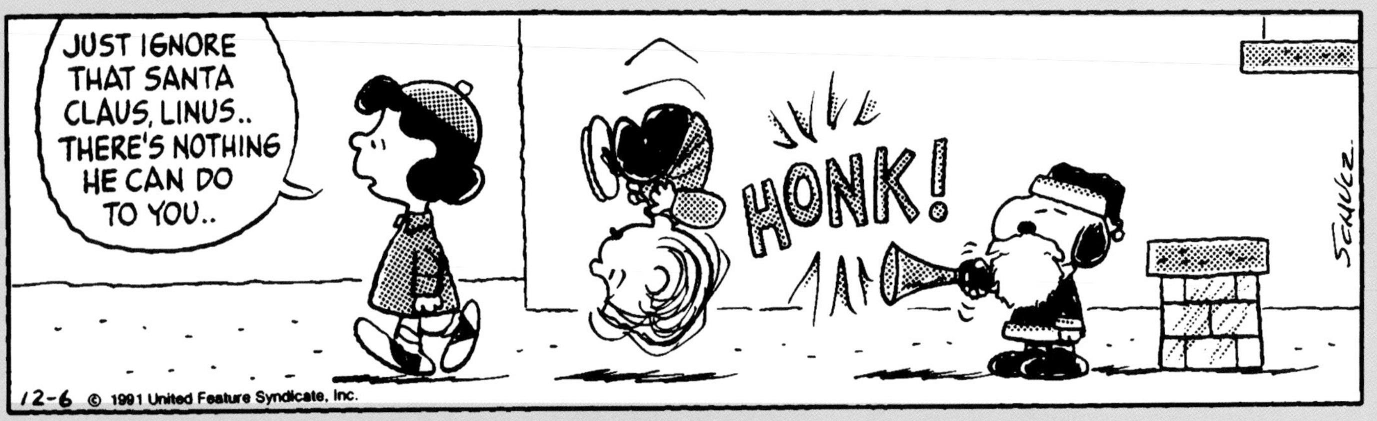
JUST IGNORE THAT SANTA CLAUS, LINUS.. THERE'S NOTHING HE CAN DO TO YOU..
HONK!
12-6 © 1991 United Feature Syndicate, Inc.

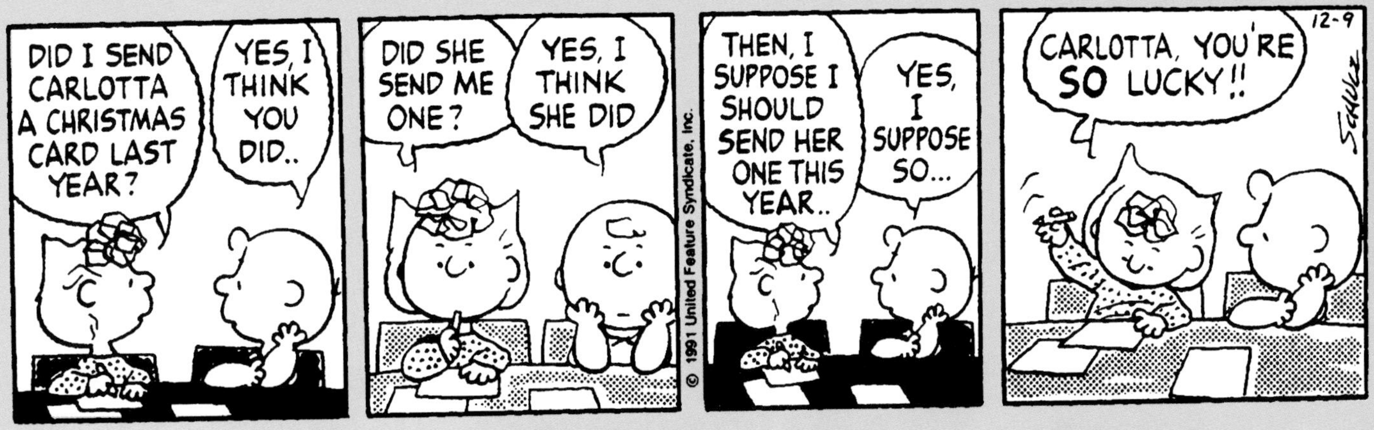
DID I SEND CARLOTTA A CHRISTMAS CARD LAST YEAR?
YES, I THINK YOU DID..
DID SHE SEND ME ONE?
YES, I THINK SHE DID
© 1991 United Feature Syndicate, Inc.
THEN, I SUPPOSE I SHOULD SEND HER ONE THIS YEAR..
YES, I SUPPOSE SO...
12-9
CARLOTTA, YOU'RE SO LUCKY!!
SCHULZ

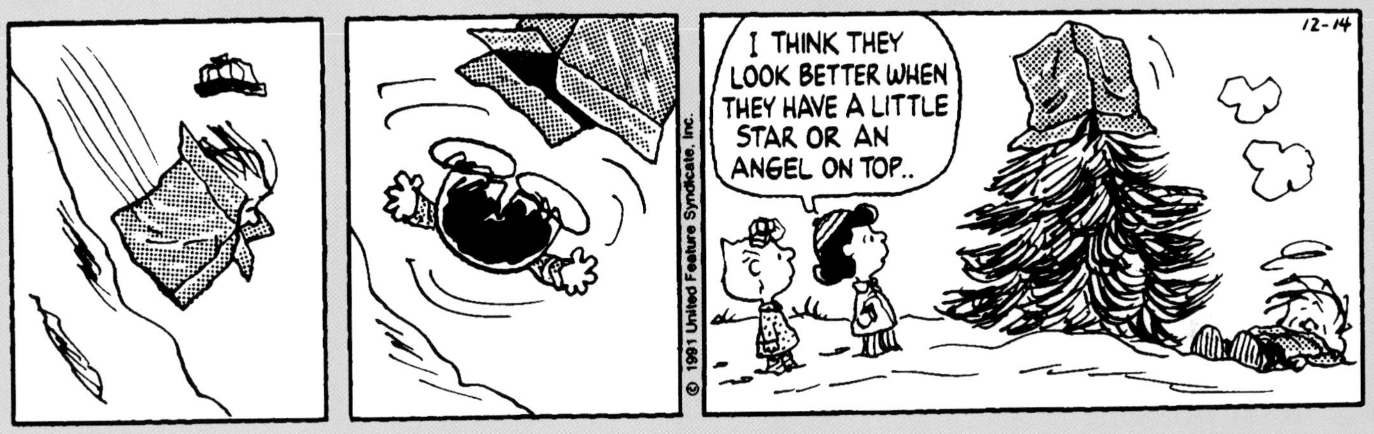
© 1991 United Feature Syndicate, Inc.
12-14
I THINK THEY LOOK BETTER WHEN THEY HAVE A LITTLE STAR OR AN ANGEL ON TOP..

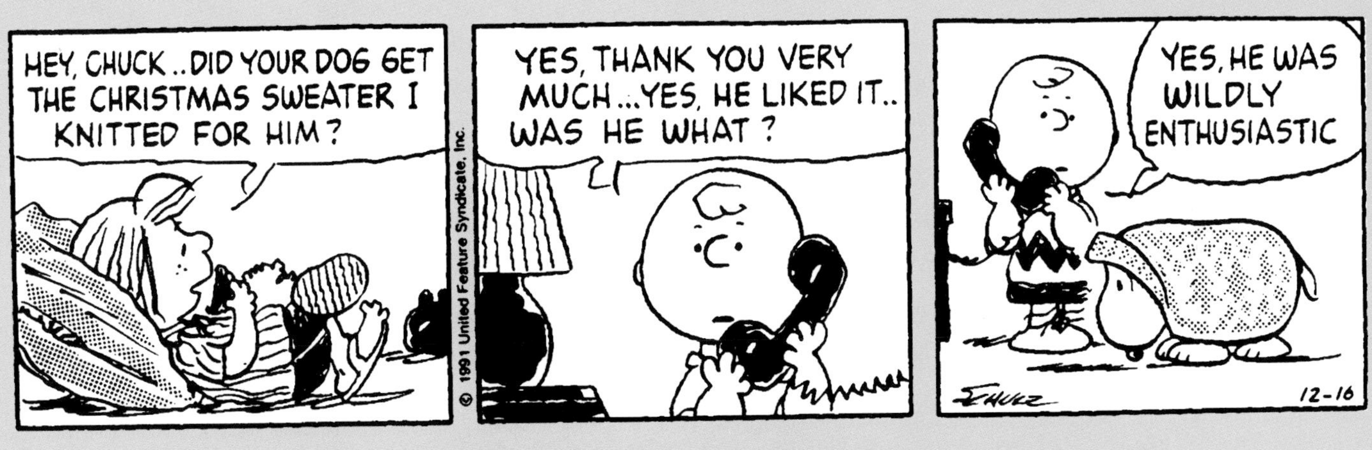
HEY, CHUCK..DID YOUR DOG GET THE CHRISTMAS SWEATER I KNITTED FOR HIM?
© 1991 United Feature Syndicate, Inc.
YES, THANK YOU VERY MUCH...YES, HE LIKED IT.. WAS HE WHAT?
YES, HE WAS WILDLY ENTHUSIASTIC
SCHULZ
12-16

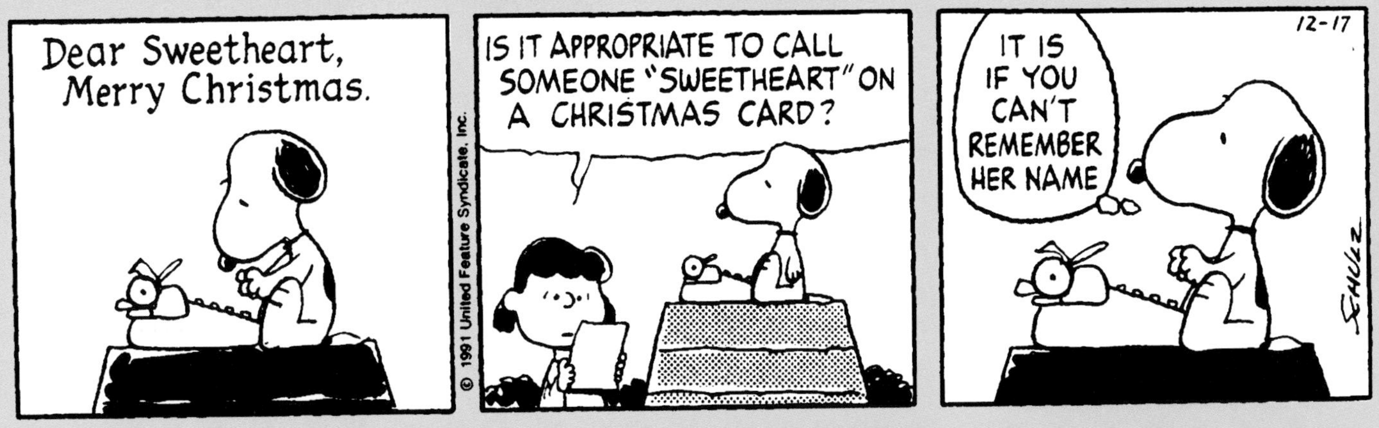
Dear Sweetheart,
Merry Christmas.
© 1991 United Feature Syndicate, Inc.
IS IT APPROPRIATE TO CALL SOMEONE "SWEETHEART" ON A CHRISTMAS CARD?
12-17
IT IS IF YOU CAN'T REMEMBER HER NAME
SCHULZ

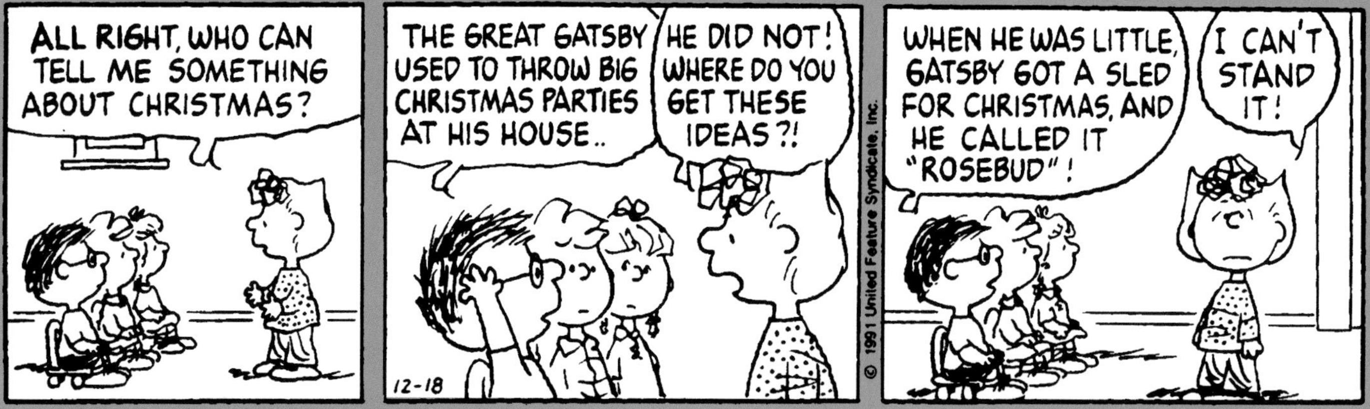
ALL RIGHT, WHO CAN TELL ME SOMETHING ABOUT CHRISTMAS?
THE GREAT GATSBY USED TO THROW BIG CHRISTMAS PARTIES AT HIS HOUSE..
HE DID NOT! WHERE DO YOU GET THESE IDEAS?!
12-18
© 1991 United Feature Syndicate, Inc.
WHEN HE WAS LITTLE, GATSBY GOT A SLED FOR CHRISTMAS, AND HE CALLED IT "ROSEBUD"!
I CAN'T STAND IT!

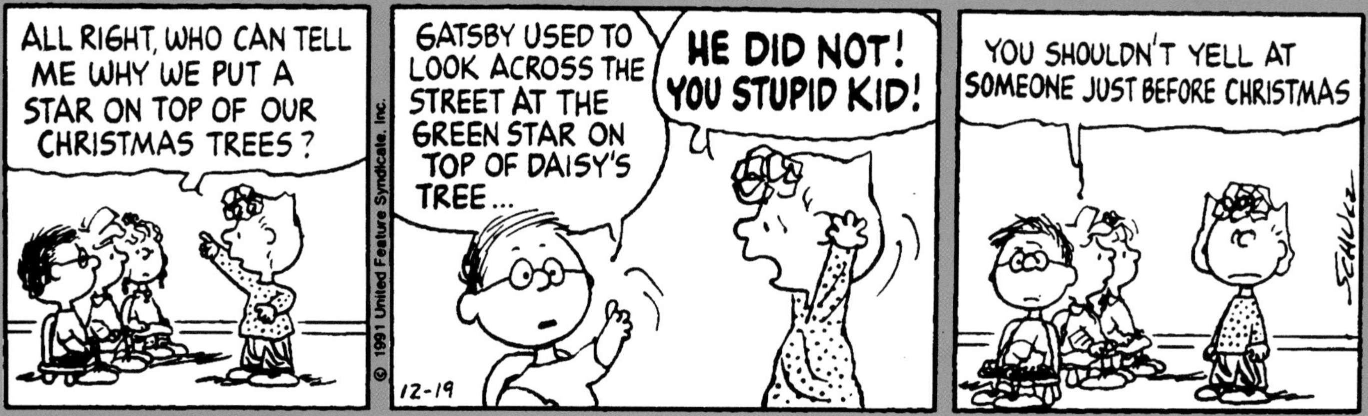
ALL RIGHT, WHO CAN TELL ME WHY WE PUT A STAR ON TOP OF OUR CHRISTMAS TREES?
© 1991 United Feature Syndicate, Inc.
GATSBY USED TO LOOK ACROSS THE STREET AT THE GREEN STAR ON TOP OF DAISY'S TREE...
HE DID NOT! YOU STUPID KID!
12-19
YOU SHOULDN'T YELL AT SOMEONE JUST BEFORE CHRISTMAS
SCHULZ

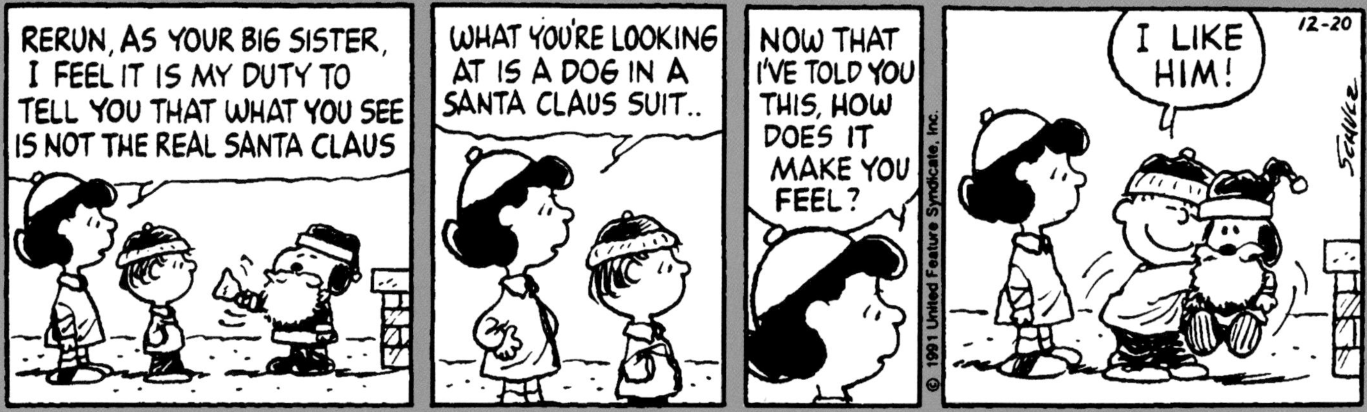
RERUN, AS YOUR BIG SISTER, I FEEL IT IS MY DUTY TO TELL YOU THAT WHAT YOU SEE IS NOT THE REAL SANTA CLAUS
WHAT YOU'RE LOOKING AT IS A DOG IN A SANTA CLAUS SUIT..
NOW THAT I'VE TOLD YOU THIS, HOW DOES IT MAKE YOU FEEL?
© 1991 United Feature Syndicate, Inc.
I LIKE HIM!
12-20
SCHULZ

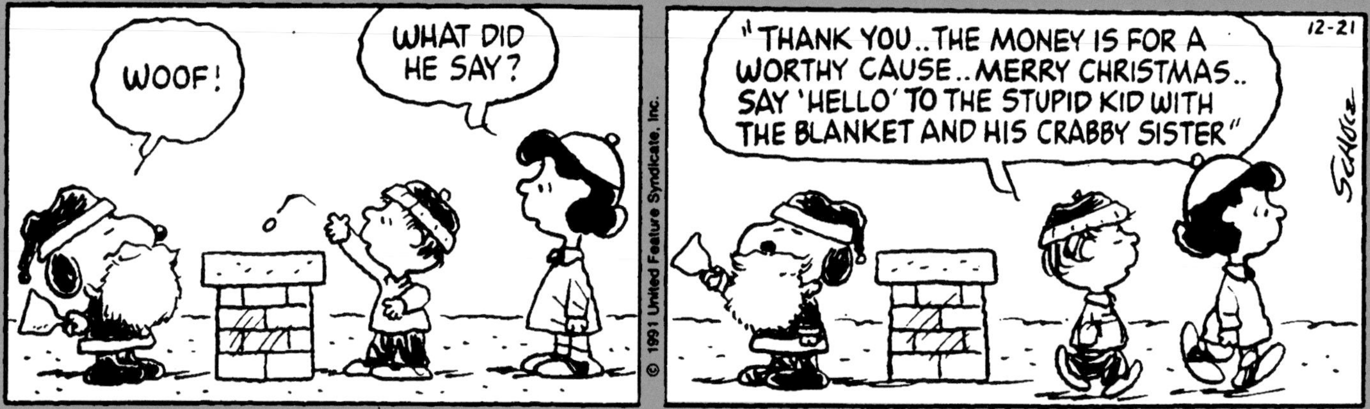
WOOF!
WHAT DID HE SAY?
© 1991 United Feature Syndicate, Inc.
"THANK YOU..THE MONEY IS FOR A WORTHY CAUSE..MERRY CHRISTMAS.. SAY 'HELLO' TO THE STUPID KID WITH THE BLANKET AND HIS CRABBY SISTER"
12-21
SCHULZ

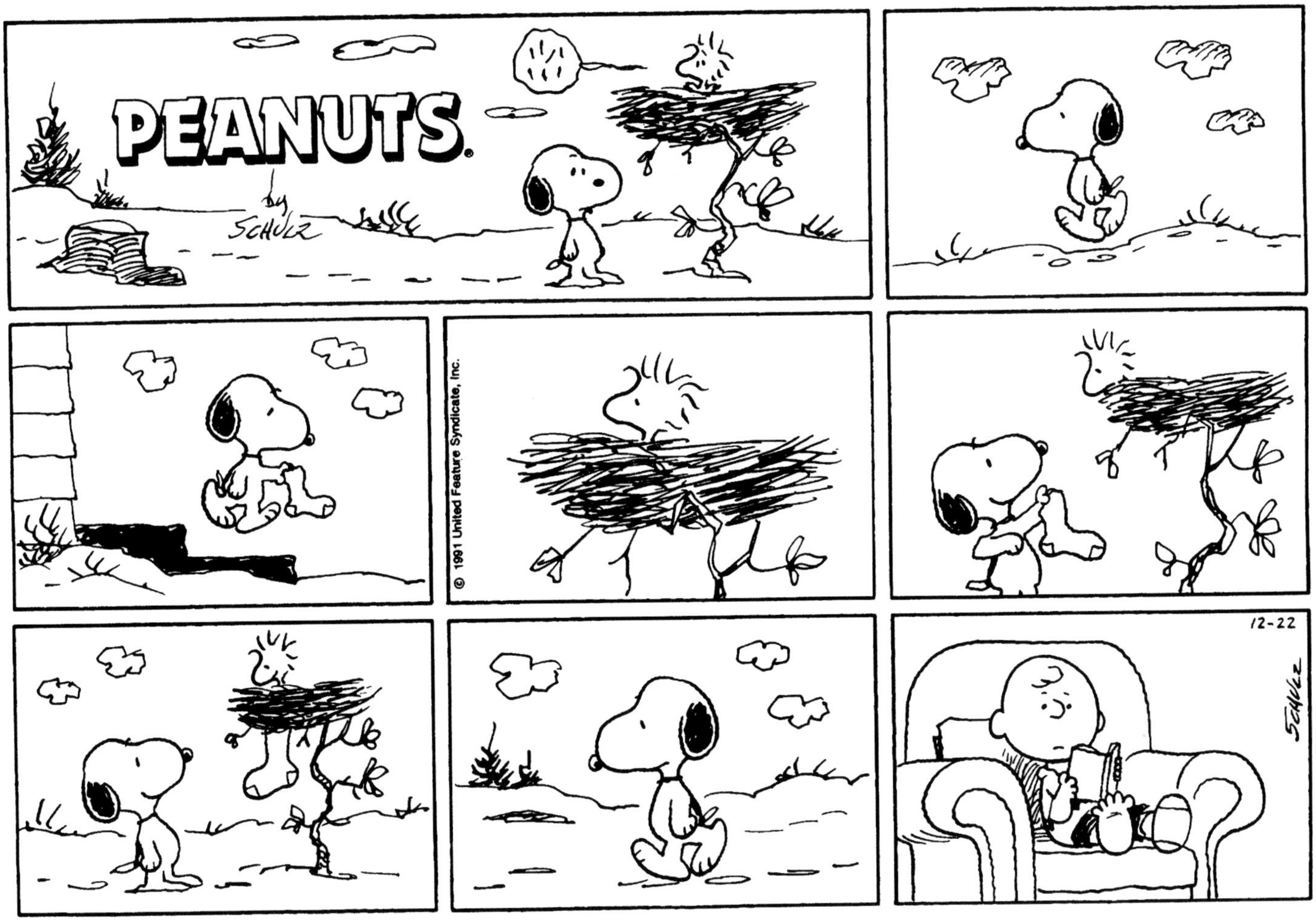
PEANUTS
by SCHULZ
© 1991 United Feature Syndicate, Inc.
12-22
SCHULZ

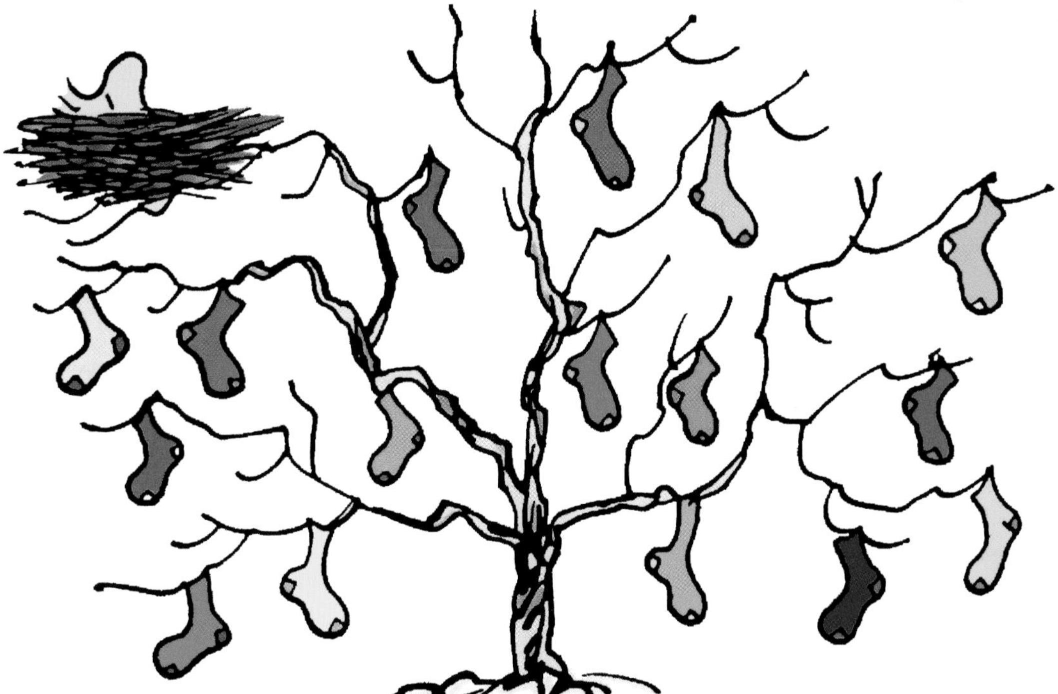

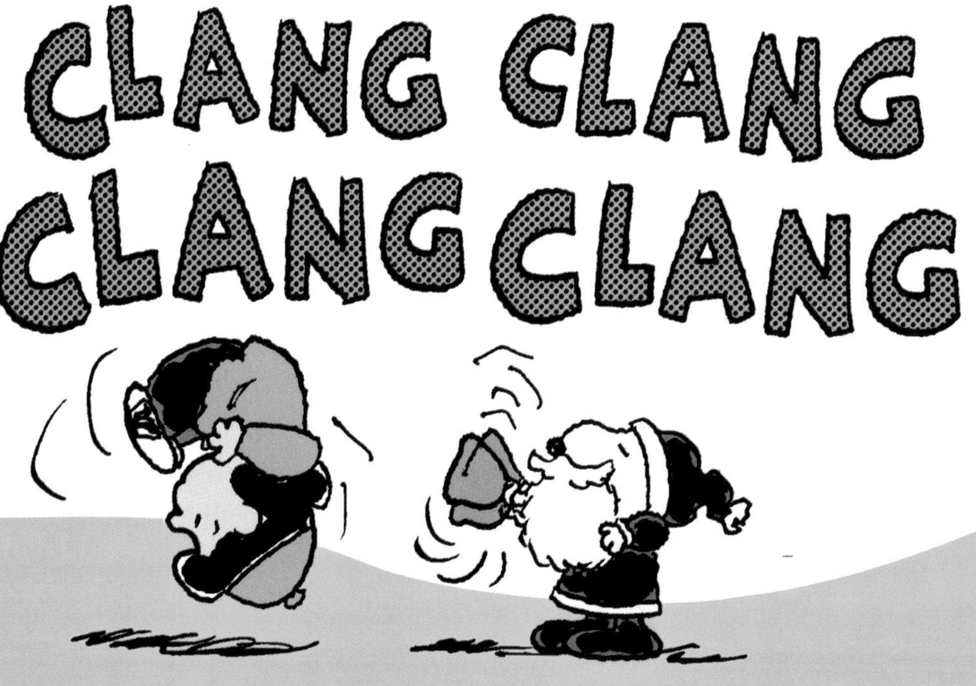
CLANG CLANG
CLANG CLANG

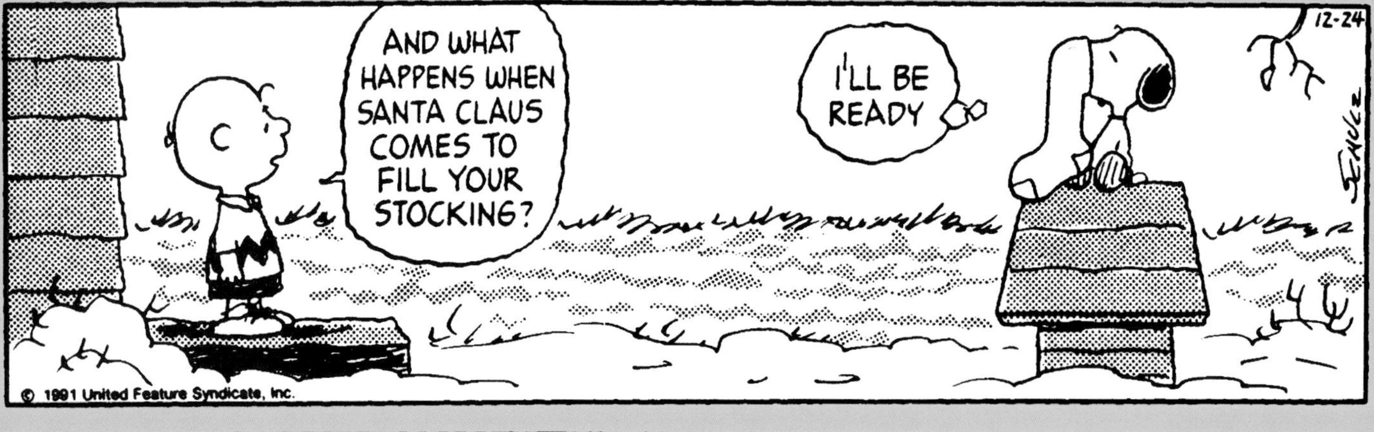
12-24
AND WHAT HAPPENS WHEN SANTA CLAUS COMES TO FILL YOUR STOCKING?
I'LL BE READY
SCHULZ
© 1991 United Feature Syndicate, Inc.

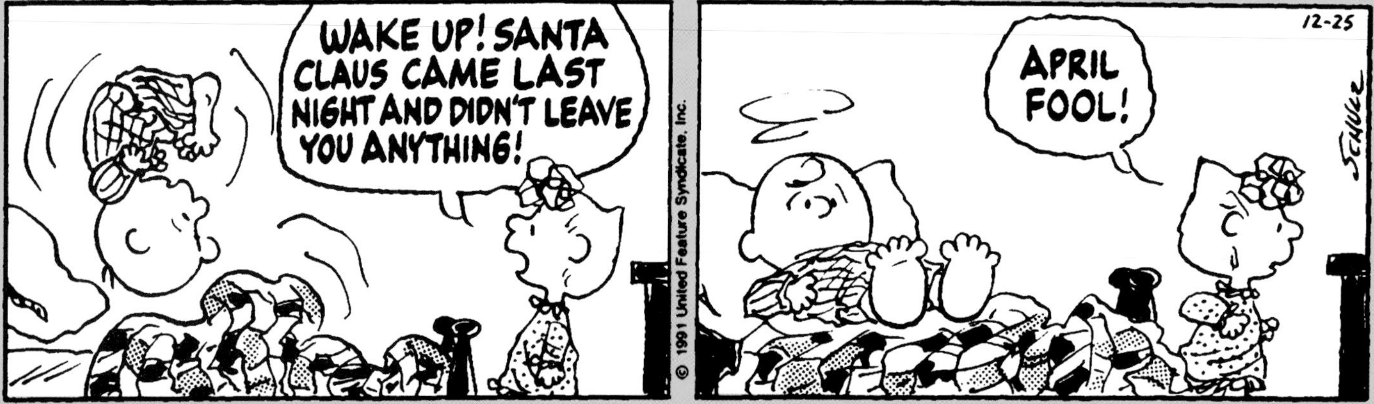
WAKE UP! SANTA CLAUS CAME LAST NIGHT AND DIDN'T LEAVE YOU ANYTHING!
© 1991 United Feature Syndicate, Inc.
12-25
APRIL FOOL!
SCHULZ

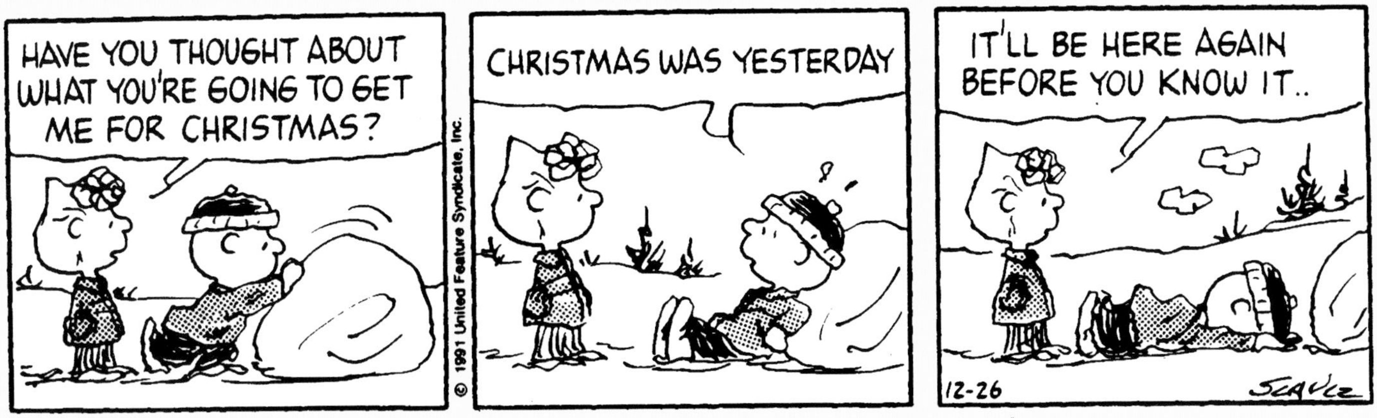
HAVE YOU THOUGHT ABOUT WHAT YOU'RE GOING TO GET ME FOR CHRISTMAS?
© 1991 United Feature Syndicate, Inc.
CHRISTMAS WAS YESTERDAY
IT'LL BE HERE AGAIN BEFORE YOU KNOW IT..
12-26
SCHULZ

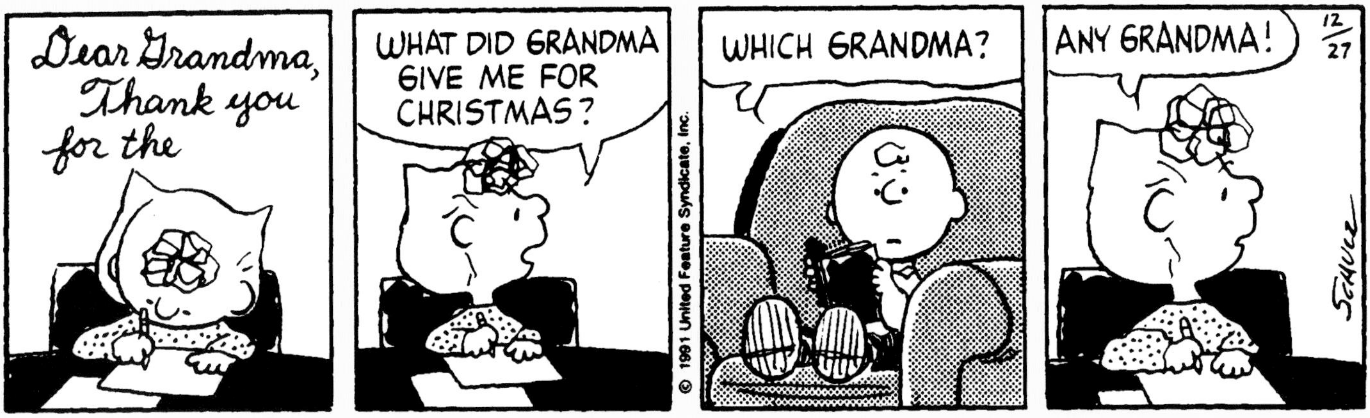
Dear Grandma, Thank you for the
WHAT DID GRANDMA GIVE ME FOR CHRISTMAS?
© 1991 United Feature Syndicate, Inc.
WHICH GRANDMA?
ANY GRANDMA!
12/27
SCHULZ

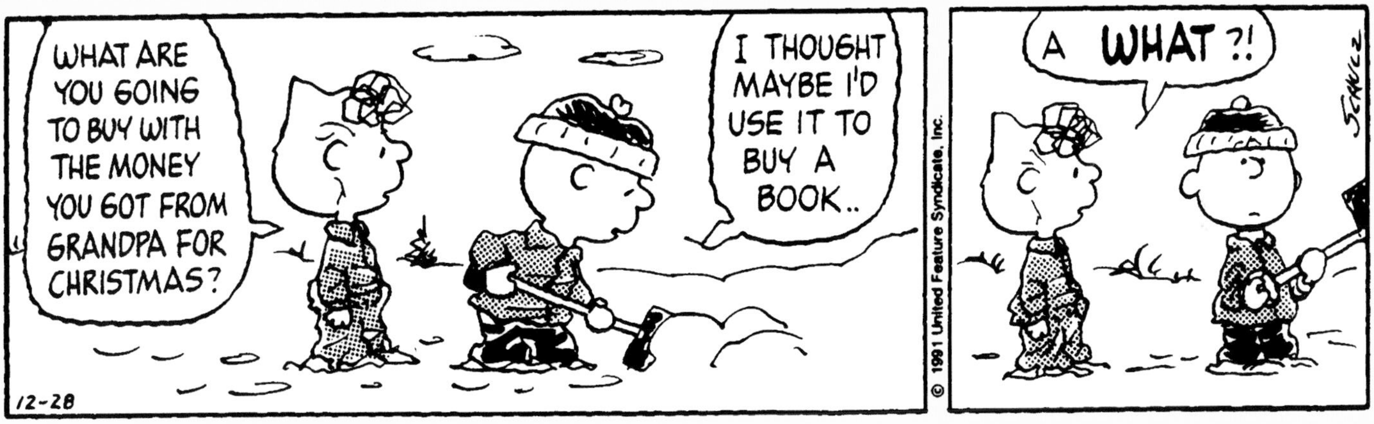
WHAT ARE YOU GOING TO BUY WITH THE MONEY YOU GOT FROM GRANDPA FOR CHRISTMAS?
I THOUGHT MAYBE I'D USE IT TO BUY A BOOK..
12-28
© 1991 United Feature Syndicate, Inc.
A WHAT?!
SCHULZ

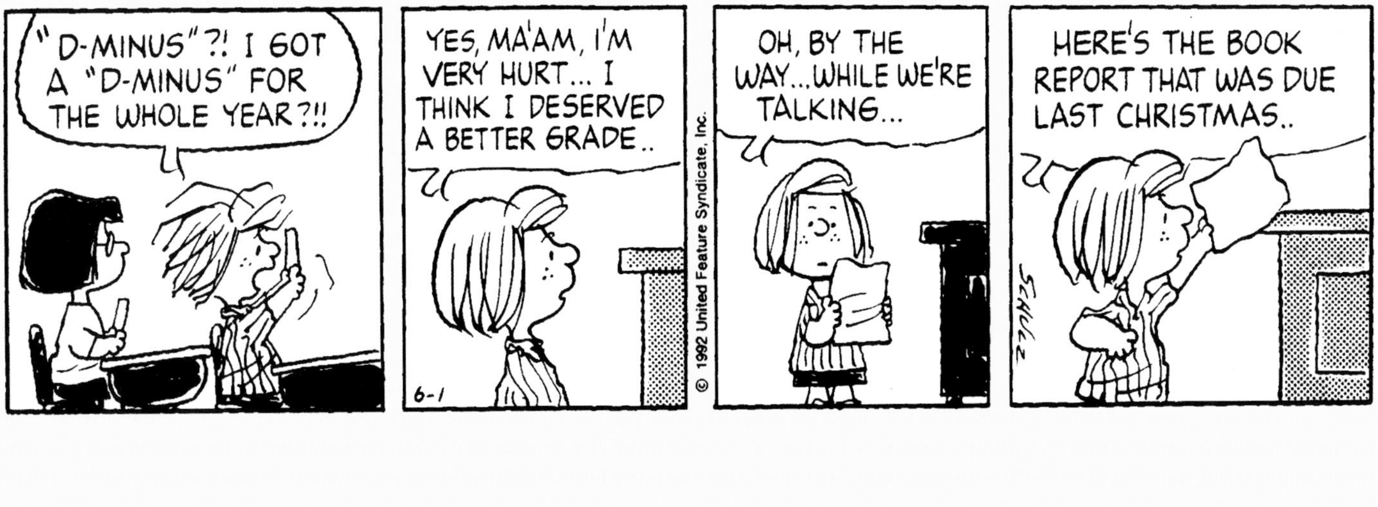
"D-MINUS"?! I GOT A "D-MINUS" FOR THE WHOLE YEAR?!!
YES, MA'AM, I'M VERY HURT... I THINK I DESERVED A BETTER GRADE..
6-1
© 1992 United Feature Syndicate, Inc.
OH, BY THE WAY...WHILE WE'RE TALKING...
HERE'S THE BOOK REPORT THAT WAS DUE LAST CHRISTMAS..
SCHULZ

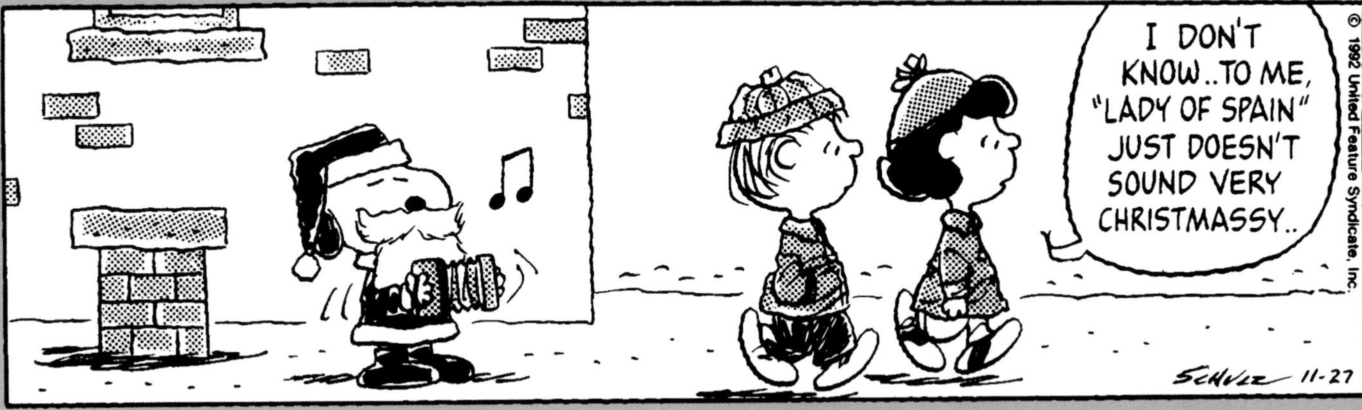
I DON'T KNOW..TO ME, "LADY OF SPAIN" JUST DOESN'T SOUND VERY CHRISTMASSY..
SCHULZ 11-27
© 1992 United Feature Syndicate, Inc.

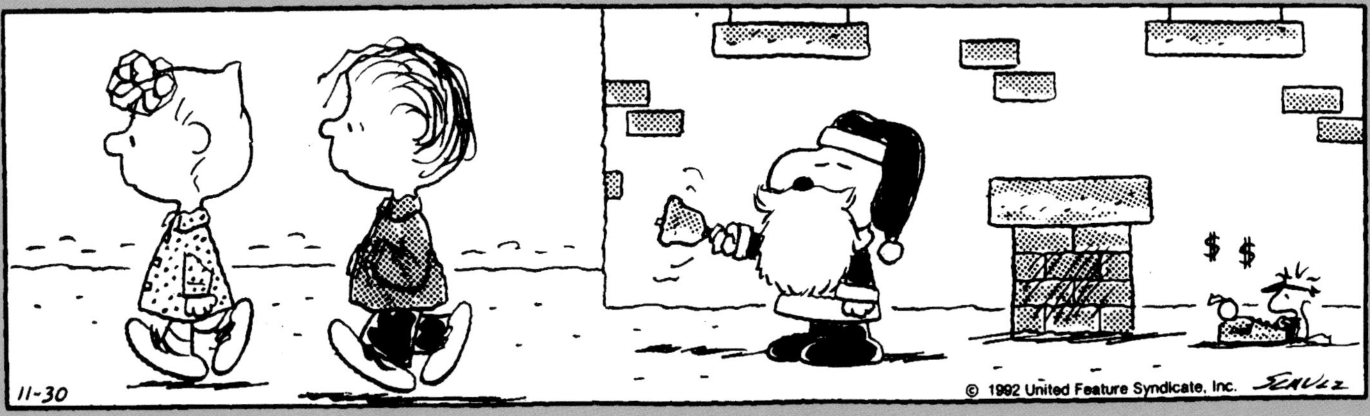
11-30
© 1992 United Feature Syndicate, Inc.
SCHULZ

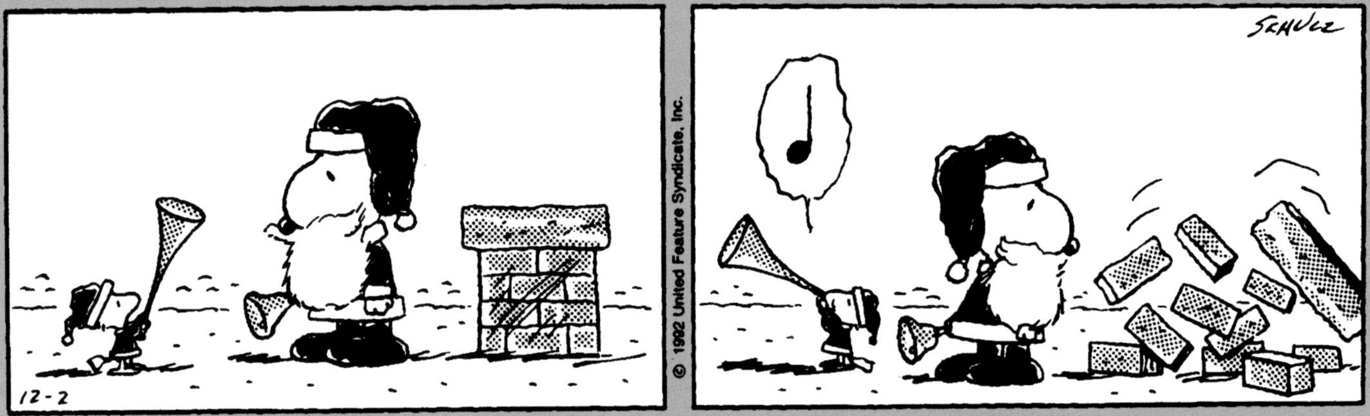
12-2
© 1992 United Feature Syndicate, Inc.
SCHULZ

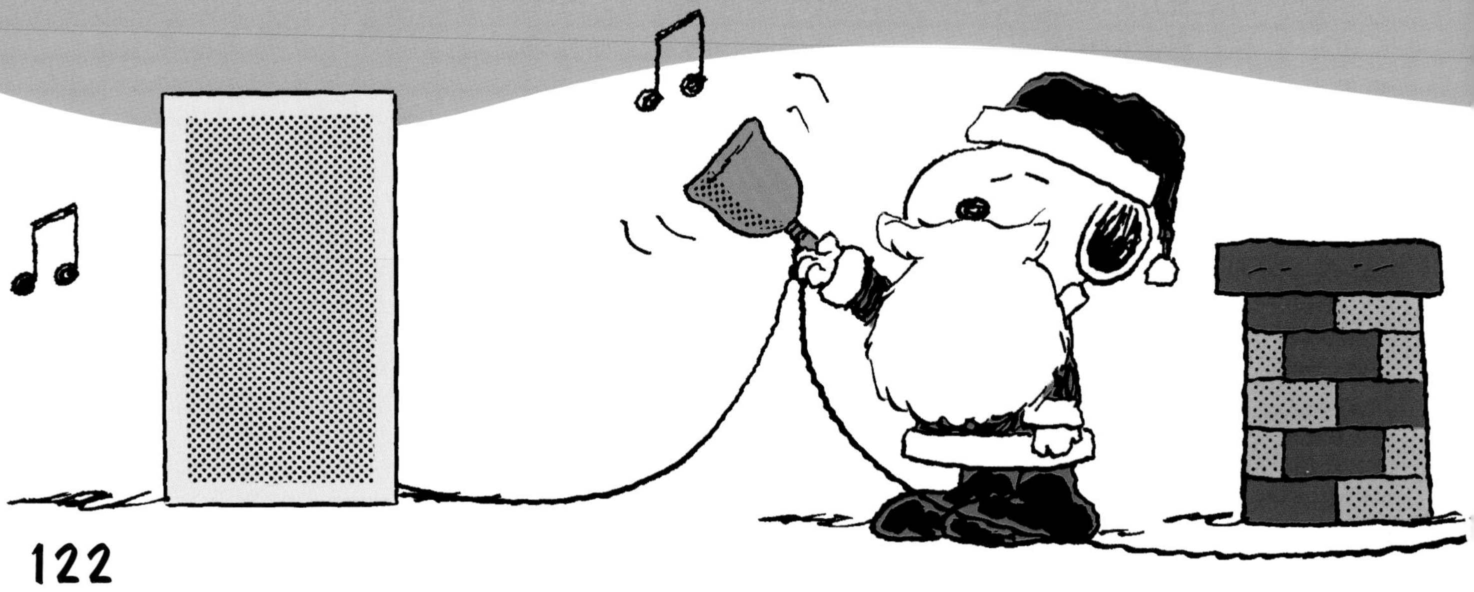

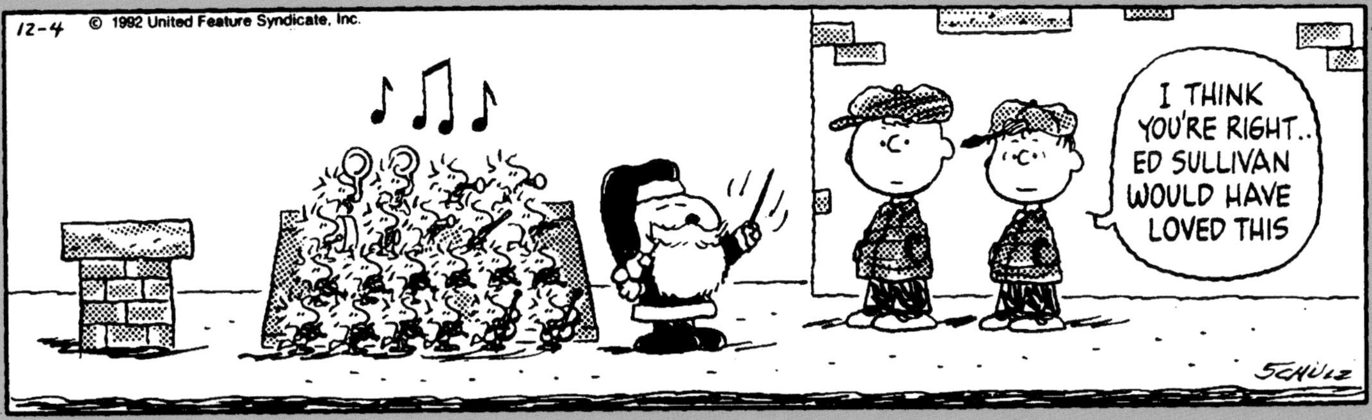
12-4
© 1992 United Feature Syndicate, Inc.
I THINK YOU'RE RIGHT.. ED SULLIVAN WOULD HAVE LOVED THIS
SCHULZ

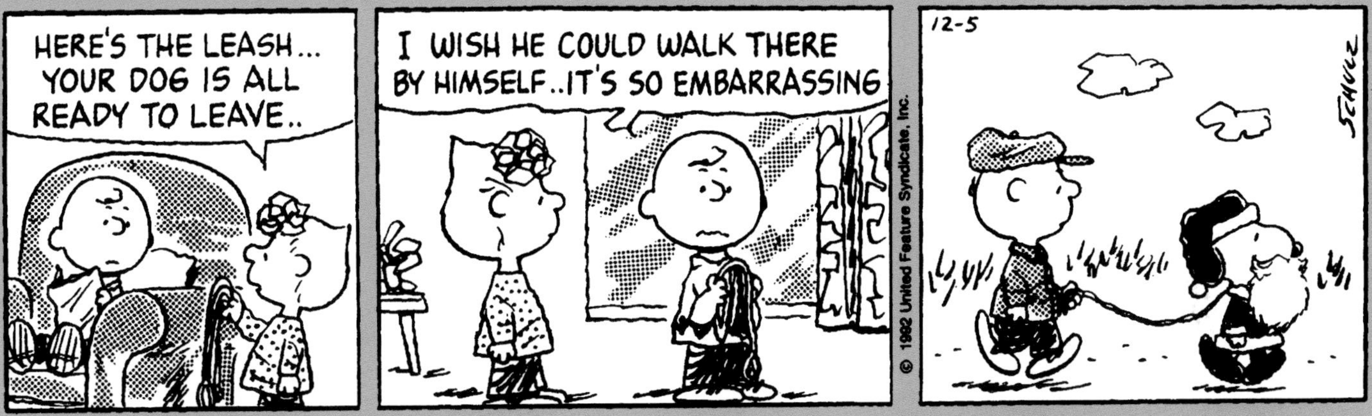
HERE'S THE LEASH... YOUR DOG IS ALL READY TO LEAVE..
I WISH HE COULD WALK THERE BY HIMSELF..IT'S SO EMBARRASSING
© 1992 United Feature Syndicate, Inc.
12-5
SCHULZ

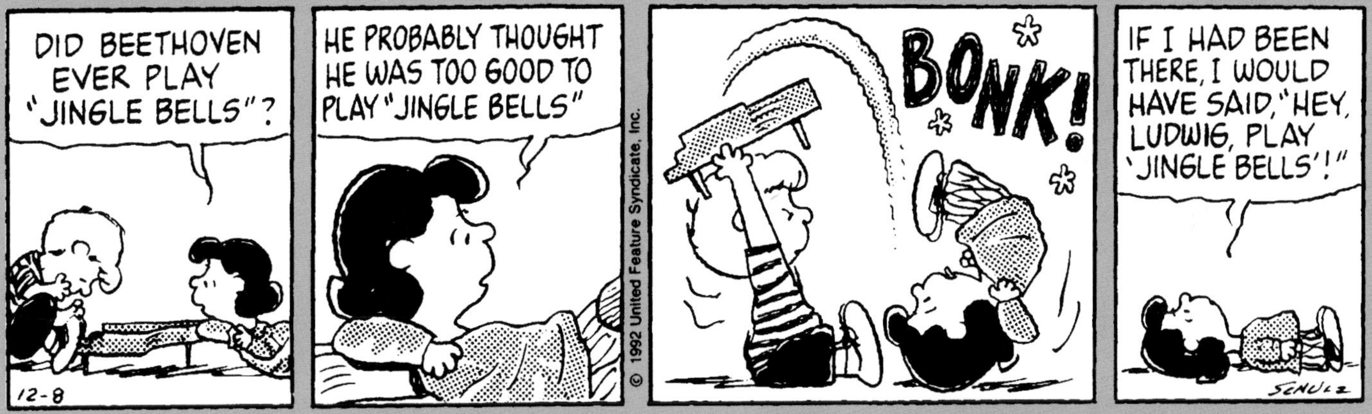
DID BEETHOVEN EVER PLAY "JINGLE BELLS"?
12-8
HE PROBABLY THOUGHT HE WAS TOO GOOD TO PLAY "JINGLE BELLS"
© 1992 United Feature Syndicate, Inc.
BONK!
IF I HAD BEEN THERE, I WOULD HAVE SAID, "HEY, LUDWIG, PLAY 'JINGLE BELLS'!"
SCHULZ

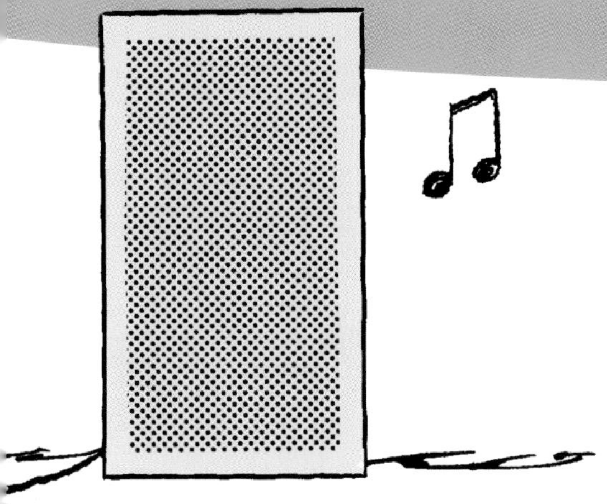

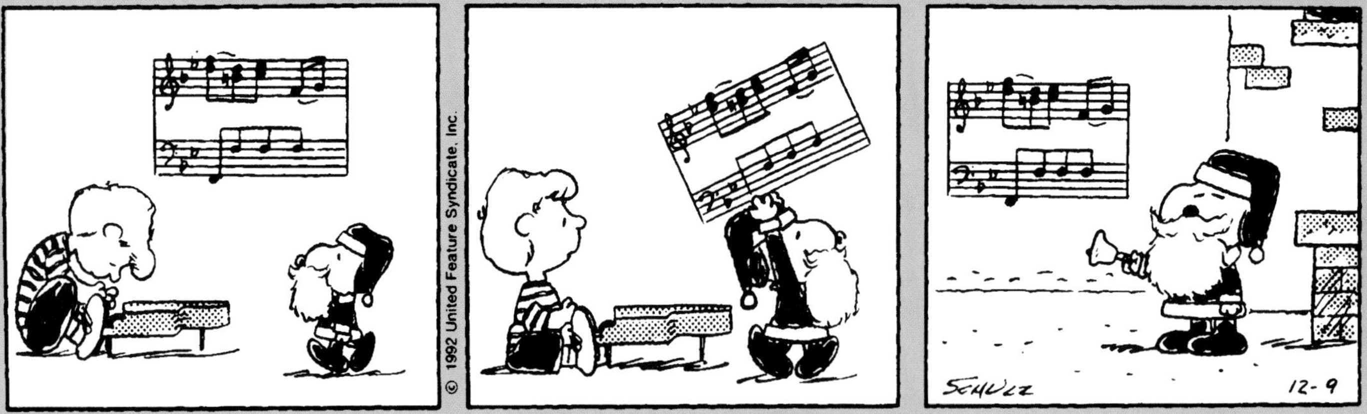
© 1992 United Feature Syndicate, Inc.
SCHULZ
12-9

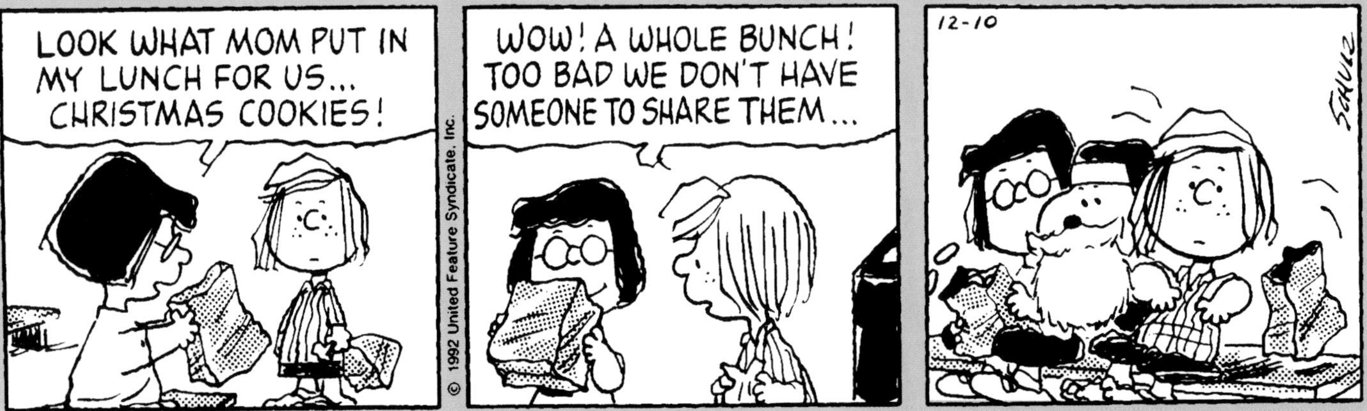
LOOK WHAT MOM PUT IN MY LUNCH FOR US... CHRISTMAS COOKIES!
© 1992 United Feature Syndicate, Inc.
WOW! A WHOLE BUNCH! TOO BAD WE DON'T HAVE SOMEONE TO SHARE THEM...
12-10
SCHULZ

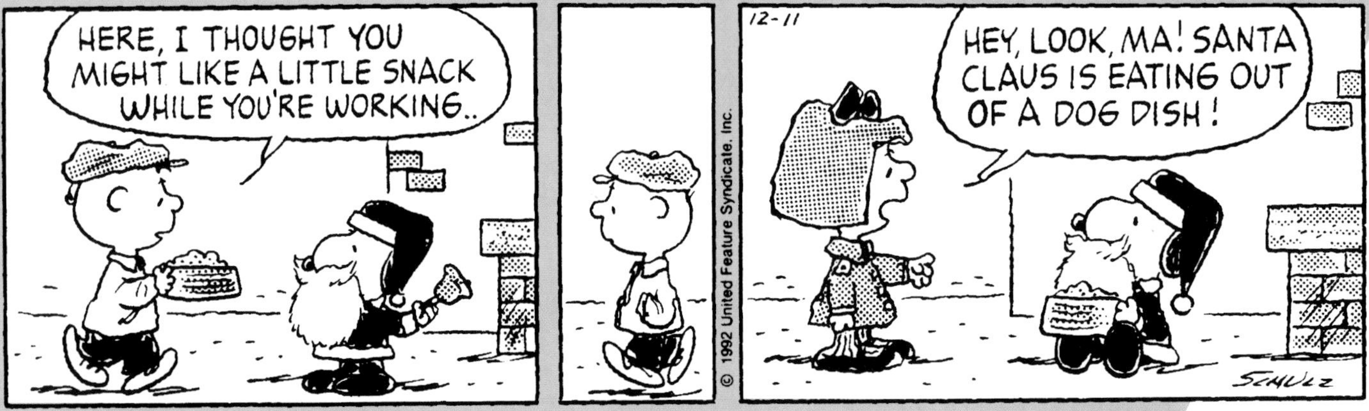
HERE, I THOUGHT YOU MIGHT LIKE A LITTLE SNACK WHILE YOU'RE WORKING..
© 1992 United Feature Syndicate, Inc.
12-11
HEY, LOOK, MA! SANTA CLAUS IS EATING OUT OF A DOG DISH!
SCHULZ

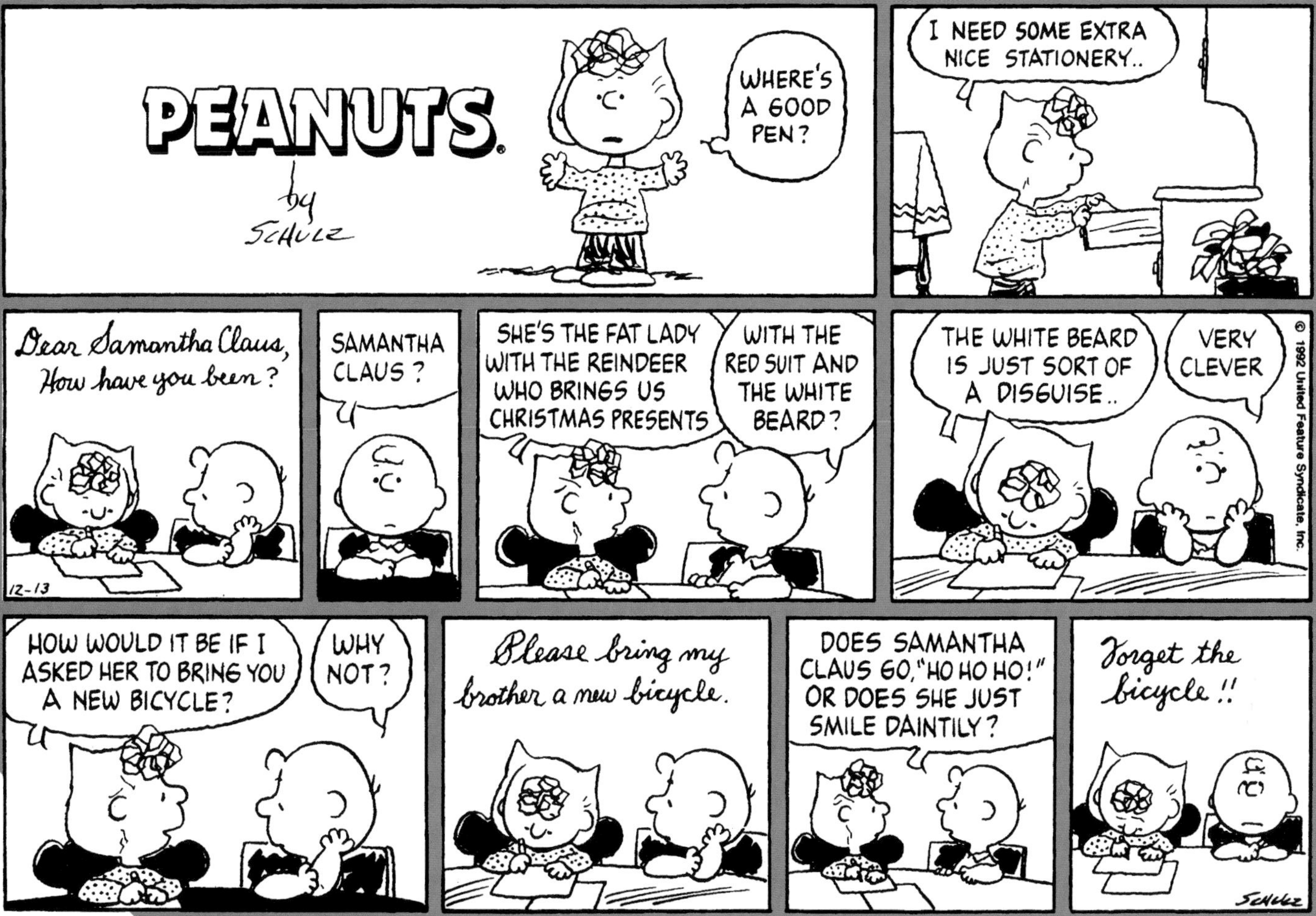

PEANUTS by SCHULZ

WHERE'S A GOOD PEN?

I NEED SOME EXTRA NICE STATIONERY..

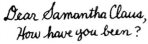

Dear Samantha Claus, How have you been?

12-13

SAMANTHA CLAUS?

SHE'S THE FAT LADY WITH THE REINDEER WHO BRINGS US CHRISTMAS PRESENTS

WITH THE RED SUIT AND THE WHITE BEARD?

THE WHITE BEARD IS JUST SORT OF A DISGUISE..

VERY CLEVER

© 1992 United Feature Syndicate, Inc.

HOW WOULD IT BE IF I ASKED HER TO BRING YOU A NEW BICYCLE?

WHY NOT?

Please bring my brother a new bicycle.

DOES SAMANTHA CLAUS GO, "HO HO HO!" OR DOES SHE JUST SMILE DAINTILY?

Forget the bicycle!!

SCHULZ

125

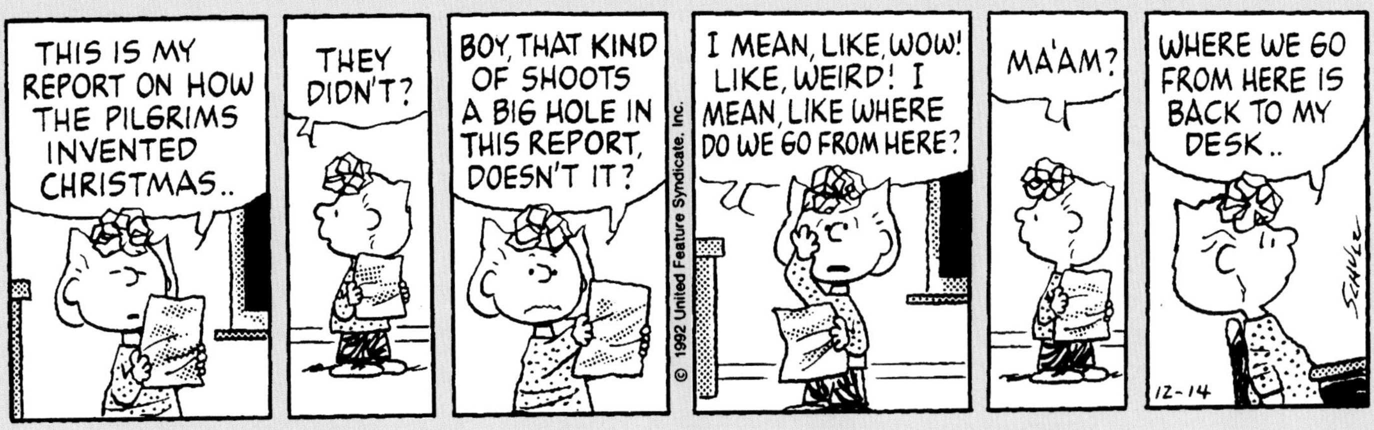
THIS IS MY REPORT ON HOW THE PILGRIMS INVENTED CHRISTMAS..
THEY DIDN'T?
BOY, THAT KIND OF SHOOTS A BIG HOLE IN THIS REPORT, DOESN'T IT?
I MEAN, LIKE, WOW! LIKE, WEIRD! I MEAN, LIKE WHERE DO WE GO FROM HERE?
MA'AM?
WHERE WE GO FROM HERE IS BACK TO MY DESK..
© 1992 United Feature Syndicate, Inc.
SCHULZ
12-14

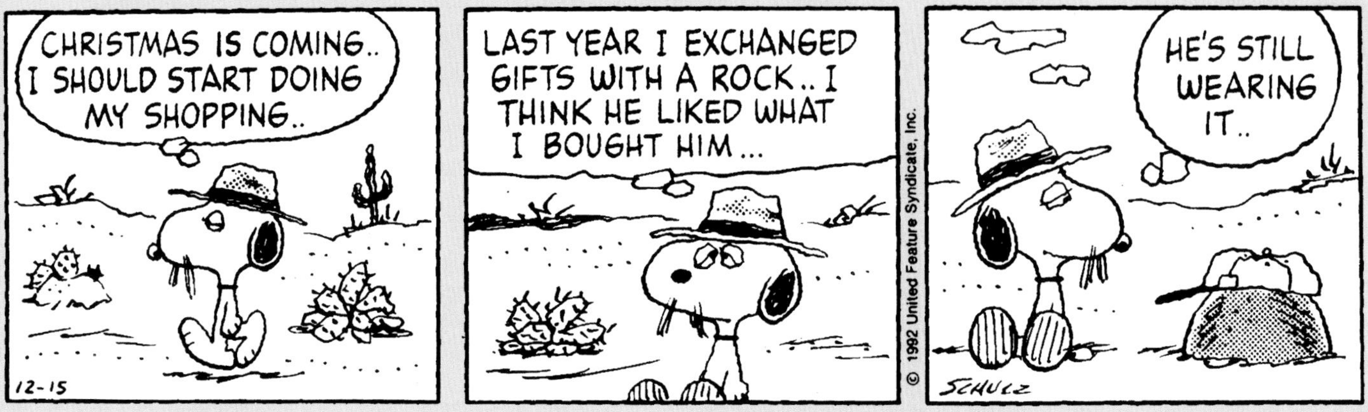
CHRISTMAS IS COMING.. I SHOULD START DOING MY SHOPPING..
LAST YEAR I EXCHANGED GIFTS WITH A ROCK.. I THINK HE LIKED WHAT I BOUGHT HIM...
HE'S STILL WEARING IT..
© 1992 United Feature Syndicate, Inc.
SCHULZ
12-15

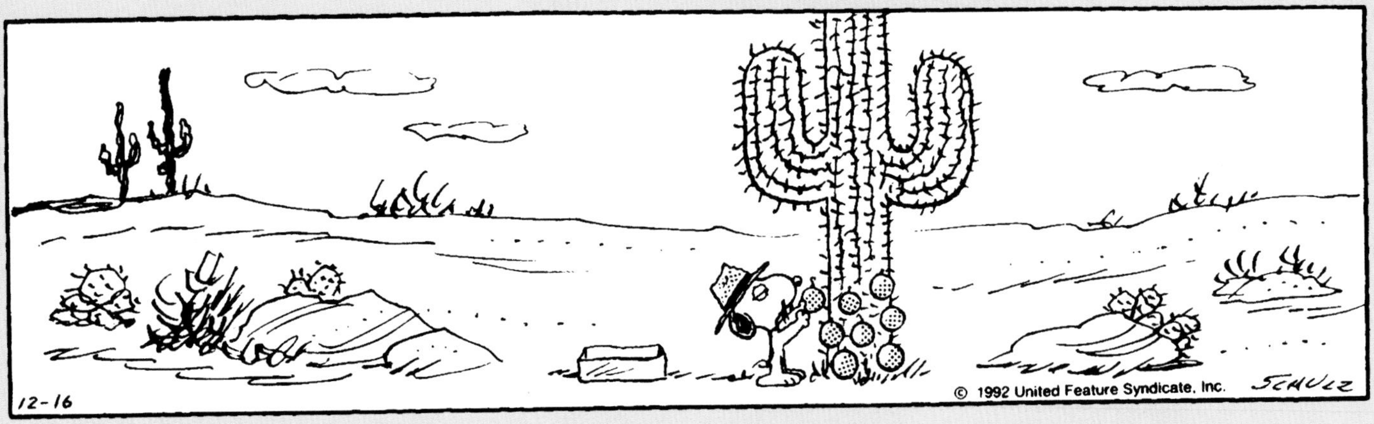
© 1992 United Feature Syndicate, Inc.
SCHULZ
12-16

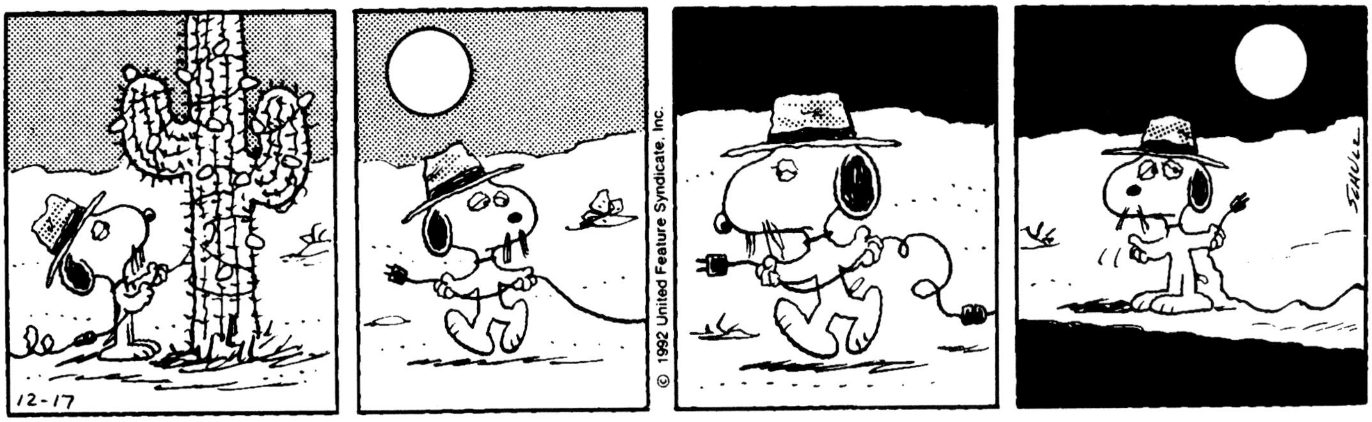
12-17
© 1992 United Feature Syndicate, Inc.
SCHULZ

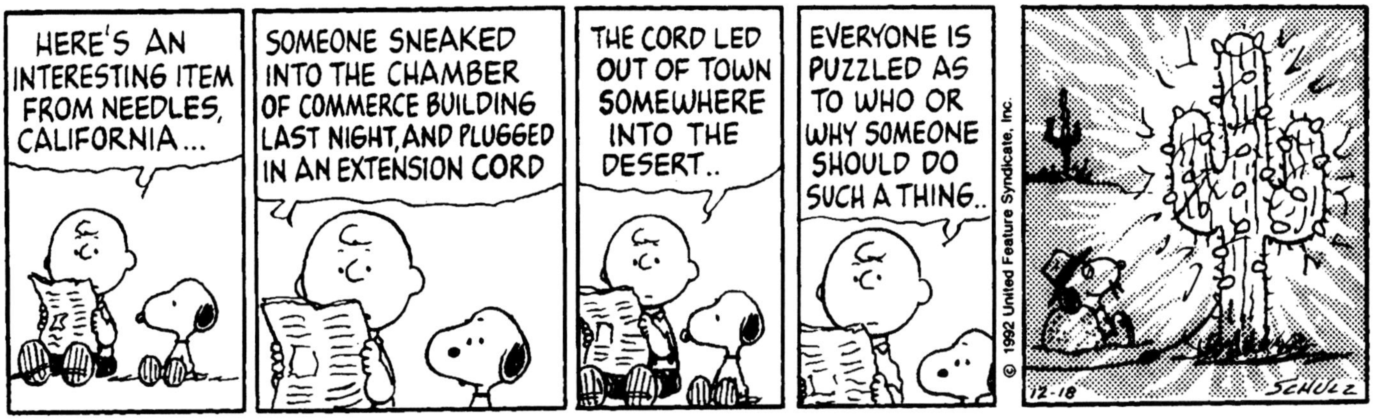
HERE'S AN INTERESTING ITEM FROM NEEDLES, CALIFORNIA...
SOMEONE SNEAKED INTO THE CHAMBER OF COMMERCE BUILDING LAST NIGHT, AND PLUGGED IN AN EXTENSION CORD
THE CORD LED OUT OF TOWN SOMEWHERE INTO THE DESERT..
EVERYONE IS PUZZLED AS TO WHO OR WHY SOMEONE SHOULD DO SUCH A THING..
© 1992 United Feature Syndicate, Inc.
12-18
SCHULZ

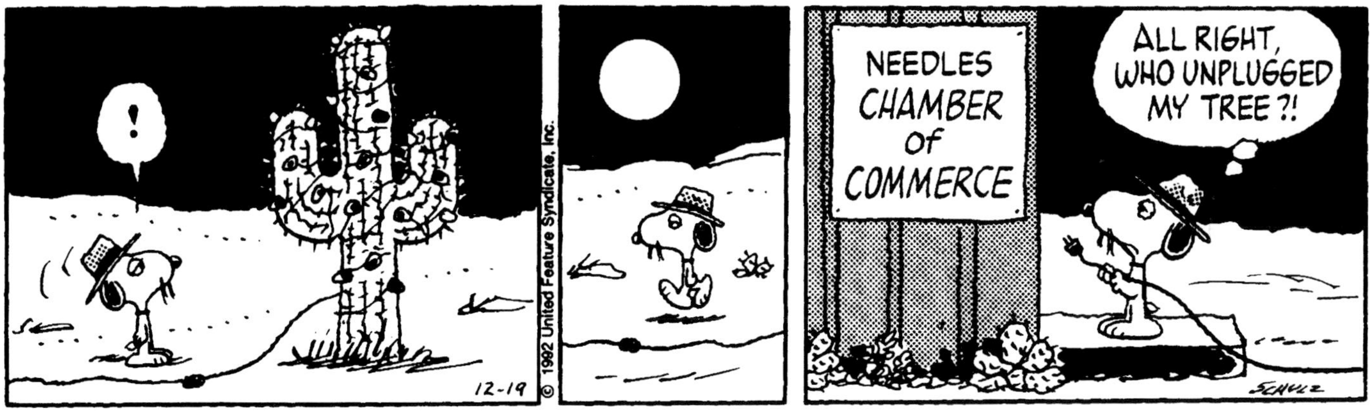
!
12-19
© 1992 United Feature Syndicate, Inc.
NEEDLES CHAMBER Of COMMERCE
ALL RIGHT, WHO UNPLUGGED MY TREE ?!
SCHULZ

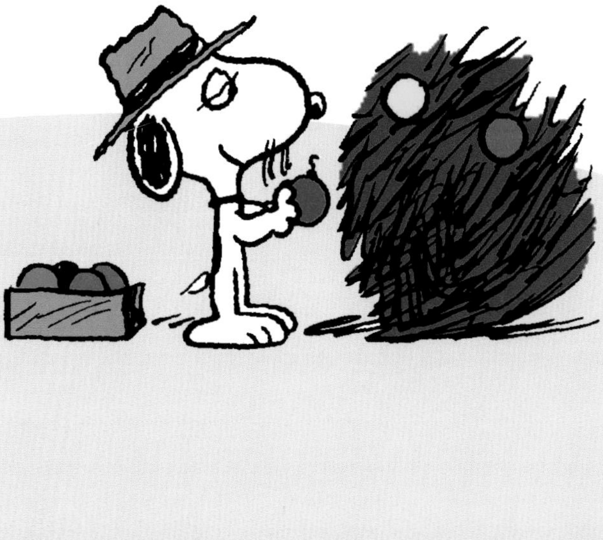

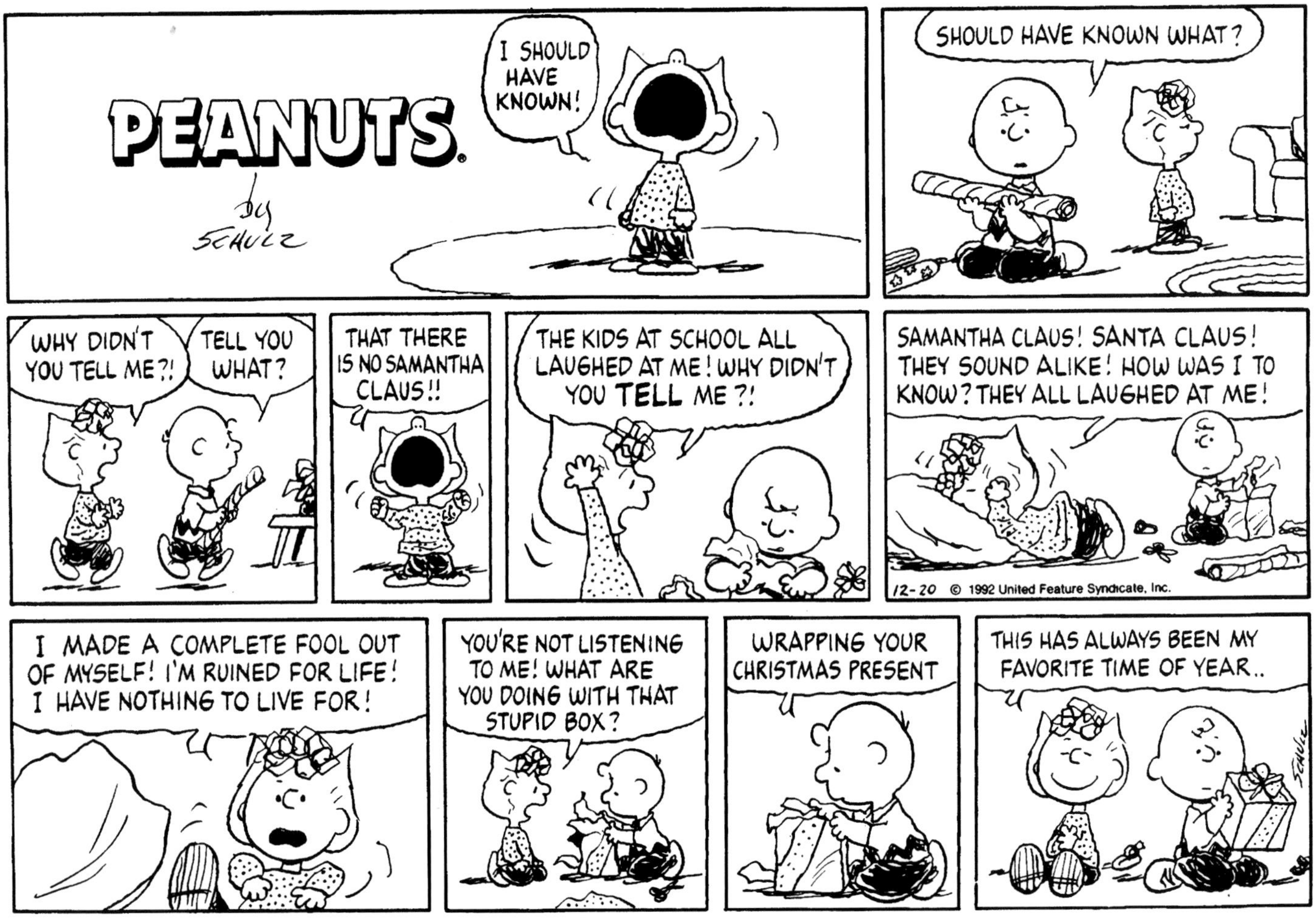
PEANUTS
by SCHULZ
I SHOULD HAVE KNOWN!
SHOULD HAVE KNOWN WHAT?
WHY DIDN'T YOU TELL ME?!
TELL YOU WHAT?
THAT THERE IS NO SAMANTHA CLAUS!!
THE KIDS AT SCHOOL ALL LAUGHED AT ME! WHY DIDN'T YOU TELL ME?!
SAMANTHA CLAUS! SANTA CLAUS! THEY SOUND ALIKE! HOW WAS I TO KNOW? THEY ALL LAUGHED AT ME!
12-20 © 1992 United Feature Syndicate, Inc.
I MADE A COMPLETE FOOL OUT OF MYSELF! I'M RUINED FOR LIFE! I HAVE NOTHING TO LIVE FOR!
YOU'RE NOT LISTENING TO ME! WHAT ARE YOU DOING WITH THAT STUPID BOX?
WRAPPING YOUR CHRISTMAS PRESENT
THIS HAS ALWAYS BEEN MY FAVORITE TIME OF YEAR..
SCHULZ

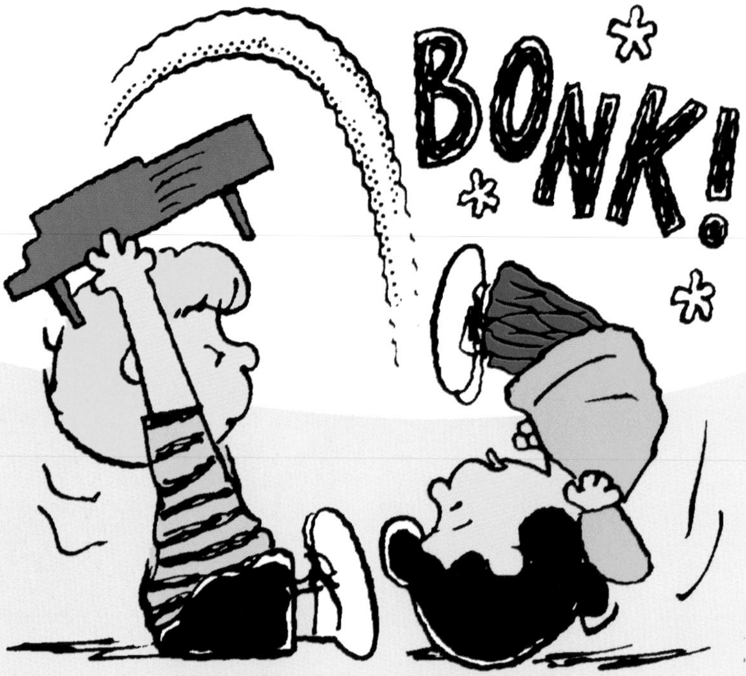
BONK!

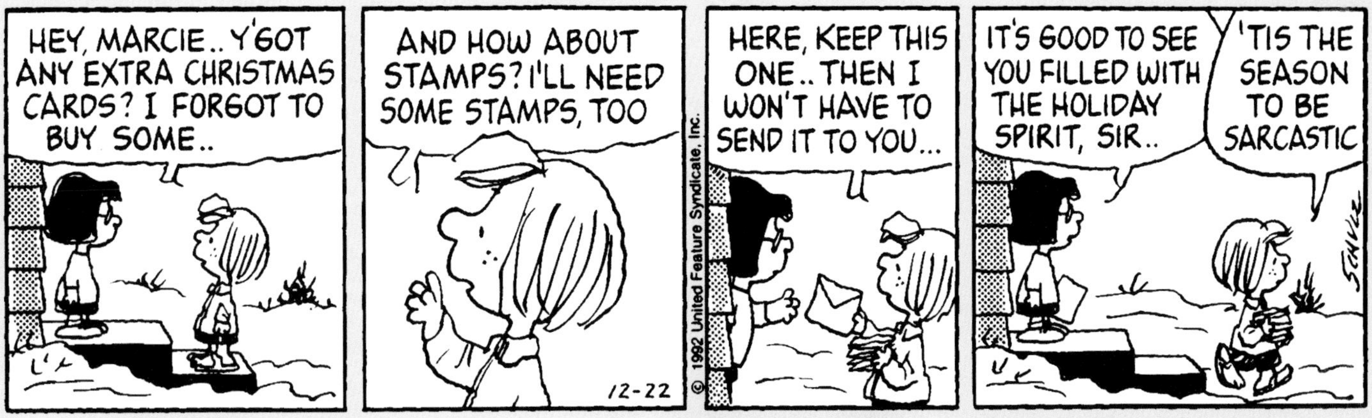
HEY, MARCIE.. Y'GOT ANY EXTRA CHRISTMAS CARDS? I FORGOT TO BUY SOME..
AND HOW ABOUT STAMPS? I'LL NEED SOME STAMPS, TOO
12-22
© 1992 United Feature Syndicate, Inc.
HERE, KEEP THIS ONE.. THEN I WON'T HAVE TO SEND IT TO YOU...
IT'S GOOD TO SEE YOU FILLED WITH THE HOLIDAY SPIRIT, SIR..
'TIS THE SEASON TO BE SARCASTIC
SCHULZ

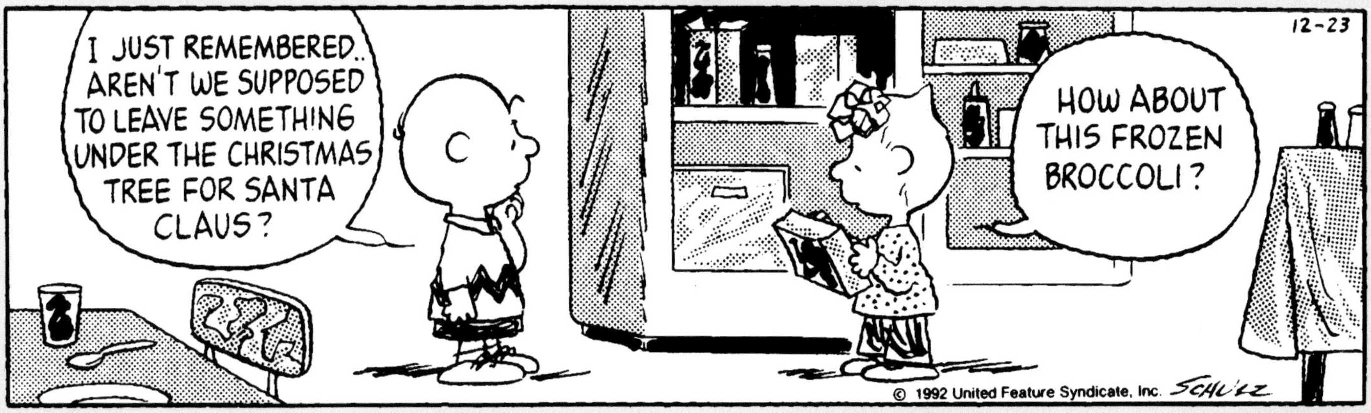
12-23
I JUST REMEMBERED.. AREN'T WE SUPPOSED TO LEAVE SOMETHING UNDER THE CHRISTMAS TREE FOR SANTA CLAUS?
HOW ABOUT THIS FROZEN BROCCOLI?
© 1992 United Feature Syndicate, Inc.
SCHULZ

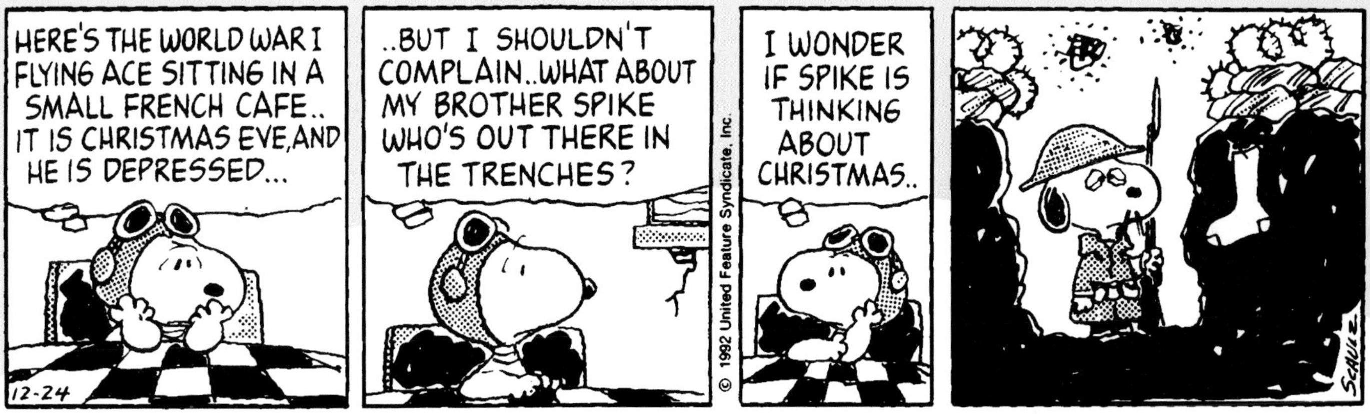
HERE'S THE WORLD WAR I FLYING ACE SITTING IN A SMALL FRENCH CAFE.. IT IS CHRISTMAS EVE, AND HE IS DEPRESSED...
12-24
..BUT I SHOULDN'T COMPLAIN..WHAT ABOUT MY BROTHER SPIKE WHO'S OUT THERE IN THE TRENCHES?
© 1992 United Feature Syndicate, Inc.
I WONDER IF SPIKE IS THINKING ABOUT CHRISTMAS..
SCHULZ

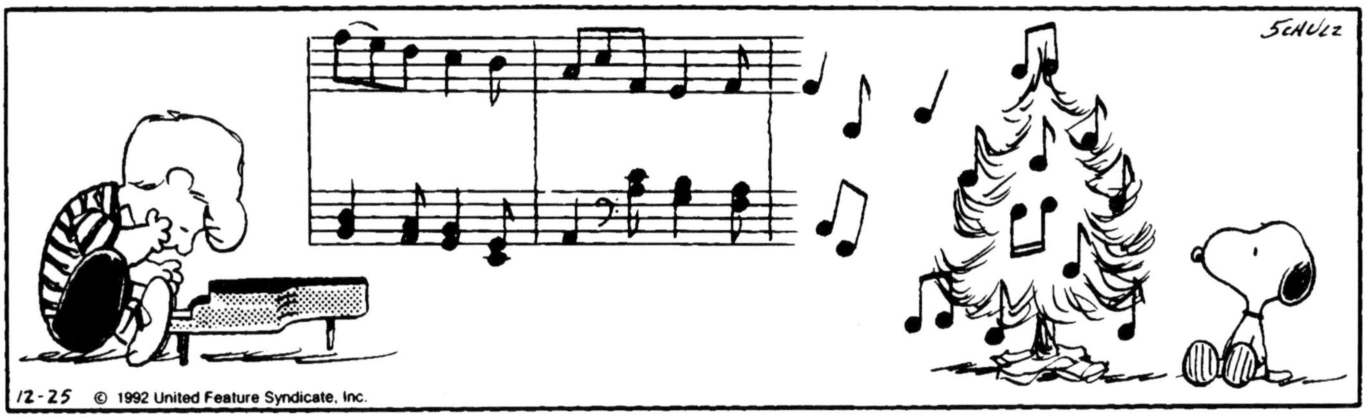
SCHULZ
12-25
© 1992 United Feature Syndicate, Inc.

PEANUTS
SCHULZ
MERCI!
WELL, LOOK HERE! IT'S SANTA! THIS IS MY LITTLE BROTHER "RERUN," SANTA...
TELL SANTA WHAT YOU WANT FOR CHRISTMAS, "RERUN"..
WELL, I'D LIKE SOME BOOKS, A VIDEO GAME, SOME IN-LINE SKATES AND MAYBE A NICE SWEATER..
THAT WAS GREAT, "RERUN"...NOW YOU HAVE SOMETHING TO LOOK FORWARD TO ON CHRISTMAS MORNING..
BEFORE WE GO ANY FARTHER, COULD I ASK YOU SOMETHING?
12-12
© 1993 United Feature Syndicate, Inc.
DID YOU KNOW I WAS TALKING TO A DOG?
SCHULZ

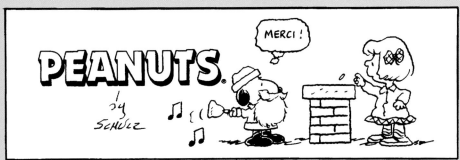

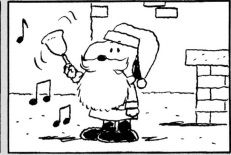

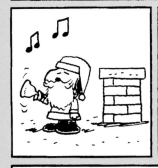

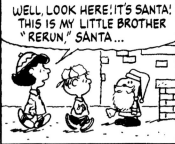

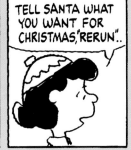

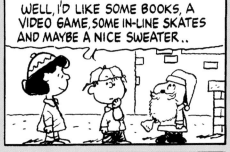

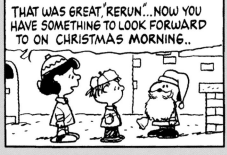

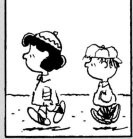

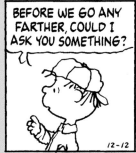

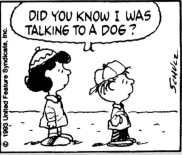

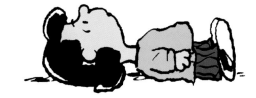

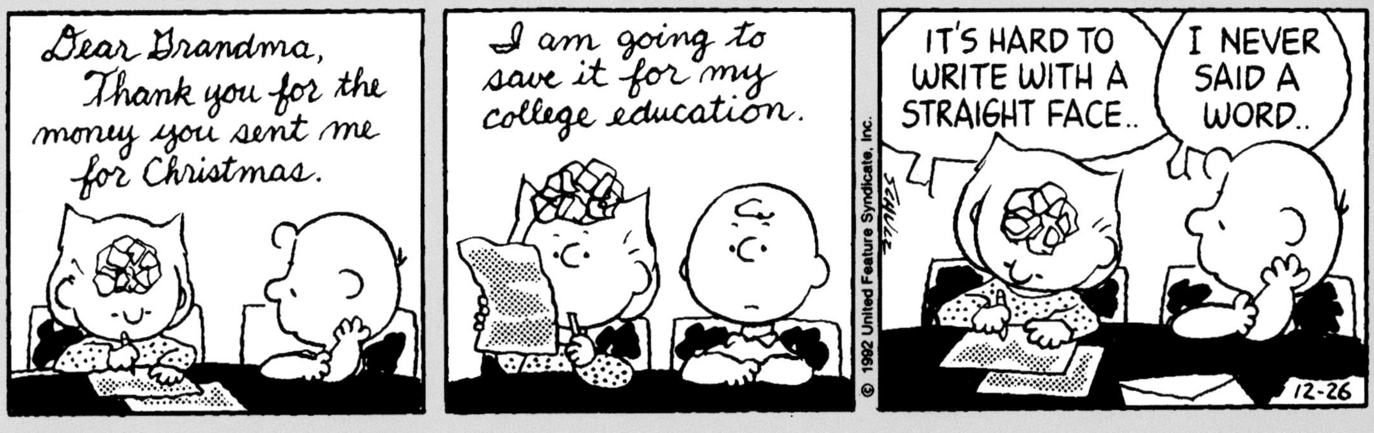
Dear Grandma,
Thank you for the money you sent me for Christmas.
I am going to save it for my college education.
IT'S HARD TO WRITE WITH A STRAIGHT FACE..
I NEVER SAID A WORD..
SCHULZ
12-26

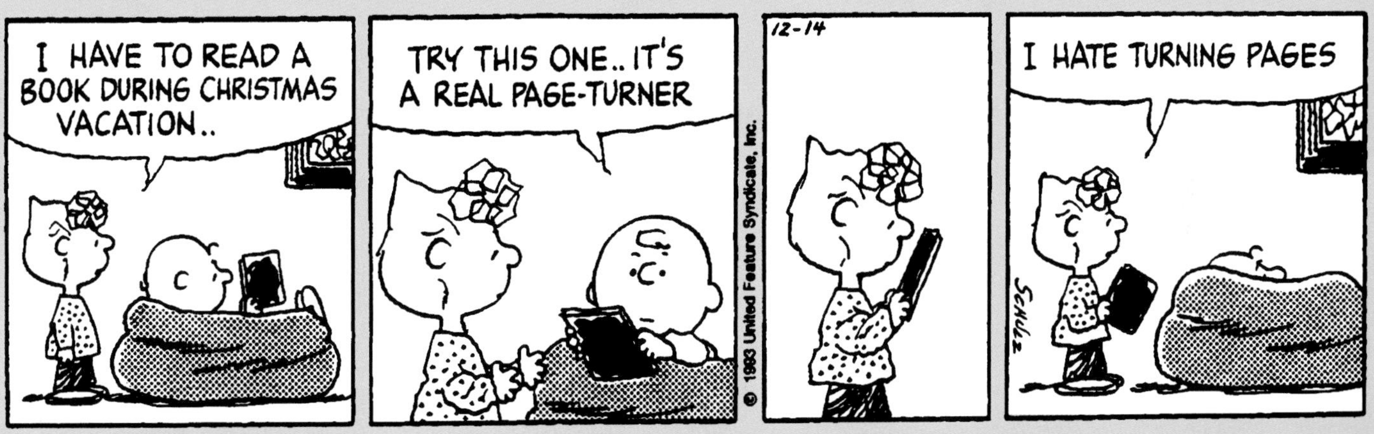
I HAVE TO READ A BOOK DURING CHRISTMAS VACATION..
TRY THIS ONE.. IT'S A REAL PAGE-TURNER
12-14
I HATE TURNING PAGES
SCHULZ

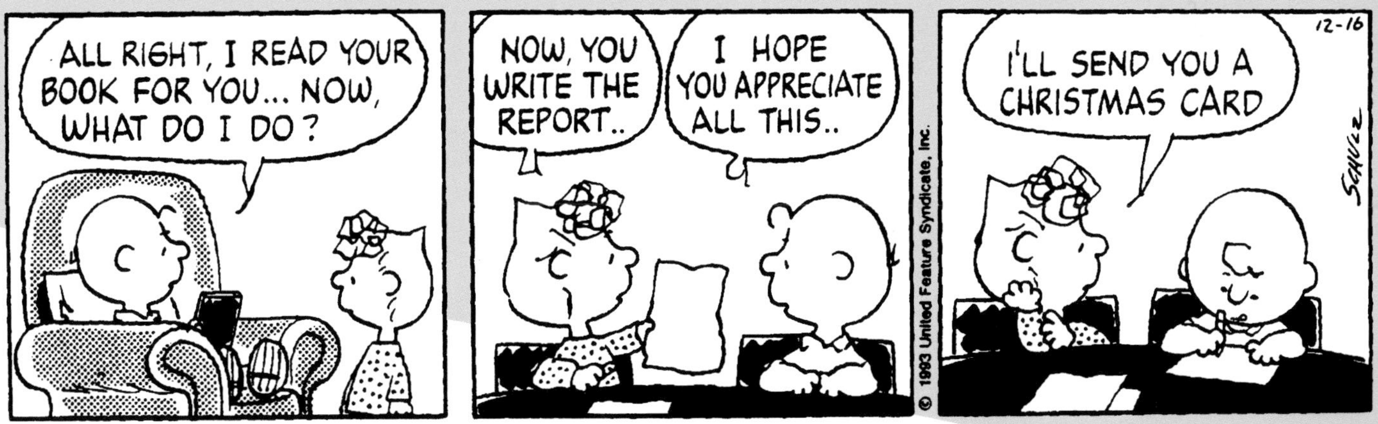
ALL RIGHT, I READ YOUR BOOK FOR YOU... NOW, WHAT DO I DO?
NOW, YOU WRITE THE REPORT..
I HOPE YOU APPRECIATE ALL THIS..
12-16
I'LL SEND YOU A CHRISTMAS CARD
SCHULZ

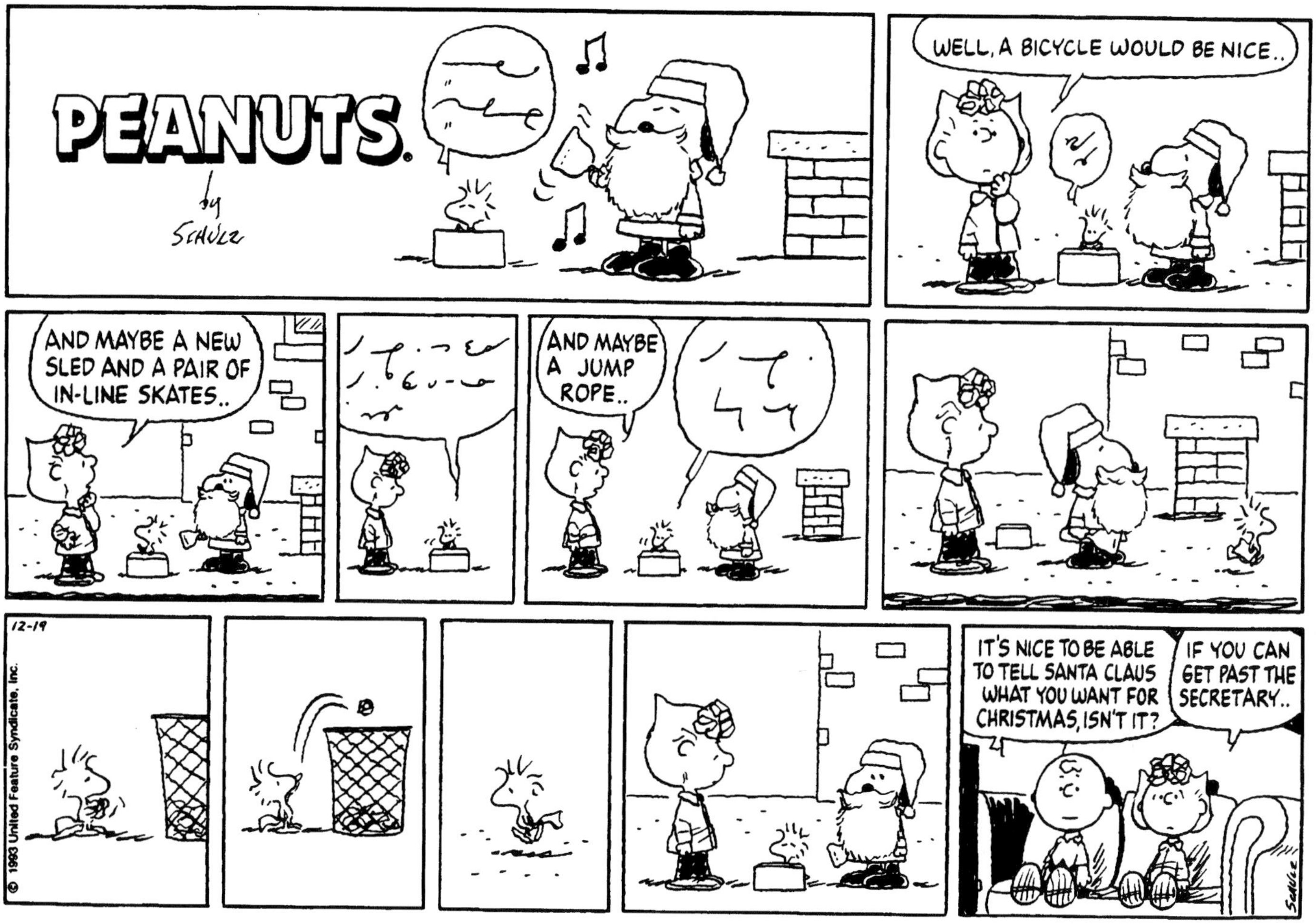
PEANUTS
by SCHULZ
WELL, A BICYCLE WOULD BE NICE..
AND MAYBE A NEW SLED AND A PAIR OF IN-LINE SKATES..
AND MAYBE A JUMP ROPE..
12-19
© 1993 United Feature Syndicate, Inc.
IT'S NICE TO BE ABLE TO TELL SANTA CLAUS WHAT YOU WANT FOR CHRISTMAS, ISN'T IT?
IF YOU CAN GET PAST THE SECRETARY..
SCHULZ

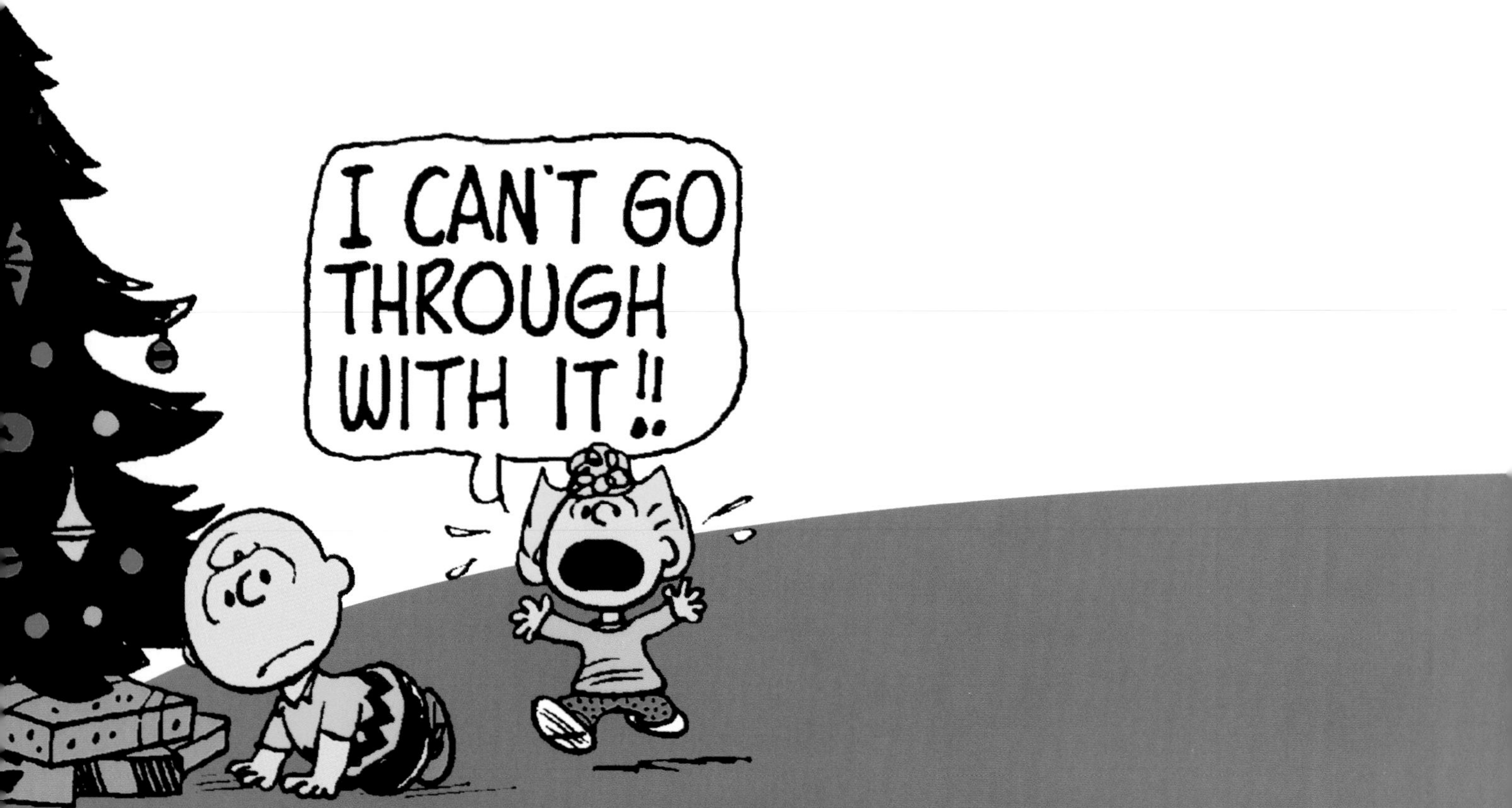
I CAN'T GO THROUGH WITH IT!!

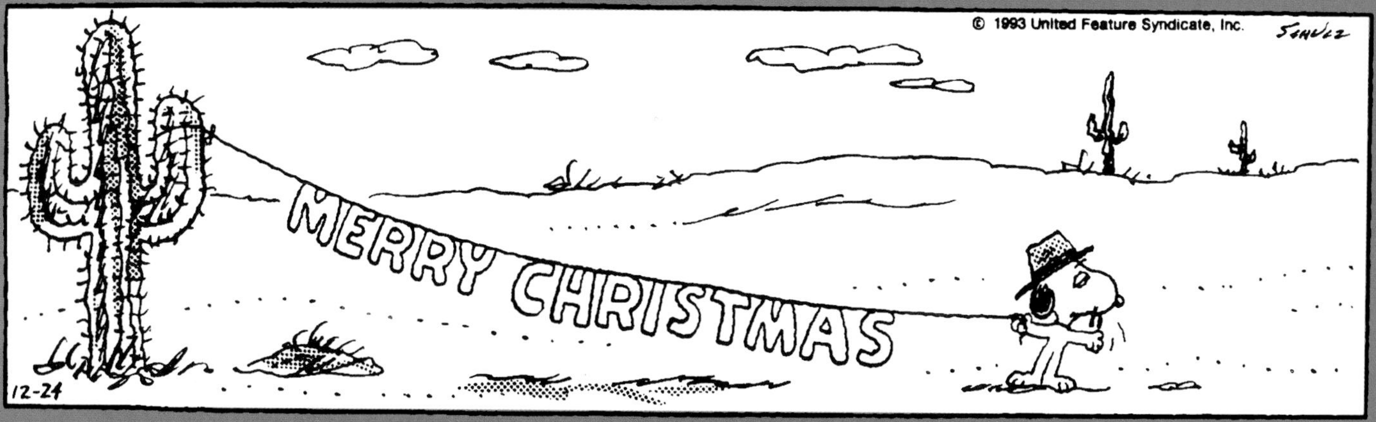
© 1993 United Feature Syndicate, Inc.
SCHULZ
MERRY CHRISTMAS
12-24

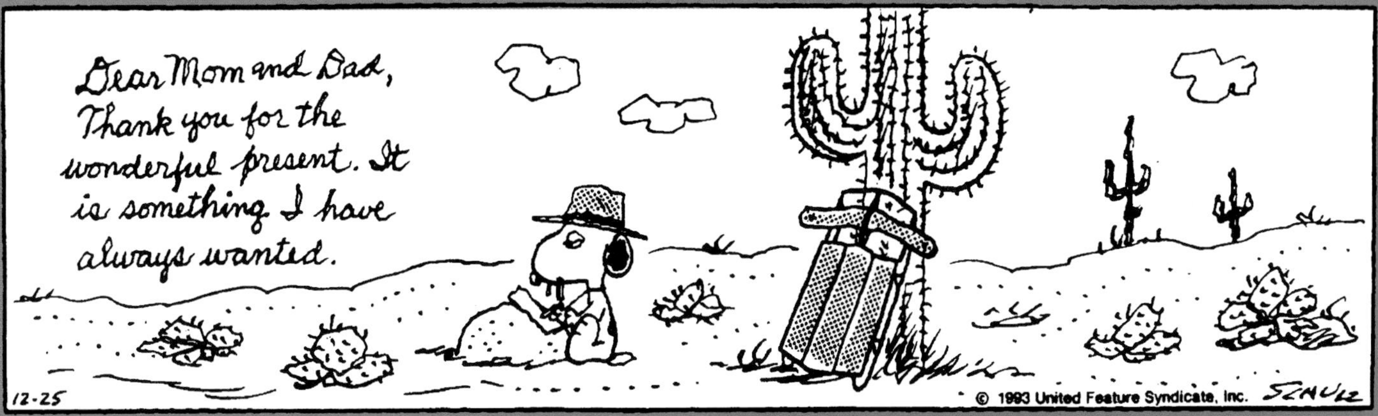
Dear Mom and Dad,
Thank you for the wonderful present. It is something I have always wanted.
12-25
© 1993 United Feature Syndicate, Inc.
SCHULZ

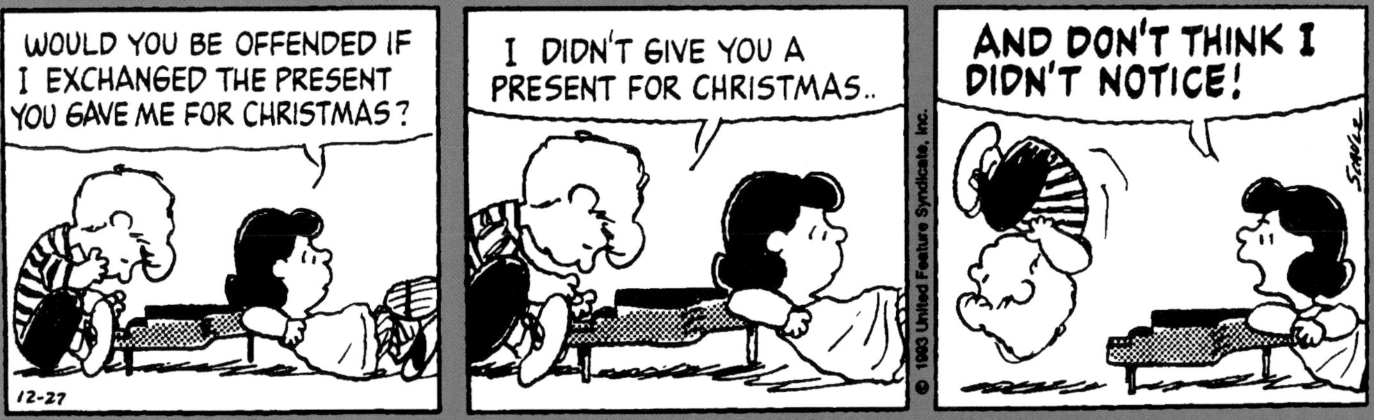
WOULD YOU BE OFFENDED IF I EXCHANGED THE PRESENT YOU GAVE ME FOR CHRISTMAS?
I DIDN'T GIVE YOU A PRESENT FOR CHRISTMAS..
AND DON'T THINK I DIDN'T NOTICE!
12-27
© 1993 United Feature Syndicate, Inc.
SCHULZ

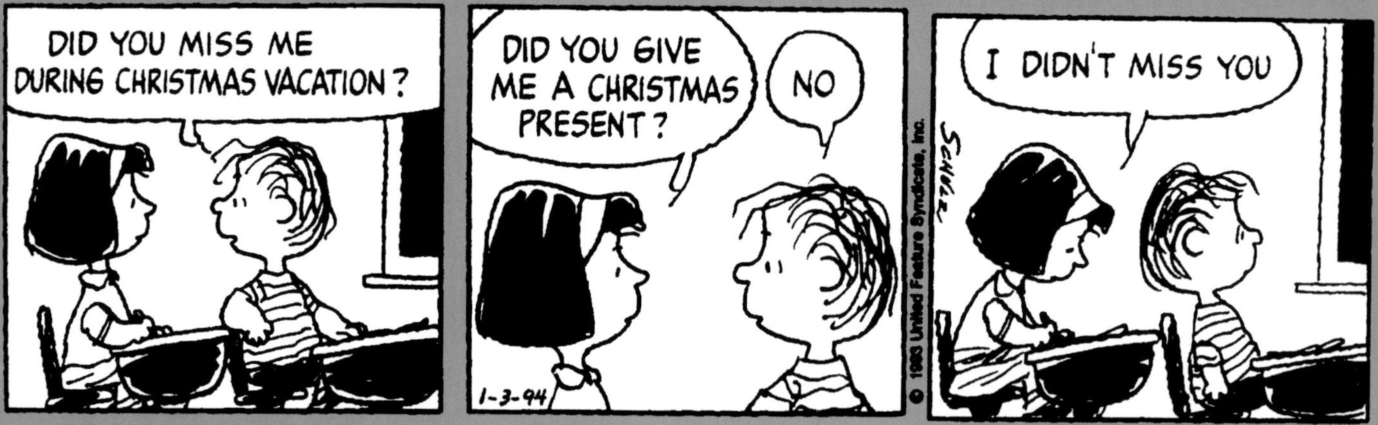
DID YOU MISS ME DURING CHRISTMAS VACATION?
DID YOU GIVE ME A CHRISTMAS PRESENT?
NO
I DIDN'T MISS YOU
1-3-94
© 1993 United Feature Syndicate, Inc.
SCHULZ

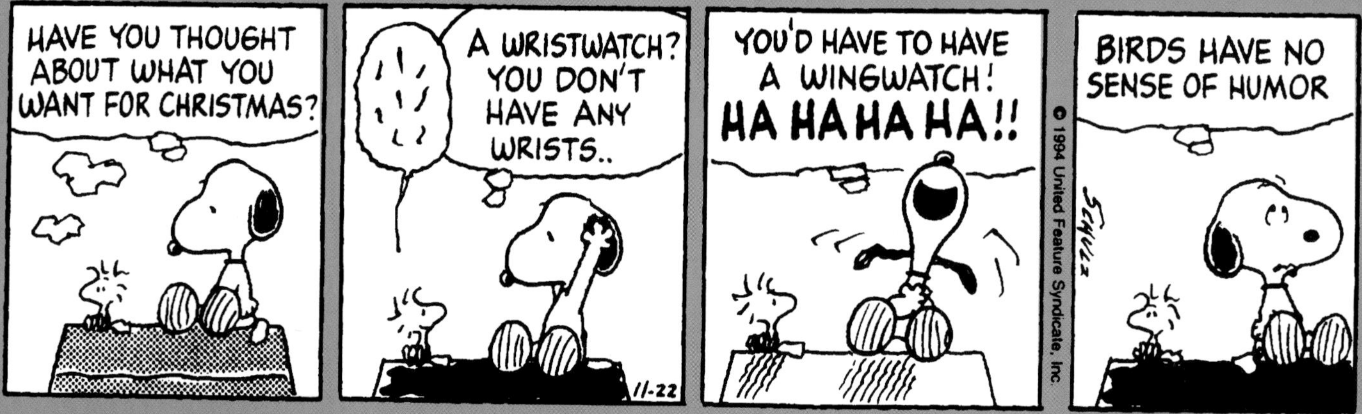
HAVE YOU THOUGHT ABOUT WHAT YOU WANT FOR CHRISTMAS?
A WRISTWATCH? YOU DON'T HAVE ANY WRISTS..
11-22
YOU'D HAVE TO HAVE A WINGWATCH! HA HA HA HA!!
© 1994 United Feature Syndicate, Inc.
SCHULZ
BIRDS HAVE NO SENSE OF HUMOR

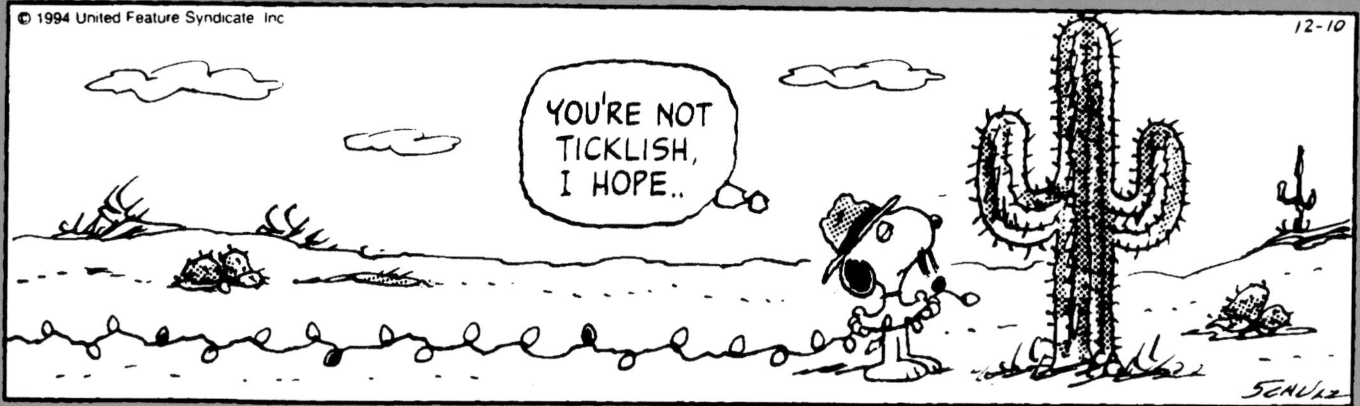
© 1994 United Feature Syndicate Inc
12-10
YOU'RE NOT TICKLISH, I HOPE..
SCHULZ

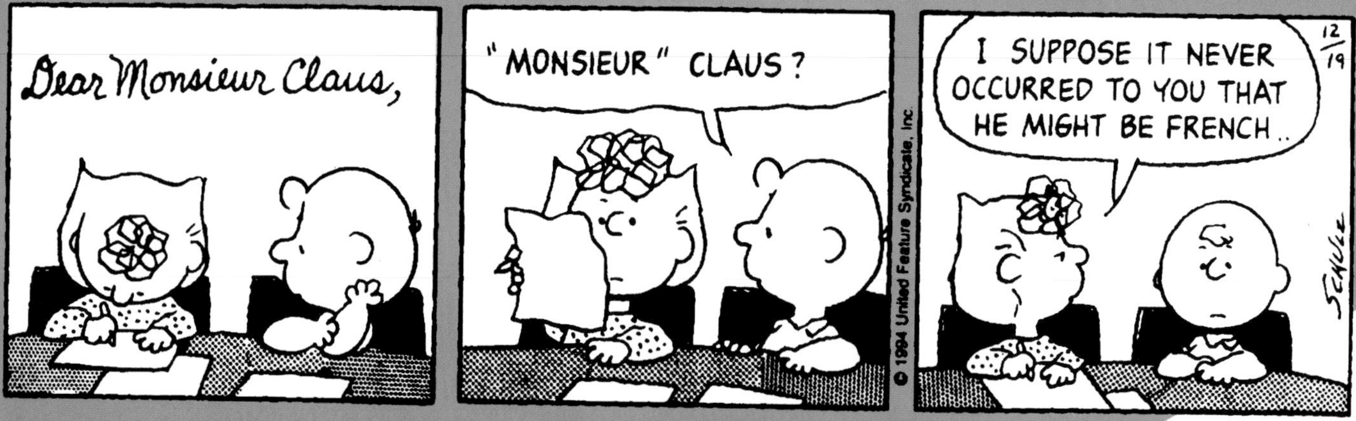
Dear Monsieur Claus,
"MONSIEUR" CLAUS?
© 1994 United Feature Syndicate, Inc.
I SUPPOSE IT NEVER OCCURRED TO YOU THAT HE MIGHT BE FRENCH..
12/19
SCHULZ

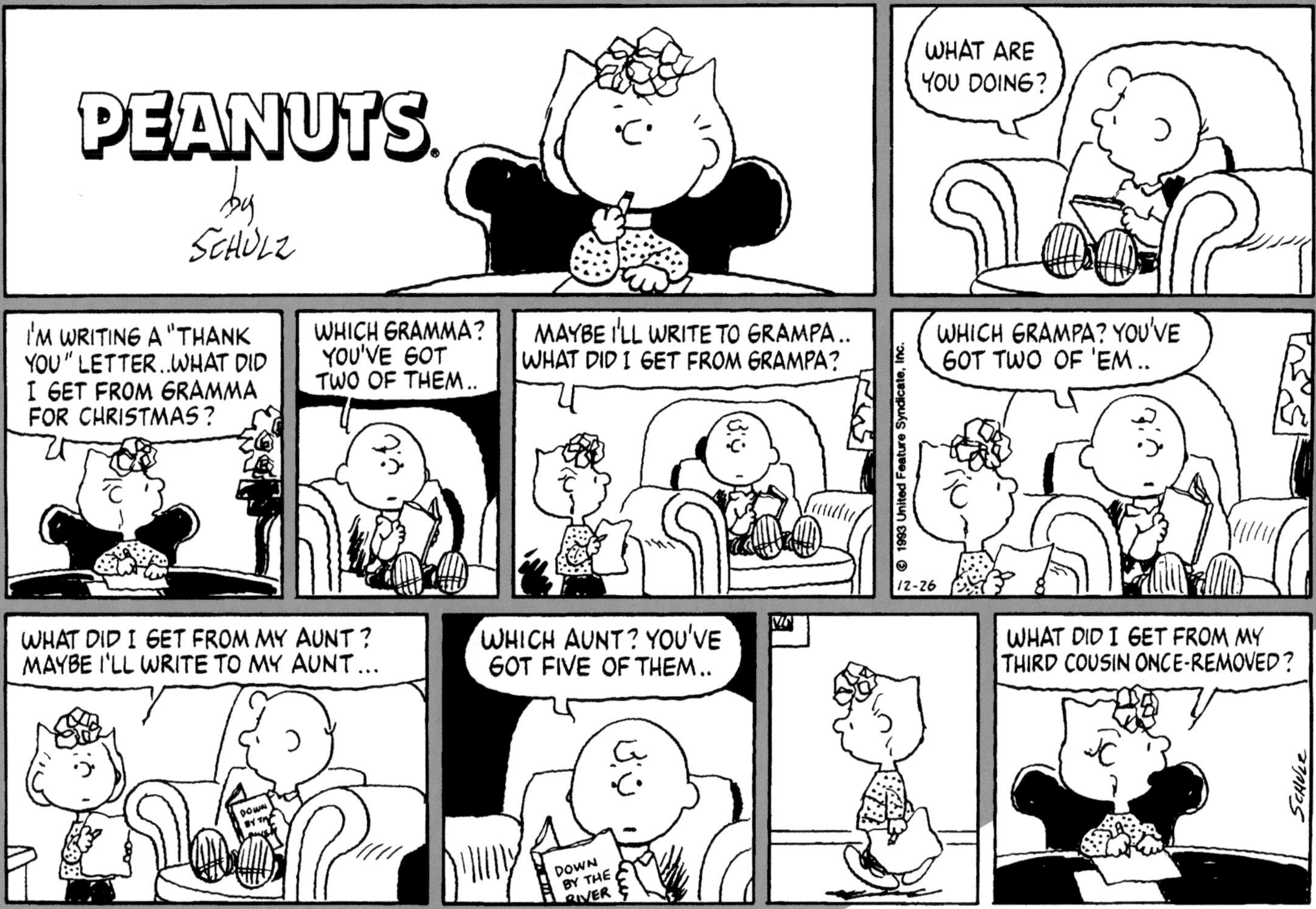
PEANUTS
by SCHULZ
WHAT ARE YOU DOING?
I'M WRITING A "THANK YOU" LETTER..WHAT DID I GET FROM GRAMMA FOR CHRISTMAS?
WHICH GRAMMA? YOU'VE GOT TWO OF THEM..
MAYBE I'LL WRITE TO GRAMPA.. WHAT DID I GET FROM GRAMPA?
WHICH GRAMPA? YOU'VE GOT TWO OF 'EM..
© 1993 United Feature Syndicate, Inc.
12-26
WHAT DID I GET FROM MY AUNT? MAYBE I'LL WRITE TO MY AUNT...
WHICH AUNT? YOU'VE GOT FIVE OF THEM..
DOWN BY THE RIVER
WHAT DID I GET FROM MY THIRD COUSIN ONCE-REMOVED?
SCHULZ

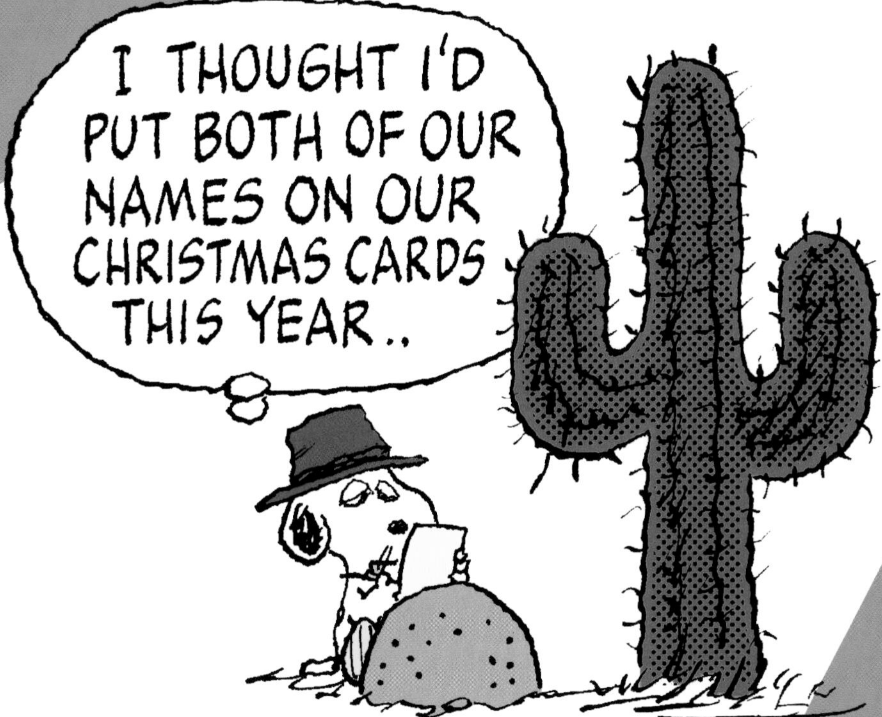
I THOUGHT I'D PUT BOTH OF OUR NAMES ON OUR CHRISTMAS CARDS THIS YEAR..

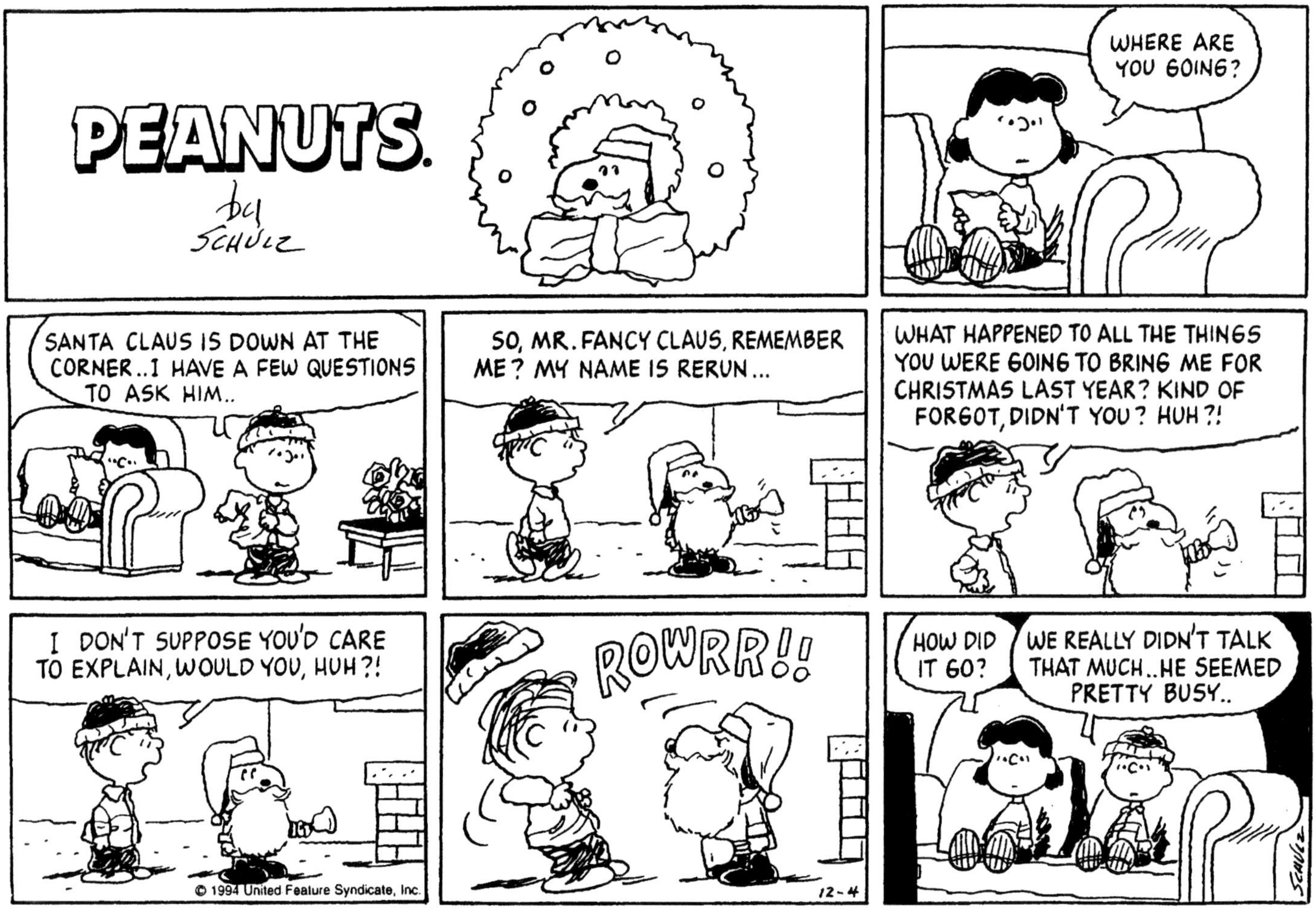
PEANUTS.
by SCHULZ
WHERE ARE YOU GOING?
SANTA CLAUS IS DOWN AT THE CORNER..I HAVE A FEW QUESTIONS TO ASK HIM..
SO, MR. FANCY CLAUS, REMEMBER ME? MY NAME IS RERUN...
WHAT HAPPENED TO ALL THE THINGS YOU WERE GOING TO BRING ME FOR CHRISTMAS LAST YEAR? KIND OF FORGOT, DIDN'T YOU? HUH?!
I DON'T SUPPOSE YOU'D CARE TO EXPLAIN, WOULD YOU, HUH?!
© 1994 United Feature Syndicate, Inc.
ROWRR!!
12-4
HOW DID IT GO?
WE REALLY DIDN'T TALK THAT MUCH..HE SEEMED PRETTY BUSY..
SCHULZ

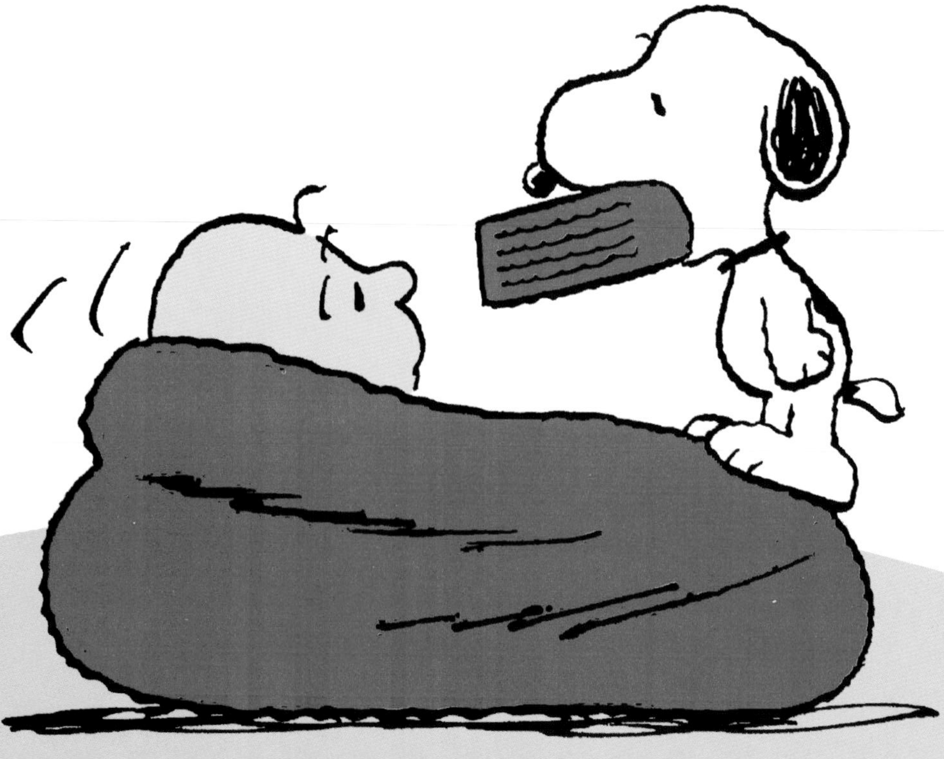

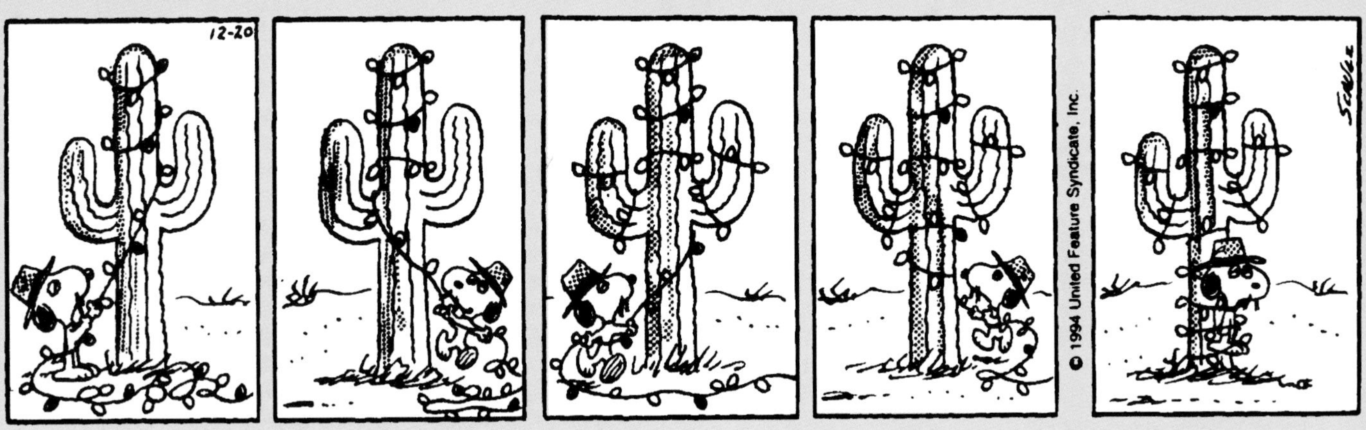
12-20
© 1994 United Feature Syndicate, Inc.
SCHULZ

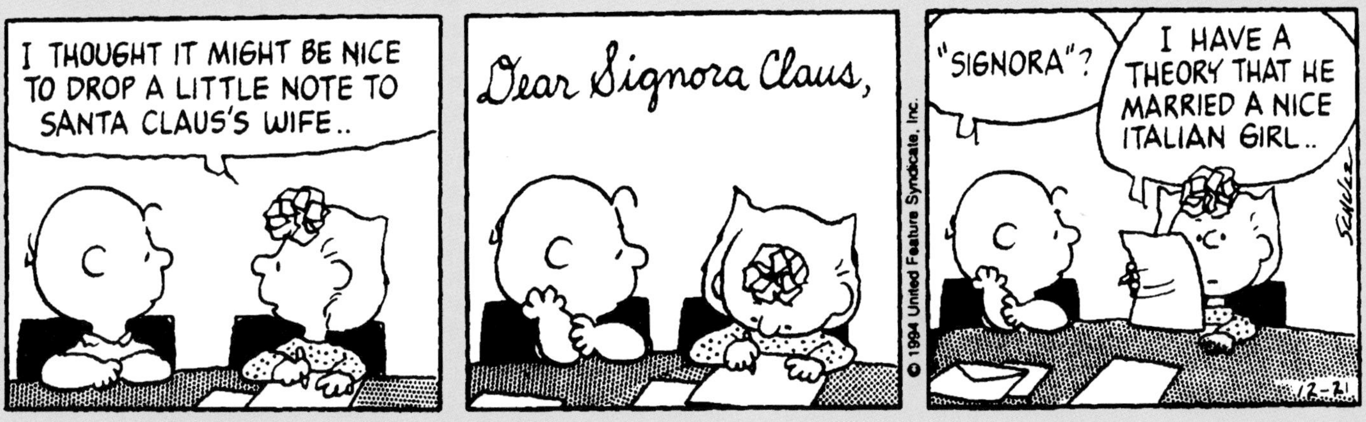
I THOUGHT IT MIGHT BE NICE TO DROP A LITTLE NOTE TO SANTA CLAUS'S WIFE..
Dear Signora Claus,
© 1994 United Feature Syndicate, Inc.
"SIGNORA"?
I HAVE A THEORY THAT HE MARRIED A NICE ITALIAN GIRL..
SCHULZ
12-21

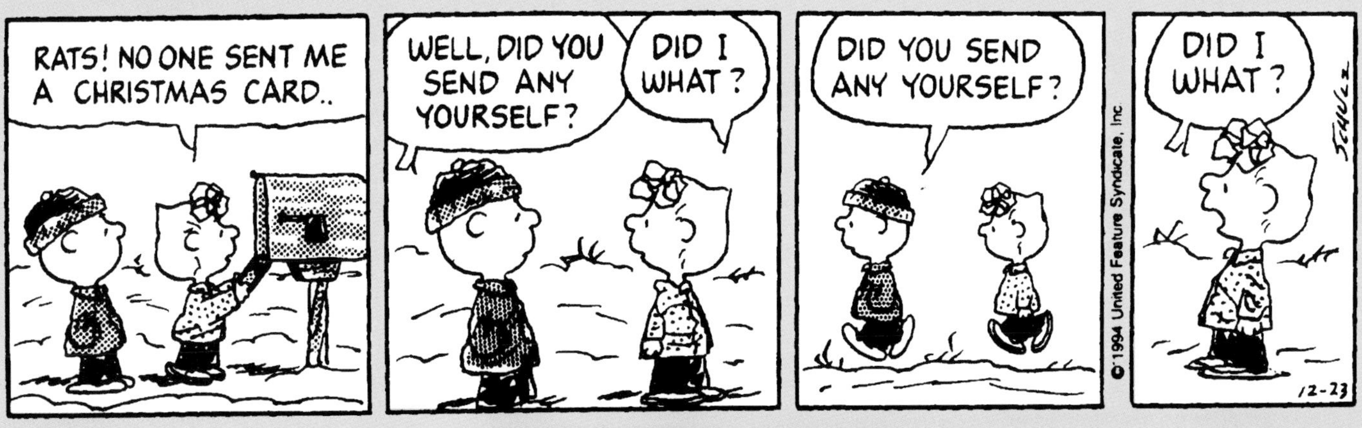
RATS! NO ONE SENT ME A CHRISTMAS CARD..
WELL, DID YOU SEND ANY YOURSELF?
DID I WHAT?
DID YOU SEND ANY YOURSELF?
© 1994 United Feature Syndicate, Inc.
DID I WHAT?
SCHULZ
12-23

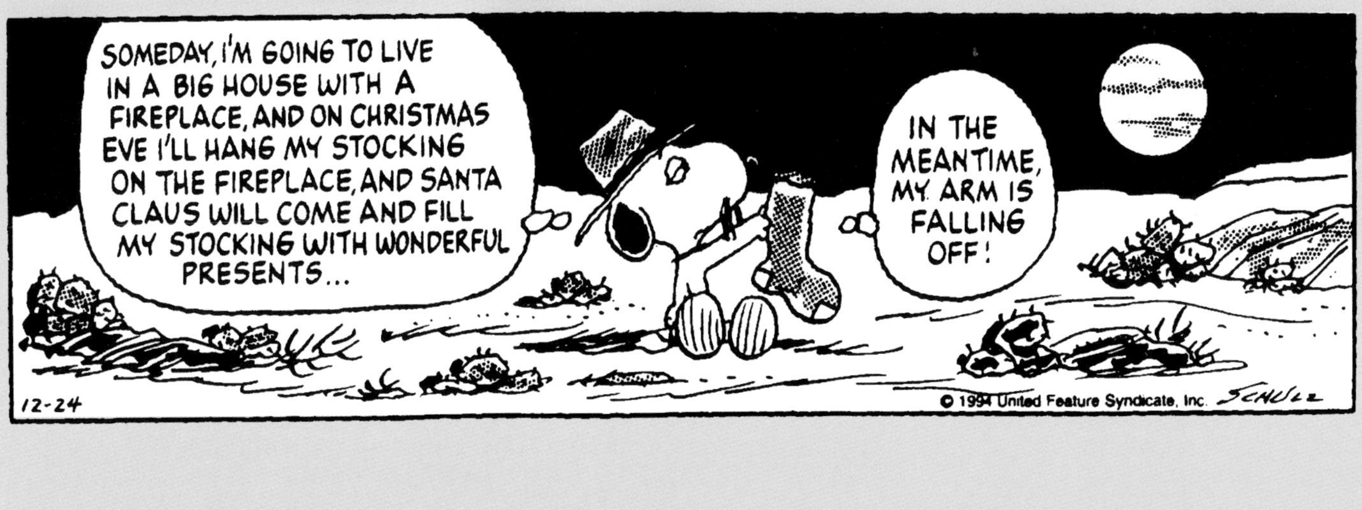
SOMEDAY, I'M GOING TO LIVE IN A BIG HOUSE WITH A FIREPLACE, AND ON CHRISTMAS EVE I'LL HANG MY STOCKING ON THE FIREPLACE, AND SANTA CLAUS WILL COME AND FILL MY STOCKING WITH WONDERFUL PRESENTS...
IN THE MEANTIME, MY ARM IS FALLING OFF!
12-24
© 1994 United Feature Syndicate, Inc.
SCHULZ

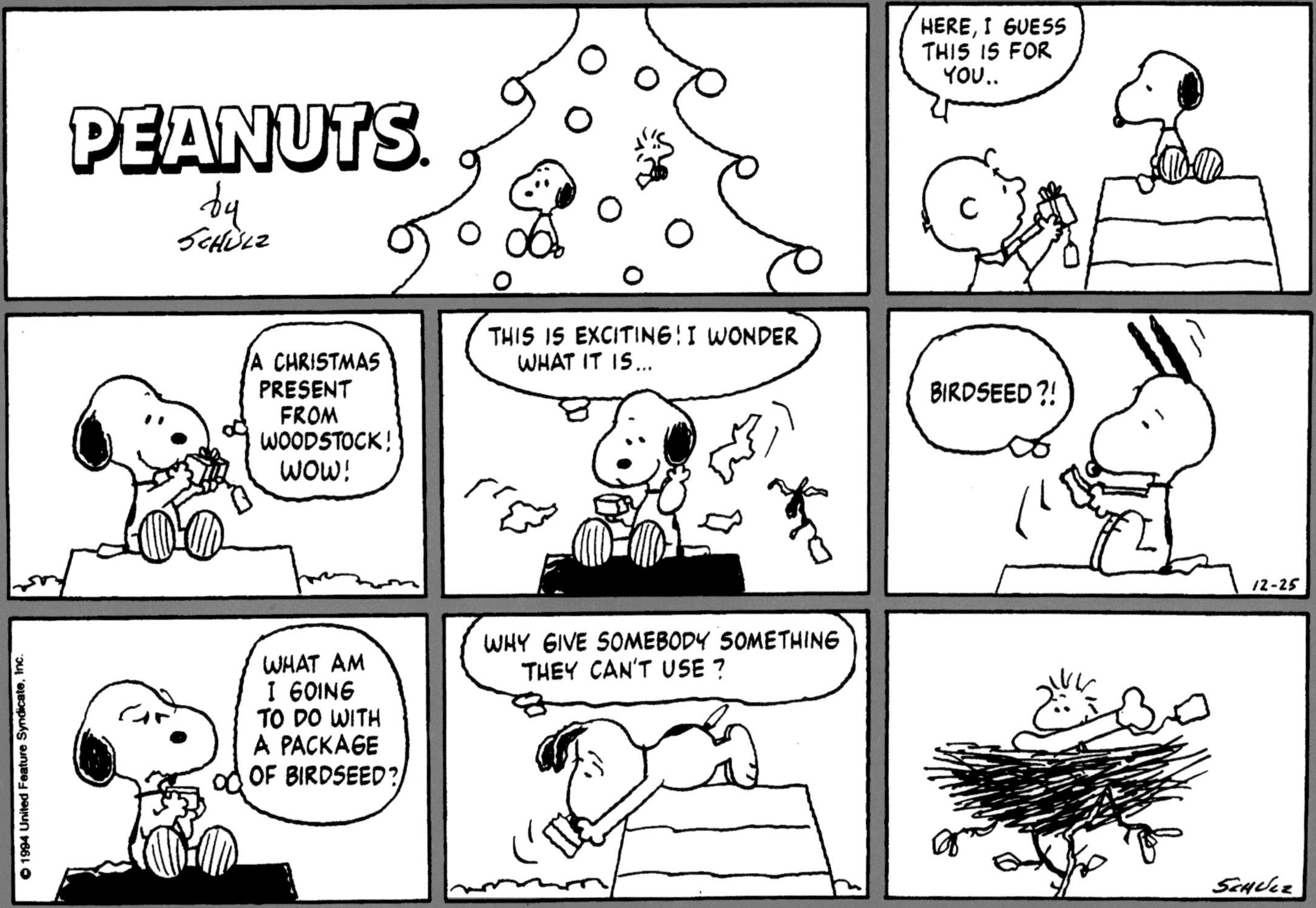
PEANUTS.
by SCHULZ
HERE, I GUESS THIS IS FOR YOU..
A CHRISTMAS PRESENT FROM WOODSTOCK! WOW!
THIS IS EXCITING! I WONDER WHAT IT IS...
BIRDSEED?!
12-25
© 1994 United Feature Syndicate, Inc.
WHAT AM I GOING TO DO WITH A PACKAGE OF BIRDSEED?
WHY GIVE SOMEBODY SOMETHING THEY CAN'T USE?
SCHULZ

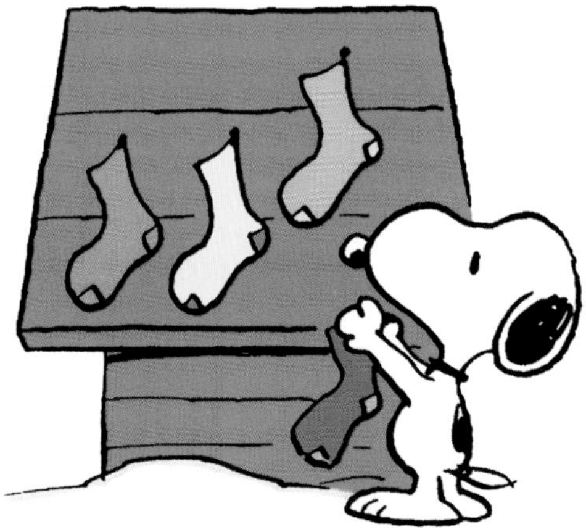

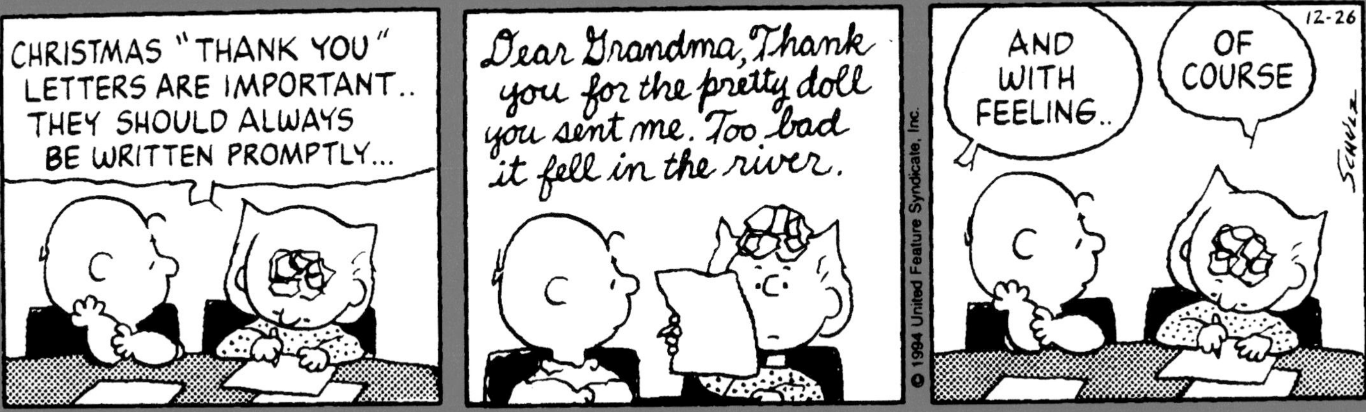
CHRISTMAS "THANK YOU" LETTERS ARE IMPORTANT.. THEY SHOULD ALWAYS BE WRITTEN PROMPTLY...
Dear Grandma, Thank you for the pretty doll you sent me. Too bad it fell in the river.
© 1994 United Feature Syndicate, Inc.
12-26
AND WITH FEELING..
OF COURSE
SCHULZ

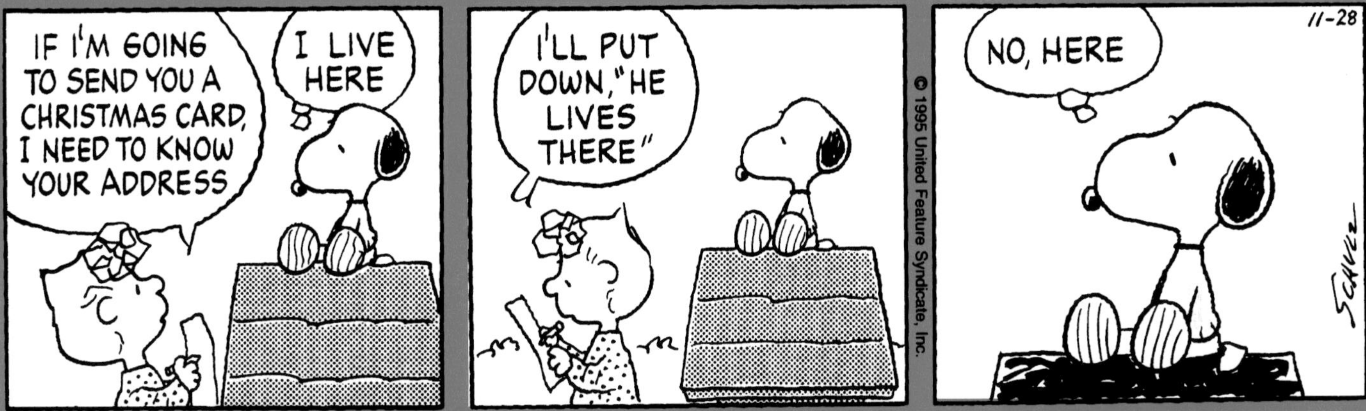
IF I'M GOING TO SEND YOU A CHRISTMAS CARD, I NEED TO KNOW YOUR ADDRESS
I LIVE HERE
I'LL PUT DOWN, "HE LIVES THERE"
© 1995 United Feature Syndicate, Inc.
11-28
NO, HERE
SCHULZ

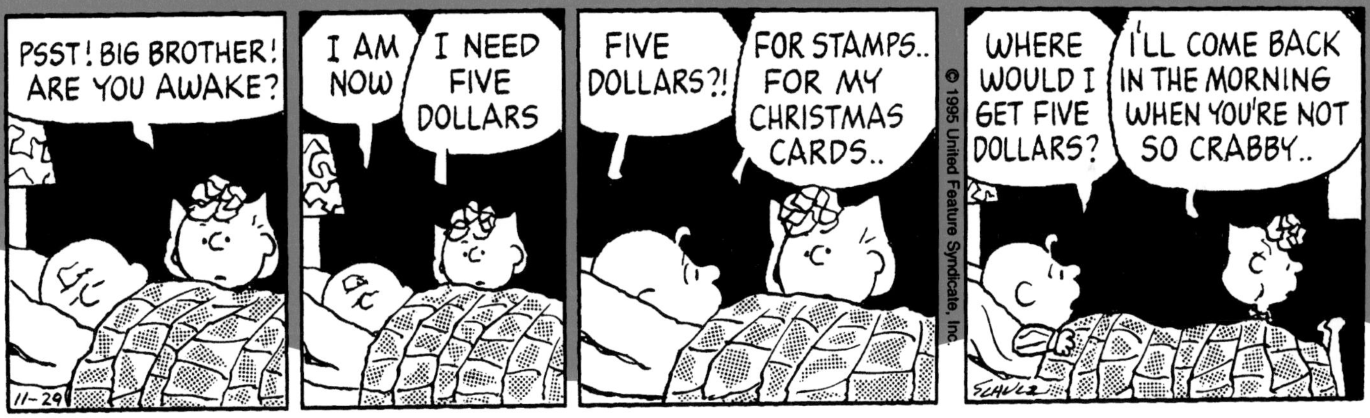
PSST! BIG BROTHER! ARE YOU AWAKE?
11-29
I AM NOW
I NEED FIVE DOLLARS
FIVE DOLLARS?!
FOR STAMPS.. FOR MY CHRISTMAS CARDS..
© 1995 United Feature Syndicate, Inc.
WHERE WOULD I GET FIVE DOLLARS?
I'LL COME BACK IN THE MORNING WHEN YOU'RE NOT SO CRABBY..
SCHULZ

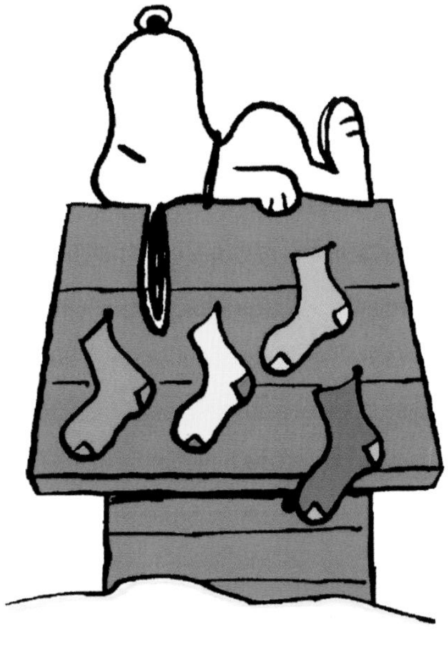

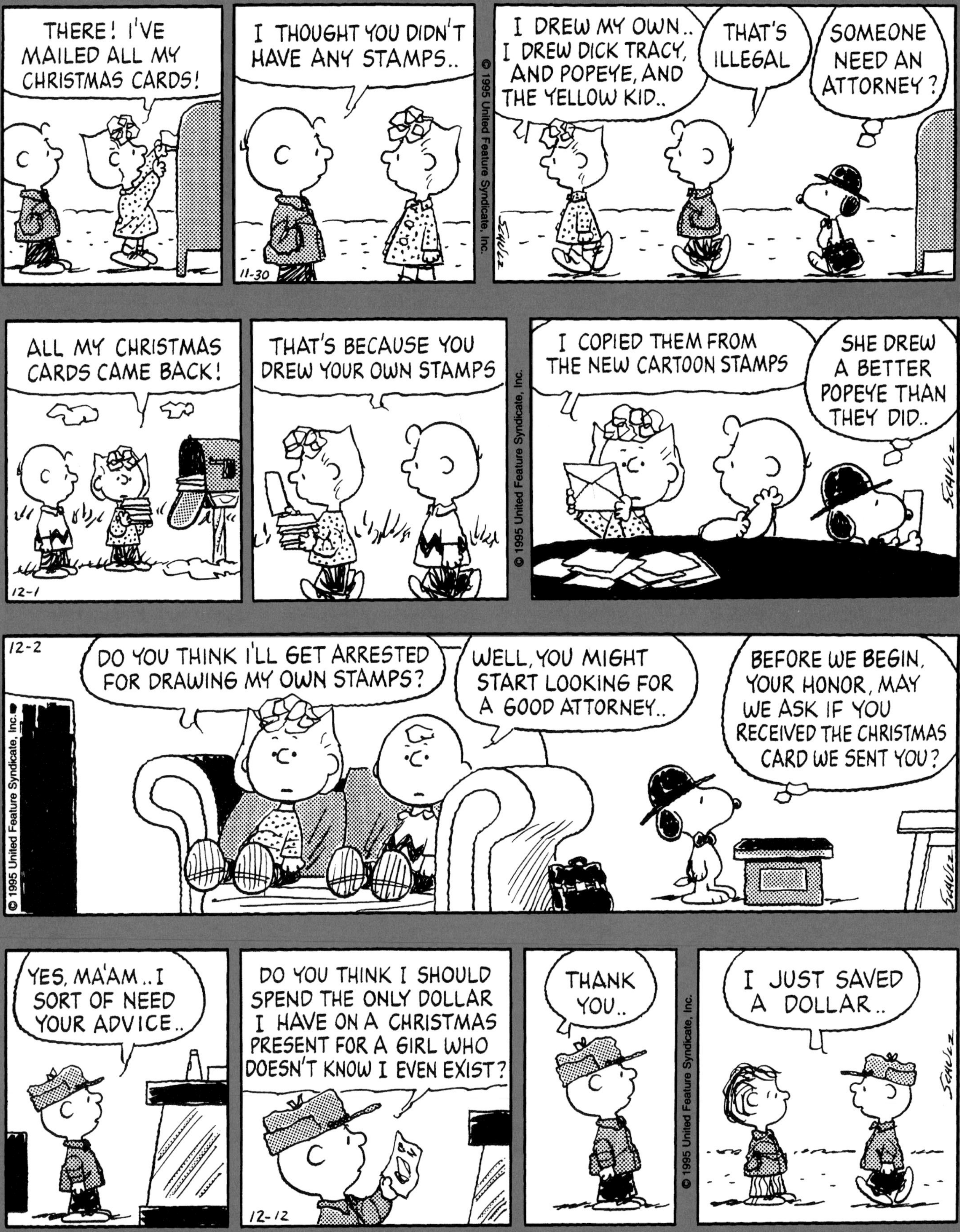
THERE! I'VE MAILED ALL MY CHRISTMAS CARDS!
I THOUGHT YOU DIDN'T HAVE ANY STAMPS..
11-30
I DREW MY OWN.. I DREW DICK TRACY, AND POPEYE, AND THE YELLOW KID..
THAT'S ILLEGAL
SOMEONE NEED AN ATTORNEY?
© 1995 United Feature Syndicate, Inc.
SCHULZ
ALL MY CHRISTMAS CARDS CAME BACK!
12-1
THAT'S BECAUSE YOU DREW YOUR OWN STAMPS
I COPIED THEM FROM THE NEW CARTOON STAMPS
SHE DREW A BETTER POPEYE THAN THEY DID..
© 1995 United Feature Syndicate, Inc.
SCHULZ
12-2
DO YOU THINK I'LL GET ARRESTED FOR DRAWING MY OWN STAMPS?
WELL, YOU MIGHT START LOOKING FOR A GOOD ATTORNEY..
BEFORE WE BEGIN, YOUR HONOR, MAY WE ASK IF YOU RECEIVED THE CHRISTMAS CARD WE SENT YOU?
© 1995 United Feature Syndicate, Inc.
SCHULZ
YES, MA'AM..I SORT OF NEED YOUR ADVICE..
DO YOU THINK I SHOULD SPEND THE ONLY DOLLAR I HAVE ON A CHRISTMAS PRESENT FOR A GIRL WHO DOESN'T KNOW I EVEN EXIST?
12-12
THANK YOU..
I JUST SAVED A DOLLAR..
© 1995 United Feature Syndicate, Inc.
SCHULZ

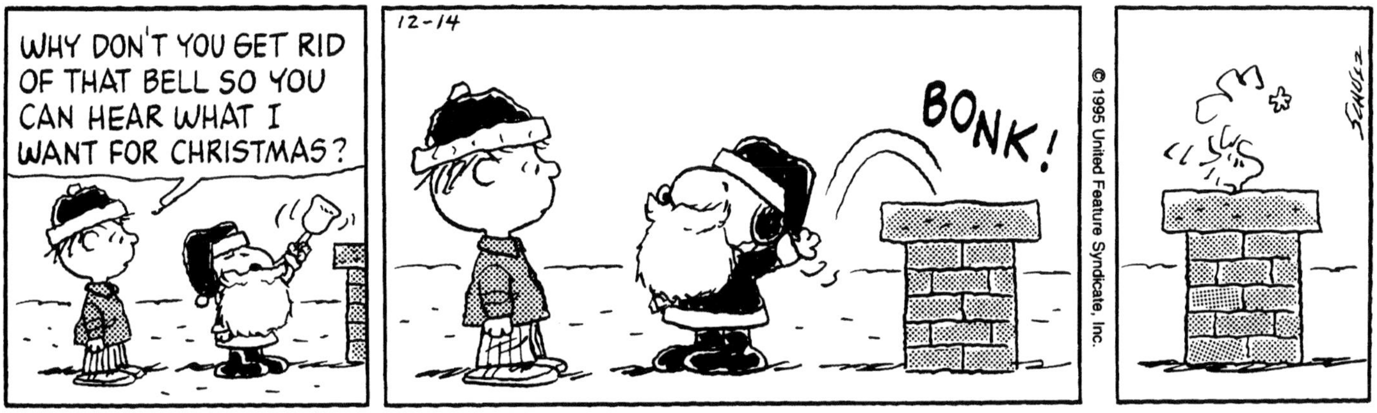
WHY DON'T YOU GET RID OF THAT BELL SO YOU CAN HEAR WHAT I WANT FOR CHRISTMAS?
12-14
BONK!
© 1995 United Feature Syndicate, Inc.
SCHULZ

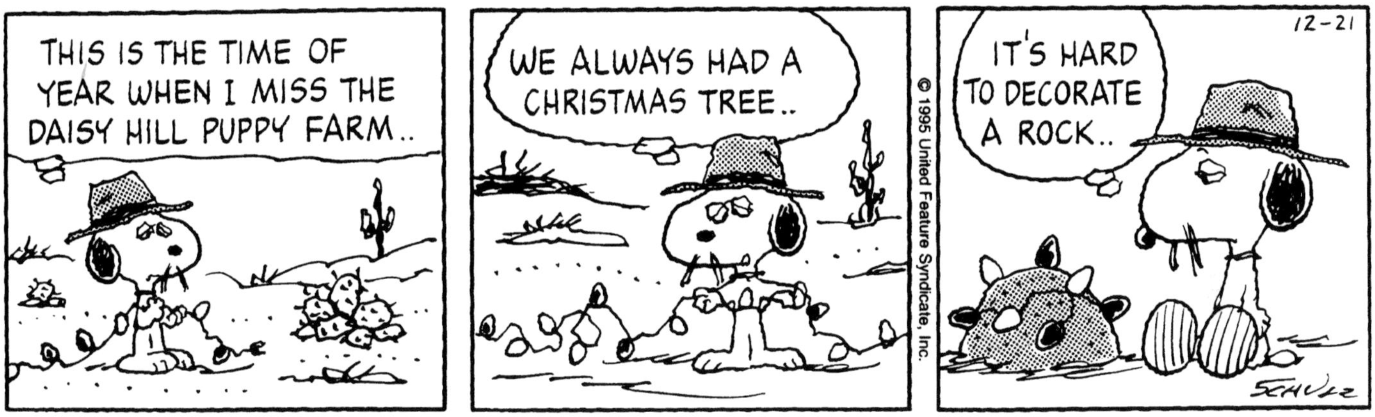
THIS IS THE TIME OF YEAR WHEN I MISS THE DAISY HILL PUPPY FARM..
WE ALWAYS HAD A CHRISTMAS TREE..
© 1995 United Feature Syndicate, Inc.
12-21
IT'S HARD TO DECORATE A ROCK..
SCHULZ

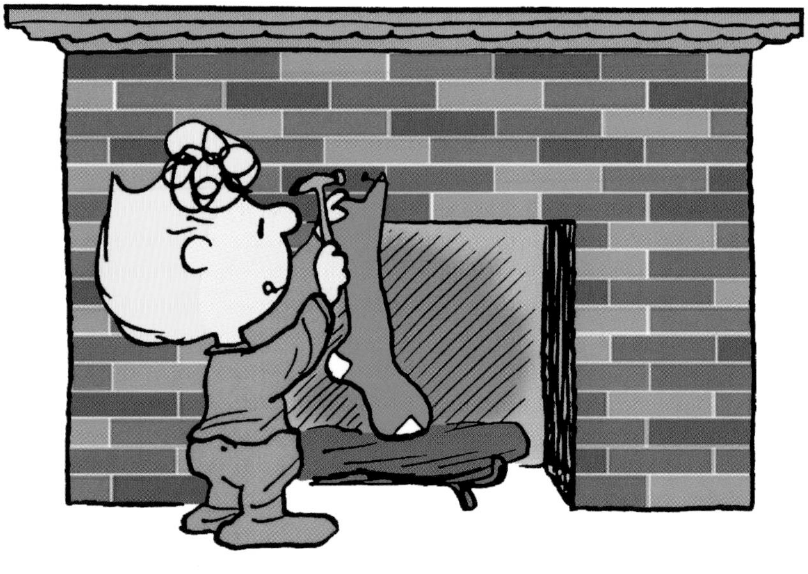

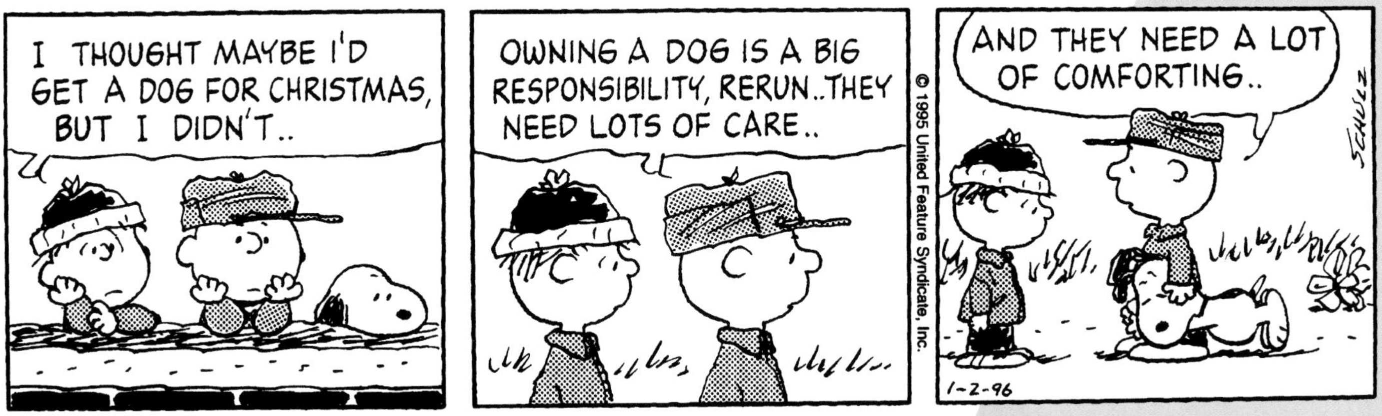
I THOUGHT MAYBE I'D GET A DOG FOR CHRISTMAS, BUT I DIDN'T..
OWNING A DOG IS A BIG RESPONSIBILITY, RERUN..THEY NEED LOTS OF CARE..
© 1995 United Feature Syndicate, Inc.
AND THEY NEED A LOT OF COMFORTING..
SCHULZ
1-2-96

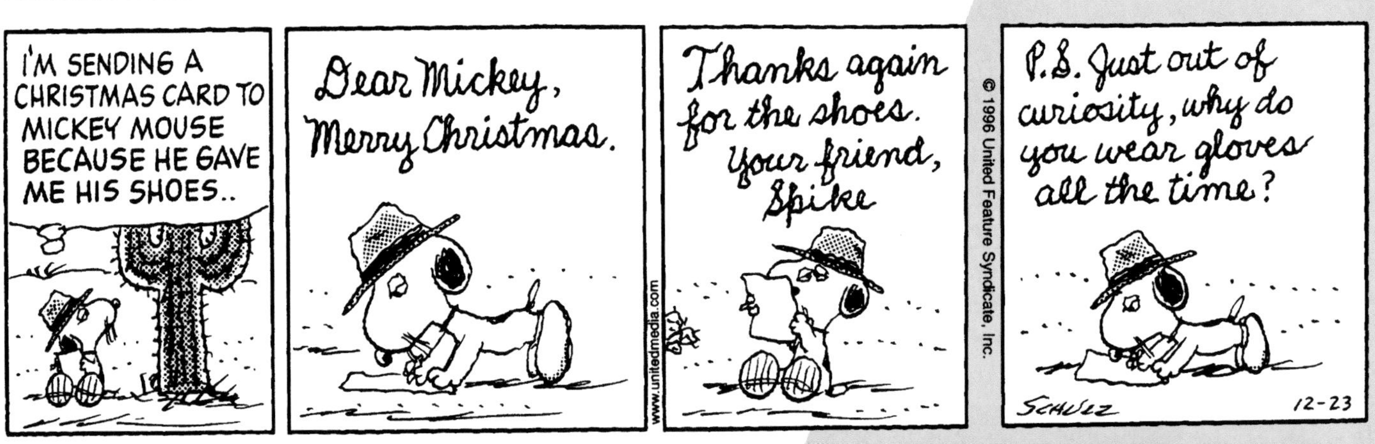
I'M SENDING A CHRISTMAS CARD TO MICKEY MOUSE BECAUSE HE GAVE ME HIS SHOES..
Dear Mickey, Merry Christmas.
www.unitedmedia.com
Thanks again for the shoes. Your friend, Spike
© 1996 United Feature Syndicate, Inc.
P.S. Just out of curiosity, why do you wear gloves all the time?
SCHULZ
12-23

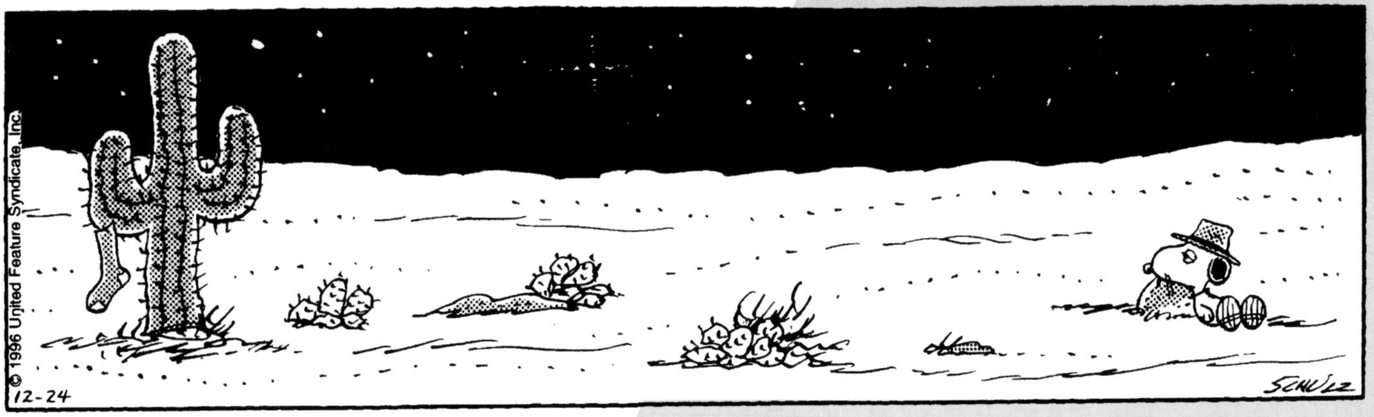
© 1996 United Feature Syndicate, Inc.
12-24
SCHULZ

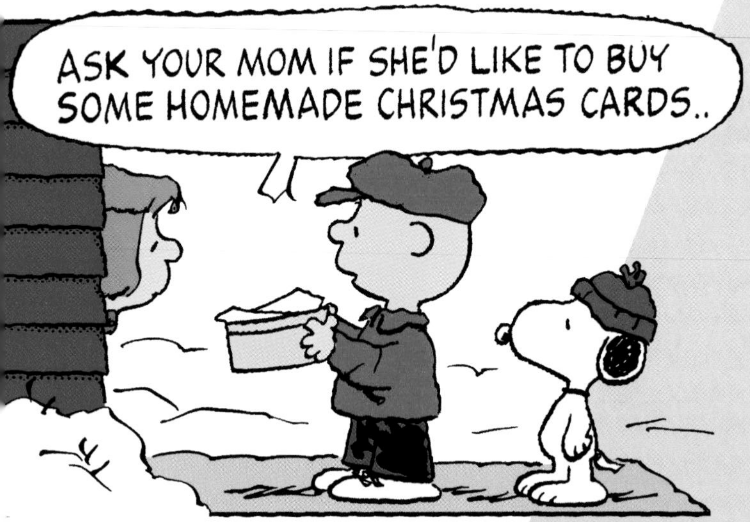
ASK YOUR MOM IF SHE'D LIKE TO BUY SOME HOMEMADE CHRISTMAS CARDS..

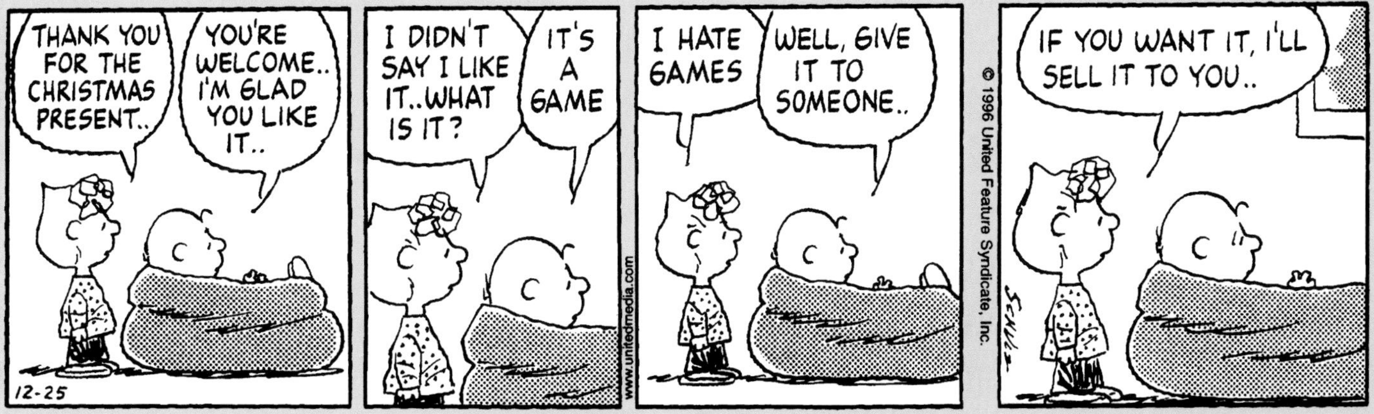
THANK YOU FOR THE CHRISTMAS PRESENT..
YOU'RE WELCOME.. I'M GLAD YOU LIKE IT..
12-25
I DIDN'T SAY I LIKE IT..WHAT IS IT?
IT'S A GAME
www.unitedmedia.com
I HATE GAMES
WELL, GIVE IT TO SOMEONE..
© 1996 United Feature Syndicate, Inc.
IF YOU WANT IT, I'LL SELL IT TO YOU..
SCHULZ

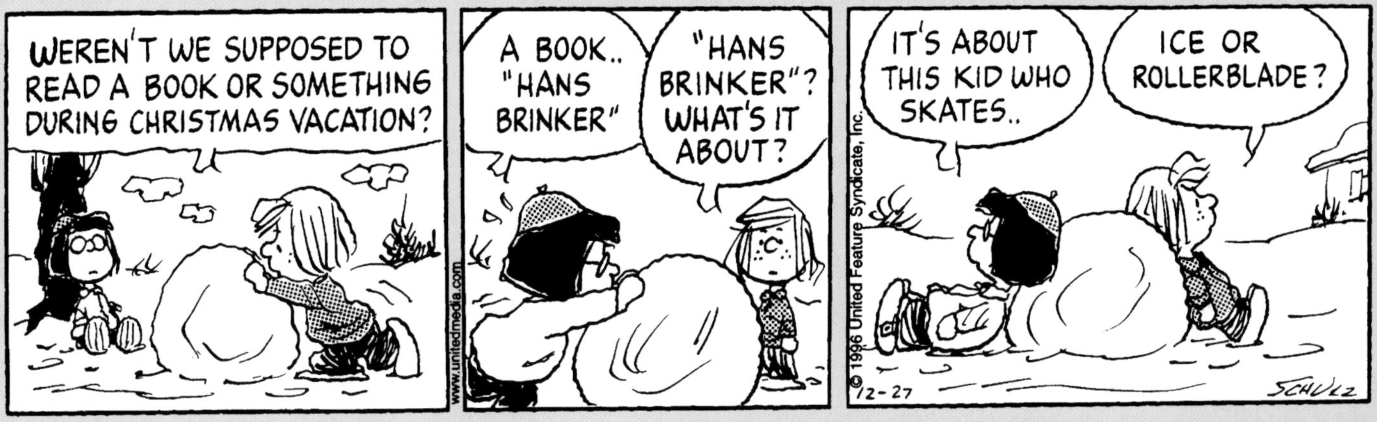
WEREN'T WE SUPPOSED TO READ A BOOK OR SOMETHING DURING CHRISTMAS VACATION?
www.unitedmedia.com
A BOOK.. "HANS BRINKER"
"HANS BRINKER"? WHAT'S IT ABOUT?
© 1996 United Feature Syndicate, Inc.
IT'S ABOUT THIS KID WHO SKATES..
ICE OR ROLLERBLADE?
12-27
SCHULZ

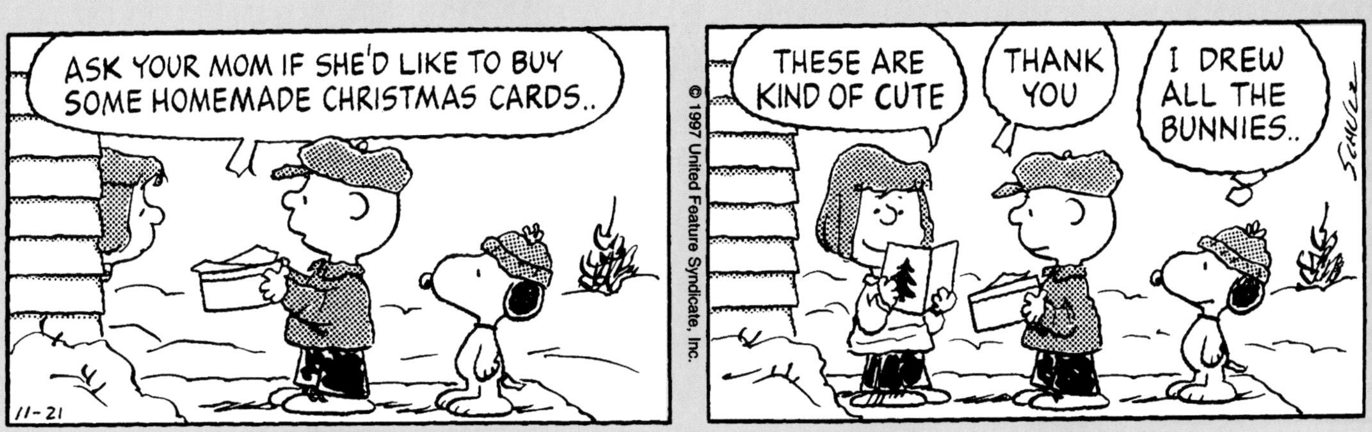
ASK YOUR MOM IF SHE'D LIKE TO BUY SOME HOMEMADE CHRISTMAS CARDS..
11-21
© 1997 United Feature Syndicate, Inc.
THESE ARE KIND OF CUTE
THANK YOU
I DREW ALL THE BUNNIES..
SCHULZ

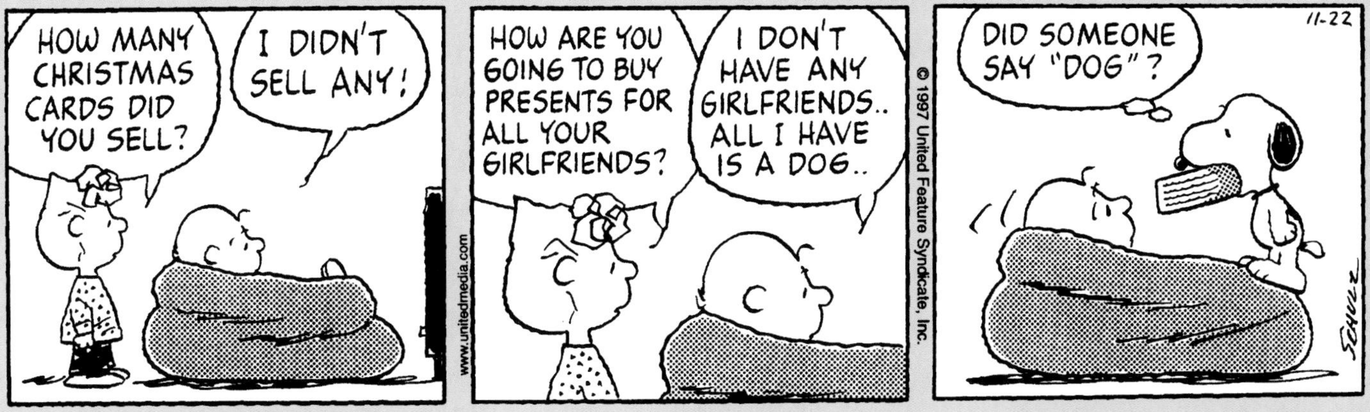
HOW MANY CHRISTMAS CARDS DID YOU SELL?
I DIDN'T SELL ANY!
www.unitedmedia.com
HOW ARE YOU GOING TO BUY PRESENTS FOR ALL YOUR GIRLFRIENDS?
I DON'T HAVE ANY GIRLFRIENDS.. ALL I HAVE IS A DOG..
© 1997 United Feature Syndicate, Inc.
11-22
DID SOMEONE SAY "DOG"?
SCHULZ

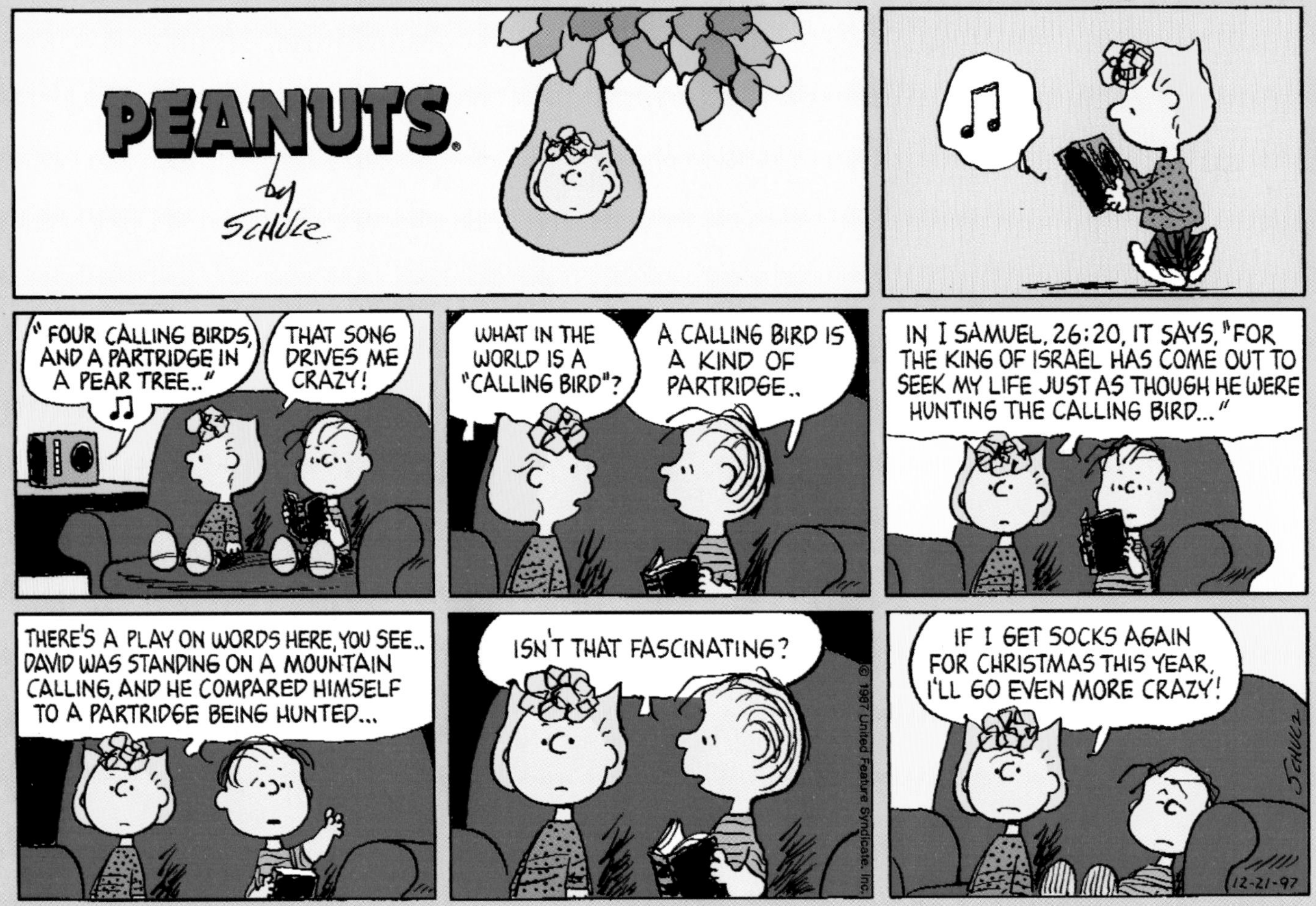
PEANUTS
by SCHULZ
"FOUR CALLING BIRDS, AND A PARTRIDGE IN A PEAR TREE.."
THAT SONG DRIVES ME CRAZY!
WHAT IN THE WORLD IS A "CALLING BIRD"?
A CALLING BIRD IS A KIND OF PARTRIDGE..
IN I SAMUEL, 26:20, IT SAYS, "FOR THE KING OF ISRAEL HAS COME OUT TO SEEK MY LIFE JUST AS THOUGH HE WERE HUNTING THE CALLING BIRD..."
THERE'S A PLAY ON WORDS HERE, YOU SEE.. DAVID WAS STANDING ON A MOUNTAIN CALLING, AND HE COMPARED HIMSELF TO A PARTRIDGE BEING HUNTED...
ISN'T THAT FASCINATING?
© 1997 United Feature Syndicate, Inc.
IF I GET SOCKS AGAIN FOR CHRISTMAS THIS YEAR, I'LL GO EVEN MORE CRAZY!
SCHULZ
12-21-97

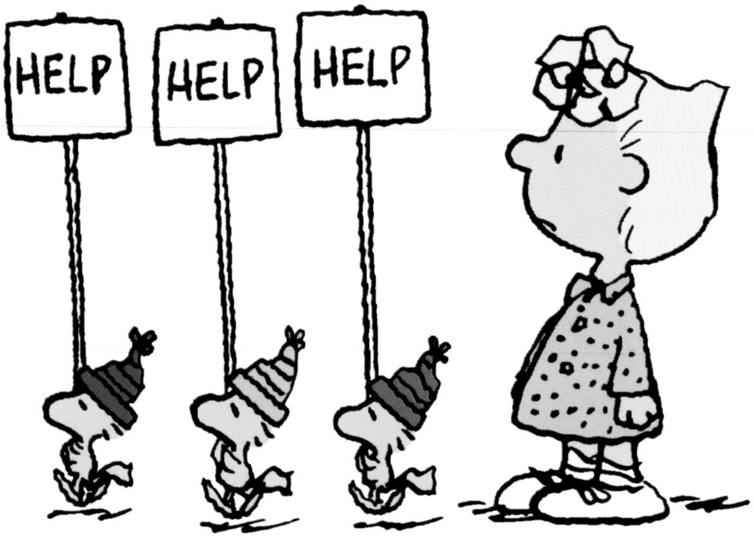
HELP
HELP
HELP

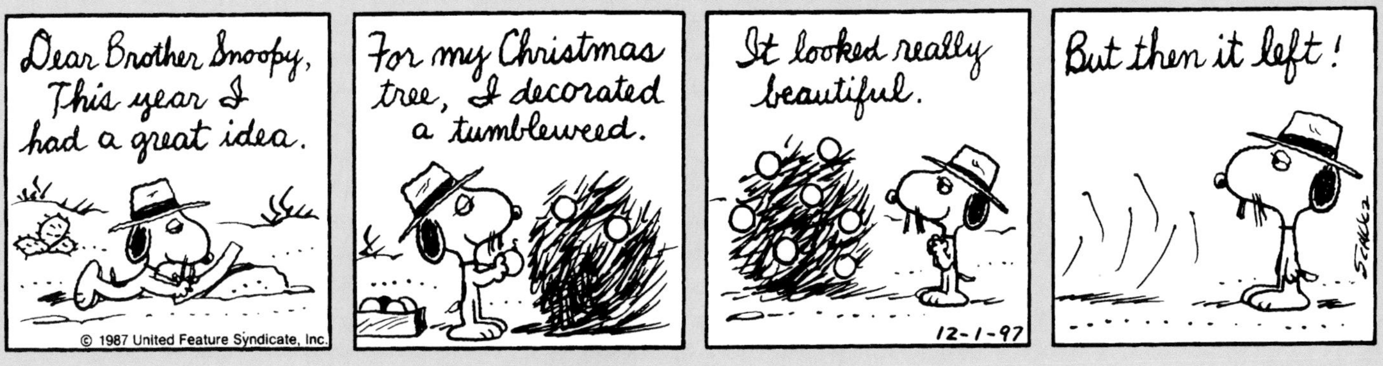
Dear Brother Snoopy,
This year I had a great idea.
© 1987 United Feature Syndicate, Inc.
For my Christmas tree, I decorated a tumbleweed.
It looked really beautiful.
12-1-97
But then it left!
SCHULZ

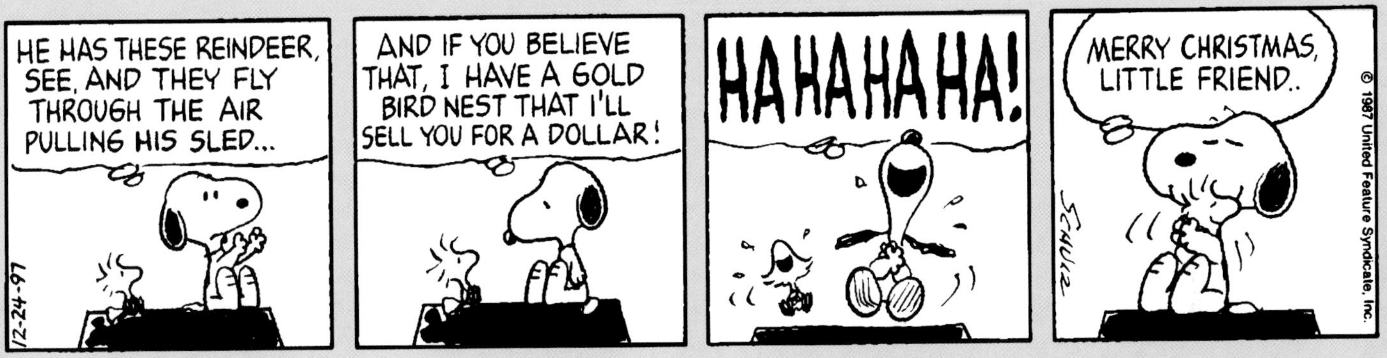
HE HAS THESE REINDEER, SEE, AND THEY FLY THROUGH THE AIR PULLING HIS SLED...
12-24-97
AND IF YOU BELIEVE THAT, I HAVE A GOLD BIRD NEST THAT I'LL SELL YOU FOR A DOLLAR!
HAHAHAHA!
MERRY CHRISTMAS, LITTLE FRIEND..
SCHULZ
© 1987 United Feature Syndicate, Inc.

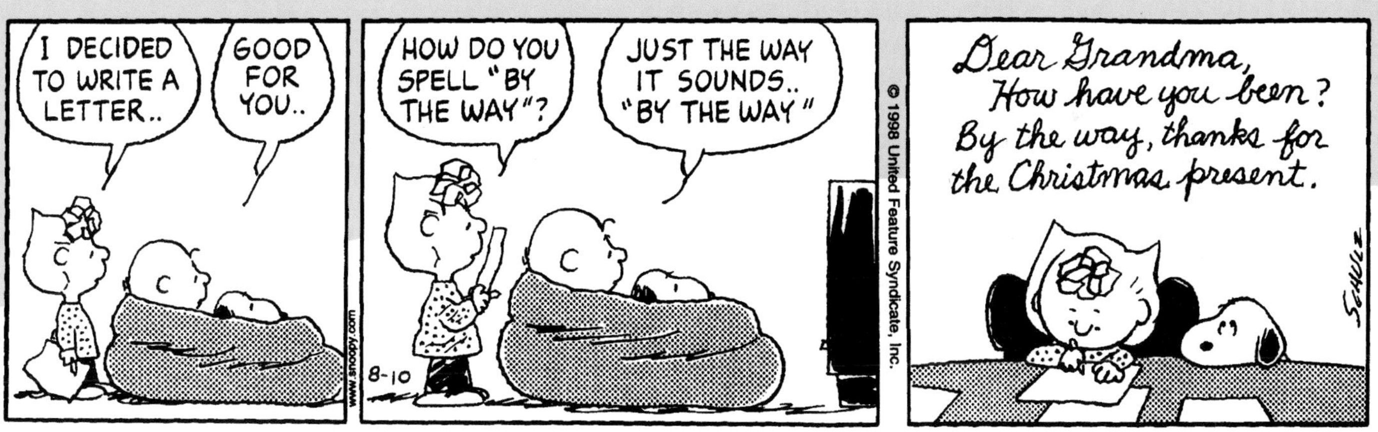
I DECIDED TO WRITE A LETTER..
GOOD FOR YOU..
www.snoopy.com
HOW DO YOU SPELL "BY THE WAY"?
JUST THE WAY IT SOUNDS.. "BY THE WAY"
8-10
© 1998 United Feature Syndicate, Inc.
Dear Grandma,
How have you been?
By the way, thanks for the Christmas present.
SCHULZ

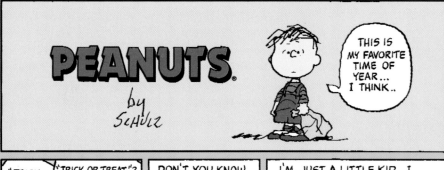

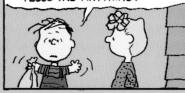

PEANUTS
by SCHULZ
THIS IS MY FAVORITE TIME OF YEAR... I THINK..
RING
"TRICK OR TREAT!"
"TRICK OR TREAT"? THIS ISN'T HALLOWEEN!
DON'T YOU KNOW WHAT MONTH THIS IS? DON'T YOU HAVE A CALENDAR?
I'M JUST A LITTLE KID.. I DON'T KNOW HOW TO READ A CALENDAR! I DON'T EVEN KNOW WHAT DAY THIS IS! NOBODY TELLS ME ANYTHING!
5-10
ALL RIGHT..HERE'S A CANDY BAR..HAPPY HALLOWEEN..
© 1998 United Feature Syndicate, Inc.
www.snoopy.com
THANK YOU
BY THE WAY, JUST SO YOU KNOW, TODAY IS MOTHER'S DAY..
IT IS?
HOW MANY DAYS 'TIL CHRISTMAS?

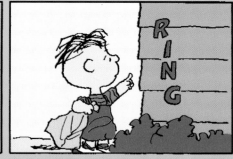

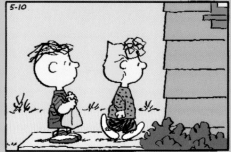

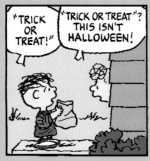

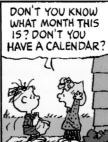

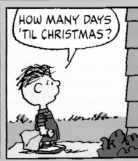

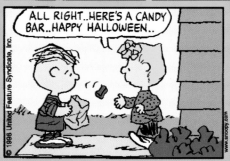

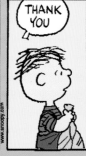

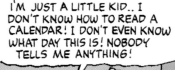

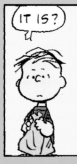

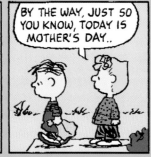

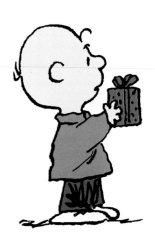

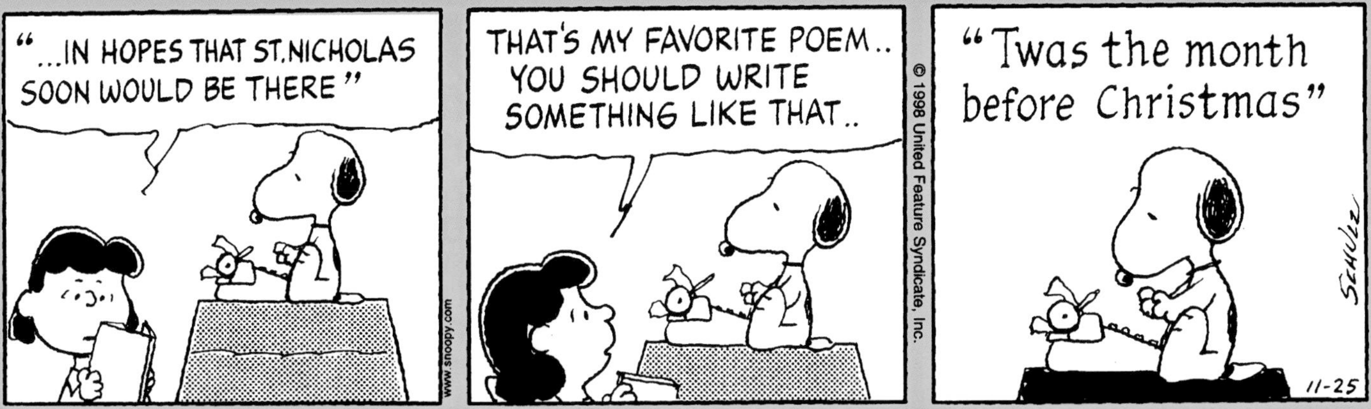
"...IN HOPES THAT ST. NICHOLAS SOON WOULD BE THERE"
THAT'S MY FAVORITE POEM.. YOU SHOULD WRITE SOMETHING LIKE THAT..
"Twas the month before Christmas"
www.snoopy.com
© 1998 United Feature Syndicate, Inc.
SCHULZ
11-25

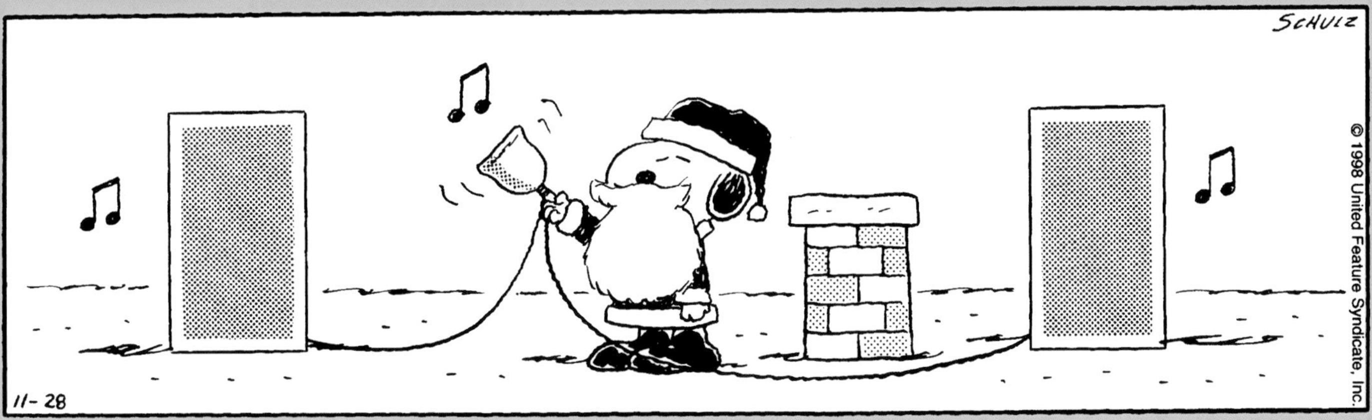
SCHULZ
© 1998 United Feature Syndicate, Inc.
11-28

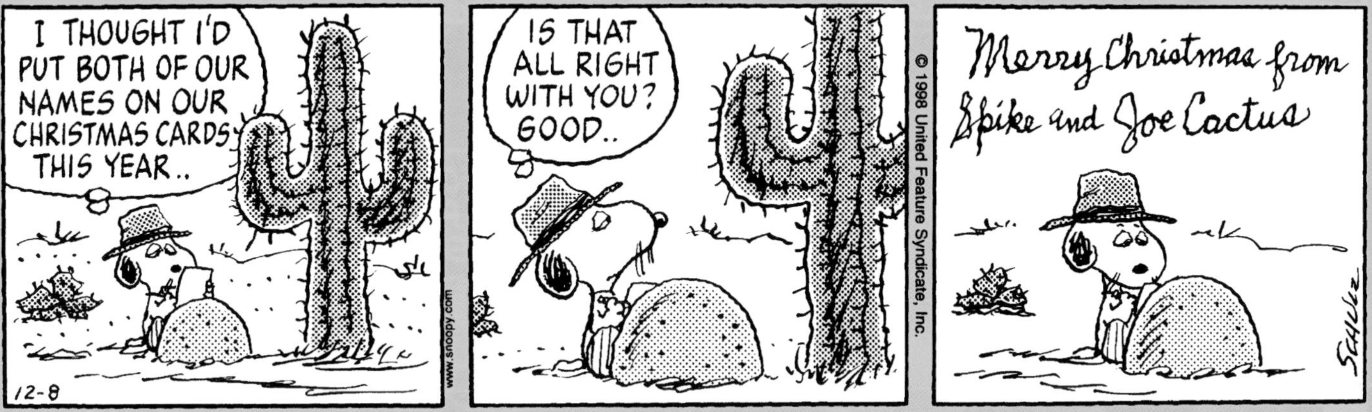
I THOUGHT I'D PUT BOTH OF OUR NAMES ON OUR CHRISTMAS CARDS THIS YEAR..
IS THAT ALL RIGHT WITH YOU? GOOD..
Merry Christmas from Spike and Joe Cactus
www.snoopy.com
© 1998 United Feature Syndicate, Inc.
SCHULZ
12-8

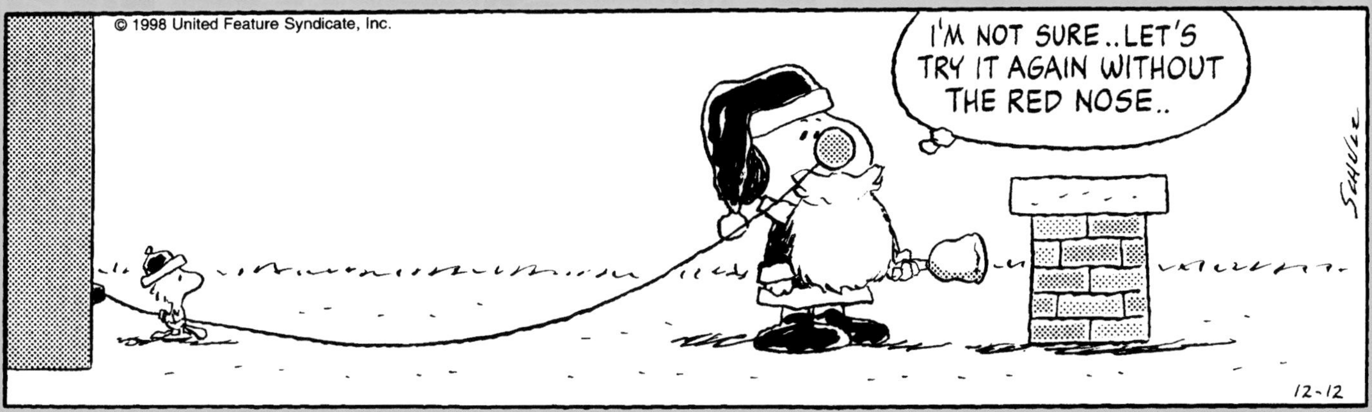
© 1998 United Feature Syndicate, Inc.
I'M NOT SURE..LET'S TRY IT AGAIN WITHOUT THE RED NOSE..
SCHULZ
12-12

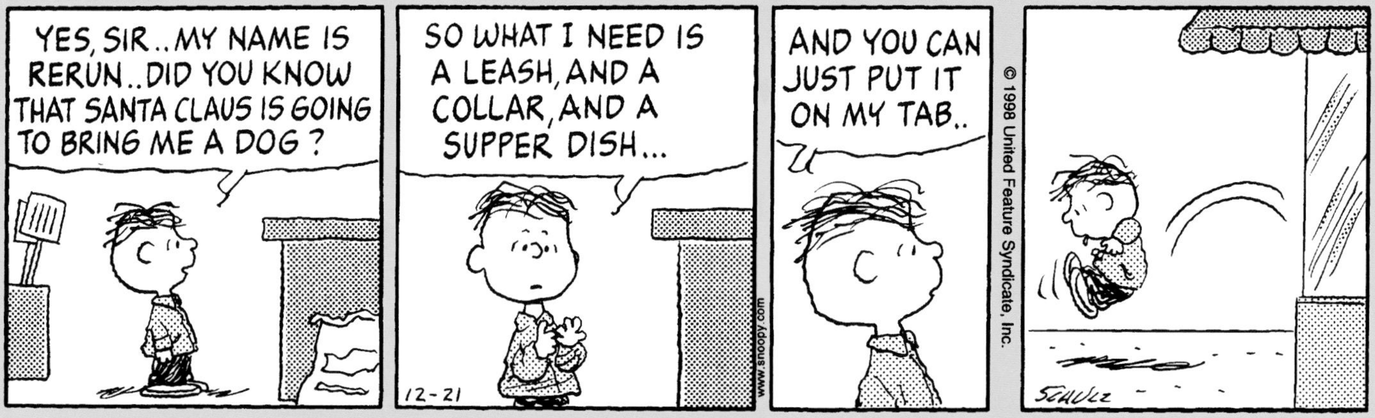
YES, SIR..MY NAME IS RERUN..DID YOU KNOW THAT SANTA CLAUS IS GOING TO BRING ME A DOG ?
SO WHAT I NEED IS A LEASH, AND A COLLAR, AND A SUPPER DISH...
12-21
www.snoopy.com
AND YOU CAN JUST PUT IT ON MY TAB..
© 1998 United Feature Syndicate, Inc.
SCHULZ

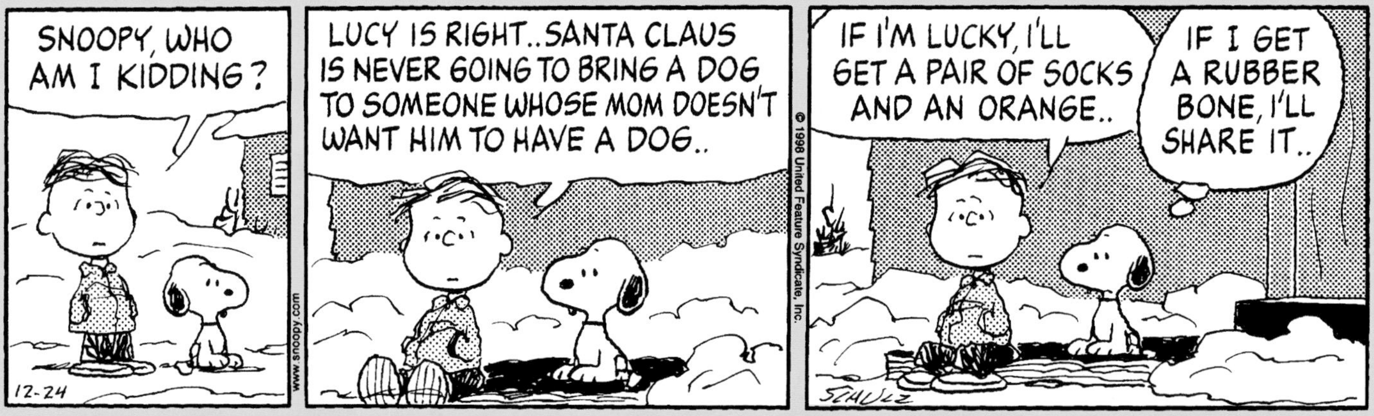
SNOOPY, WHO AM I KIDDING?
12-24
www.snoopy.com
LUCY IS RIGHT..SANTA CLAUS IS NEVER GOING TO BRING A DOG TO SOMEONE WHOSE MOM DOESN'T WANT HIM TO HAVE A DOG..
© 1998 United Feature Syndicate, Inc.
IF I'M LUCKY, I'LL GET A PAIR OF SOCKS AND AN ORANGE..
IF I GET A RUBBER BONE, I'LL SHARE IT..
SCHULZ

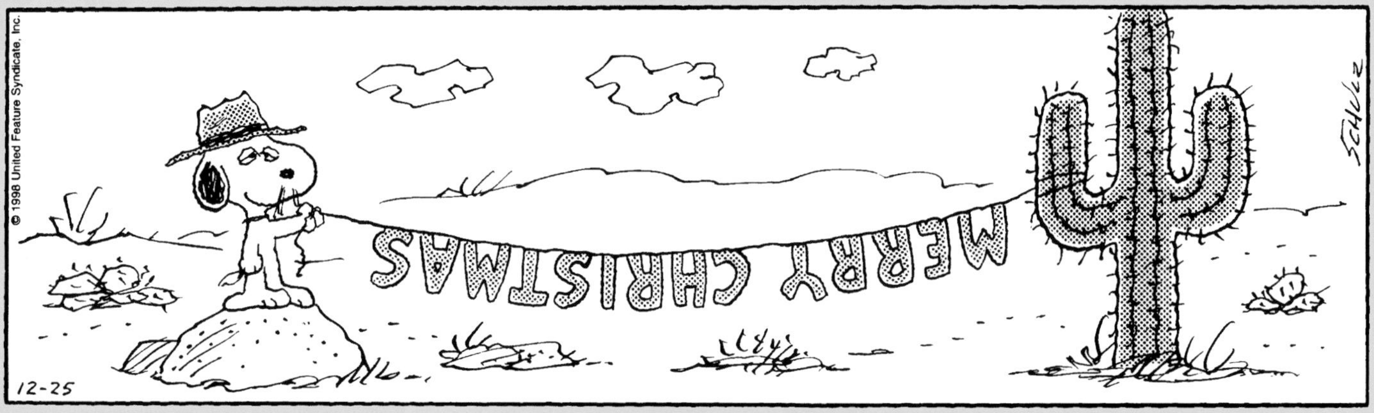
© 1998 United Feature Syndicate, Inc.
MERRY CHRISTMAS
SCHULZ
12-25

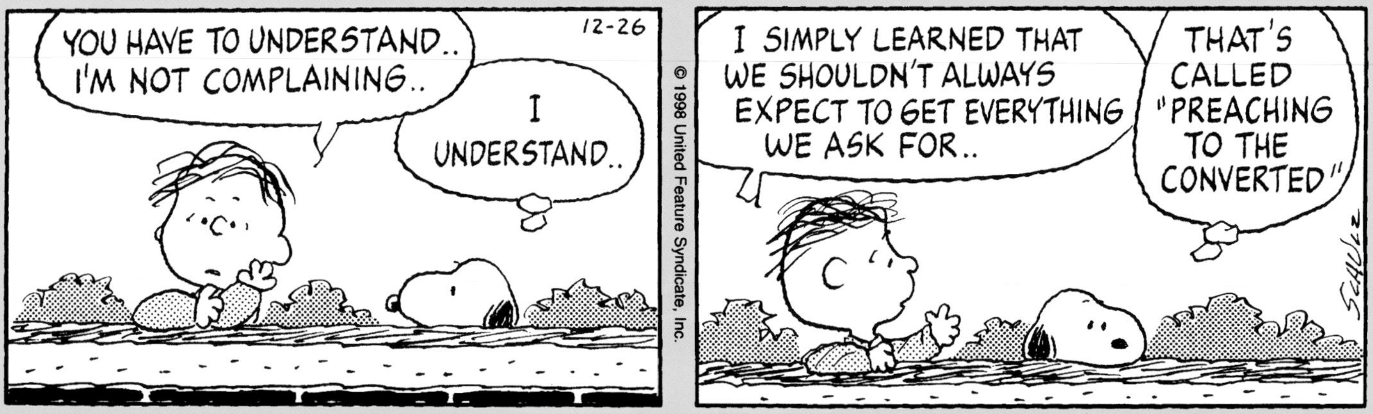
12-26
YOU HAVE TO UNDERSTAND.. I'M NOT COMPLAINING..
I UNDERSTAND..
© 1998 United Feature Syndicate, Inc.
I SIMPLY LEARNED THAT WE SHOULDN'T ALWAYS EXPECT TO GET EVERYTHING WE ASK FOR..
THAT'S CALLED "PREACHING TO THE CONVERTED"
SCHULZ

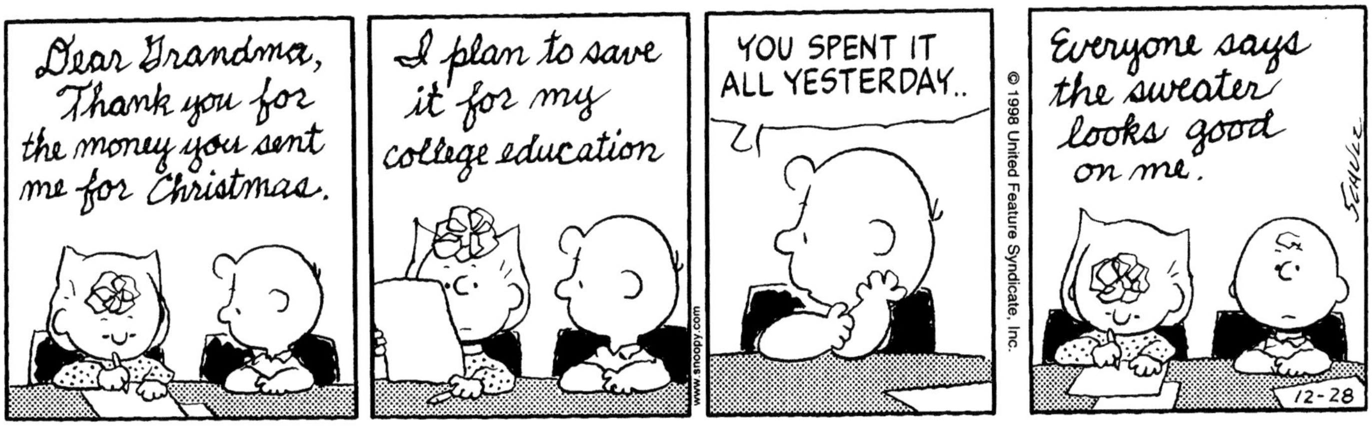
Dear Grandma, Thank you for the money you sent me for Christmas.
I plan to save it for my college education
YOU SPENT IT ALL YESTERDAY..
© 1998 United Feature Syndicate, Inc.
www.snoopy.com
Everyone says the sweater looks good on me.
12-28

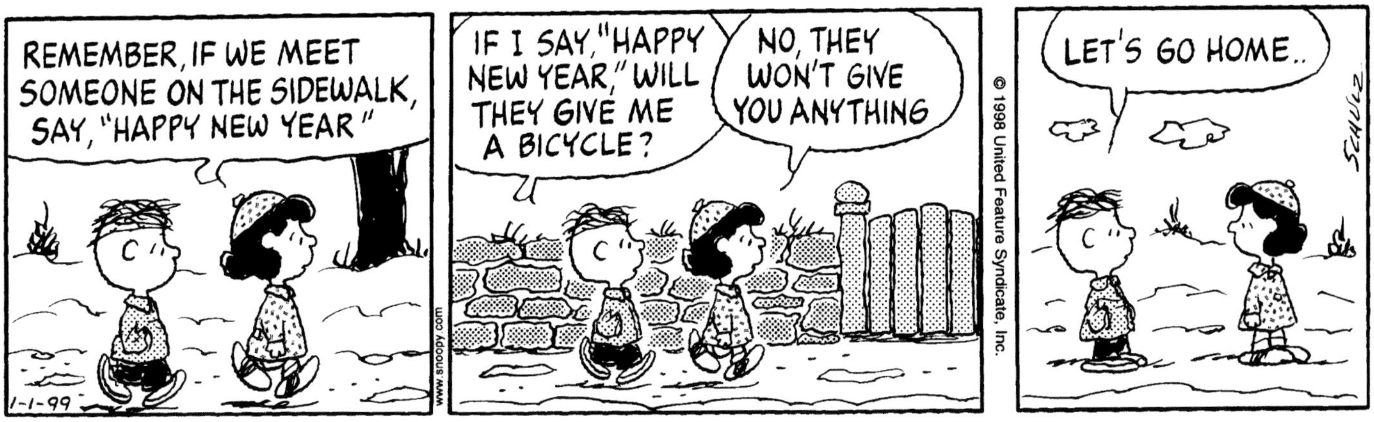
REMEMBER, IF WE MEET SOMEONE ON THE SIDEWALK, SAY, "HAPPY NEW YEAR"
1-1-99
www.snoopy.com
IF I SAY, "HAPPY NEW YEAR," WILL THEY GIVE ME A BICYCLE?
NO, THEY WON'T GIVE YOU ANYTHING
© 1998 United Feature Syndicate, Inc.
LET'S GO HOME..

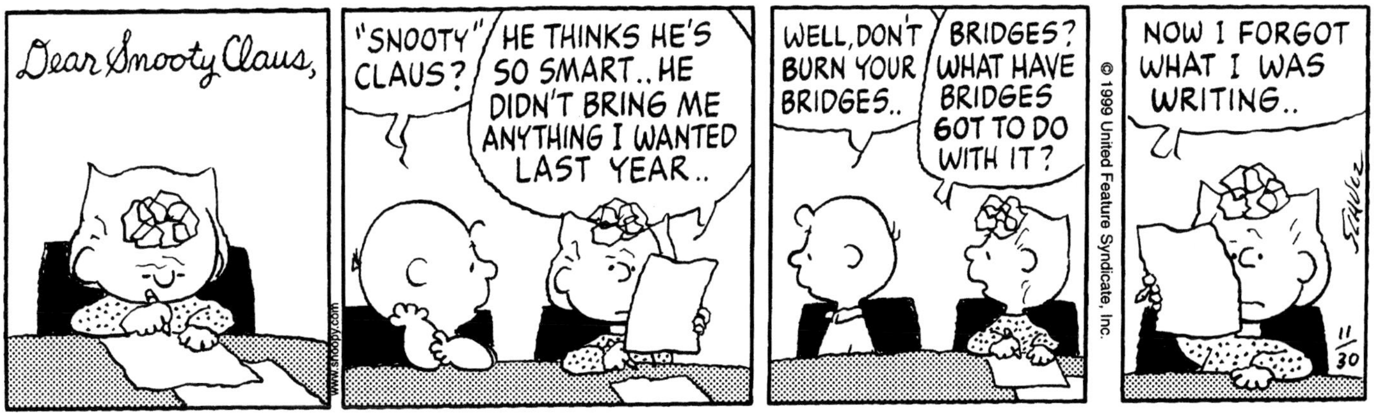
Dear Snooty Claus,
www.snoopy.com
"SNOOTY" CLAUS?
HE THINKS HE'S SO SMART.. HE DIDN'T BRING ME ANYTHING I WANTED LAST YEAR..
WELL, DON'T BURN YOUR BRIDGES..
BRIDGES? WHAT HAVE BRIDGES GOT TO DO WITH IT?
© 1999 United Feature Syndicate, Inc.
NOW I FORGOT WHAT I WAS WRITING..
11/30

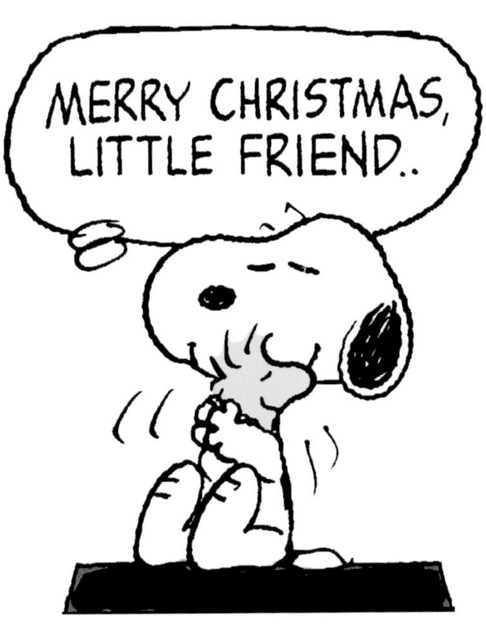
MERRY CHRISTMAS, LITTLE FRIEND..

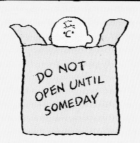

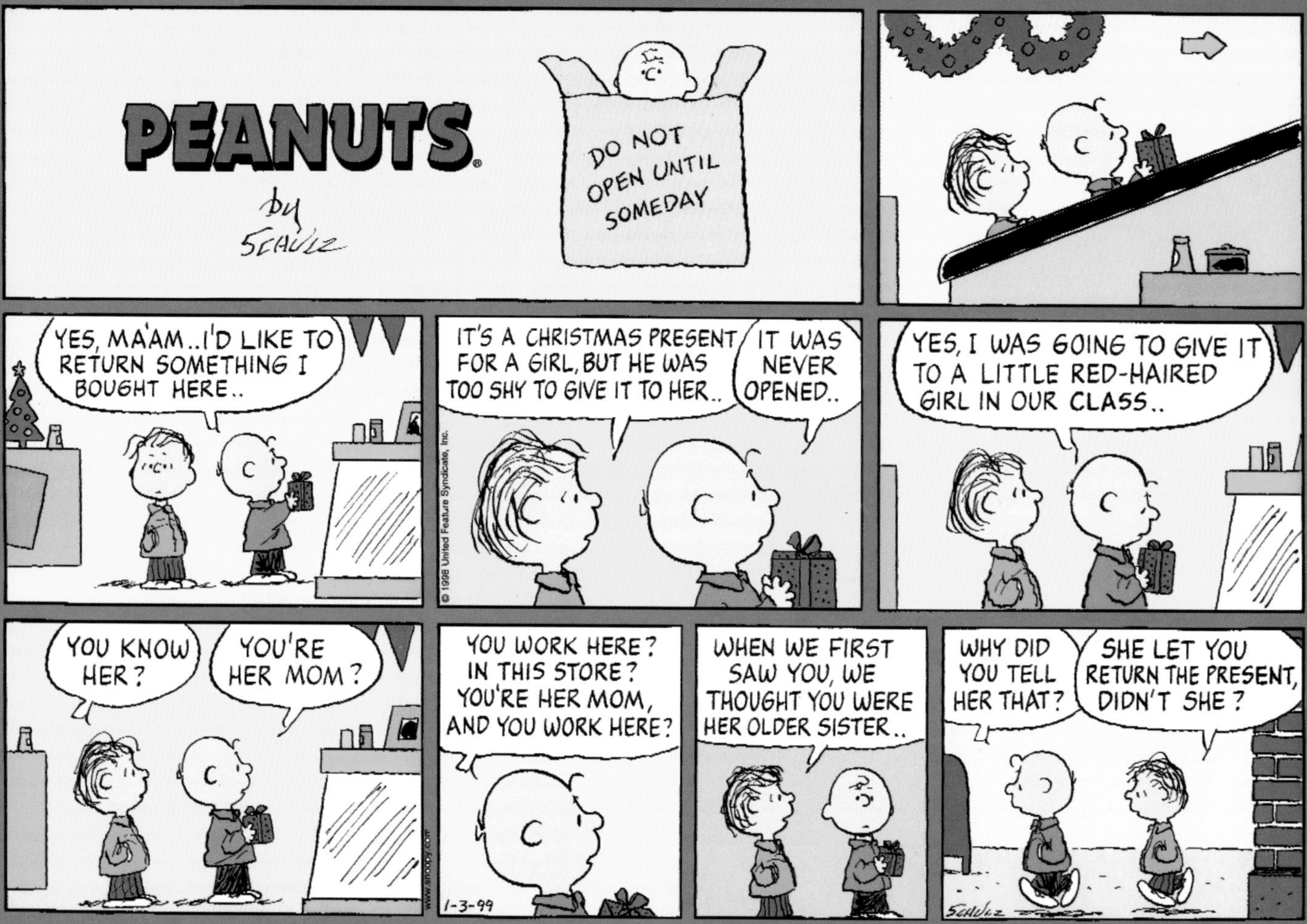

PEANUTS
by SCHULZ
DO NOT OPEN UNTIL SOMEDAY
YES, MA'AM..I'D LIKE TO RETURN SOMETHING I BOUGHT HERE..
IT'S A CHRISTMAS PRESENT FOR A GIRL, BUT HE WAS TOO SHY TO GIVE IT TO HER..
IT WAS NEVER OPENED..
© 1998 United Feature Syndicate, Inc.
YES, I WAS GOING TO GIVE IT TO A LITTLE RED-HAIRED GIRL IN OUR CLASS..
YOU KNOW HER?
YOU'RE HER MOM?
www.snoopy.com
YOU WORK HERE? IN THIS STORE? YOU'RE HER MOM, AND YOU WORK HERE?
1-3-99
WHEN WE FIRST SAW YOU, WE THOUGHT YOU WERE HER OLDER SISTER..
WHY DID YOU TELL HER THAT?
SHE LET YOU RETURN THE PRESENT, DIDN'T SHE?
SCHULZ

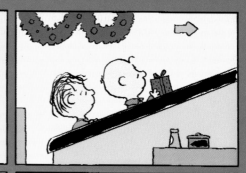

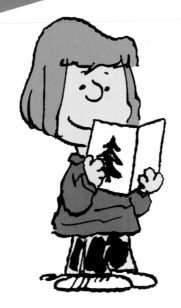